ENDŌ SHŪSAKU

In his book, Mark Williams takes the first focused look in English at the complex and challenging *oeuvre* of Endō Shūsaku, one of the most important of contemporary Japanese novelists. Williams rejects the facile notion that Endō started out sceptical about the possible spiritual meeting of East and West and replaces it with a sophisticated, compelling argument for a process of reconciliation between opposites that is at the core of much of Endō's writing. I find this a refreshing, engaging and persuasive argument that will allow a new level of understanding of this superb writer's work.
  Van C. Gessel, Dean, College of Humanities and Professor
  of Japanese, Brigham Young University

Endō Shūsaku is probably the most widely translated of all Japanese authors. In this first major study of Endō's work, **Mark B. Williams** moves the discussion on from the well-worn depictions of Endō as the 'Japanese Graham Greene', and places him in his own political and cultural context. Through a discussion covering all Endō's major novels, the picture painted by Williams is of an author building on his native Japanese tradition in pursuit of a more universal literary portrayal of the individual engaged in his or her unique 'process of individuation'. Bringing to light the enduring legacy of an author who has contributed as much as any Japanese writer of his generation to an unmasking of the unsustainability of talk of an 'East–West divide', this volume will be of great value to all those interested in Japanese literature.

Mark B. Williams is Senior Lecturer in Japanese Studies at the University of Leeds.

THE NISSAN INSTITUTE/ROUTLEDGE JAPANESE STUDIES SERIES

Editorial Board

J. A. A. Stockwin, *Nissan Professor of Modern Japanese Studies, University of Oxford and Director, Nissan Institute of Japanese Studies*

Teigo Yoshida, *formerly Professor of the University of Tokyo, and now Professor, Obirin University, Tokyo*

Frank Langdon, *Professor, Institute of International Relations, University of British Columbia, Canada*

Alan Rix, *Professor of Japanese, The University of Queensland*

Junji Banno, *Institute of Social Science, University of Tokyo*

Leonard Schoppa, *University of Virginia*

Other titles in the series:

THE MYTH OF JAPANESE UNIQUENESS,
Peter Dale

THE EMPEROR'S ADVISER: SAIONJI KINMOCHI AND PRE-WAR JAPANESE POLITICS,
Lesley Connors

A HISTORY OF JAPANESE ECONOMIC THOUGHT,
Tessa Morris-Suzuki

THE ESTABLISHMENT OF THE JAPANESE CONSTITUTIONAL SYSTEM,
Junji Banno, translated by J. A. A. Stockwin

INDUSTRIAL RELATIONS IN JAPAN: THE PERIPHERAL WORKFORCE,
Norma Chalmers

BANKING POLICY IN JAPAN: AMERICAN EFFORTS AT REFORM DURING THE OCCUPATION,
William M. Tsutsui

EDUCATION REFORM IN JAPAN,
Leonard Schoppa

HOW THE JAPANESE LEARN TO WORK,
Ronald P. Dore and Mari Sako

JAPANESE ECONOMIC DEVELOPMENT: THEORY AND PRACTICE,
Penelope Francks

JAPAN AND PROTECTION: THE GROWTH OF PROTECTIONIST SENTIMENT AND THE JAPANESE RESPONSE,
Syed Javed Marwood

THE SOIL, BY NAGASTSUKA TAKASHI: A PORTRAIT OF RURAL LIFE IN MEIJI JAPAN,
translated and with an introduction by Ann Waswo

BIOTECHNOLOGY IN JAPAN,
Malcolm Brock

BRITAIN'S EDUCATIONAL REFORM: A COMPARISON WITH JAPAN,
Mike Howarth

LANGUAGE AND THE MODERN STATE: THE REFORM OF WRITTEN JAPANESE,
Nanette Twine

INDUSTRIAL HARMONY IN MODERN JAPAN:
THE INVENTION OF A TRADITION,
W. Dean Kinzley

JAPANESE SCIENCE FICTION: A VIEW OF A CHANGING SOCIETY,
Robert Matthew

THE JAPANESE NUMBERS GAME: THE USE AND UNDERSTANDING OF
NUMBERS IN MODERN JAPAN,
Thomas Crump

IDEOLOGY AND PRACTICE IN MODERN JAPAN,
Roger Goodman and Kirsten Refsing

TECHNOLOGY AND INDUSTRIAL DEVELOPMENT IN PRE-WAR JAPAN,
Yukiko Fukasaku

JAPAN'S EARLY PARLIAMENTS 1890,
Andres Fraser, R.H.P. Mason and Philip Mitchell

JAPAN'S FOREIGN AID CHALLENGE,
Alan Rix

EMPEROR HIROHITO AND SHOWA JAPAN,
Stephen S. Large

JAPAN: BEYOND THE END OF HISTORY,
David Williams

CEREMONY AND RITUAL IN JAPAN: RELIGIOUS PRACTICES
IN AN INDUSTRIALIZED SOCIETY,
Jan van Bremen and D. P. Martinez

UNDERSTANDING JAPANESE SOCIETY: SECOND EDITION,
Joy Hendry

THE FANTASTIC IN MODERN JAPANESE LITERATURE:
THE SUBVERSION OF MODERNITY,
Susan J. Napier

MILITARIZATION AND DEMILITARIZATION IN CONTEMPORARY JAPAN,
Glenn D. Hook

GROWING A JAPANESE SCIENCE CITY: COMMUNICATION IN
SCIENTIFIC RESEARCH,
James W. Dearing

ARCHITECTURE AND AUTHORITY IN JAPAN,
William H. Coaldrake

WOMEN'S GIDAYŪ AND THE JAPANESE THEATRE TRADITION,
A. Kimi Coaldrake

DEMOCRACY IN POST-WAR JAPAN,
Rikki Kersten

TREACHEROUS WOMEN OF IMPERIAL JAPAN,
Hélène Bowen Raddeker

JAPANESE-GERMAN BUSINESS RELATIONS,
Akira Kudō

JAPAN, RACE AND EQUALITY,
Naoko Shimazu

ENDŌ SHŪSAKU,
Mark B. Williams

JAPAN, INTERNATIONALISM AND THE UN,
Ronald Dore

LIFE IN A JAPANESE WOMEN'S COLLEGE,
Brian J. McVeigh

ON THE MARGINS OF JAPANESE SOCIETY,
Carolyn S. Stevens

THE DYNAMICS OF JAPAN'S RELATIONS WITH AFRICA,
Kweku Ampiah

THE RIGHT TO LIFE IN JAPAN,
Noel Williams

THE NATURE OF THE JAPANESE STATE,
Brian J. McVeigh

SOCIETY AND STATE IN INTER-WAR JAPAN,
Elise K. Tipton

JAPANESE–SOVIET/RUSSIAN RELATIONS SINCE 1945,
Kimie Hara

GREEN POLITICS IN JAPAN,
Lam Peng-Er

ENDŌ SHŪSAKU

A literature of reconciliation

Mark B. Williams

London and New York

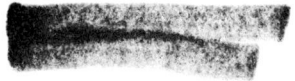

First published 1999
by Routledge
11 New Fetter Lane, London EC4P 4EE

Simultaneously published in the USA and Canada
by Routledge
29 West 35th Street, New York, NY 10001

© 1999 Mark B. Williams

Typeset in Times by Routledge
Printed and bound in Great Britain by Biddles Ltd,
Guildford and King's Lynn

All rights reserved. No part of this book may be reprinted or reproduced or utilised in any form or by any electronic, mechanical, or other means, now known or hereafter invented, including photocopying and recording, or in any information storage or retrieval system, without permission in writing from the publishers.

British Library Cataloguing in Publication Data
A catalogue record for this book is available from the British Library

Library of Congress Cataloging in Publication Data
Williams, Mark B.
Endō Shūsaku: A literature of reconciliation / Mark B. Williams.
p. cm. – (Nissan Institute/Routledge Japanese Studies series)
includes bibliographical references and index.
1. Endō Shūsaku, 1923–1996 2. Criticism and interpretation.
I. Title. II. Series.
PL849.N4Z95 1999
895.6'35–dc21 98–30573 CIP

ISBN 0-415-14481-7

TO IKUKO

CONTENTS

Series editor's preface	xi
Acknowledgements	xv
Introduction	1
1 Towards Reconciliation	25
2 White Man, Yellow Man	58
3 The Sea and Poison, Wonderful Fool, The Girl I Left Behind	76
4 Silence	105
5 The Samurai	130
6 Scandal	166
7 Deep River	191
Afterword	220
Appendix A: A brief biography of Endō Shūsaku	225
Appendix B: Synopses of the works discussed	227
Notes	242
Selected Bibliography	258
Index	272

SERIES EDITOR'S PREFACE

Japan, as the new century approaches, is going through a turbulent period, in which some of her most entrenched institutions and practices are being increasingly questioned. The financial crisis which began in the latter half of 1997 – but whose origins go back several years earlier – gravely affected Japan, as well as other Asian countries. Quite apart from the economic and political implications of recession, widespread bankruptcies, increasing unemployment and a falling yen, the crisis was having a considerable impact on the psychology of ordinary Japanese people. They had been accustomed to steadily increasing prosperity and the international respect generated by the successes of their politico–economic model. Now, however, they were coming to wonder whether attitudes and ways of doing things that had been central to their outlook over several decades were still appropriate to the disturbingly unstable world in which they now found themselves. One straw in the wind was a hugely popular soap opera aired on Fuji Television in the spring of 1998, entitled *Shōmu 2* (General Affairs Section 2), in which a group of women office workers egotistically assert their rights as individuals and challenge time-honoured working practices. By challenging the prevailing atmosphere of inefficiency, refusal to face up to responsibilities, conformity, sexual harassment of women and mindless deference to hierarchy, this feisty group of 'office ladies' succeed in saving the company from bankruptcy.

However much of a caricature the Fuji TV soap opera may be, it is symptomatic of a spreading sense that all is not right in what used to be seen as an unbeatable set of methods for running society. Grave though the crisis being faced by Japan was as the century approaches its close, the impressive human and material resources that the country is still able to command are advantageous in the struggle to overcome the crisis. Whatever might be the outcome at the economic level, however, a troubling intellectual problem remains. Few can doubt that radical reform is needed, but if this reform is simply to be a case of conformity with the norms of an America-centred global economy (following the principles of the free market and egotistical individualism), where does that leave the status of Japanese values? History suggests that simple acceptance of foreign models is an unlikely outcome, and that ultimately a creative solution might emerge, mixing external with indigenous elements. To follow this process over the coming years should be an intriguing task.

The Nissan Institute/Routledge Japanese Studies Series seeks to foster an informed and balanced, but not uncritical, understanding of Japan. One aim of the series is to show the depth and variety of Japanese institutions, practices and ideas. Another is, by using comparisons, to see what lessons, positive or negative, may be drawn for other countries. The tendency in commentary on Japan to resort to outdated, ill-informed or sensational stereotypes still remains, and needs to be combated.

One of Japan's most widely read – and most widely translated – modern novelists is Endō Shūsaku, who died in 1996. Unusually for Japanese literary figures, Endō was a Christian, having been baptised into the Roman Catholic faith at the age of eleven. As Dr Williams shows in his superb analysis of Endō's literary pilgrimage, he was on the one hand a devout adherent of his faith and influenced by it in his choice of subject matter and approach, but on the other a writer of novels, not theological tracts. Over his work as a whole, but in particular in his best-known later novels *Silence*, *The Samurai* and *Deep River*, the theme of redemption is prominent in Endō's approach to his characters, though it is a concept of redemption that manifests itself in various, even contradictory, ways. Like all first-rate novelists, Endō, during his literary career, developed an understanding of human psychology in its disturbing complexity. As Williams shows, he was also concerned to demonstrate that mundane, or flawed, individuals sometimes possess the capacity to transcend their basic nature, and rise to a higher ethical plane.

In terms of our earlier discussion in this Preface, Endō encapsulates in a particularly sharp and interesting form the psychological dilemma of Japanese separate identity under challenge. Being a Catholic writer – and thus part of the 'monotheistic West' – but Japanese – and thus part of the 'polytheistic East' – he was able to

SERIES EDITOR'S PREFACE

reflect in a wonderfully creative fashion on Japan's long-standing dialectic between universality and separateness.

J.A.A. Stockwin
Director, Nissan Institute of Japanese Studies,
University of Oxford

ACKNOWLEDGEMENTS

In the course of writing a book of this kind, one inevitably incurs debts of gratitude to more people than it is possible to mention by name. I am nevertheless delighted to be in a position to acknowledge at least some of the individuals who have helped me along the way. The others will know that their contribution to this process has been greatly appreciated.

I was introduced to Endō's literature during my days as one of only four students enrolled on the Japanese undergraduate programme at Oxford University. My first thanks should therefore be addressed to my tutors there, and in particular to Brian Powell and James McMullen, both of whom were highly influential in changing me from a freshman who, however keen, had not the slightest knowledge about Japan, into a graduate with a working knowledge of the language and literary heritage of Japan.

It was during the course of my graduate studies at the University of California at Berkeley, however, that my interest in contemporary Japanese literature was truly fired – and chief responsibility for this must rest squarely on the shoulders of my ever-willing adviser, Van Gessel. As will be evident from the number of footnotes in the ensuing study referring to his work, Van was highly influential in determining the direction ultimately assumed by my studies at Berkeley – and in particular in my decision to write my Ph.D. dissertation on the influence of Christianity on the twentieth-century literary scene in Japan. From the moment I approached him to see whether this would be acceptable as a dissertation topic, I received nothing but encouragement and constructive feedback on my work from Van. Indeed, without that invitation from Van to join him for dinner with Endō on the eve of the conferment of the latter's honorary doctorate from the University of California at Santa Clara in 1985, my studies would, in all probability, have proceeded down a completely different path. Once my decision to

ACKNOWLEDGEMENTS

focus on Endō had been made, however, Van was joined by two others on my dissertation committee and my thanks are due to Haruo Aoki and Stephen Knapp for their willingness to sit down and discuss ideas with me as the chapters emerged.

My final year as a graduate student in Berkeley was spent as an exchange student in the Department of Literature at the University of Tokyo where I benefited considerably from the counsel of several of the faculty, most notably, Professor Noyama Yoshimasa. At the same time, this period of study in Japan would not have been possible without the generous funding that I received for this purpose from Monbushō, the Japanese Ministry of Education.

After a year in Japan, I planned to return to Berkeley to write up the dissertation, but events conspired against this and I found myself, in the Autumn of 1988, on the faculty of the Department of East Asian Studies at the University of Leeds. Although teaching and administrative commitments were not altogether conducive to the task in hand, I never received anything less than total support for my research from my colleagues in the department; in particular, my thanks are due to Penny Francks and other colleagues from the Japanese section who have covered for me during the various sabbatical absences I have been fortunate to receive.

The vast majority of my research in Japan since 1988 has been conducted as a Visiting Research Fellow affiliated to the Institute of Asian Cultural Studies at International Christian University in Tokyo. My thanks in this regard are due especially to Professors Masayoshi Uozumi and Bill Steele, Directors of the Institute who looked after me and arranged for me to present the results of my research at seminars and lectures during my various visits – and to the British Academy, the Japan Foundation, the Japan Foundation Endowment Committee and the Daiwa Anglo-Japanese Foundation, all of whom helped to fund these ventures on different occasions. My debts at ICU extend beyond the doors of the Institute, however, and it is a special privilege to be able to record my particular appreciation for all that has been done to further my research by ICU Professor and Vice President, Saitō Kazuaki. I first met Professor Saitō during my time at Tokyo University and it has been largely as a result of this connection that I have made ICU my first port of call in Japan these past ten years. It was also thanks to Professor Saitō, serving in his capacity as President of the Society for the Study of Christian Literature in Japan, that I became involved in the discussions of this group and, wherever possible, I have tried to coincide my visits to Japan with the annual meetings of

ACKNOWLEDGEMENTS

this Society. The conversations prompted by these meetings have invariably proven challenging and I have benefited in no small measure from the advice and friendship received from various members of the Society, notably Professors Yamagata Kazumi and Ono Kōsei.

There remains, however, one further contact without whom my studies would certainly not have assumed the form they have. From the moment of our first meeting in California, Endō was active in support of my work. It was at his encouragement that I undertook translations of two of his novels, *Ryūgaku* (Foreign Studies) and *Watashi ga suteta onna* (The Girl I Left Behind). It was thanks to funding directly procured by Endō himself (in co-operation with Kenzō Kogi at the Global Youth Bureau in Tokyo) that I was able to make two further visits to Japan in 1991 and 1993. And it was at Endō's instigation that I became involved in the monthly meetings of the Society for the Study of Christian Arts in Tokyo. Most important for me, however, was the time that Endō was always able to make for me out of his incredibly busy schedule – time that was spent in a whole range of fascinating discussions, the conversation invariably stimulated by the delicious cuisine to which he treated his visitors. I can only say that if literary prizes were to be awarded on the basis of the author's choice of Chinese restaurant, then Endō would have received all the prizes going at an early stage in his career! One final word of thanks is due to the Endō family – and to Endō's widow, Junko, in particular – for provision of the photograph of Endō that appears on the front cover and for the permission, willingly granted, for me to translate from the Japanese and cite sources from her husband's work wherever required.

My greatest thanks, however, must be reserved for my long-suffering family. Without the dare (and opinions are divided as to whether this was initiated by my sister or my father!) to mention my passing interest in studying Japanese at my initial university interview, which was ostensibly for a place to read French and German, my fascination with Japan would presumably have faded into oblivion. And certainly there were times following graduation when, without the encouragement of my parents in particular, I would have opted for a slightly more secure future than that which, at the time, appeared to be available to graduate students in Oriental Studies. Sadly, my mother died before I could complete this manuscript, but she knew – and my father still knows – the extent of the influence they have both exerted on my studies. My thanks also to my parents-in-law in Tokyo; without their support and willingness to

ACKNOWLEDGEMENTS

accommodate us, often at short notice, those research trips would have been much more difficult to arrange. My children, Naomi, Ken and Mari, have suffered gamely and with commendably little complaint those frequent occasions when 'daddy is working upstairs'. But it is to my wife, Ikuko, that my greatest thanks are due. Without her commitment to my work – including those years when she provided financial support to her impecunious graduate student husband – none of this would have been possible. This has in a real sense been a joint venture – and it is only fitting that this book be dedicated to her.

Finally, I should like to acknowledge all the help I have received from the editors of the journals, *Japan Christian Review* and *Japan Forum*, who have allowed me to incorporate into Chapters 5 and 6 of this study material from articles published in their journals – and from my publishers at Routledge. Vicky Smith, in particular, has been supportive of this project from the outset and has accepted the inevitable missed deadlines with customary good cheer.

The debts are very real. Far be it for me, however, to impute any accountability for the ensuing work to any of the above. Responsibility for this, including all translations from the Japanese originals, except as otherwise noted, rests with me.

INTRODUCTION

> The more inner and the less outer life a novel presents, the higher and nobler will be its purpose....Art consists in achieving the maximum of inner motion with the minimum of outer motion; for it is the inner life which is the true object of our interest.
>
> (Arthur Schopenhauer)

A quick glance at the dust jackets of the various editions of the fictional narratives of Endō Shūsaku serves to pigeon-hole the Japanese author along lines that have remained virtually unchanged since publication of his widely acclaimed *Chinmoku* (Silence; trans. 1969) in 1966. Both the Japanese originals and their English translations have come to be accompanied, almost by default, with some reference to Endō as a 'Japanese Catholic author' struggling to 'plant the seeds of his adopted religion' in the 'mudswamp' of Japan. And, where space permits, such depictions are invariably supported by the sobriquet that remained *de rigeur* until his death in September 1996: that of Endō as the 'Japanese Graham Greene'.[1]

These portrayals are certainly convenient; and, in their own way, they can be seen as encapsulating the literary concerns of an author whose baptism into the Catholic tradition at the age of 11, however expedient, was clearly influential in determining the literary direction that he would subsequently pursue. At the same time, however, there are dangers implicit in such depictions. Quite apart from the oversimplifications and misunderstandings that tend to accrue in the light of such, at best, loosely defined portrayals, there is a danger, evidenced in much of the critical discussion of Endō's *oeuvre*, of placing an inordinate emphasis on a series of 'foreign' influences and of thereby locating him outside his native tradition. Before turning to Endō's own literary production, therefore, a brief

INTRODUCTION

consideration of his position within the tradition of the *shōsetsu*, the Japanese term invariably used to translate the concept of 'the novel', is required.

It was the critic Miyoshi Masao, in his study of 'the whole discourse of the modern Japanese novel as it is conducted in the United States, and to a lesser extent in Japan as well',[2] who drew attention to the tendency, when reading an 'exotic' text in the West, to resort to one of two techniques. In such cases, suggests Miyoshi, some readers deploy a 'strategy for domestication' whereby they 'exaggerate the familiar aspects of the text and thereby disperse its discreteness in the hegemonic sphere of first world literature'.[3] Alternatively, they adopt a 'plan for neutralization...by distancing the menacing source': they dismiss these texts as 'strange,... "delicate," "lyrical," or "suggestive," if not "illogical," "impenetrable" or "incoherent"[4].' For Miyoshi, the issue runs deep and, in the case of Japan, is seen as the result of a failure to emphasise the clear differences between the novel on the one hand and the *shōsetsu* on the other. Indeed, Miyoshi goes further: not only do differences exist, but the *shōsetsu* is 'the reverse of the novel', an argument Miyoshi supports in the following manner:

> Rather than a 'credible fabrication which is yet constantly held up as false', the *shōsetsu* is an incredible fabrication that is nonetheless constantly held up as truthful. Art is hidden, while honesty and sincerity are displayed.[5]

The gauntlet was picked up by Edward Fowler in *The Rhetoric of Confession*, a study of the *shishōsetsu* genre of confessional literature that has so dominated the twentieth-century Japanese prose narrative tradition. To Fowler, the issue at stake was clear: 'the basic difference [between the classical western narrative and the Japanese *shishōsetsu*] derives from the fact that the *shōsetsu* itself – that Japanese word we glibly translate as "novel" – also differs fundamentally from western narrative'. The challenge, he suggests, is 'to distance *shōsetsu* from "novel" while collapsing the perceived distinctions between *shōsetsu* and *shishōsetsu*'.[6] What was required, in short, was the alternative methodology for reading the *shōsetsu* which Miyoshi had earlier advocated, one that allowed for interpretation of the *shōsetsu* 'as a confluence of narrative possibilities as inherited by the Edo period and later writers whose perception and response, dream and realization, were guided and defined by the constraints of their times'.[7]

As Fowler and Miyoshi are the first to acknowledge, the implications of this call are considerable. For, if we are to heed this advice, not only is there a need for a radical rethink of the 'rhetoric of confession' upon which the *shishōsetsu* is premised; there is a concomitant requirement to revisit a whole series of Japanese authors who have traditionally been pigeon-holed, again all too 'glibly', as heavily indebted to Western influences, as somehow belonging outside the native narrative tradition – and, by extension, as indebted to techniques espoused by the western novel. Quite apart from the questions raised by textualist critics with regard to the notion of 'influence' (which, as James Fujii has pointed out, 'suffers from the problem of privileging the person or work "influenced" and also fails to account for more than naive unidirectional effects'),[8] the attempt to locate such works within the Japanese tradition of the *shōsetsu* is surely well-heeded. To persist with Fujii's logic, 'we might be better served by abandoning a static model of binary influence in favor of a view that accounts for what was and is a dynamic process of often self-reflective engagement with otherness'.[9] To be sure, in seeking to divest such texts of some of their intercultural baggage, there is a danger that we will end up merely relocating them in some other equally one-sided liminal site by replacing such 'foreign' influences with some equally unidirectional influences from within the *shōsetsu* tradition. Whilst attempting to avoid such drastic over-rectification, however, we can at least continue the process of strengthening the structural supports upon which the *shōsetsu* has been established.

One such author who would surely benefit from reappraisal as a writer of *shōsetsu* is Endō Shūsaku, a writer whose identification with Western literary tradition was, in large measure, self-induced. Thus, even before publication of his first work of creative fiction, Endō had gone on public record acknowledging his literary debt to the series of 'French Catholic authors' who had represented the primary focus of his studies both as an undergraduate at Keiō University and, later, as one of the first Japanese students to study in France after the war. In the aptly named 'Katorikku sakka no mondai' (The Problems confronting the Catholic Author, 1947), for example, in addition to the widely discussed 'influence' of Mauriac, Endō also recognises the significance on his own subsequent literary direction of various other French novelists, including Paul Bourget, Henri Bordeaux, Gide, Proust, Charles du Bos, Julien Green, Emile Baumann, Paul Claudel and Georges Bernanos.[10]

It is hard to exaggerate Endō's literary debt to European letters.

However, reinterpretation in the light of the caveats proffered by Fowler, Miyoshi and Fujii provides interesting insights into an author more deeply imbued in the *shōsetsu* tradition – and more readily identifiable as building on the pre-war *shishōsetsu* tradition – than is generally acknowledged. It is to this tradition that we now turn – in an attempt, albeit brief, to locate Endō more squarely within this tradition than previously suggested. More specifically, we shall be identifying Endō as inheritor of the trend towards an increasingly subjective focus in the pre-war *shishōsetsu* and as at the forefront of a tradition of fractured narrative perspective to which the *shishōsetsu* gave way in the wake of Japan's defeat in the Pacific War.

In search of selfhood

In theory, any attempt to relocate Endō within the *shōsetsu* tradition is going to take us back to the earliest exemplars of the genre, which can be traced back to the early Meiji era (1868–1912).[11] In the discussion that follows, however, particular emphasis will be placed on the claim, advanced by Karatani Kōjin in his seminal study, *Nihon kindai bungaku no kigen* (Origins of Modern Japanese Literature), that the origins of the genre are closely linked to the discovery attributed to a series of authors in the third decade of Meiji (the 1890s): the 'discovery of interiority'. At the one level, Karatani is here merely reiterating the common depiction of the literature of this period as 'a literature of self-definition'; and in suggesting that 'the theme of the exploration of the modern self, however diverse its articulations, dominates discussions of modern Japanese literature',[12] Karatani would appear to be simply echoing the conventional wisdom. For Karatani, however, the main focus remains the extent to which this 'discovery of interiority' represented an influencing factor on the direction subsequently assumed by the literature of 'self-definition' – and it is in these terms, he suggests, as precursors of a move towards a more complex narrative of the self, that the contribution of this group of *fin de siècle* authors is best considered. Of even greater significance in our attempt to contextualise the prose fictions of the postwar Endō is the view, expounded by Karatani, of the emerging vision of the presence of an 'alternative self' – of what Karatani describes as the 'self...severed from the self'[13] – as integral to the ensuing prose narrative tradition. This vision of the divided self – of authors engaged in consideration of the ramifications of this 'discovery of interiority' – will be cited during the course of this study as characteristic of the art of the *Daisan no shinjin* (third generation of new authors) to which Endō was affiliated – one that distinguishes this literary group from their precursors in the pre-war *shishōsetsu* tradition. More specifically, in the critical studies of the various Endō narratives that follow, this trait will be singled out as integral to the author's attempt to depict composite individuals as protagonists of his works.

So let us return to Karatani – to the caveat he offers in the wake of his acknowledgement of the centrality of exploration of the modern self to discussions of modern Japanese literature. Having made this assertion, Karatani continues:

> Yet it is laughable to speak of this modern self as if it were purely a mental or psychological phenomenon. For this modern self is rooted in materiality and comes into existence...only by being established as a system.[14]

To Karatani, this system had emerged in the early Meiji period – in the form of the movement towards the 'unification of written and spoken language' (*genbun itchi*). Reversing the traditional assumption that 'it was the needs of the inner self that gave rise to the *genbun itchi* movement', Karatani suggests rather that 'it was the formation of the *genbun itchi* system that made possible the so-called "discovery of self"',[15] by a series of writers epitomised by Kunikida Doppo and his literary mentor, Kitamura Tōkoku. In Karatani's estimation, then, it was with this generation of writers that the *shōsetsu* attained 'spontaneity', a spontaneity linked to the belief that 'interiority and self-expression were self-evident' and 'brought into being through a sense of the presence of one's own voice to which one listens'.[16] It was this willingness to listen to their own voice that Karatani cites as leading to the vision of the divided self – of the 'self...severed from the self' evidenced in the ensuing literary tradition:

> The illusion that there is something like a 'true self' has taken deep root. It is an illusion that is established when writing has come to be seen as derivative and that voice which is most immediate to the self, and which constitutes self-consciousness, is privileged. The psychological person, who begins and ends in interiority, has come into existence.[17]

INTRODUCTION

The implications for the twentieth-century Japanese *shōsetsu* are far-reaching. For, as Karatani acknowledges, the emergence of the system that facilitated the 'discovery of self' was directly linked to a further development – the emergence of the literary form of the confession – that enhanced the trend towards interiority. As Karatani argues, 'it was the literary form of the confession – confession as a system – that produced the interiority that confessed, the "true self"'.[18]

As Dennis Washburn claims in his recent study of the concept of 'the modern' in Japanese fiction, in thus highlighting 'the fundamental dichotomy between the rhetorical devices of the confession and the "true self" those devices supposedly reveal',[19] Karatani has here isolated a significant feature of the confessional mode that has so dominated the twentieth-century Japanese prose narrative tradition. In identifying the origins of this process very clearly with the group of writers who emerged on the literary scene in the 1890s, moreover, Karatani has sought a more rigid assessment of the contribution of this generation all too frequently dismissed as 'mere precursors' of the Naturalist tradition in Japan. A brief examination of the direction assumed by their quest for interiority – and, in particular, of the concept of the *naibu seimei* (inner life) as espoused by Tōkoku, the foremost spokesman of the group – should suffice to reinforce Karatani's suggestion of the far-reaching ramifications of their discovery of selfhood.

Born around the time of the restoration of Imperial rule in 1868, here was a generation of writers weaned on the notion of individualism introduced into Japan in the 1870s and convinced that the existence and values of the individual were valuable in their own right and, as such, worthy of respect. Following centuries of suppression under the neo-Confucian orthodoxy that informed the preceding Tokugawa era, it was only in the wake of the reforms implemented by the new Meiji oligarchy that the individualist culture upon which the vision of the self as spontaneous and irrational was premised could take root. At the same time, disturbed by official attempts to equate private interests with public responsibilities, these writers, initially active in their support of the People's Rights movement of the 1880s, found themselves in the aftermath of the constitution promulgated in 1889 increasingly moved to withdraw from the public sphere and to focus instead on the individual as independent, ethical and moral subject. The result was an increasing tendency to focus on themselves as protagonists for their fictions – protagonists who consequently existed in an abstract situation of freedom where they were able to pursue sensual awakening away from the dictates of society.

The inward turn assumed by these writers can be seen in large measure as a reaction to the gradually evolving notion of the limited political subject. Equally significant to this process was the contribution of Christianity, whose espousal of the uniqueness of the individual's 'inner life' struck a chord with a group of writers driven by a determination to pursue and understand the self. Inspired to develop the new ideal of self-cultivation in the hope thereby of promoting the spirit of freedom and independence amongst the Japanese of the day, here was a generation whose attraction to what the critic Ian Watt sees as essentially 'an inward, individualist and self-conscious kind of religion' has been viewed,[20] by Fowler and others, as the result of more than mere coincidence.[21] To be sure, as we shall see in the consideration of Kitamura Tōkoku's notion of the 'inner life' that follows, there is a danger in this regard of overestimating the influence of the particular tenets of the Christian faith as reintroduced by the Western missionaries in the latter half of the nineteenth century and of overlooking the effect of traditional Japanese culture rooted in the aesthetic life and in nature in the formulation of the Japanese version of selfhood. Yet in providing these authors with the encouragement to explore a more autonomous and private realm, Christianity can nevertheless be seen as a guiding force in determining the approach to selfhood adopted, not merely by this generation of turn of the century writers, but of so many Japanese authors. More significantly for the purposes of this study, Christianity will be seen as integral to the formulation of the vision of the 'inner self' evidenced not merely by Endō, but by several of his colleagues in the *Daisan no shinjin* coterie.

As noted above, however, at the vanguard of this movement towards interiority was Tōkoku, an author described by Mathy as 'the first writer in Japanese history to explore seriously the nature and potentialities of self and to try to integrate a philosophy of self into an over-all view of life'.[22] In view of the constant political pressure to conform and the frequent reminders of the need to 'benefit mankind' in all his endeavours,[23] Tōkoku's contribution to the 'discovery of the self' was indeed remarkable – especially when viewed against the reality of his suicide in 1894 at the age of 26. Disillusioned by his own efforts and those of his peers to influence the course of events through the People's Rights Movement in the 1880s, Tōkoku turned increasingly to his pen as a means of asserting the selfhood of the individual freed from the strictures of shogunal rule. In this he may not have been alone. In advocating a spirit of freedom founded upon the principle of the 'inner life', however, Tōkoku succeeded, in the words of one critic, in fanning a 'new spirit of individualism that spread with great contagion to enflame the hearts of the youth of the age'.[24] In so doing, he contributed more to the 'discovery of interiority' than any other author of the age. As such, although an extended discussion of his literary legacy is beyond the scope of a study of this nature, a brief examination of the salient elements of his philosophy of 'inner life' should nevertheless serve to identify this as integral to the vision of selfhood inherited by subsequent generations of authors in Japan.

In identifying the search for the spirit of the Universe – 'the spirit of freedom' – as essential to the process of individual awakening, Tōkoku was conforming to the call for greater *dokuritsu* (independence) in the context of democracy amongst the Japanese of the day. As Janet Walker has noted, however, in contrast to the social and political focus of earlier advocates, such as Fukuzawa Yukichi, Tōkoku was more concerned with the religious and spiritual connotations of the concept. And whereas earlier calls had been for the nurturing of 'good, responsible citizens', for Tōkoku, the ultimate goal of the political, social and philosophical revolution that had been set in motion in the wake of the Meiji Restoration in 1868 had to be viewed in terms of 'awaken[ing] the spiritual selfhood of the individual'.[25]

To the majority of his generation, such awakening tended to be viewed in the context of the pursuit of economic goals. For Tōkoku, however, such goals could never be anything but temporary; instead, he cited spiritual goals which, in contributing to the harmony of the universe, were eternal. And these, in turn, could be achieved only through cultivation of the 'inner life' which, in directing the sights of the individual to the eternal goals of selfhood and harmony, represented the sole path to true freedom.

The concept is first explored in 'Ninomiya Sontoku Ō' (Ninomiya Sontoku, the Wise, Old Man), a short essay in which Tōkoku praises Ninomiya, a low-ranking official in the Meiji government, for living in accordance with the 'inner life'. Couched in terms of self-development through self-reliance, the 'inner life' is here introduced as the key to self-understanding – in that it enables the individual to reconcile the various levels of his being and, in so doing, to begin the process of regeneration. The logic is pursued in a subsequent essay, 'Kakujin shinkyū-nai no hikyū' (The Heart, a

INTRODUCTION

Holy of Holies), in which Tōkoku focuses on the *kokoro* (lit. the heart, the focus of the individual), which he divides into two layers: the 'outer *kokoro*' (the superficial level which tends to represent the extent of the individual's search for understanding) and the 'inner *kokoro*' (the level to which the individual must aspire in order to achieve self-definition). As Mathy suggests,

> To a person in the first sanctuary such things as the gospel, salvation, resurrection are only words; these can only be understood by the man who has penetrated into the Holy of Holies.[26]

At this stage in his career, Tōkoku's vision of the 'inner life' is couched in specifically Christian terminology. As Janet Walker has suggested, however, in stressing the need for spiritual selfhood to ensure harmony in life, the notion is ultimately 'intersected with traditional Eastern ideals of the sage and the enlightened man, to emerge finally, leavened by Emerson's transcendentalist philosophy, as an intellectual and spiritual vision of man in the context of democracy'.[27] At the same time, moreover, it is important to acknowledge the extent to which exposure to Christianity as a young man, far from leading Tōkoku to reject his native cultural ethos, resulted rather in a concerted attempt to accommodate this within Japanese tradition. We shall detect a similar conviction as evidenced by Endō in the chapters that follow. At this stage, however, let us remain with Tōkoku's assertion of the primary responsibility of the literati: the definition of this inner world. 'Man must by all means respect his [inner *kokoro*]; he must make it distinct; he must make it straight, he must make it clear, and he must make it public', he argued.[28] To Tōkoku, it was only in this way, by emphasising the experience of the heart, that the individual could come into contact with the 'spirit of the universe'; and it was only by thus placing supreme emphasis on the absolute value of Truth that he could challenge his own selfish ego. It was here that the artist came into his own: it was his duty to 'give voice to this inner life. No ordinary observation will do; he must penetrate through to the inner life of things [by means of] inspiration'.[29]

The challenge was clear. And it is difficult to exaggerate the influence of Tōkoku's theory of the 'inner life' on subsequent generations of Japanese writers. As the first concerted attempt to define the self in terms of the self, Tōkoku had identified a philosophy of idealistic humanism that not only set him aside from his literary predecessors, but was to serve as inspiration to his literary successors. As Mathy concludes:

> There is a remarkable continuity between [Tōkoku] and those who came after. By anticipating in his work the themes and problems that were to occupy later writers, he well deserves the title of forerunner which has been given him by Japanese critics.[30]

At the time of his death, the extent of this legacy may not have been immediately acknowledged by Doppo and the group of writers on whom Tōkoku's literary mantle subsequently fell (limited largely to those involved with the journal, *Bungakkai,* in which Tōkoku had expounded his philosophy). Within a very short time, however, the challenge of couching the concept of the 'inner life' in more specifically literary terms had been readily assumed – to the extent that Karatani suggests that: 'the mainstream of modern Japanese literature continued along lines set forth by Doppo....All the germs of the literature which was to be produced by the next generation were contained in the writing of Doppo'.[31]

Another to be mentioned in this regard is Shimazaki Tōson, an author whose admiration for Tōkoku as friend and mentor was quickly acknowledged and whose portrayal of the awakening of the individual in his ground-breaking first work of prose fiction, *Hakai* (Broken Commandment, 1906; trans. 1974) represents a literary embodiment, from the viewpoint of a single individual, of the territory that had been appropriated by Tōkoku: the inner life of the modern Japanese individual. But whereas Tōkoku limited his depiction of this realm to theoretical pronouncements, Tōson drew upon his skills of observation of those around him to explore in depth his vision of the individual as 'inheritor of a future of free selfhood that he has struggled consciously to achieve'.[32] The vision was inspiring – especially for those steeped in the Meiji drive towards self-definition – and contributed considerably to the emergence in the first decades of the twentieth century of various philosophies that arose from the need to satisfy the demands of those seeking to cultivate the self.

The other author we must mention briefly in our survey of developments with regard to approaches to selfhood during the early twentieth century is Natsume Sōseki, described by Fowler as 'perhaps the *only* Meiji or Taishō writer to comprehend fully the meaning of individualism in Japanese society'.[33] Much has been made of Sōseki's theory of individualism, encapsulated in his essay, 'Watashi no kojinshugi' (My individualism), in which the author insisted that developing individualism and assertion of the self entailed concomitant requirements to respect the individuality of others and to acknowledge the duties and responsibilities that accompany such new-found power. For many, such focus on the potential of the individual – and the valorisation of self-preoccupation (*jiko hon'i*) with which this is accompanied – has led to charges of this as representing a fundamentally antisocial gesture. But, as Jay Rubin points out, Sōseki is vigorous in his admonition against unbridled self-assertion: in focusing on the rights and duties of the individual, he was seeking rather to reaffirm the continued and growing validity for the author of the ideal of respect for the uniqueness of each individual.[34] To be sure, the Sōseki protagonist tends to be depicted as enduring the consequences of his own egotism; and, as Susan Napier has suggested, 'the sense of the self as alienated from its past, present and future, forced into various manifestations, but all largely negative' pervades his work.[35] In the light of the author's claim that the pursuit of individuality must be accompanied by respect of the individuality of others, however, such suffering comes to assume its own rationality as the logical consequence of egotism.

The question of identity is thus integral to Sōseki's art and it is in his mastery of human psychology, particularly in his mature novels, as analysis of character and motivation for action come to assume a greater prominence, that his contribution to the emergence of the *shōsetsu* as a literary form heavily imbued with the search for interiority is most readily evidenced. In contrast to the narratives of those of the Naturalist tradition, Sōseki's determination to avoid mirroring himself in his art is pronounced. For all the carefully crafted distance between author and his fictional constructs, however, and in spite of the jealously guarded distance between himself and his readers, there is, as Howard Hibbett has argued, an 'intensity of feeling beneath the polished surface [of his texts that] suggests a strong emotional involvement with his material'.[36]

The concept of the *kindai jiga*, which Irmela Hijiya-Kirschnereit describes as 'that ominous "modern self"'...a new notion of a modern, liberated individual [which] is said to have formed, albeit on a more or less subconscious level, a major driving force' in determining the direction assumed by the prose narrative form in twentieth-century Japan,[37] had taken root. The decades that followed saw writers working to appropriate the private self with unprecedented tenacity and, as they came increasingly to focus on themselves and their own immediate worlds, so Naturalism came to be identified as the rallying point for the inward turn taking place within the *shōsetsu*. As the critic, Donald Keene, has noted, 'in Japan, the most salient feature of Naturalist writing was the search for the individual'.[38] The search was, in large measure, a solitary exercise, one rooted in a literary world divorced from mainstream society. But there was an intensity about this preoccupation with the notion of the self as an 'enigmatic, yet essential, new reality'[39] that was to exercise considerable influence on the direction assumed by the twentieth century *shōsetsu* form. As Suzuki argues in *Narrating the Self*, a radical reconsideration of what the author depicts as 'I-novel discourse', 'the notion of the..."self" – referred to by a cluster of terms such as *jiga*, *jiko*, *jibun*, *kojin*, and *watakushi* – became a privileged, master signifier'.[40] Of greater significance, however, suggests Suzuki, is that this remained a signifier 'whose signifieds remained vague and fluid. For those Meiji writers who aspired to "represent" the new "reality" of the self in "concrete form," there were still no established assumptions about what the individual self might represent'.[41]

As Suzuki suggests, the vagueness was, in part, an inevitable consequence of the attempts by Tōkoku, Doppo, Tōson and others of their generation to represent the new paradigms of reality that had taken shape 'through the assimilation and naturalization of literary representation in Western literature'.[42] At the same time, however, Suzuki reiterates the necessity, advanced by Miyoshi, Fowler and others in their considerations of the peculiar characteristics of the *shōsetsu*, of locating the issues of modernity and selfhood firmly within the native intellectual tradition. More important to the development of the twentieth-century *shōsetsu* than the question of how subsequent Japanese authors appropriated the concept of the modern self from foreign sources, therefore, was the manner in which this was revamped by subsequent generations of Japanese authors within the *shōsetsu* tradition – a tradition increasingly epitomised by authors intent on a literary portrayal of the search for the sense of interiority that, in general, remained the *sine qua non* for an understanding of the often tenuous relationship between the individual and the society from which he found himself increasingly distanced. The concept has proven remarkably durable and, as Janet Walker acknowledges:

> If one links the novel to the spread of the ideal of individualism, both in its social and political manifestations and in

the less obvious internal transformations,...one cannot help remarking the strength and endurance of the tradition of the subjective novel, and the progressive depth of revelation of the inner self that it has [subsequently] attained.[43]

The strength and endurance of the tradition of the subjective novel is indeed impressive and this tendency to privilege 'that voice which is most immediate to the self' certainly provided a significant impetus to those authors of the pre-war *shishōsetsu* tradition in their determination to record personal experience with absolute sincerity. The resulting obsession with unmediated reality has been subjected to a gamut of interpretations – from those, like Kume Masao, who regarded the *shishōsetsu* as 'the core of literary art (in the true sense of the word), its true path, its essence',[44] to those, such as Nakamura Murao and Ikuta Chōkō, who deplored the 'bad tendency towards a one-sided emphasis on everyday life' (*nichijō seikatsu o henjū suru aru keikō*).[45]

For all the lack of consensus concerning the relative merits of the *shishōsetsu* as a literary form, however, the aims of the genre were largely accepted: there was general agreement on the vision of the *shishōsetsu* expounded by Uno Kōji, and subsequently developed by Itō Sei, as a form created out of the 'deepest self' (*mottomo fukai watakushi*) and, as such, 'the most natural form for Japanese writers'.[46] With the tradition of scrutiny of the self as an isolated figure in society and emphasis on the need to follow the inner self now firmly established, the main function of the author was consequently to give literary expression, as accurately and faithfully as possible, to that which came to be seen in terms of the 'genuine self' (*honmono no watakushi*).[47] The reader, in turn, responded to such protestations of sincerity and, despite the absence of any formal 'autobiographical contract' which Philippe Lejeune cites as integral to such referential reading,[48] was encouraged by various textual signals to assume a fundamental factuality that encouraged a reading of these texts as author faithfully revealing his 'genuine self'. The emphasis at this point, though, must be on the image of author *giving literary expression to* the self, of his *faithfully recording* his 'genuine self'. For it is in this regard, as a literature in which the reporting of actual perceptions and sensations and the honest portrayal of lived experience remains paramount, with little attempt to analyse or define this self, that the depiction of the *shishōsetsu*, hinted at by Walker, as but one stage, however influential, in the attainment of 'progressive depth of revelation of the inner self' is best supported.

For Walker, as noted above, the tradition has proven remarkably durable: in the passage cited above, she discerns a trend towards 'progressive depth of revelation of the inner self' that persisted up through Ōe Kenzaburō's *Kojinteki na taiken* (A Personal Matter, 1964; trans. 1969).[49] As she readily accepts, however, the example is arbitrary: there is any number of narratives that could be cited, from the post-war literary tradition, of *shōsetsu* that build on the inward turn effected in the pre-war *shishōsetsu* and, in so doing, pursue the search for interiority with, if anything, renewed intensity. It is in this regard that the literature of the *Daisan no shinjin* will be portrayed as coming into its own. For whilst it may well be true, as Uno Kōji suggested, that the traditional *shishōsetsu* enabled the author 'to "plumb the depths of the self" in a way that the ordinary novel, fettered by its conventions of "fictionalization", could not',[50] it should be noted that there is a world of difference in 'plumbing the depths' in search of a more vivid and accurate portrayal of the individual in splendid isolation and a similar determination, which we will be attributing to the *Daisan no shinjin*, which nevertheless enabled the author better to define this self in social context. The remainder of this Introduction will thus be devoted to an examination of the fundamentally different approach to 'revelation of the inner self' adopted by this group of post-war writers[51] – an approach epitomised, as we shall see, by the determination to give literary expression to the sense of the 'self...severed from the self' through focus upon individual protagonists struggling to come to terms with the existence of their own perceived double. In so doing, we shall be highlighting several qualities of their art that will enable us to identify Endō as an author more deeply imbued with the literary ethos of this generation than is often acknowledged.[52]

Picking up the pieces

The debates concerning the obligation of the author to limit his literary world to the sphere of personal experience raged remorselessly during the 1920s and early 1930s. The 1930s, however, saw the burgeoning supremacy of military dictates – and, as war spread to the mainland of Asia, so writers came increasingly to confront the reality of the call for a literature that was in harmony with the national effort and purpose. And just as those authors whose sympathies remained with a Marxist world view found themselves increasingly rounded up and faced with the demand to commit *tenkō* (political conversion) in return for their freedom, so those authors of the *shishōsetsu* tradition, whose works tended to be of such limited perspective and so closely identified with the experiences of one central figure as to seem of little concern to the censors, were nevertheless subjected to considerable reassessment. Authors, particularly those of the Shirakaba-ha (White Birch society) who had remained so confident of the intrinsic interest – even the practical value – of their portrayals of events drawn largely from personal experience, now found themselves increasingly challenged, their absolute faith in themselves as artists shaken as they were obliged by events outside their control to question their very identities as writers.

The debate in the 1930s concerning the future of the *shishōsetsu* therefore occurred spontaneously, an inevitable consequence of the burgeoning call for conformity. For some, there would always be a future for an 'honest and earnest record of the author's struggle with his fate'.[53] By the mid-1930s, however, there existed an increasing number of critics convinced that the *shishōsetsu* had run its course, at least in its present guise. Convinced that the form as it stood had entered a cul-de-sac, critics led by Yokomitsu Riichi called for a radical rethink – and, in so doing, issued a plea for a modern, 'pure' novel, one in which the central focus would be ' "self-consciousness" (*jiishiki*) or the "self that sees itself" in a modern age that had "destroyed the hitherto accepted notions of the psyche, the intellect, and the emotions" '.[54] The cry was taken up by Kobayashi Hideo who, in attacking the *shishōsetsu* for 'lack[ing] the power to conceptualize the impasse between the individual and society or the issue of the self in flight from the instability of life',[55] concluded his attack on the status quo with the following, oft-cited – and, as we shall see, prophetic – observation:

> The time has come for writers again to engage the problem posed by the self. Will they come to believe that an unvanquished 'I' still exists within them?...
>
> The *watakushi shōsetsu* (*shishōsetsu*) may have died, but have we really disposed of the self? Perhaps the *watakushi shōsetsu* will appear again in a different form. Such is the possibility, so long as Flaubert's famous equation – 'Madame Bovary, c'est moi' – remains in force.[56]

The call, in short, was for a re-evaluation of the aims of the *shishōsetsu* – for a move beyond the overwhelming emphasis on accurate and, where possible, verifiable portrayal of events drawn from the author's life[57] – towards a form that would allow for expression of the increased concern for definition of the self in social context. The decade that followed – the decade of the Pacific War – was hardly conducive to such radical rethinking of literary values. With the end of the war in 1945 and the arrival of Occupation forces eager to interfere as little as possible with such aspects of indigenous culture, however, the call to 'squash *shishōsetsu*'[58] was taken up with renewed intensity. Hijiya-Kirschnereit sums up the prevailing sentiment in the following terms:

> In the 1950s...*shishōsetsu* was accused of spiritual meanness, social abstinence and 'hermit-like isolation' (Kuwabara Takeo), 'privatism' and 'passive conformity,' retreating from public responsibility (Maruyama Masao) and the name of the genre was given derogatively a purely symbolic meaning.[59]

It was one thing to attack the *shishōsetsu* form as dated and ill-suited as a means of expressing the sense of modern selfhood. It was quite another to suggest amendments that might render the *shōsetsu* more amenable to post-war consciousness. One critic particularly influential in this regard was Itō Sei, who cited the author's 'inner voice' (*uchinaru koe*) as integral to the modern novel – and called for an assessment of subsequent trends in the *shōsetsu* form to be based on the extent to which the author succeeded in giving expression to this 'voice'. Itō can here be seen attacking a perceived lack of psychological depth in the pre-war *shishōsetsu*. At the same time, moreover, he was at pains to cite the dearth of fictional disguise within the form as the factor most influential in frustrating the free expression of this 'inner voice'. Suzuki sums up Itō's comparison between the *shishōsetsu* and its European counterparts in which this voice finds clearer expression in the following terms:

> The European novelists required 'fiction' (*kyokō*) as a 'mask' in order to extract and explore the 'pure essence' of their 'inner self'; the more sincerely these European novelists attempted to confess, the more they concealed themselves in fiction. By contrast, the Japanese authors revealed their natural selves directly without any 'extraction or abstraction'.[60]

The call for revitalisation of the *shōsetsu* form through augmented

INTRODUCTION

attention paid to exploration of the 'pure essence' of the 'inner self' would no doubt have possessed a ready appeal to both authors and readers for whom the potentialities of a literature of unmediated reality had largely been exhausted. In view of the situation in which these authors found themselves in the immediate post-war period, however, the need for reconsideration was all the more acute. Here was a nation reduced, quite literally, to ruins, a country with little alternative but to confront the urgent task of rebuilding. The psychological scars of defeat were aptly summed up by General McArthur in the following terms:

> Their whole world crumbled. It was not merely an overthrow of their military might, not merely a great defeat for their nation, it was the collapse of a faith, it was the disintegration of everything they had believed in and lived by and fought for. It left a complete vacuum morally, mentally and physically.[61]

For all these victims of war, confusion reigned, a confusion that found expression in a variety of guises within literary circles. Some, unable or unwilling to plumb their own all too painful recent experience took the opposite route – towards a literature of the fantastic in which they worked out their explorations of the self against such textual elements as dreams, ghosts and doppelgängers.[62] Others of the so-called *sengoha* (post-war) grouping, many of whom carried the additional stigma of having succumbed to the pressure to commit *tenkō* in the 1930s, determined to 'endure' the rigours of daily existence whilst somehow trying to make sense of the war by coming to terms with its root causes.[63] In this, they found inspiration either in Marxism or in the existential philosophy of the likes of Camus and Sartre, concerns which, in large measure, added a strongly ideological tenor to their depictions of life among the ruins.

There was, however, another generation of writers, that which would subsequently be labelled as the *Daisan no shinjin*, whose literary productions in the aftermath of war stood in stark contrast to the above responses. Critics disagree as to the exact membership of this group, although the names of Yasuoka Shōtarō, Kojima Nobuo, Shimao Toshio, Yoshiyuki Junnosuke and Miura Shumon are generally listed as founder members.[64] There was, however, one other latecomer to this grouping, Endō Shūsaku, whose delayed assimilation into the coterie was in part attributable, as we shall see,

17

to his physical absence from the Tokyo literary scene during the group's formative years.

The typical *Daisan no shinjin* member was only a few years younger than the *sengoha* affiliates. Those were all-important years, however. For having been born towards the end of the Taishō era (1912–26), here was the first generation of Japanese authors to have come of age under wartime conditions. Too young to have known anything but life on a war footing and educated in accordance with the increasingly militaristic code in the 1930s, here was a generation for whom the inexorable drift towards World War II hostilities had come to represent normalcy. They were, in short, as the critic Yamamoto Kenkichi suggests, a 'generation which [was] in every sense a product of the war'.[65]

Such information is of more than mere biographical interest. For, as I shall argue with specific reference to Endō, no assessment of the changes effected on the narrating self in the post-war *shōsetsu* is possible without acknowledgement of the ambiguous position in which Endō and his peers found themselves in the wake of defeat in 1945. On the one hand, glad to have survived at all, they were obliged to set about the task of restoring some semblance of normalcy to their lives. At the same time, even for those who, like Endō, had missed out on front-line action on medical grounds, the experience of war had left them scarred and, all too often, unsure how to cope with life in post-war reality. Their concerns in the immediate post-war period were, in short, those addressed in the so-called *shutaisei* debate concerning the role of the reconstituted individual in the democratic society that occurred between 1947–8. Epitomising the awareness of the need for positive self-definition that was essential for the survival of democracy in the volatile context of Occupation, here was a group of authors who would take advantage of their unique perspective to capture in their fictions the mood of troubled introspection and preoccupation with the sense of self that was characteristic of Japan's intellectual climate of the time.[66]

The sense of rootlessness experienced by this generation has been meticulously documented by Van Gessel. Disturbed by their own feelings of ambivalence and consequently unable to apply themselves wholeheartedly to the task of reconstruction being pursued, so assiduously and conspicuously, by their peers in the economic sector, they chose, whether consciously or not, to shift the focus back to the mundane events of their own small worlds. In this, as Gessel suggests, they succeeded in a very real sense in giving expression to the spirit of the age:

However much Japan may have boasted of the initial miracles, beneath the surface a gnawing sense of inferiority and guilt continued to flow. It was this spirit that the Third Generation captured in their literature.[67]

Far more than existential crises, then, it was the very real constraints of everyday life that were of primary concern to the average Japanese readers of the day – and it was to this new public sentiment that the *Daisan no shinjin* strove to give voice. In this, the legacy of the pre-war *shishōsetsu* is readily apparent – leading to inevitable depictions of these narratives as representing a second wave of the *shishōsetsu*.[68] For all the similarities, however, there is a marked difference in narrative focus in these post-war narratives – a distinction that, as Torii acknowledges elsewhere, seeks to 'capture and internalise experience from a different vantage point than that used by the first and second generations of post-war writers – from a point deeper in the recesses of the human psyche'.[69] The obsession with petty human activity certainly persists; indeed many of these authors established their reputations with Akutagawa Prize-winning works that focus, with an intensity to match that of the most self-obsessed *shishōsetsu*, on their own immediate trials and anxieties. The difference, however, lies in the use made by these authors of such material. For the author of the pre-war *shishōsetsu*, as we have noted, the desire to avoid fabrication – to see art as 'the recreation of the life of a single individual'[70] – was all-consuming. Encouraged to produce ever more detailed factual depictions of their immediate lives, the intrinsic value of these facts as in some way indicative of a higher truth was rarely questioned. And whilst writers such as Shiga Naoya regularly bemoaned the impossibility of revealing the whole 'truth' concerning a given incident, such concerns were nevertheless turned to their advantage – as such disclaimers were used, paradoxically, to heighten the sense of verisimilitude of the portrayal on offer. To be sure, these authors were aware of the inevitability of exercising a degree of editorial control over their material in their recreations of the 'facts' depicted. In deciding which incidents – which 'facts' – to withhold, however, they were able to augment the appearance of absolute faithfulness to reality.

As noted above, it was a similar determination on the part of the *Daisan no shinjin* to draw on their own 'factual' experience as material for their narratives that encouraged comparisons with the pre-war *shishōsetsu*. What such comparisons fail to acknowledge, however, is the attempt by the latter to move beyond recreations of reality and to remove the material drawn from real life to a new dimension – to create 'truths' that transcended these 'facts'. We shall return to this issue in the next chapter in the discussion of Endō's use of the technique of *oki-kae* (transposition). At this point, let us simply note the author's determination to maintain a clear distinction between 'facts' and 'truths':

> I have no intention of writing down facts (*jijitsu*). If I did, the result would no longer be a novel. Rather, to write a novel is to record truths (*shinjitsu*), not facts. Thus, having examined those around me, I analyse them...and gradually the character germinates....The art of creating a novel is to use 'truths' to reconstruct 'facts': real 'facts' themselves are totally unimportant to the novelist.[71]

In one sense, Endō is here addressing an issue that had long been prominent in literary circles in Japan; indeed, his concern is reminiscent of the debate concerning the respective roles exercised by 'actuality' and 'reality' initially aired in the open discussion that occurred between Mori Ōgai and Tsubouchi Shōyō, the so-called *botsurisō-ronsō* (debate about submerged ideas) that occupied the pages of the literary journals in Japan towards the end of 1891. At the same time, however, in drawing this distinction, he is giving expression to the post-war reality of the *shōsetsu* that was shared by his peers in the *Daisan no shinjin* and by their readers who no longer assumed that what they were reading represented factual accounts of personal experience. More than the 'facts' on which their narratives are based, then, there was a new concern, a determination to discern behind these depictions of mundanity an 'inner truth', one more closely related to the lives of the individuals caught up in these dramas. The concern now was to portray these dramas as taking place, not simply within the narrow confines of the world of the author–protagonist, but in the context of a broader society in which the actions of the individual have more far-reaching repercussions. As the critic, Akiyama Shun argues,

> Their literature doesn't simply depict a small segment of society; it reveals society changing at a given moment – and highlights concerns with depictions of the individual in that society....It offers a deeper perspective on those individuals caught up in mundane reality.[72]

It was the critic, Kobayashi Hideo in his famous 1935 discussion of the *shishōsetsu* who cited the absence of the tradition of a 'socialised self' as a defining feature of the genre.[73] Devoid of concern for the place of the individual within society, it is the absence of the sense of the author assimilated into the community, he suggests, that represents the essential distinction between the *shishōsetsu* and European counterparts as works of personal fiction by such as Goethe and Gide. The consequences were predictable: as Fowler notes, without awareness of any confrontation between society and the individual – with 'society' comprising no more than those people who had a direct impact on the author's sensibilities – these writers could hope for 'nothing more than technically brilliant depictions of...themselves living in studied isolation....[They] were left to seek a kind of "self-purification" achieved by recording one's mental state'.[74] In short, the protagonists of these pre-war *shishōsetsu* tend to act alone, convinced that it is only thus, devoid of extraneous distractions, that they are in a position to present the unmediated reality of their lives that their readers had come to expect.

The vision of the self isolated from social interaction led the critic Nakamura Mitsuo to talk in terms of the 'deformed I' of the *shishōsetsu*.[75] As Ueda Miyoji suggests, however, there is a paradox at work here: the more the authors of the *shishōsetsu* tradition had chosen to explore their own inner landscapes, the more 'the self had come to exist as believable reality'.[76] All this changed with the *Daisan no shinjin*, however – as increased concern for the social implications of their scenarios resulted in 'the self being reduced to a small, unreliable being'.[77] The *shishōsetsu* may have been restricted in scope. It was nevertheless possessed of a driving force – a desire to affirm the supremacy of selfhood – which, however self-serving, provided the critical impetus for practitioners of the genre. For the *Daisan no shinjin*, however, such confidence in the supremacy of their own selfhood had been shattered, leading to the following sobering assessment of their prospects by the critic Yamamoto Kenkichi in a roundtable discussion of the time:

> I feel as though we have seen the emergence of a truly lost generation. Compared with the *sengoha* who were motivated by idealistic concerns, they appear to have rejected mental effort and adopted a negative stance in their attempt to accept reality passively.[78]

The comment was made in 1955, at a time when the future for the *Daisan no shinjin* did indeed appear bleak. Significantly, however, Yamamoto's somewhat pessimistic assessment is followed immediately by a cursory remark that, in retrospect, appears to epitomise the very real contribution of the group:

> It is precisely because they represent a new generation of writers that the *Daisan no shinjin* are in a position, whilst maintaining their passive stance, to assert a new literary self (*bungaku-jō no atarashii jiko o shuchō dekiru*).[79]

It is this 'new literary self' – one that incorporated a sense of the self being brought into much clearer awareness of, and interaction with, the world around them – that represents the main distinction between the pre-war *shishōsetsu* and the narratives of the *Daisan no shinjin*. In addition to the self, there is now an 'other' (*tanin/tasha*) to be taken into consideration, and personal experience as depicted in their fictions is introduced, less by way of assertion of the supremacy of the self, more in an attempt to discern there the keys for an understanding of the nature of interpersonal relationships.

The consequences of this shift are significant – and extend beyond a severing of the intimate author–protagonist relationship characteristic of the pre-war *shishōsetsu*, as author comes to identify with more than one 'focus figure',[80] and to allow the sensibilities of more than one character to intrude. For inherent in this recognition of the existence of the 'other' is a rejection of the inability which the *Daisan no shinjin* attributed to their *shishōsetsu* forebears to acknowledge a greater complexity to the process of recording human experience – and their concomitant 'failure to delve beyond the psyche in their portrayals of human nature'.[81] For the *Daisan no shinjin*, then, the need to locate their explorations of the self in the process of active engagement with the 'other' was paramount and their fictions reveal a growing propensity to highlight alternative characters who, in serving as foils to the focus figure, are ideally placed to alert the protagonist to his/her own social shortcomings.

At the one level, the desire to incorporate the existence of an 'other' into their narratives required little more than an expansion of the range of the narrative focus. Increasingly disturbed by the feelings of ambivalence implicit in their identities as both survivors of war and yet uncertain how to contribute to the process of reconstruction, however, the sense of this 'other' as existing, not as an alternative, independent individual, but as an integral part of their own complex being, took root. The self as participant in the drama of coping with the reality of post-war 'normality' remained centre stage. More and more, however, this being found himself confronted with another self – a *mō hitori no jibun* – whose presence he struggles, in vain, to deny. The tension was portrayed by Yasuoka Shōtarō, a leading member of the coterie, in the following terms,

> There seems to be 'another me' (*betsu no, mō hitori no watashi*) who is feeding my family and paying my taxes – and this serves as a constant reminder to me of my lack of integrity.[82]

It is hard to imagine a pre-war *shishōsetsu* writer such as Shiga Naoya diluting his belief in artistic integrity through introduction of such an alternative self. The division between the self and this 'other' self is nevertheless central to the narrative design of the *Daisan no shinjin* – and nowhere more extensively evidenced, as we shall see, than in the narratives of Endō. For the group as a whole, however, the need to determine a narrative perspective better suited to portrayal of this self in conflict with this 'other self' was keenly felt. A spontaneous and highly subjective narrative voice may have served its purpose in the *shishōsetsu*. With the *Daisan no shinjin* authors increasingly intent on highlighting the conflict within the self, however, there was a need for a greater degree of objectivity in the positioning of their narrators. And as, more and more, these authors determined to forge their literary worlds out of this tension, so they found themselves increasingly drawn to question the reliability of the perspective offered by their own narrators. The result was a series of texts in which the hitherto privileged position of the narrator was seemingly wilfully undermined by the presence of an alternative perspective on characters and events – a perspective that, by definition, served to cast doubt on previously inviolable visions of 'truth' and 'reality'.

The fiction to emerge from this re-evaluation has been categorised by one critic as 'a literature of dual perspectives'.[83] Portraying 'a good portion of the fiction written in Japan since its defeat in World War II' as attempts to 'attack...and crush...the strong, confident literary self that stood at the center of prewar Japanese fiction', Gessel defines the resulting texts in the following terms:

INTRODUCTION

> Like the picaresque fiction produced in post-war Germany, these Japanese works involve an expanded, often splintered, range of perspective and point of view; questioning of the narrator's reliability and authority to speak by his own alter ego; and a new, invigorating dosage of irony. These stories are told both in the voice of the narrator, who relates his personal experience in much the same manner as the creators of *shishōsetsu* who dominated the realm of fiction before the war, and in the voice of the narrator's doppelgänger – his 'spirit double' – who infuses the text with a critical commentary or provides an ironic view of the narrated events.[84]

In the study of the Endō texts that follows, much will be made of the contribution of this 'splintered perspective' to the portrayal of protagonists struggling to come to terms with this 'other self' – with a deeper level of their being than that to which they had previously assented. The Endō protagonists are engaged in a remorseless quest, a search for greater understanding, not merely of the motivating force behind their seemingly impulsive behaviour, but, by extension, of the relationship between their conscious self – the persona that they have traditionally presented to society – and this 'other self', symbol of the unconscious being in which such actions appear rooted. Troubled by the malice that they discern within themselves and obliged to acknowledge their powerlessness to exercise control over this realm increasingly dismissed as 'unfathomable', they find themselves in direct confrontation with this '*mō hitori no jibun*', whose presence becomes increasingly undeniable.

In pursuit of these ends, such a splintered perspective is highly appropriate. Without such an alternative – without the 'critical commentary' entrusted to 'the voice of the narrator's *doppelgänger*' – the portrayal of individual protagonists struggling to come to terms with the existence of another self would inevitably lack for objectivity; the depiction of their journeys toward greater self-understanding would, of necessity, be deprived of a certain psychological verisimilitude. Yes, the initial discovery is often painful. But as one by one they come to acknowledge this other self as an integral part of their being and to appear, as such, as increasingly composite individuals, so they appear less and less troubled by the often conflicting agendas they come to discern in the depths of their being.

With this in mind, let us move to direct consideration of the author whose works represent the focus of this study.

1
TOWARDS RECONCILIATION

> What a piece of work is a man, how noble in reason, how infinite in faculties, in form and moving how express and admirable, in action how like an angel, in apprehension how like a god: the beauty of the world, the paragon of animals – and yet, to me, what is this quintessence of dust?
> (*Hamlet*, Act 2, sc. ii)

> We have tacitly assumed, for some centuries past, that there is *no* relation between literature and theology. This is not to deny that literature – I mean, again, primarily works of the imagination – has been, is, and probably always will be judged by some moral standards.
> (T.S. Eliot)

> If it has been believed hitherto that the human shadow was the source of all evil, it can now be ascertained on closer investigation that the unconscious man, that is, his shadow, does not consist only of morally reprehensible tendencies, but also displays a number of good qualities, such as normal instincts, appropriate reactions, realistic insights, creative impulses, etc.
> (C.G. Jung)

The discussion in the second half of the Introduction described, in broad brush strokes, the distinctive features of the literature of the *Daisan no shinjin*, the group with which Endō found affiliation on his return from his period of study in France. Critics have, as noted, played down the significance of this 'nominal' affiliation,[1] choosing rather to identify Endō as engaged in a somewhat lonely literary pursuit in search of a form of Christianity better suited to the Japanese spiritual climate than that he had inherited with his baptism into the Catholic tradition, undertaken largely at his mother's instigation, at the age of 11. The reasons for this critical response are not difficult to discern. Not only is there an overwhelming tendency, pervading the author's entire *oeuvre*, to address in his literature the questions raised by his faith; equally, there is at first glance very little to link Endō's diligently researched and carefully crafted portrayals of characters who bear little overt resemblance to the author who created them with the seemingly indefatigable emphasis on young male protagonists who appear to double with their authors, at least in physical and autobiographical detail, that characterises the works of other members of the group.

The distinction is marked, the jealously guarded distance between Endō as author and the protagonists who occupy the pages of his narratives seemingly at complete odds with the portrayals of protagonists, all too readily interpreted as self-portraits, in the works with which fellow members of the coterie established their reputations. The portrayal of the directionless Shintarō struggling to come to terms with the reality of his dying mother in Yasuoka Shōtarō's *Kaihen no kōkei* (A View by the Sea, 1959; trans. 1984); that of Shunsuke desperately seeking to halt the fragmentation of his family in Kojima Nobuo's *Hōyō kazoku* (Embracing Family, 1966); that of Toshio helpless to stem his wife's psychological disorder occasioned by his own marital infidelity in Shimao Toshio's *Shi no toge* (The Sting of Death, 1960–77): the seemingly overt attention to autobiographical detail in such works, repeated in each case in a string of short stories ostensibly focusing on the same events in the author's personal lives, seems a far cry from even the earliest Endō narratives. Here, in contrast we shall see a variety of protagonists, ranging from a French student-turned-Nazi collaborator, through a doctor implicated, however vicariously, in the wartime experiments in vivisection on Allied POWs, to a Western missionary desperately seeking to circumvent the ban on all Christian proselytisation imposed by the Tokugawa shogunate between 1600 and 1867. In short, in contrast to the proliferation of protagonists in the texts of the other members of the *Daisan no shinjin* who appear to echo the factual reality of the lives of the artists who created them (whether delivered as first- or third-person narratives), Endō's corpus seems devoid of attention to such autobiographical detail. Not only is his *oeuvre* notable for a marked dearth of first-person narratives,[2] but the various protagonists are clearly distinguished from their models, even where these are identifiable.

To cite but one example, as Endō himself remarked with reference to the various wives who populate his works:

> [In the creation of a particular character], I obviously take certain traits from various people: for example, my portraits of my wife are actually an amalgam of various traits stemming from my observation of various wives.[3]

In view of the superficial distinctions between Endō's narratives and those of his peers in the *Daisan no shinjin*, the tendency to downplay the significance of his affiliation with the coterie is understandable. And it is certainly true that, for all the close personal friendships he forged with several of its members,[4] Endō remained at best a fringe contributor to the formal activities of the group. But here we are merely scratching the surface: a consideration of the qualities attributed to the group in the Introduction to this book suggests a greater degree of affinity between Endō and his peers – one born of a mutual determination to probe deeper into the psychological worlds of their protagonists – than is readily acknowledged. It is to these points of common interest – and, in particular, to Endō's very real contribution to examination of the literary possibilities of these shared concerns – that this discussion will now turn.

In the Introduction, much was made of the tendency, shared by the various members of the *Daisan no shinjin*, to focus on the inner horizons of their creations through more consistent observation of the artistic distance separating author and protagonists than is evident in many of the pre-war *shishōsetsu*. The commitment was shared by Endō, whose determination to fathom the psychology of his characters is, with the arguable exception of Shimao Toshio's portraits of his protagonists struggling to come to terms with the concept of the previously unconscionable 'future' following his aborted *kamikaze* mission, unrivalled within the group. For Endō, the challenge for all his narrators was to highlight the 'deep inside of man',[5] a challenge that can be directly attributed to the author's vision of the composite human being as summarised in a 1988 interview:

> Man is a splendid and beautiful being and, at the same time, man is a terrible being as we recognised in Auschwitz – God knows well this monstrous dual quality of man.[6]

The portrayal is of the individual as representing an amalgam of conflicting forces, the implicit challenge to Endō, as author, being the need to seek a literary reconciliation of the conscious and unconscious elements within human nature. As we shall see, the attempt can be seen as the defining moment of Endō's *oeuvre*. The effect of this attempt, however – the portrayal of protagonists engaged in the gradual process of coming to terms with a deeper level of their being than that to which they had previously assented – is reminiscent of a similar tendency that pervades the literature of the *Daisan no shinjin*.

We are talking here of Endō as an author at the forefront of the move towards assertion of a 'new literary self', a process already identified as integral to an understanding of the narratives of the *Daisan no shinjin*. Of even greater relevance to our current discussion is the extent to which, in pursuit of this goal, Endō conforms to the model, depicted in the Introduction, of the *Daisan no shinjin* authors exercising greater care in the positioning of their narrators, in an attempt thereby to give voice to the full extent of the conflict within the self. For Yasuoka, for Shimao and the other members of the *Daisan no shinjin*, as we have noted, the ensuing 'splintered perspective' contributed to the overall depiction of characters engaged in constant confrontation with an 'other' – whether as an independent being or as an alternative facet of the self with whom the protagonist seeks reconciliation. Nowhere, however, is the technique used as extensively, or with such effect, as in the Endō narrative as, in work after work, the 'voice of the narrator's doppelgänger – his spirit double' results in a subversion of initial character depictions and a reassessment of narrated events. The 'critical commentary' provided in this way is integral to Endō's design and, as such, we shall be returning to this aspect of the author's art later in this chapter. At this stage, however, let us remain with the *Daisan no shinjin* – with a consideration of other narrative elements, identified in the Introduction as representative of the group, which serve to locate the Endō *shōsetsu* more readily within this remit than is often acknowledged.

One aspect, cited in the Introduction as distinguishing the literature of the *Daisan no shinjin* from their precursors in the pre-war *shishōsetsu*, was the emergence, in the former, of a truly 'socialised self'. In contrast to the earlier protagonists who remained, on the whole, isolated from social interaction, there is a concern for the social implications of their scenarios in the works of the *Daisan no shinjin* that leads to portrayal of protagonists who accept their status as insignificant entities in a much broader social spectrum. The generalisation certainly appears to hold true for the Endō narrative. Whether it be the protagonists of several of the earlier works, troubled by a social conscience in the wake of their instinctive responses to confrontation with the forces of evil,[7] the foreign missionary, Rodrigues in *Silence*, whose actions are dictated, in large measure, by concern for the outcome of his actions on the Japanese whose destinies rest largely in his hands, or the self-effacing Ōtsu in Endō's final novel, *Fukai kawa* (Deep River, 1993; trans. 1994), the Endō protagonist is acutely aware of his membership of a larger society. As such, he is rarely tempted to determine the course of his actions without reference to the implications of this on those with whom his destiny is linked.

Closely tied to this determination to look beyond the immediate worlds of his protagonists is the tendency, again identified earlier as a distinguishing feature of the *Daisan no shinjin* text, to allow the sensibilities of more than one 'focus figure' to dominate his dramas. The Endō protagonist is an elusive figure, the novel in which a single protagonist is identified at the outset as the fulcrum around which the subsequent drama will revolve and whose perspective subsequently dominates the entire text the exception rather than the rule. Instead, the Endō narrative tends to cater for a variety of 'focus figures', each of whom is provided with the opportunity, however rare, to assume centre stage and whose perspective consequently dominates, if only briefly. The technique used to give expression to these varying voices may vary – from the exchange of letters in *Shiroi hito* (White Man, 1955), through the alternating diary extracts of Yoshioka and Mitsu in *Watashi ga suteta onna* (The Girl I Left Behind, 1964; trans. 1994) and the carefully considered juxtaposition of the perspectives of Velasco and Hasekura in *Samurai* (The Samurai, 1980; trans. 1982), to the overt division of *Deep River* into chapters devoted to the worlds, not merely of Ōtsu and Mitsuko, the purported protagonists, but of a series of other fellow tourists on the trip to the Ganges.[8] The effect in each case, however, is similar: by virtue of the introduction of the perspectives on narrated events of a series of 'protagonists' – by implicitly questioning the validity of any single perspective – the author attributes a more universal significance to his narratives than he would have achieved with a single-focus narrative style.

There remains, however, one further characteristic that provides a powerful link between Endō and his contemporaries in the coterie. The distinction between 'factual reality' and remaining 'true' to the dramas as they evolve even whilst emphasising the distance between author and protagonist was cited in the Introduction as central to the discussions of the evolution to the *shōsetsu* effected by the *Daisan no shinjin* in general in the immediate post-war period. The issue was to prove crucial to Endō in his attempts to portray, by means of imaginative reconstruction, the 'truth' surrounding his own, intensely personal, spiritual journey. In all but a few cases, the protagonists of his narratives may bear little overt resemblance, in terms of physical and autobiographical detail, to Endō himself. For all this, however, there is a degree of empathy, an identification with the pains and struggles that his protagonists experience as an inevitable part of their journeys toward greater self-awareness no less intense than that of the other authors in the group. The details of the events depicted – the agonising choices with which so many of his protagonists are confronted – may bear little resemblance even to the archival records that represent the wellspring of so much of Endō's literary production, let alone to anything that the author may have personally experienced. For all their 'fabrication', however, there is an underlying 'truth' to the events, one that is close to the author's heart. Indeed, as Endō admitted in an interview with the critic, Kazusa Hideo, even in the case of those protagonists who ultimately succumb to the force of evil, there is an empathy between author and protagonist born of a sense of shared spiritual turmoil:

> If I had been confronted with the decisions faced by [the Nazi collaborator in *White Man*, by Suguro in *Umi to dokuyaku* (The Sea and Poison, 1957; trans. 1972) or by Rodrigues in *Silence*], who am I to say that I would not have responded as they did?[9]

The Endō protagonist is, in this sense, remarkably 'true' to the reality of the author's personal experience. More specifically, however, the empathy achieved with his protagonists is a powerful testimony to the consistency with which Endō has indeed sought to pursue the doubts occasioned by his own spiritual journey in his fictional narratives. Before examining the texts themselves, therefore, let us briefly consider the salient elements of the journey upon which the author embarked on that December day in 1933 when, at the behest of his mother and aunt, he agreed to go through with the ritual of baptism into the Catholic tradition.

Unforeseen consequences

As Endō himself was the first to admit, the full significance of the baptismal vows was lost on the young boy. The following depiction of events of that day may benefit from more than thirty years of hindsight. It nevertheless serves to encapsulate a sense of the frivolity with which Endō and his friends viewed the entire ceremony, a frivolity disturbed only by frustration at the enforced abandonment of the game of soccer they had been enjoying before being summoned inside to take part in the service:

> I was baptised along with several other children from the neighbourhood on Easter Sunday. Or more precisely, since this was not an act taken of my own free will, perhaps I should say that I was forced into baptism. At the urging of my aunt and my mother, I went along with the other children and, despite my predilection for disturbing the class, eventually succeeded in memorising the catechism. As such, the event was generally viewed as the baptism of a mischievous young boy. When the French priest came to that part of the baptism service in which he asked, 'Do you believe in God?', I felt no compunction in following the lead set by the other boys and replied, 'I do'.
>
> It was as though we were engaged in conversation in a foreign language in which my reply to the question, 'Do you want to eat this sweet?' was 'I do'. I had no idea of the enormity of the decision I had just taken. And I did not stop to think of the consequences on my entire life of these two simple words.[10]

The more Endō sought to dismiss the incident as a childish charade, however, the more he was obliged to attribute a greater significance to this event than he had initially recognised – and consequently to acknowledge a greater complexity to his being than suggested by this description of events of that day. Increasingly concerned that this one act, however insignificant it may have seemed at the time, would continue to haunt him, Endō determined to come to a clearer understanding, both of the cultural underpinnings of his newly acquired faith and of the implications for his understanding of human nature. The result was the decision to pursue a degree in French literature at Keiō University, with specific focus on the works of Mauriac, Bernanos and other French authors of Catholic persuasion. During the almost three years Endō spent in the early 1950s as one of the first Japanese students to study in France after the cessation of World War II hostilities, increasing frustration at his perceived inability to bridge the cultural divide he had come to discern between East and West was reinforced. Thereafter, the author's ultimate repatriation on medical grounds only served to enhance the perception of the need for recognition of the integral nature of all aspects of his being in the formulation of his vision of the composite self. In an interview offered some years after his return to Japan, Endō was to encapsulate the issue in the following terms:

> The confrontation of my Catholic self with the self that lies underneath has, like an idiot's refrain, echoed and re-echoed in my work. I felt I had to find some way to reconcile the two.[11]

For Endō, however, the process of reconciliation represented a very personal challenge – and led to a recognition of the need to redefine his faith in a manner that would account for the various tensions he had come to discern within his being. The result is a vision of Catholicism that clearly reflects the image of the individual as a composite of often conflicting forces:

> It seems to me that Catholicism is not a solo, but a symphony. It fits, of course, man's sinless side, but unless a religion can find a place for man's sinful side in the ensemble, it is a false religion. If I have trust in Catholicism, it is because I find in it much more possibility than in any other religion for presenting the full symphony of humanity. The other religions have almost no fullness; they have but solo parts. Only Catholicism can present the full symphony. And unless there is in that symphony a part that corresponds to Japan's mudswamp, it cannot be a true religion. What exactly this part is – that is what I want to find out.[12]

The desire to reconcile his adopted faith with his own cultural heritage is clearly evidenced in this comment, the author's consequent determination to define the faith in terms with which he and his fellow Japanese could more readily identify leading him to conclude that:

God must be found on the streets of Shinjuku or Shibuya, too – districts which seem so far removed from Him....It will be one of my tasks to find God in such typical Japanese scenes....If I succeed in doing that, my 'Western suit' will no longer be Western, but will have become my own suit.[13]

The image of Christianity as an 'ill-fitting suit' imported from the West was one with which Endō had long struggled, although by the time he produced his article with that title in 1967, the tone was less one of desperation born of the seeming impossibility of having Christianity take root in Japan, more an attempt to establish the pattern required if this ill-fitting garment were to be tailored into something more appropriate to his requirements. In this, Endō was by no means alone: the concept of 'indigenisation' of Christianity – the very terminology clearly locating the process in its historical context – is one to have been addressed in theological and literary circles in Japan ever since the return of the Christian missions in the early Meiji era following the rigidly enforced ban on all overt proselytisation during the Tokugawa era. In this regard, one can point to the literary contributions of the authors, already discussed in the Introduction – authors such as Tōkoku, Doppo, Tōson and Sōseki – as providing the literary foundations upon which future generations of authors, including Akutagawa Ryūnosuke, Masamune Hakuchō, Arishima Takeo and Dazai Osamu, would subsequently build and which would lead to the generation of post-war writers, epitomised by Endō, who remained determined to address in their fiction the issues raised by their faith.[14]

Endō's self-acknowledged search for a Japanese version of Christianity is thus firmly rooted in the twentieth-century Japanese philosophical tradition. For Endō and his fellow artists seeking to address the issue from a literary perspective, however, the perception of the vast gulf between the 'monotheistic' West and the 'pantheistic' East[15] has been further exacerbated by the perceived necessity of coming to terms in their literature with a further opposition inherent in their situation – that between their identity as adherents of the 'religion of the West' on the one hand and their careers as literary artists on the other. Defining the consequent tension in terms of a 'trichotomy',[16] Endō portrays this perception of a threefold opposition in the following terms:

> As a Christian, a Japanese and an author, I am constantly concerned with the relationship and conflict created by

these three tensions. Unfortunately, I have yet to reconcile and create a certain unity between these three conditions in my mind and, for the most part, they continue to appear as contradictory.[17]

At first glance, the desire to identify and isolate various aspects of the human composite would appear to fly in the face of contemporary psychological theory. Why, one may well ask, was Endō so concerned with the need to posit a tension of conflicting forces in a manner that suggests mutual incompatibility rather than representing these as a symbiosis of interrelated forces? Instead of the vision of a 'trichotomy' of mutually exclusive facets to human identity, have not others in similar circumstances been led to adopt a more holistic perspective depicting these, not as contradictory but as complementary elements of the composite being? For Endō, however, the depiction of such tension was essential – not as the basis of a fundamentally negative vision of human nature as an amalgam of ultimately irreconcilable forces, but as precursor of the attempt, integral to his literature, to highlight the essentially paradoxical interdependence he increasingly came to discern as at work within the individual. The paradoxical attempt to forge a link between characteristics initially established as opposing forces of some binary tension represents a recurring theme in the novels to be analysed in this study of Endō's literature – and it is on this aspect of the author's art that much of the ensuing discussion will focus.

For all its seemingly exclusive categorisation, therefore, Endō's depiction of the individual as torn between a series of conflicting identities provides an invaluable key to locating the link between a series of works that would appear, at first glance, to have little in common. Before considering the connection between the early works, in which the author's struggle with the question of identity appears to occupy centre stage, and his more recent novels, in which such issues have been superseded by a more studied examination of the role of the human unconscious, however, let us briefly consider the significance on Endō's fictional products of his examination of the implications of his identity as a novelist of Christian persuasion.

As suggested by the title of the essay with which he marked his emergence on the literary scene, 'Katorikku sakka no mondai' (The Problems Confronting the Catholic Author, 1947), Endō's study of the writings of a series of French Catholic authors during his university days led to the perception in their works of a potential conflict between the 'desire, as author, to scrutinise human beings' and 'the Christian yearning for purity'.[18] There followed a series of essays, some produced while still at university, in which he outlined his vision of these novelists as confronting the conflicting demands of their faith and their chosen careers as authors. The issue is encapsulated by Endō in the following extract:

> Normally, an author hopes that his work will induce a sense of artistic excitement in the soul of his reader. But he will not be plagued by a nagging fear that the evil human world he has created may sully the reader's soul. It is probably no exaggeration to claim that the average author is upheld by a belief, however unconscious, that anything can be condoned in the name of art.
>
> The Catholic author, however, finds himself confronted by the following Biblical verse, from Mark 9: 42: 'Whosoever shall offend one of these little ones that believe in me, it is better for him that a millstone were hanged about his neck, and he were cast into the sea.' The doubt that never left Mauriac's mind was precisely the fear that the gloomy world he had created might draw his reader closer to the world of sin, by granting him a glimpse of Evil.
>
> In which case, mindful of the harsh rejoinder of Christ, 'If thy hand offend thee, cut it off; if thy eye offend thee, pluck it out', does the author have a responsibility to remove the very essence of his work out of concern for his audience?[19]

As Endō was the first to recognise, however, the authors here under scrutiny were concerned more with literary creativity than with theology. The distinction for Endō – as for his French mentors – was vital and from the outset, he was at pains to acknowledge both the overriding need for the creation of 'living human beings' and the obligation, as author, 'to understand not only the characters' psyche and personality, but also their true flavour, their pains and struggles, everything about them'.[20] The distinction lay at the heart of his vision of his art and, as evidenced by the following assessment of the role of the 'Christian author', Endō was determined to distinguish between those for whom literature remained a vehicle for proselytisation and those, with whom he himself could more readily identify, for whom artistic integrity remained of paramount importance:

> Catholic literature involves not a literary portrayal of God and angels, but must limit itself to scrutiny of human beings. Besides, the Catholic writer is neither saint nor poet. The goal of the poet and saint is to focus all his attention on God and to sing his praises. But the Catholic writer must remember not only that he is a writer, but also his duty to scrutinise the individual....
>
> If, for the sake of creating a truly 'Catholic literature', or for the purpose of preserving and propagating the Catholic doctrine, the personalities of the characters in a novel are subjected to artifice and distortion, then the work ceases to be literature in the true sense of the word.[21]

Endō's desire to forge his artistic world through consideration of the dramatic tension that ensues when religion and literature are placed in opposition is readily apparent in such comments. Equally in evidence, moreover, is the author's conviction that it is only in examining the violent internal struggles within the individual that the author can highlight the integral relationship that exists between the two. Acknowledging the inherent danger that the 'Christian author' will be prevented, through a sentimental attitude towards religious motifs, from a deeper probing of human nature, Endō is here giving expression to his belief that, provided that the author persists with the examination of the fundamental essence of his characters rather than seeking to lead them in a particular direction, then the potential for a literature born of this duality remains.

For Endō at this stage, the issue was mainly of interest as part of his wider examination of the novels of the French authors who represented the primary focus of his studies. Increasingly, however, he found himself obliged to acknowledge the lengthy tradition upon which such literature was premised:

> The psychoanalytical self-examination of Freud and Bergson, the novelistic technique and psychology of contradiction that permeates the works of Dostoevsky, the question of self-integrity in Gide and the techniques of Proust are problems that the Catholic authors after Bourget and Bordeaux could not deny, issues with which they had to grapple and which had to be overcome. Even if this conflicted with the goal of proselytisation, these authors adopted such techniques in that they contributed to the science of human observation. At that time, these

new Catholic writers sensed an urgent need to remove themselves from the lofty heights of 'apologetic literature' and to examine 'godless man' as human beings....

Catholic writers under the influence of the likes of Freud, Bergson, Proust and Joyce 'look at the innermost recesses of human existence' and, 'in shining the spotlight on the soul of one who, though possibly appearing no different at the superficial level from fellow-members of twentieth century society, in fact represents a unique individual', they must scrutinise the secrets, the sins and the evils within the soul of their characters. On such occasions, the more they are able to get beneath the surface of their characters, the more intimacy they will come to feel with them. They must come to feel a sense of empathy with their sins and evils. But [these authors] are also Catholics; and, as believers in the Christian gospel, is there not a danger that they will be polluted through examination of these sins, through the intimacy and empathy they develop with these? Doesn't this pose a threat to their fulfilment as unique human beings?[22]

Here and elsewhere, the determination to avoid a betrayal of his duties as an author of creative fiction through resort to an 'apologetic literature' is evident. But there is a distinction between avoiding a direct focus on proselytisation in one's writing and seeking to incorporate themes born of one's faith on the other. Motifs raised by the author's faith are never far beneath the surface of this literature, for, as Endō himself argued:

> I don't seek Christian material as the basis for my novels: it is just that my environment and themes are Christian; the environment in which I was raised had a distinctly Christian flavour to it, and so, inevitably, I became embroiled with Christian material and themes. I am certainly not writing in order to proselytise or to spread the gospel....If I were, my works would definitely suffer as literature.[23]

Once more, Endō was by no means alone in this assessment: the comment is reminiscent of the claim to struggle with the same perceived tension between theology and literature made by another author, Graham Greene: 'I am not a Christian author. It is just that

Catholic padres happen to populate the pages of my works.'[24] To Endō, Greene and others, the danger was that the literary text would be relegated to secondary importance by the author's determination to convey a particular 'message'. Equally, however, such authors were aware of the concomitant need to avoid seeking within their work the possibility of salvation, either for their creations or for themselves. As Endō commented later in a subsequent discussion:

> I believe that when writing, all authors nurse an unconscious sense that they will thereby be liberated, even saved. But if, on completing the work, they realise that that is not the case, isn't that the sign of a great work?[25]

The determination to avoid succumbing to a sentimental attitude towards religious motifs – and to persist with the examination of the fundamental essence of his characters rather than seeking to force them into a ready mould – represents a constant in the literature of Endō. It also leads to a body of works that conforms very closely to the conclusion ventured by the critic, Boyce Gibson, in his discussion of the religious aspect of the literature of another author involved in a similar quest, Fyodor Dostoevsky:

> Unlike the Christian thinker, [the Christian artist] cannot, as he explores situations, focus on what lies beyond them. He does not, for example, write novels about God; he writes them about people in their perplexities about God. He may, indeed he cannot but, reveal his personal convictions, but it will be dissolved in the structure of the novel; it is the people, with their unfulfillments, their stresses, their defiances and also their complacencies and compromises, and their exposure to the light which they may accept or decline, who absorb his attention. It is not his business to explore the universe, but rather, if he has the power, to convey it; what he explores is character.[26]

With this assessment, Gibson is clearly not attributing to Dostoevsky any monopoly on the exploration of 'character'. In his suggestion of a link between the spiritual struggles in which so many of Dostoevsky's creations are embroiled and his attention to 'people with their unfulfillments, their stresses, their defiances and also their complacencies and compromises', however, Gibson highlights an element of Dostoevsky's art that has exercised a profound influence on the literary ethos, not merely of Endō but of other members of the above-mentioned generation of post-war writers with ties to the Christian church.[27] For Dostoevsky, Endō and others, therefore, the spiritual dimension of their exploration of human nature through their fictional constructs is not to be dismissed lightly and Endō, in particular, was at pains to stress from the outset the link he had come to discern between the desire to fathom the complexity within the individual and the tendency he had identified in the writings, not only of Dostoevsky, but of the various French novelists he had considered at length, to focus on the realm of the unconscious. For Endō, the more such authors sought to explore human nature in their novels, the more they were confronted with this inner realm, leading him to conclude:

> The Catholic author views this world as a shadow of the supernatural world, and, even whilst observing human psychology, he will detect, behind the 'second dimension' psychology of Freud, Bergson and Proust, the 'third dimension' of which Jacques Rivière happened to make mention. As a result, the Catholic writer can conceive as reality the introduction of the supernatural world into the world of human interaction, even if the non-Catholic reader is apt to misinterpret this as a distortion of reality.[28]

The concept of the 'third dimension' was one to which Endō would make repeated reference in his subsequent writing, the conviction that focuses on the psyche of his creations resulted in confrontation with some 'third dimension' within his characters leading to increasing consideration of the nature of the realm of the unconscious. The connection he had come to see between his faith and this territory, already evidenced in the above citation, was never far beneath the surface, the more he sought to portray a greater profundity to his characters, the greater the emphasis on characters driven by forces beyond their conscious understanding or control. As Endō noted in a more recent study:

> Nowadays, it may be possible to discuss ideology without resort to the question of the unconscious; but it is not possible to consider literature and religion in that way.... Religion is more than the product of the intellect; it is a product of the subconscious transcending all intellectualisation and consciousness.[29]

The belief lies at the heart of Endō's attempt to penetrate the 'deep inside of man'. It also suggests a link between a series of novels and short stories, written over a period of four decades, that might appear, at first glance, to have little in common. The reader of the earliest stories, *Shiroi Hito* (White Man) and *Kiiroi hito* (Yellow Man), both 1955 – and even of early novels such as *The Sea and Poison*, *Obakasan* (Wonderful Fool, 1959; trans. 1974) and *The Girl I Left Behind* – may indeed struggle to identify the connection between these and Endō's most recent novels, *Sukyandaru* (Scandal, 1986; trans. 1988) and *Deep River*, whether from the standpoint of subject material or its treatment. When viewed as a concerted attempt to probe ever deeper behind the persona, the continuum does, however, emerge and the novels consequently assume their position as the rungs of a carefully crafted ladder. At this point, therefore, let us turn our attention to an examination of the protracted focus on the inner worlds of the various protagonists of Endō's narratives.

Into the shadows

Having recognised the integral relationship between his faith and the unconscious, Endō was equally aware of the need, as author, to refrain from seeking to unravel the complexities of this realm in his literature. The question consequently presented itself of the means available to the author by which to probe the unconscious – and to render this in his fiction. The issue is that pursued by Dorrit Cohn (1978) in her penetrating study, *Transparent Minds*, and it is interesting to note the extent to which the Endō narrative conforms to the model established by Cohn. As such, let us begin our discussion of the techniques employed to this end by Endō with a brief consideration of the various narrative modes cited by Cohn as available to the author in the presentation of the psychological dramas experienced by his/her protagonists.

For Cohn, the three techniques that dominate attempts at rendering consciousness in the third-person prose narrative form are subsumed under the headings of psycho-narration, quoted monologue and narrated monologue. All three represent means whereby the author adds to the complexity of the psychological portraits on offer, but in each case, the distinctive approach results in a differing perspective on the worlds created. Cohn herself summed up these differences as follows:

> Psycho-narration summarizes diffuse feelings, needs, urges; narrated monologue shapes these inchoate reactions into virtual questions, exclamations, conjectures; quoted monologue distills moments of pointed self-address that may relate only distantly to the original emotion.[30]

Turning first to psycho-narration, the narrator's discourse about the protagonist's consciousness, Cohn suggests that it is in its verbal independence from self-articulation that the technique proves most effective:

> Not only can it order and explain a character's conscious thoughts better than the character himself, it can also effectively articulate a psychic life that remains unverbalized, penumbral, or obscure. Accordingly, psycho-narration often renders, in a narrator's knowing words, what a character 'knows' without knowing how to put it into words.[31]

Psycho-narration comes into its own, therefore, as a means of articulating the sub- or unconscious nature of the psychic states the author narrates. Moreover, as the most direct path to the sub-verbal depth of the mind, the technique is invaluable in shifting the narrative from *inter*personal to *intra*personal relationships. The trait is all-pervasive in the Endō narrative – and, as we shall see, the consequent shift from 'the manifest social surface of behavior to the hidden depth of the individual psyche'[32] lies at the heart of the author's portrayal of protagonists engaged upon their own journeys of self-discovery.

The effect induced by insertion of quoted monologue – of intense scrutiny of a character's mental discourse – will vary depending on the extent to which such inner discourse is separated from its third-person context. Traditionally restricted to the form of the audibly soliloquising voice (with the attendant sense of rationalisation or self-deceit that this entails), Cohn argues that, 'in the novels of Dostoevsky and other late Realist writers, direct citation of a character's thoughts is no longer restricted to isolated moments explicitly set aside for extended contemplation or inner debate...but accompanies his successive encounters and experiences'.[33] Again, the Endō *shōsetsu* conforms to Cohn's model – with the quoted monologue carefully integrated into the surrounding narrative text. More specifically, the Endō narrative is replete with the literary device, cited by Cohn as a common means of incorporation of such monologue into an extended narrative depiction – that of characters assailed by the presence of an increasingly incontrovertible 'inner voice'. In the chapters that follow, we shall encounter numerous examples of protagonists obliged to reconsider particular courses of action in deference to a voice they perceive as emanating from their unconscious being. As Cohn acknowledges, 'the *audition* of [such a] voice...is one of the conventions of third person fiction, and partakes in the larger convention of the transparency of fictional minds'. Cohn's rejoinder at this point is, however, of considerable importance: 'But that inner voice *itself* is a generally accepted psychological reality, and by no means a literary invention.'[34] The point was not lost on Endō, whose protagonists respond to this 'inner voice' with an intensity born of an awareness of the futility of attempting to repudiate it. The initial instinct to seek to overrule this voice is clearly present as Gaston, Rodrigues, Suguro and other protagonists contemplate their responses to this challenge. All, however, ultimately accept the need for a more considered approach – with the result that they end up paying greater heed to this than they would initially have countenanced.

Even a cursory reading of a representative sample of Endō's works will reveal the propensity of Cohn's third technique for rendering consciousness in fiction: that of narrated monologue. Enabling the author to reproduce verbatim a character's own mental language – in the guise of the narrator's discourse – the technique is cited by Cohn as holding a midpoint between the other two:

> rendering the content of a figural mind more obliquely than the former, more directly than the latter. Imitating the language a character uses when he talks to himself, it casts that language into the grammar a narrator uses in talking about him, thus superimposing two voices that are kept distinct in the other two forms.[35]

The Endō narrator takes maximum advantage of this technique for rendering a character's thoughts in his own idiom while maintaining a basic third-person referent and it is to this that the augmented sense of author–narrator–protagonist empathy noted above can perhaps best be attributed.

Cohn's thesis serves as a valuable key to an understanding of the issue of narrative presentation of the layers of consciousness of his protagonists that was of critical concern to Endō. Let us turn now, however, to consideration of various influences of a more immediate nature that were to determine the nature of the author's response to this challenge.

Such a discussion must surely start with reference to an author to whom Endō himself invariably acknowledged a literary debt: François Mauriac. Endō's attraction to what he saw as Mauriac's ability to achieve psychologically credible protagonists precisely by refraining from the temptation to identify the various layers of consciousness within his characters is evident in the series of short essays he produced at the outset of his career. The issue is subsequently addressed at length in *Watashi no aishita shōsetsu* (A Novel I Have Loved, 1985), a work whose title represents an open acknowledgement of the author's enduring fascination with Mauriac's classic work, *Thérèse Desqueyroux*, and in which Endō develops his belief that it is only by leaving the workings of the psyche as an 'unfathomable chaos' that the author can succeed in penetrating the realm of the unconscious. Far from imposing an arbitrary order and logic onto the psyche of his creations, he argues, it is his duty as author to sculpture his characters 'without passing judgement on their intellectual or moral values'.[36]

The portrayal suggests an author at the mercy of the unconscious. But what of the nature of the contents he discerned within this unfathomable chaos? The issue is critical – for it is the move from a fundamentally negative view of the unconscious (as 'a swamp that houses our desires and urges which, though present in our subconscious, must remain suppressed and unexpressed'[37]) towards a concomitant recognition of the realm as 'the place in which God's love is exercised on mankind'[38] that the image of the individual as an amalgam of seemingly conflicting forces is rooted. To Endō, this recognition of the dual nature of the unconscious was derived, in part at least, from a similar progression he had come to discern in the literature of Mauriac and led to portrayal of a realm in which 'our desire for Good conflicts with our penchant for Evil, in which our appreciation of Beauty conflicts with our attachment to the Ugly'.[39]

Having acknowledged this fundamental tension within the unconscious, Endō was now in a position to view the human exterior as 'the entrance to the inner being'.[40] The vision is one, not of incompatibility, but of a fundamental interdependency and derives, in large measure, from the author's increasing interest in the image of the individual as depicted by Carl Jung. Endō himself was the first to acknowledge the influence on his work of the Jungian vision of the individual;[41] indeed, much of the above-mentioned work, *Watashi no aishita shōsetsu*, represents a critical study of *Thérèse Desqueyroux* from a Jungian perspective. Particularly in the light of the protracted assessment of this vision in Endō's later works, however, the influence would appear paramount. And the process is not limited to Endō's 'mature' work: in retrospect, a similar approach can be seen even in the earlier novels, works that predate the author's self-acknowledged period of intensive study of the writings of Jung following composition of the award-winning *The Samurai*. Viewed thus, even the earlier Endō protagonists can be seen as engaged in a process of increasing self-awareness as they seek to reconcile various elements within their being which are initially portrayed as standing in opposition but which are eventually acknowledged as of equal importance in the definition of the 'whole' individual.

In the analysis of the novels that follows, it is this process at work on the texts that will be emphasised. As one by one Endō's characters come to recognise within themselves an amalgam of conscious and unconscious forces, so the conclusion that both are an equal element of the 'integrated' individual is reinforced. At the same time, as they come increasingly to be depicted as complex personalities, so the image of characters seeking a balance of previously opposing forces is developed. In this sense, the characters are embarked on a journey – a journey towards 'wholeness' – that conforms closely with the 'process of individuation' as defined by Jung:

> I use the term 'individuation' to denote the process by which a person becomes a psychological 'in-dividual', that is, a separate, indivisible unity or 'whole'. It is generally assumed that consciousness is the whole of the psychological individual. But knowledge of the phenomena that can only be explained on the hypothesis of unconscious psychic processes makes it doubtful whether the ego and its contents are in fact identical with the 'whole'....There is plenty of evidence to show that consciousness is very far from covering the psyche in its totality.[42]

Having recognised the duality within the individual, Jung subsequently stressed the need to avoid taking a stand in which the individual becomes wholly identified with one or the other pole. For, as he argued later in this same essay:

> Conscious and unconscious do not make a whole when one of them is suppressed and injured by the other. If they must contend, let it at least be a fair fight with equal rights on both sides. Both are aspects of life. Consciousness should defend its reason and protect itself, and the chaotic life of the unconscious should be given the chance of having its way, too – as much of it as we can stand. This means open conflict and open collaboration at once. That, evidently, is the way human life should be. It is the old game of hammer and anvil: between them the patient iron is forged into an indestructible whole, an 'individual'. This, roughly, is what I mean by the individuation process.[43]

As a result of being possessed of both flesh and spirit, reason and emotion, what is needed is a balance in which a reconciliation between previously opposing forces can be effected. The goal of this journey, this process of individuation, is thus to locate a new centre within the individual – one which is neither conscious nor unconscious, but which partakes of both. This is the 'Self', a concept that Jung chose to define in the following terms:

> If the unconscious can be recognised as a co-determining factor along with consciousness, and if we can live in such a way that conscious and unconscious demands are taken into account as far as possible, then the center of gravity of the total personality shifts its position. It is then no longer in the ego, which is merely the center of consciousness, but in the hypothetical point between the conscious and unconscious. This new center might be called the Self.[44]

The definitions provide a useful key to an understanding of Endō's attitude towards his creations – as suggested by the plethora of characters within his work who become increasingly aware of an inner voice urging them to reconsider their conscious instincts. Such characters typically experience psychological uncertainty before ultimately succumbing to this inner, more powerful force. When reassessed in the light of such Jungian definitions, however, this can be viewed as an integral part of the process of integration upon which each is embarked. Without this, their 'Self' would remain subsumed by their ego and the unconscious side of their being would continue to represent a negative force, a Satanic voice, set up in absolute opposition to the voice of their conscious being. That this is not the case is testimony to Endō's determination to achieve total reconciliation – and to his acceptance of Jung's more positive view of the unconscious:

> The unconscious is not a demoniacal monster, but a natural entity which, as far as moral sense, aesthetic taste, and intellectual judgment go, is completely neutral. It only becomes dangerous when our conscious attitude to it is hopelessly wrong. To the degree that we repress it, its danger increases. But the moment the patient begins to assimilate contents that were previously unconscious, its danger diminishes.[45]

As Endō's characters come, increasingly, to listen to the voice of their unconscious, therefore, so they come to conform to Jung's claim that it is 'only the man who can consciously assent to the power of the inner voice [who] becomes a personality'.[46] At the same time, moreover, the more they come to plumb the depths of their inner being, the more they are confronted by a realisation of the amalgam of positive and negative forces at work there. The discovery is often painful, as evidenced by the number of protagonists who struggle to come to terms with the growing conviction that thoughts that come to them at moments when their self-confidence has plumbed new depths are as integral an element of their entire being as those, more positive, qualities with which they had hitherto chosen to confront society.

At this point, the challenge confronting Endō as a novelist engaged in a protracted examination of the realm of the unconscious is clear. In probing the inner being of his creations, Endō was committed to a concerted attempt at reconciliation of the seemingly opposing qualities that he discerned there. In so doing, however, Endō found himself increasingly conscious of the above-mentioned need to 'feel a sense of empathy with the sins and evils' he discovered there – hence his depiction of the 'third dimension' as 'the territory of demons' and his conclusion that 'one cannot describe man's inner being completely unless he closes in on this demonic part.'[47] Once more, in his self-assessment as an author whose ultimately optimistic evaluation of human nature was dependent, paradoxically, on a series of depictions of characters confronted by the murkier side of their being, the influence of Jung is readily discernible. More specifically, it is a relatively simple task to identify several sections of the critical study, *Watashi no aishita shōsetsu*, as drawing on Jung's assertion that:

> Evil needs to be pondered just as much as good, for good and evil are ultimately nothing but ideal extensions and abstractions of doing, and both belong to the chiaroscuro of life. In the last resort there is no good that cannot produce evil and no evil that cannot produce good.[48]

To Jung, the conclusion to be drawn from this claim was of the need to acknowledge the archetype of the Shadow as standing in opposition to the persona. Defining this as 'the "negative" side of the personality, the sum of all those unpleasant qualities we like to hide, together with the insufficiently developed functions and the contents of the personal unconscious',[49] Jung was at pains to stress this as representing a vital aspect of the integrated individual. For as he acknowledges elsewhere:

> Unfortunately there can be no doubt that man is, on the whole, less good than he imagines himself or wants to be. Everyone carries a shadow, and the less it is embodied in the individual's conscious life, the blacker and denser it is. If an inferiority is conscious, one always has a chance to correct it. Furthermore, it is constantly in contact with other interests, so that it is continually subjected to modifications. But if it is repressed and isolated from consciousness, it never gets corrected, and is liable to burst forth suddenly in a moment of unawareness.[50]

As noted earlier, however, it was Jung's vision of the realm of the unconscious as incorporating, not merely the 'negative' side of personality suppressed from the conscious being, but also a more positive force to which Endō has found himself drawn. In particular, as a Christian, Endō has been attracted to the Jungian image of the unconscious as the source of religious experience – as 'the medium from which religious experience seems to flow'.[51] The conception of 'God as at work, not only in our beautiful parts but over our sullied parts, our sins'[52] clearly owes much to this basic premise. Equally, moreover, it is in the ensuing vision of the individual as torn between two conflicting forces that the tendency to focus on the 'demonic' in a paradoxical quest for a more positive quality within the human composite can be seen as rooted. The result is a technique, evidenced throughout Endō's literature, that can be described as one of paradoxical inversion – a process whereby the author seeks to highlight that element in his protagonists which holds out against societal norms in a deliberate attempt to illuminate the antithetical potential for rebirth in beings who appear irreparably fallen. The consequent fusion of oppositions conforms closely to the description of this process offered by the Jungian psychologist, Erich Neumann:

> At the polar points, consciousness loses its faculty of differentiation and in this constellation can no longer distinguish between positive and negative. In this way, it becomes possible for a phenomenon to shift into its opposite.[53]

Clearly, the technique is by no means limited to the literature of Endō. Indeed, the process can be seen as derived in large measure from the author's determination, discussed above, to seek within his work a poetics of literature rather than a consistent theology. In his use of the device of paradoxical inversion as a primary means of highlighting the internal tensions within his creations, however, Endō has succeeded in elevating dialectic investigation to a level of sophistication rarely evidenced by his literary forebears in Japan.

The fascination with the darker side of human nature is evident in Endō's earliest fiction and, as shown by the discussion in Chapter 2 of Endō's two early novellas, *White Man* and *Yellow Man*, this frequently assumes the guise of examination of the potential evidenced by the Endō protagonist to inflict pain and suffering on his fellow man.[54] The depiction of the protagonist of *White Man* collaborating with the Gestapo interrogation and torture of his friends in the French Resistance, of Suguro and his fellow interns seemingly intoxicated by the gruesome experiments into vivisection on American POWs as depicted in *The Sea and Poison*, of Tanaka's inexplicable identification with the more outrageous aspects of the lifestyle of the Marquis de Sade as portrayed in *Ryūgaku* (Foreign Studies, 1965; trans. 1989): all appear designed to suggest a morbid fascination with the nature of Evil *per se*.

As suggested by the above discussion, however, to interpret the novels thus is to overlook the paradoxical intent behind these portrayals. And, as evidenced by the conviction offered by Father Durand in Endō's early novel, *Kazan* (Volcano, 1960; trans. 1978), in his admission that 'if a man doesn't feel guilty of any sin, he doesn't have to depend on God',[55] there are occasions when Endō's fictional constructs appear to encroach, over explicitly, into the discussion of the nature of this reversal. Reviewed in the light of this technique, however, such depictions do call for reassessment: the tendency to focus on the ugly, the frightening and the grotesque can now be recognised as stemming rather from a conviction of the impossibility of portraying the potential for salvation without an understanding of its antithesis, the 'demonic' element within mankind. Once more, Endō cites Mauriac as his model, with explicit reference to the latter's belief that:

> The writer has a duty to expose human nature, sullied as it is by sin. But, in the depths beyond this sin exists something in which the Christian places implicit trust. This is another ray of light that purifies and sanctifes the sin before the author's own sceptical gaze. The author should bear witness to this light.[56]

Endō proceeds to equate this 'ray of light' with a 'twilight glow reminiscent of a Rembrandt painting – the light of God's grace',[57] an image highly effective in accounting for the paradoxically positive effect induced, on occasion, by Endō's depiction of even the darkest of acts. In thus removing the focus from the portrayal of baser human instincts to a concentration on plumbing, ever deeper, the inner being of the protagonists capable of such inhuman behaviour, Endō has introduced a variety of images, to be discussed in the ensuing chapters, designed to suggest this 'ray of light'. In so doing, and the more he has honed this technique, the more he has come to identify this as the means available to himself as author to introduce issues of a spiritual nature into his literature. This, in turn, has led to his uncompromising assertion in his more recent work that:

> Evil and faith are similar....Take lust, for example. In structural terms, there is no difference between the psychology of lust and the psychology of faith. They are locked in a relationship of interdependence, as two sides of a coin. And it is in the search for some link between the two that religion and literature come together
>
> In other words, in keeping with the principle that 'all roads lead to Rome', I have come to view all evil as a perverted image of the search for Christ.[58]

The comment epitomises the mysterious power that Endō had come to locate at the heart of the unconscious, a power that elsewhere in the same study Endō portrays as the 'X-like quality urging the individual towards discipline and balance'.[59] The notion of the 'X-like quality within man' represents another constant refrain in Endō's corpus; he even used this as the title of one of his essay collections.[60] Reminiscent of Jung's depiction of the psyche as a 'regulatory system' that renders the reconciliation of seemingly opposing forces not merely feasible, but an entirely natural phenomenon, the concept reflects the author's attempt to redefine the 'demonic part' resident in the unconscious in terms designed to highlight the spiritual drama he was seeking to create. As Endō proceeded to point out, however, the concept is equally the product of a vision of literature as a means of restoring inner equilibrium to the unconscious – of both author and reader – that is again derived from his study of various Jungian archetypes:

> The stories and images created by our unconscious are the ultimate proof that our hearts are consistently seeking out this 'X'. Needless to say, this 'X' is not death and destruction – but life, that which elevates our lives – the Being which I personally refer to as Jesus.[61]

The conclusion provides an invaluable insight into the author's view of narrativity. The more he has probed the workings of the unconscious, the more he has come to see this 'X-like quality' as an indispensable stimulus for the 'narrative-creating archetype'[62] within the artist – and to view this as an unconscious force without which the author is unable to give conscious representation to his, or her, inner being. Acknowledging his debt to the study of narratology by the Japanese psycholinguist, Izutsu Toshihiko – and citing, in particular, the latter's claim that 'the images of the unconscious are embellished and subsequently develop into a tale'[63] – Endō subsequently gave expression to this vision in terms designed to highlight the role exercised by the archetype in the creation of all literature:

> Having come into contact with the author's unconscious, a 'fact' is embellished and developed into a tale – into an image and a 'truth' transcending the original 'fact'.[64]

The literary technique to emerge from this process is frequently described by Endō as that of 'transposition'. A clear reflection of the author's vision of the art of the novelist as involving, not a recreation of reality but rather the removal – the 'transposition' – of material born of real life to a different dimension, together with the gradual and imperceptible replacement of one figure with another. More specifically in the Endō narrative, the process involves a gradual minimalising of the disparity between beings traditionally assigned to differing dimensions and an ever-increasing acknowledgement of the need for his creations to look ever deeper within their inner being for resolution of the conflicts with which they find themselves confronted. As the author recognised in *Watashi no aishita shōsetsu*:

> Behind the technique of transposition lies the conviction that salvation is to be found, not in some distant place separated from us by a vast expanse of open sky, but within our own being – in the dirtiest and most mundane part of our being.[65]

The implications for the Endō narrative are readily apparent. The more the author has sought to provide concrete form to the process whereby his creations arrive at a greater sense of self-awareness, the more he has probed the unconscious thoughts and motivations that continue to guide their actions. At the same time, consistent focus on this inner realm has resulted in an ever-increasing tendency to blur the distinction between the conscious and unconscious realms, initially portrayed as in polar opposition. The ensuing process represents a fusion, a resolution of dichotomies accompanied by a growing awareness of some unconscious aspect of the being as it is gradually brought into *rapprochement* with a conscious element that lies at the heart of the process of individuation. It is only in addressing such oppositions that the individual is in a position to continue this journey; and it is only in effecting a resolution of qualities that appear to be irreconcilable that he/she is able to move towards a more 'integrated' being.

But at this point we must return to the literature – to an examination of the various dichotomies, all of which can be seen as symbols of this fundamental human duality that Endō seeks to fuse during the course of his novels. In large measure, these can be identified with specific novels and, as such, discussion of Endō's challenge on a particular opposition is best introduced in the appropriate chapter. Before turning to the texts themselves, however, a brief consideration of the more significant examples of such fusion during the course of Endō's works is in order.

Of these, perhaps the most discussed with regard to Endō's literature is that between East and West. Stemming from Endō's adoption of what he perceived of at the time as a 'Western' religion and his decision to pursue his studies in French literature, the two poles are initially established in a series of early essays epitomised by 'Kamigami to kami to' (The gods and God, 1947) as separated, at least at the superficial level, by an unbridgeable divide. At this stage, confronted by perception of an unfathomable gulf between the 'pantheistic' (*kamigami*) East and the 'monotheistic' (*kami*) West and tempted to attribute the illness that led to premature abandonment of his studies in France and his subsequent protracted hospitalisation in Japan to his unsuccessful attempt to confront the 'great flow' of European tradition, the author would appear to be engaged in a deliberate attempt to establish a clear-cut opposition. The definitions ventured in 'The Gods and God' and other early essays, therefore, brook no compromise: the challenge as here presented is that of bridging the perceived divide between the 'pantheistic' world of the East in which 'everything (e.g. Nature, the gods, etc.) represents an amalgam and extension of the individual and in which the individual remains but a part of the whole' and the 'monotheistic' world of the West in which 'there exists an absolute distinction and division between God, angels and the individual that represent a fundamental condition of existence'.[66]

The same trend is equally evident in Endō's early fiction: the titles of the two early novellas, *White Man* and *Yellow Man* would appear to represent a similarly cut-and-dried distinction. Once more, however, the fact that the author is not simply engaged in a lament at the impossibility of effective cross-cultural communication is to be inferred from the earlier discussion of the process of paradoxical inversion – and closer examination of the works themselves suggests just such a technique operating at the textual level. As such, the more characters are confronted by this seemingly unfathomable divide, the more they come to view the East and West, less as irreconcilable opposites, more as elements of a dynamic tension in which the one is ultimately only definable in terms of the other. Inevitably, the process is gradual. The growing optimism concerning the possibility of reconciliation evident within the texts is, however, distinctive, leading to the author's recent admission:

> As a result of continuous consideration of the concept of the unconscious in my literature, I am now convinced that meaningful communication between East and West is possible.

I have gradually come to realise that, despite the mutual distance and the cultural and linguistic differences that clearly exist in the conscious sphere, the two hold much in common at the unconscious level.[67]

Another opposition subjected to a similar process of fusion within Endō's *oeuvre* is that between strength and weakness, poles which, for Endō, have derived in large measure from consideration of the distinction between those 'strong' Christians who were willing to martyr themselves for their faith during the era of Christian persecution in early seventeenth-century Japan and those 'weaklings' who, unwilling or unable to sacrifice themselves in this way, ended up according with the Shogunate's wishes and performing the act of *efumi* by placing their foot on a crucifix (*fumie*) in an outward act of apostasy. The issue is one with which Endō has consistently struggled and has resulted in an identification with the generations of *Kakure* (Hidden) Christians forced, not only to perpetuate their faith in secret, but to live with the stigma of being branded as 'weaklings' as a result of their having succumbed to the overwhelming pressure to apostatise.[68] The more Endō was to consider the lives of these *Kakure*, obliged to live with the sense of ignominy and shame at having defiled the image of Christ whom they continued to venerate, the more he came to question the traditional dismissal of the *Kakure* as 'weak' apostates rather than as possessed, paradoxically, of the strength to live the rest of their lives in full knowledge of this act of betrayal and to seek rather to portray the existence of an innate relationship between the two forces. The result is a series of characters, initially epitomised by Gaston in *Wonderful Fool* and Mitsu in *The Girl I Left Behind*, who are portrayed as weak and powerless – but human; and it is in stressing their humanness that Endō seeks to locate within his 'weak' characters an inner vigour and consequent capacity for acts of strength. Significantly, in so doing, such characters are not suddenly endowed with qualities which they did not formerly possess. Rather, in casting increasing doubts upon the initial categorisation of such characters, Endō seeks to hint at the potential within such characters to influence, not only their own destinies but also the lives of those with whom they come into contact. Only gradually is the paradox unravelled. But, as the very qualities that were initially seen as signs of weakness come to be seen as the potential source of ultimate salvation, so the fusion of the traditional opposition between 'strength' and 'weakness' is reinforced.

In the Endō text, the opposition between strength and weakness assumes a variety of guises that will be discussed in the analysis of the novels themselves. In particular, however, as suggested by the author's study of the fate of the *Kakure* Christians, the concept is frequently embodied in the suggestion of a fundamental link between two other qualities traditionally placed in opposition: that between faith and doubt. Inspired, in part at least, by the author's own spiritual journey, this has led to a series of novels in which the most profound faith appears only to be expressible through the language of doubt and scepticism – in a manner reminiscent of Dostoevsky's depiction of the dark, sceptical soul of Ivan Karamazov as countered by portrayal of the pure soul of Alyosha. The resulting suggestion of chaos, in which the one is required to support the other, enables the author seeking to capture the hearts of his characters at the moment of greatest internal drama – as their inner beings are wracked by fundamental doubts concerning the underpinnings of their lives – to highlight the potential for fusion between forces initially perceived as in opposition.

Endō's reader is confronted with several further examples of this technique, each designed to bring into question any absolute categorisation of human nature. The gradual merging of a total absence of sin-consciousness with an awareness of the pangs of conscience occasioned by Evil (as evidenced, for example, in *The Sea and Poison*), the ability of characters reduced to the depths of despair to discern the paradoxical potential for hope in the form of the ray of light shining through the darkness (as evidenced, for example, in *Silence*): all now come to be seen as contributing to the process of fusion as outlined above, the cumulative effect being that the reader is encouraged to reserve judgement on initial, seemingly unassailable impressions.

As noted earlier, the vision of human nature to emerge from this process of reconciliation is fundamentally optimistic, if complex. The more Endō penetrates the inner worlds of his protagonists – the more he seeks to isolate the 'X-like' quality present within even the most mundane of his characters – the more he is in a position to hint at the potential they all possess to influence their own destiny through greater self-awareness. To be sure, there are occasions when the Endō protagonist appears intent on self-destruction, times when these creations appear unable to make sense of, let alone to control, their own inner tensions and uncertainties. The consequent vision of the inner world as a battleground, especially for forces of a psychic nature, is, however, deeply rooted in Jungian psychology, the ensuing depictions of characters embroiled in psychological uncertainty reminiscent of Jung's portrayal of humans as irrational beings, driven by subtle, unknown and unknowable psychic motives.

Once more, the task for Endō as novelist was to present this vision of the divided self in literary terms and, as suggested by the number of Endō's characters, especially in his later novels, who find themselves confronted by '*mō hitori no jibun*' (another self), Endō too found himself increasingly drawn to portrayal of this tension through examination of the concept of the *doppelgänger*.[69] Frequently expressed in terms of characters engaged in a desperate search for *hontō no watashi* (the real me) or *hontō no anata* (the real you), Endō's interest in this division – and his attempts to portray this *alter ego* as representing the positive side of the Shadow archetype as defined by Jung – is introduced in overt terms in the title of the 1968 short story, 'Kagebōshi' (Shadows; trans. 1993). Here, the more the young protagonist probes the 'real' person behind the public mask assumed by his former pastor, the more aware he becomes of a certain facet of the priest's personality with which he has yet to come to terms.

The concept of the *doppelgänger*, or *bunshin* (lit. divided self), is one which we shall be considering in some detail in the discussion of the novel *Scandal* in which portrayal of the shadowy figure who continues to haunt the protagonist, Suguro, conforms closely to the model established for the double by Carl Keppler in his in-depth analysis of what he describes as the 'literature of the second self'. In Chapter 6, therefore, we shall consider the extent to which Suguro and the 'impostor' he encounters accord with Keppler's prescription of 'an inescapable two that are at the same time an indisputable one'.[70] Let us limit the discussion at this stage, however, to a few words about the manner in which, in the portrayal of characters who become ever more aware of a deeper level of their being that they are ultimately unable to keep suppressed, the Endō narrative mirrors accurately the process at work in all fiction of the second self as delineated by Keppler.

Rodrigues in *Silence*, Hasekura and Velasco in *The Samurai* and, more explicitly, Suguro and Madame Naruse in *Scandal*, Ōtsu and Mitsuko in *Deep River*...Endō's fiction provides a steady stream of characters who experience varying degrees of success in coming to terms with perception of their own divided selves as a result of engagement with *mō hitori no jibun*. Confrontation with this 'other self' results in an invasion of the previously unquestioned self-sufficiency and peace of mind of protagonists, and it is in this sense, in bringing about a moral development in these characters, that they conform to Keppler's depiction of the second self of the 'conscious ego'.[71]

Portraying the process set in motion as a result of such confrontation as a 'reconciliation of absolute irreconcilables',[72] Keppler describes the consequent awakening effected within protagonists in such circumstances in the following terms,

> The 'I' one ordinarily supposes oneself to be in the everyday world is not the only tenant in the house of self...this house is far larger than one has imagined, full of shadowy recesses and corridors, but full of wonder as well.[73]

The passage represents an apposite encapsulation of the process at work in Endō's narratives. Gradually convinced during the course of the novels of the need to acknowledge this other self as an integral part of their whole being, Endō's protagonists come increasingly to accept that their earlier faulty or incomplete perception of themselves and others was the result of failure to come to terms with this 'other self'. The pain inherent to the process is never glossed over. The overall effect, however, is that of an adventure of reconciliation, an adventure symbolised by the experience of encountering the second self that accords with Keppler's encapsulation of all such narratives:

> If we compare the first self before his experience of the second with the same first self after the experience...we will see that in most cases...it has yielded a great deal....In the vast majority of cases the harm done to the first self by the second is harm as catastrophic as harm can be....[But] it is a harm that stirs awake, that lances through the comfortable shell of self-complacency or self-protection, that strips away all masks of self-deception, that compels self-awareness and in the agony of the process brings self-enlargement.[74]

The passage could have been written with the literature of Endō in mind, and, as we shall see in the discussion of individual texts that follow, each can be seen as supporting Keppler's claim that 'every second self story...is to one degree or another a story of shaping... [a story of] the growth of the first self'.[75]

In examining the personalities to emerge from Endō's fiction, therefore, the reader cannot but be struck by the 'growth' occasioned within the various protagonists – and the consequent depiction of human nature conforms closely to the vision, outlined at the beginning of this chapter, of man as a 'splendid and beautiful being and, at the same time,...a terrible being'. In the considerations that follow of the journeys towards greater self-understanding upon which each of these is engaged, therefore, so the view of these as embarked upon their own 'process of individuation' will be developed. The discoveries that each makes along the way will inevitably differ and the extent to which the author succeeds in maintaining the focus on this process of growth will, of necessity, be determined, in part at least, by the narrative considerations discussed earlier. As a concerted attempt to penetrate the public facade and to expose the alternative facets of the divided self that lurk behind this veneer, however, Endō's work represents an invaluable addition to the corpus of literary texts in Japan devoted to consideration of this aspect of human nature.

It is in this sense that I have chosen to refer to Endō's literary corpus as a 'literature of reconciliation', and the texts analysed below have all been selected as exemplars of this trend. Discussed in chronological order in an attempt to highlight this continuum, it is as elements of the consistent search for reconciliation of the self, initially presented as torn between conscious and unconscious forces, that the various novels will be considered. All but the first novellas are available in English translation but, for those unfamiliar with Endō's work, synopses of all the works discussed in this study are included as Appendix B. But at this point, let us allow the texts to speak for themselves.

2
WHITE MAN, YELLOW MAN

Oh, East is East, and West is West, and never the twain shall meet
Till Earth and Sky stand presently at God's great Judgement Seat;
But there is neither East nor West, Border, nor Breed, nor Birth,
When two strong men stand face to face, though they come from the ends of the earth!

(Rudyard Kipling)

Well, sir, if I'm no more a Christian, then I can't be telling no lies to my torturers when they asks me whether I am a Christian or not, for God himself has stripped me of my Christianity on account of my intention alone and even before I've had time to say a word to my torturers. And if I've already been degraded, then in what manner and with what sort of justice am I to be called to account as a Christian in the next world for having denied Christ, when for my intention alone I've been stripped of my baptism even before I had denied him? If I'm no longer a Christian, I cannot possibly deny Christ, for there's nothing more left for me to deny.

(*The Brothers Karamazov*)

Endō was 27 years old when he boarded the *Marseille* on 5 June 1950 at the port of Yokohama, bound for France and a period of research ostensibly into the writings of the French Catholic authors that had represented the primary focus of his university studies. The author's own accounts of the journey itself reveal the despair and ignominy experienced by the group of young Japanese students travelling as representatives of a nation still under Allied Occupation towards a world with which full Japanese diplomatic relations had yet to be restored. By all accounts, the heat and the stench that these 'pioneer' Japanese students were forced to endure in their fourth-class berth deep in the bowels of the *Marseille* represented a humiliating experience and one that was to reinforce the sense of distance between East and West that Endō and so many of his generation had come to experience as a result of events of the Pacific War and the ensuing Occupation.[1]

As noted earlier, for Endō, as a Japanese youth who, though never actually experiencing life at the front, had spent his formative years confronted by the increasing tension between Japan and the Western Allies in the late 1930s and early 1940s, perception of this distance was deep-rooted. As Christian, moreover, the vision of the barrier between the 'monotheistic' West and the 'pantheistic' East had only been reinforced by the constant rejections as believer in the 'enemy religion' that he had been forced to endure during the wartime years. Far from the baptism he had received as a child of 11 serving as a catalyst enabling the young man to effect a reconciliation in his mind between East and West, it had served rather to highlight the perceived division between the two. And far from the vision of Christianity as of universal significance, at this stage at least, Endō came to view his faith as the embodiment of a Western spiritual drama with which he, as Japanese, struggled to empathise.

For Endō at the time, the implications of this perceived East/West distinction were far-reaching. In particular, as he argues in the early essay devoted to consideration of this divide, 'The gods and God', Endō was to categorise this perceived gulf as implying that 'Western artists, even those who reject Christianity are nevertheless rooted in a monotheistic world',[2] and to conclude that the spiritual choice confronting all members of this culture is consequently a straightforward decision between acceptance or rejection of God. The contrast with the pantheistic model is clear: as Endō points out later in the same essay, even the act of rejection entails a paradoxical affirmation of the existence of the being thus denounced – an affirmation that he saw as absent from the 'pantheistic' tradition in which the individual was apt to deny the very existence of a single divinity.

The distinction here established between rejection and denial is significant, serving as it does to highlight the opposition that Endō presents in the early essays between 'active' Western culture (in which 'the lines of demarcation between a series of oppositions are clearly delineated') and the 'passive' Eastern tradition (in which 'existential distinctions are far less in evidence and which consequently places far greater emphasis on the erosion of such barriers').[3] Indeed, to Endō, it was the vision of the Eastern tradition as devoid of the drama created by the tension of such oppositions that accounted for the difficulties that he saw Japanese authors as having traditionally experienced when seeking to borrow from the Western literary tradition. Rooted in a literary ethos that tended to ignore a Western dialectic approach, such Japanese authors had struggled, in Endō's eyes, to come to terms with such oppositions and were consequently less well equipped to address the tensions between spirit and flesh, logos and pathos, that lie at the heart of this approach. Instead, in that they addressed one half of such dichotomies whilst ignoring the other, Endō viewed such authors as having failed to establish a credible tension within their literature, leading all too readily to works that lack true drama and that consequently appear one-dimensional.[4]

Confronted with this perception of an unfathomable East/West divide, Endō's decision to travel to France can be viewed as a very personal commitment to address this perceived gulf in an attempt to overcome such boundaries. However, initial evidence from the two novellas derived most immediately from this experience, *White Man* and *Yellow Man*, both published in 1955 shortly after the author's enforced return to Japan, would suggest that, far from effecting such a resolution, the author returned with an enhanced conviction of the impossibility for effective communication across the cultural divide. Indeed, in choosing to posit an apparent opposition between East and West in the very choice of titles of these two works, Endō actively encourages interpretation of these as separated by an unfathomable gulf. It was this same impression that Endō appeared intent on conveying in the speech delivered upon acceptance of the prestigious Akutagawa Prize for Literature conferred upon the first of these two novellas:

> Even after reaching the age when I could enjoy foreign literature, I was constantly torn between the world of the 'white man' with its long tradition of God and the world of the 'yellow man' in which it made little difference whether God existed or not.[5]

Taken at face value, the inference to be drawn from this comment is that, in choosing to depict the world of 'white man', the first of these two works represents an attempt to highlight a variety of dichotomies in the 'monotheistic' West in an attempt to establish a readily identifiable East/West polarity. Particularly when viewed in conjunction with the subsequent novella, *Yellow Man*, the temptation is to view this as a literary attempt to highlight the inferiority complex of the 'yellow man' in the face of the clearly defined delimitations of the world of the 'white man'.

To interpret this project in this way, however, is to ignore the process of 'paradoxical inversion' at work here – a paradox rooted in the apparent implication that, in order to portray the world of the 'yellow man' with its absence of polarity, the author was first obliged to establish this clear-cut dichotomy between the two realms by first depicting the world of 'white man'. It is here that the true irony of these two works is to be found. For in suggesting the existence of a neatly delineated confrontation between East and West, Endō can here be seen conforming to the very Western dialectic that he claimed, in 'The gods and God' and other essays of the period, to view as lacking from his own cultural identity and which he cites as the chief obstacle to successful intercultural communication.

At the superficial level, therefore, the pair of novellas may indeed suggest an irreconcilable opposition. The more one examines the nature of this polarity, however, the more it becomes evident that the focus rests, not on the fundamentally irredeemable aspects of two opposing traditions, but rather, in both cases, on the dark secrets that the protagonists – and here it is significant that the protagonists of both these works are Westerners – initially seek to ignore but are ultimately obliged to address. In so doing, the paradoxical desire to challenge the very qualities that lie at the heart of the East/West dichotomy becomes increasingly evident. In short, having established the parameters of the physical opposition, the author is paradoxically better equipped to penetrate behind the facade and to focus, rather, on the internal drama of his creations. The technique of fusion as depicted in the previous chapter thus provides a means to hint at the true complexity of human nature; it also provides the author with a forum to examine the various paradoxes that he had raised in his earlier essays.

But what of the texts themselves? To what extent do these represent the author's initial attempts to focus upon the 'fallen' elements within his creations in a paradoxical attempt to hint at their potential for greater self-awareness? And how closely does the development portrayed by the various characters during the course of these novellas conform to the Jungian model for the 'process of individuation'?

White Man

Turning first to *White Man*, the story itself focuses on Nazi atrocities in wartime France, using these as a compelling symbol of 'man's inhumanity to man'. In keeping with the technique of paradoxical inversion, however, far from this being portrayed as aberrant behaviour perpetrated in defiance of natural human instinct, the occasion of the Nazi overthrow of Lyons and the subsequent torture of those connected with the Resistance is depicted as 'the day when this world would tear off the *mask of civilisation and progress* to expose its *true countenance*', a day when 'the world would recapture its *fundamental essence*'.[6] And to the first-person protagonist, as he watches the seemingly indiscriminate round-up of those who happened to be on the streets of Lyons at the time, the Nazis appear to be exhibiting, again, not exceptional callousness, but 'basic human instincts' (p. 54).

At this stage in the story, the conclusions to be drawn with regard to human nature appear unremittingly pessimistic, the focus on Nazi brutality seemingly designed to highlight a latent potential for Evil within the human condition. True to the process of paradoxical inversion at work on the Endō text, however, such depictions are not simply dismissed as expressions of despair over the inhuman Nazi impulse towards Evil. Rather, as intimated by the protagonist's subsequent conclusion that those rounded up were the victims of '*gūzen*' (chance) – and more specifically of '*setsuri*' (a term traditionally reserved for the concept of 'divine providence') (p. 74) – the author hints at his intention of seeking to focus on such inhuman behaviour, not as a depiction of Evil *per se*, but in the hope of thereby alluding to the potential for reform within even the darkest of beings.

At the heart of this design lies the portrayal of the first-person protagonist, a young Frenchman who is himself unable to account for his decision to collaborate with the Nazis as a Gestapo interpreter. At the superficial level, the protagonist conforms very closely to the 'Western' stereotype as defined in the author's earlier essays. Attributing his penchant for cruelty to a series of childhood experiences and to the personalities of his parents – more specifically to the excessively Puritanical outlook of his mother combined with the total lack of parental concern evinced by his father – he is shown, for all his outward bravado, as clearly possessed of that distinguishing feature of 'white man's' society: a consciousness of sin. Equally, the more he embroils himself in the world of Evil (by co-operating with the Gestapo), the clearer is his understanding of the options confronting, not only himself, but also those with whom, like it or not, his life is inextricably linked. As he contemplates the dilemma, both physical and mental, confronting Jacques and Marie-Terèse, the two friends from his college years who are brought before him as victims of Nazi aggression and who are faced with an impossible choice between torture and the ignominy of capitulation, for example, the alternatives appear clear:

> This night, the two of them were ultimately to be confronted with a choice: to betray or be betrayed. Equally, I would learn whether I would win or lose against Jacques – no, not just against Jacques, but against Christians, the revolutionaries and against [my former professors]. (p. 75)

Again, however, the text itself appears designed to belie such simplistic categorisation, this being suggested by the frequent resort to expressions – the use of conjunctions such as *shikashi*, *keredomo*, *ni mo kakawarazu* ('but', 'and yet', 'nevertheless') is particularly prominent – that reinforce the impression of the protagonist responding to given situations with a reaction that represents the inverse of what is expected, either by those around him or by his own conscious being. With the protagonist frequently driven by the 'intense heat' or 'the grey, leaden sky' (images to which Endō resorts throughout his *oeuvre* to accompany the sudden and unexpected surfacing of previously suppressed instincts) to actions that surprise even himself, the consequent portrayal is of a man determined to penetrate the facade he had traditionally revealed to society and to examine the contents of his inner being, regardless of their nature.

Again, in keeping with the model outlined above, the process involves, not a radical change in personality, rather a growing acceptance of a greater complexity to the protagonist than is initially in evidence – a complexity suggested early in the text in the protagonist's acknowledgement of 'the torturer within [him]self' and of his ability, manifest even as a child, 'to adjust [himself] to the image that everyone held of him' (p. 16). For years, therefore, as he had gone about his daily life as a child growing up in Lyons and subsequently as a promising young student at the local university, the protagonist had succeeded in conforming to the image of the pious and hard-working young man that had been so encouraged by the upbringing he had received at the hands of his doting mother. It is thus with a certain pride that he confesses that she had ultimately died 'without knowing the dark secrets of her son,...in the arms of her angel-like son' (p. 49).

His mother, for one, had never succeeded in penetrating the protagonist's social facade and the latter, for his part, had sought diligently not to disabuse her of this image. And yet, as the text comes increasingly to focus on a deeper level of the protagonist's being, so the image is strengthened of a young man who rebels in the face of pressure to conform to this puritanical vision of Christianity, not through any conscious desire to oppose his mother, but as a result of more powerful emotions stemming from his unconscious being. At the rational, conscious level, the protagonist never questions his mother's basic good intentions. As suggested by a series of unfathomable reactions to events, however, his outward expressions of filial piety are frequently challenged by the text, leading gradually to the depiction of a man more willing to acknowledge the unconscious as equally integral to the human composite as the conscious elements.

The process of gradual erosion of the initial image of the protagonist is marked in the text by a series of oxymorons, expressions in which the fundamental contradiction serves paradoxically to raise awareness of deeper realities within the protagonist. The first such example occurs in the depiction of the protagonist as a boy surprised by his own reaction as he watches the family maid beating a dog. At once troubled by the 'joy of lust', which he confesses to experiencing in the face of such cruelty, he is obliged to concede: 'My awakening to lust was accompanied by the *pleasure of cruelty*' (p. 14, my emphasis).

Such a reaction is far removed from the world of piety in which his mother in particular had sought to nurture him. Far from representing a temporary aberration, however, such conflicting emotions intensify, with the result that, as he watches members of the Resistance engaged in a desperate battle with their Gestapo torturers, he comes to acknowledge that:

> When they clenched their teeth, there were times when the faces of the victims looked *beautiful* as, *unable to endure the pain*, they cried out. (pp. 59–60, my emphasis)

The protagonist's subsequent conclusion that 'even the voices of those being beaten suggested they felt a certain *lustful joy at being beaten*' (pp. 60–1, my emphasis) defies all the protagonist's attempts at rational comprehension. As a literary symbol, designed to highlight the various oppositions within the human condition to which the author is here seeking to draw attention, however, the image is highly effective.

The theme of the individual confronted with unfathomable, unconscious impulses is one to which Endō would constantly return throughout his career. At the same time, it is closely linked with another concept that would subsequently be developed into a major motif of Endō's literature: the belief in the 'indelible marks' that all humans leave on the lives of all those with whom they come into contact, however briefly. Try as he might to erase certain memories and individuals from his mind, therefore, the Endō protagonist is frequently troubled by the realisation that such chance encounters cannot be simply dismissed as irrelevancies from the past: having once come into contact, these fellow human beings become an intrinsic part of the complex life journey of these characters, memories of shared experiences liable to resurface at the least expected moment.

In *White Man*, the concept is introduced by Monique, a college friend of Marie-Terèse who tries to convince the latter that her excessive dependence on Jacques is misplaced. 'What possible connection does he have with your life?' (p. 36), she asks in an attempt to persuade Marie-Terèse to attend a dance in defiance of Jacques' wishes. But as the text consistently emphasises, such ties cannot simply be severed: as fellow human beings whose paths through life *have* crossed, each has left 'indelible traces' on the other and, as such, each influences the other, if not necessarily always at the conscious level, then at the level of the unconscious.

On the one hand, the theme can be seen as a reflection of the nature of interpersonal relationships. As emphasised by Jacques, a student at theological seminary, however, the issue is viewed as equally applicable with regard to the individual's relationship with God. To Jacques in his current circumstances, the 'indelible marks' left by his encounter with God are readily acknowledged. For the protagonist who is seeking to distance himself from the creed that he sees as having been 'imposed' upon him by his over-zealous mother, the issue is indeed one of which he is painfully aware: the more he seeks to deny the influence of Jacques' God on his life, the more he finds himself confronted with a nagging sense of uncertainty. At the time, Jacques' testimony that 'even if you don't think about God, He is always thinking of you' (p. 33) fails to find a responsive chord within the protagonist. But the more he attempts to ridicule this assessment, the more the text itself appears to undermine his apparent conviction.

Initial evidence that the protagonist's attempts to deny any role for God in his life are destined to failure is provided shortly after the friends agree to go their separate ways upon graduation. For all his attempts to convince himself that such friends are now firmly rooted in the past, the protagonist nevertheless finds himself drawn to seek out Jacques and Marie-Terèse on learning that they have moved into a nearby convent. Visiting the convent, he finds the two deep in prayer, and is immediately driven to dismiss them as hypocrites who 'listen vacantly to the sermons, but pay no attention to the message of the cross in front of them' (p. 51). To the protagonist at that moment, a vast gulf appears to separate the world of the convent and the reality of his own life experience. But the more he tries to convince himself that these Christians are ignoring reality, the more the text emphasises the protagonist's growing awareness of God working through his cynicism. As such, the more he tries to block his ears to the words whispered to him by the Christ on the cross in front of him, the more he comes to sense 'Christ beginning to tempt [him], beginning with those aspects of [his] being most likely to respond positively' (p. 51).

At this stage, however, such an instinctive reaction remains anathema to the protagonist and, in a desperate attempt to deny such whisperings, he proceeds to embroil himself ever more in the world of Nazi inhumanity. Paradoxically, however, the more he plumbs the depths of Evil – and the more intoxicated he becomes with the 'pleasure of cruelty' as he co-operates in the Nazi interrogation of his two former comrades – the more he is obliged to acknowledge, not merely the unseverable tie that links the three of them as a result of their shared pasts, but also the presence of 'a being transcending my will' (p. 74), whom he now sees as the only possible explanation for the 'indelible traces' they have left on each other's lives. At the same time, he is left with the inescapable concern:

> It was not me who placed the three of us on the experiment table with a pair of tweezers like abandoned dolls and forced this gamble upon us. It was definitely not me. But, if not me, then...(p. 75)

In deliberately leaving the question unanswered, the passage hints at a growing self-awareness within the protagonist – and, during the subsequent torture scene, the text alludes to several instances in which the protagonist is indeed confronted by emotions stemming from a deeper level of his existence. Most significant in this regard is his reassessment of both Marie-Terèse and Jacques in the light of their confrontation with torture.

In the case of Marie-Terèse the process is indicated in the portrayal of the protagonist's gradual realisation of a hidden dimension to this woman whom he had always dismissed as 'looking like a clown' (p. 41), as a woman with 'an emaciated face covered in spots' (p. 76). The more he stares at Marie-Terèse as she awaits her torturers, however, the more he is obliged to acknowledge a begrudging respect for her inner strength (in volunteering to take the torture upon herself rather than seeing Jacques tortured on her behalf). As he does so, the protagonist comes to acknowledge the presence of a fundamental beauty and 'purity' (*junpakusa*) (p. 79) to Marie-Terèse that he had hitherto overlooked. Only now are the qualities leading to Marie-Terèse's depiction as a 'saint' (*seijo*) (p. 78) in evidence. Only now is there a clear suggestion of a spiritual dimension to Marie-Terèse beyond that of the purely physical.

A similar intent can be discerned behind the portrayal of Jacques, a man whose increasing kindness towards the protagonist is met with a burgeoning callousness by the latter. The more Jacques tries to come alongside the protagonist, the more the latter is driven to interpret Jacques' concern for others as a sign of weakness – and to seek to deny the existence of any relationship between the two of them. As noted above, however, such attempts at denial are doomed to failure and, try as he might to ignore the 'indelible traces' each has left on the other, the protagonist cannot escape the conclusion that Jacques had 'come dancing back to influence my destiny' (p. 74). At the conscious level, the former may be able to bring himself to collaborate in the Gestapo interrogation of Jacques. But it is in his spontaneous reaction to the latter's death that the true nature of the tie that unites the two men becomes evident. Far from the callous insensitivity betrayed in his physical actions, the protagonist's response is further evidence of a deeper level to his being in which Jacques' death represents a profound loss:

> When I lost my mother, I didn't feel anything like this. It was as though I had loved Jacques for years, had subsequently been betrayed in that love, and had finally lost it. (p. 80)

The more the protagonist tries to resist such unconscious impulses – the more he attempts to turn his back on Jacques and his own past – the more he becomes aware of a human 'essence' (*honshitsu*)

(p. 63) that cannot be removed, even in the face of torture. At the same time, the protagonist is here engaged in a process designed to highlight the intrinsic paradox inherent within his attempt to turn his back on the spiritual values that his mother had sought to inculcate within him: it is as a consequence of this process that he comes to accept that the very act of abandonment represents an implicit recognition of the existence of a being that demands either acceptance or rejection. It is this same theme that is developed in the companion novella, *Yellow Man,* and it is to this work that the focus of this discussion will now turn.

Yellow Man

As noted earlier, the decision to locate the action of *Yellow Man* firmly within Eastern culture represents more than simply a desire to switch the focus from 'white man' operating within Western society to 'yellow man' operating within Eastern society. Nevertheless, in establishing a seemingly clearly defined polarity between East and West, the author appears intent on encouraging interpretation of this work as an expression of the inferiority complex of 'yellow man' and, to this end, on the surface at least, the text places considerable emphasis on a very clear-cut East/West dichotomy, of which all the characters are aware. As such, not only does the novella introduce the added dimension of 'white man' interacting with 'yellow' characters but in the very construction of the story, in which passages from the diary of the disgraced, 'white' priest, Durand, are interspersed with sections from the letter written by the 'yellow' student, Chiba, himself a lapsed believer, to Durand's former mentor, Father Brou, Endō appears intent on dwelling upon the impossibility of effective communication between the two worlds.

The perception of this unfathomable chasm is immediately acknowledged by Chiba who, at this level, conforms closely to the model of the 'yellow man' as outlined in the section from 'The gods and God' discussed earlier. During the course of the opening pages of his letter to Father Brou, a letter in which he finally brings himself to open his heart to his former priest, secure in his belief that the latter's arrest as a member of the 'enemy' race renders his confession irrelevant, Chiba therefore acknowledges the absence of all three sensibilities (towards sin, God and death), which the author had delineated in his earlier essays as the three primary distinguishing features of 'pantheistic man'.[7] Thus, in the space of the first five pages, Chiba is led to the following three conclusions:

1 'I didn't understand the true nature of sin. Or perhaps it would be more accurate to say that I had no *consciousness of sin*' (p. 86).
2 'It was then [as I studied the illustrated Bible you had lent me] that I learned that *God* was a white blond like you' (p. 88).
3 Strangely enough, to me, *death* seemed neither terrifying nor imminent' (p. 89, my emphases).

Throughout the novella, this dimension of the portrayal of Chiba as conforming to the 'yellow' stereotype is maintained. Attributing his moral weakness to his wretchedness as a 'godless' Japanese, he claims to experience, not a sin-consciousness, but a 'deep-rooted sense of fatigue' (p. 87). Such a depiction stands in stark contrast to that of Durand who, despite suffering the ignominy of excommunication following discovery of his affair with the Japanese woman, Kimiko, on whom he had taken pity following a disastrous flood, nevertheless retains a powerful sense of his identity as a 'white man'. To the end therefore, he is obliged to admit:

> Whilst rejecting God, I cannot deny His existence. He has penetrated to the very core of my being. And yet...all the Japanese coped quite well without God. They could live in a carefree manner, unconcerned by, and insensitive to, the church, the pain of sin and the hope of salvation – everything that we 'white people' see as fundamental to the human condition. (p. 148)

The message appears clear. For all his increased identification with the 'yellow world' following his eviction from his position of authority in the 'white world', the choice for the 'white' Durand remains stark: to accept or to reject God. In contrast to Chiba who, to the end, retains his belief that 'to us "yellow people", there is no distinction between light and dark...nothing could be further divorced from us "yellow people" than the pure white world of those like [Father Brou]' (p. 154), therefore, Durand is portrayed as unable to divest himself of those personal attributes that stem from his heritage as member of the 'white world'.

Seen in this light, the identification appears over-overt, the characters over-restricted by their stereotypical moulds. However, in keeping with the model outlined in Endō's early essays and developed in *White Man*, it is precisely through establishment of such a clearly defined opposition that the author is able to hint at the intrinsic paradox at work in the story.

In *Yellow Man*, as in *White Man*, therefore, having established a clear opposition, the focus subsequently rests, less on the nature of the distinction, more on the internal drama that exists on both sides of the divide and on the process of reconciliation that ensues as this drama unfolds. In so doing, especially in focusing on the dark secrets of the soul of the 'white' Durand, the author once more challenges the very dichotomy that appears so unquestionable. The superficial distinctions between Chiba and Durand may never be challenged. But in the increasing emphasis on the link that unites these two men as fellow renegades struggling to come to terms with the existence of the 'indelible marks' that the church, as their former spiritual home, has left on their lives, the text draws attention to a deeper level of their beings at which the two men are closely linked. Significantly, at this level, far from the depiction of two men engaged in a vain struggle to overcome their differences as representatives of opposing cultures, the focus is on the points of common interest, even though both remain unaware of these at the conscious level. Whilst nowhere denying these differences, therefore, it is at this deeper level that the portrayal of Durand developing increasingly into the kind of man with whom Chiba can identify as more in tune with the 'yellow' psyche is developed. And it is at this level that Chiba is led to acknowledge the former as the kind of person 'we feel we can understand' (p. 154).

For all the superficial type-casting, therefore, neither of the characters at the heart of this purported opposition fits as neatly into his pre-assigned mould as he himself would like to think. Herein lies the inherent paradox within *Yellow Man*, a paradox that, in retrospect, is evidenced throughout the novella.

First indications of this process at work appear in the opening section of Chiba's letter to his former pastor – in the portrayal of a youth who, for all his attempts to convince himself that God is no longer a part of his life, nevertheless finds himself drawn from Tokyo back to Kansai, scene of his childhood – and symbol of the days when he had been a regular worshipper at Father Brou's church. In acknowledging that, in Kansai, he was 'searching in vain for [his] childhood self' (p. 92), Chiba himself appears to be seeking a distance between his current self, as medical student in Tokyo, and his former self who had been caught up in the world of 'white man'. Thanks in part to the alternative perspective on Chiba that is provided by Durand's diary, in part to recognition of the process of paradoxical inversion operating on the text, however, the reader is gradually confronted with a deeper level of Chiba's being which, far from lacking a consciousness of sin, is experiencing the pain of sin at a more profound level. As the text progresses, therefore, so increasingly the reader comes to sense that what is lacking in Chiba is not so much a consciousness of sin *per se*, but rather an inability to respond to his own sin, since it is operating at the level of the unconscious. The result is the portrayal of a man who, whilst claiming to be firmly rooted in the world of 'yellow man', is unable simply to forget his childhood connection with the 'white man's' world and whose actions consequently appear to be increasingly inspired by the very consciousness of sin that he claims to lack.

At the schematic level, this paradox is incorporated into the very structure of the story: there is an inherent contradiction in choosing to present Chiba's perspective on events in the form of a lengthy letter to his former mentor, a letter in which Chiba is at pains to deny the existence of any connection between himself and the recipient. Were the connection between the two men truly broken – were Chiba truly lacking in any sense of sin-consciousness – such a letter, particularly such a heartfelt letter, would be superfluous. In short, in the very act of writing to Father Brou, Chiba unconsciously betrays the very qualities he is seeking to disclaim.

Several incidents during the course of the novella appear designed to highlight this same inherent paradox. As he gazes at the house occupied by Durand and Kimiko, for example, Chiba reveals that, far from an inability to discern sin, his senses are finely attuned to the existence of this very aspect of human nature:

> That sickly smell in Father Durand's house was definitely not that of old, rotten furniture. Rather, *if there is a smell to sin*, if there is a smell to hatred, jealousy and curses, then it was that smell, wasn't it? That acrid smell...still remained. (p. 122, my emphasis)

A similar dimension to the text is revealed in a subsequent incident in which, confronted by a dying student at his uncle's hospital, Chiba's emotional response again belies his seemingly callous reaction. Faced with the need to push the alarm bell to summon the nurses, Chiba claims:

> It was not just physical fatigue. Something leaden and heavy held down my hand and prevented the desire to push the button from surfacing. (p. 136)

Despite repeated denials that he experienced any sense of guilt as a result of his inaction, however, Chiba's unconscious reaction to this incident is reflected in the fact that he feels drawn to offer such frequent denials – and in the need he felt to report this matter in his letter to Father Brou. Why, if the incident were of no significance to him, does he keep harping back to it in this way? And why, if he were really so unconcerned about the episodes from his past, was he so determined to set the record straight in his letter?

Such scenes, in which Chiba's pronouncements to Father Brou appear to be undermined by his unconscious impulses, recur, the overall effect being to bring into question the claim that lies at the heart of Chiba's letter – that he has severed all ties with Father Brou and the church. During the course of his account of events, Chiba is at pains to defend his claim that:

> What possible connection can there be between myself and the world of Durand and Brou? Sooner or later, we all end up going our own way. (p. 123)

The more he tries to convince himself of the great chasm that exists between his world and that of 'white man', however, the more this other world comes to influence his thoughts, his actions – indeed, his entire life. The conclusion he eventually reaches relates to the 'indelible marks' discussed earlier:

> Even when lying down on a bed like a patient afflicted with T.B., we send out ripples to those around us. This is a weird and strange fact. (p. 140)

The comment goes a long way towards highlighting the increased self-awareness within Chiba. At the same time, moreover, it serves to emphasise the distance between himself and the other 'yellow people' in the novella. His acknowledgement of these 'marks' thus stands in stark contrast to the view expounded by Kimiko who, unable to fathom Durand's continued pangs of conscience regarding the church, is drawn to conclude:

> Why don't you just forget God and the church?...You left the church, right? So why do you keep worrying about it all the time? (p. 130)

To Kimiko, Durand's continued concern is indeed hard to fathom and her subsequent advice to Durand represents the natural culmination of such logic:

> It makes no difference now, however much you sin. Just keep on in the same way until your soul is worn down by the weight. If you do that, you'll become insensitive to death and sin, just as we yellow people are. (p. 143)

Kimiko has manifestly failed to acknowledge the cumulative nature of human experience and her suggestion, however well-intentioned, only serves to augment the mental conflict with which Durand finds himself confronted.

The contradictions inherent within Durand are evident from the outset – in the portrayal of a man who, having travelled to Japan in the hope of introducing his God into a fundamentally 'godless' environment, ends up succumbing to what he views as the irreconcilable tension between the two cultures – only to find his life increasingly influenced by the very church he has been obliged to reject. The more he tries to turn his back on the church, the more he finds himself drawn back to secretly observe the church services. And the more he seeks to convince himself that God is no longer part of his life, the more he is troubled by thoughts of the 'resonances of [his] fear of Hell' (p. 127). Confronted by Kimiko's encouragement to simply 'forget God and the church', therefore, Durand is in no position to comply. The marks left on his life by the church cannot simply be erased and he is forced to admit:

> During the eight years since I rejected God and left the church, I have been plagued by thoughts of divine retribution as though living in a nightmare. I tried to hate, even to deny the church that excommunicated me. But *I was totally unable to forget God*, even for one minute. (p. 130, my emphasis)

On the one hand, Durand's inablity to dismiss the concept of God from his life serves to locate him, very firmly, within the 'white' world. At the same time, paradoxically, it is this very inability simply to obliterate his past that accounts for his increasing sense of jealousy directed at the Japanese whose 'insensitivity to God' enables them to exist free of the pangs of conscience with which he remains burdened. Jealousy in turn leads to feelings of empathy –

and to development of the portrayal of a man whose human 'weakness' paradoxically serves to establish him as a potential source of reconciliation between the two seemingly opposing worlds.

Durand's role as mediator is clearly crucial; but it is only gradually, as he continues with his acts of betrayal of Father Brou (even in the face of the latter's continued financial and psychological support) that this paradoxically optimistic aspect of the portrayal of this fallen priest becomes apparent. By the end, however, there is evidence of a man who, while continuing to be troubled by his perception of the church's refusal to acknowledge specific cultural needs, nevertheless appears to have plumbed a deeper level of his being at which some form of effective communication may be realisable. In opposing Father Brou's traditional, 'Western' approach to mission, therefore, Durand is now in a position to argue:

> Aren't you looking on the church in Europe with all its tradition and the church in Japan with none of that in the same light?...Your methods are too uniform, concerned only with the end result. Just think for a moment of your average Japanese. Does he need God? Can he really visualise Christ?...
>
> Do you really think your God can plant shoots in this swamp, amongst this 'yellow' race? You have failed to notice that the look in the eyes of the 'yellow' people is the same as that you have seen in Chiba and Kimiko. Your ignorance is due to the fact that you have not been tainted by their sin, that you have never sullied your white hands. But in violating Kimiko, I stumbled across *the secrets of their soul*. (pp. 145–6, my emphasis)

The passage pre-empts the vision of Japan as a 'swamp' in which Christianity can never take root offered by Endō in the novel, *Silence*, written some ten years later. At the same time, in highlighting Durand's increasing awareness of the need to understand 'yellow man' at a deeper level, this comment reinforces the self-assessment of the former priest as a man who has not so much abandoned God, but rather been abandoned by God. In so doing, he rejects the 'aggressive, active' stance, cited earlier as representative of Endō's depiction of the world of 'white man'. Instead, in stumbling across the secret of the soul of those in his host culture, Durand conforms more to the 'passive' stance Endō had attributed to 'yellow man'.

It is this same 'passive' stance that categorises Durand's relationship with Kimiko. Far from love at first sight, the couple drift into their affair, influenced more by the 'dampness unique to Japan' (p. 113) than by any passionate desire. The two meet in the aftermath of the great Kansai flood – as Kimiko finds herself homeless and forced to take advantage of the charity that Durand had offered her on learning of her plight. As the latter stares at Kimiko following the overdose she takes in desperation on learning that Durand has arranged to send her away for the next stage of her rehabilitation, therefore, Durand's instinctive reaction is to pray – to the very God whom he saw as having abandoned him – on behalf of this 'lonely woman' (p. 113). Immediately, however, his attention is drawn to the paradoxical realisation that 'she was far from lonely' – that she is blessed with a total absence of 'those forced dark and contorted shadows that we Europeans love to call despair or loneliness' (pp. 113–14).

In keeping with the paradoxical intent behind these stories, therefore, it is at this moment – as his eyes are opened to a greater appreciation of his own abject circumstances – that Durand embarks along the path to a greater appreciation of a deeper truth than that which had hitherto ordered his life. His assessment of Kimiko at this moment is that 'he had never seen a face so divorced from God' (p. 114). But it is through his relationship with this same woman and the influence that she, as symbol of the 'godless' world, comes to exert on his life that Durand is led to a clearer understanding of a deeper level to his being at which his affiliation with the world of the church would continue with renewed intensity.

As suggested by the above discussion, the ground for Endō's subsequent career had been prepared by these two novellas. Several of the motifs that would be developed at greater length in subsequent novels had been introduced and, though the literary technique would inevitably be refined, it is possible to discern, even in these earliest works, those elements of Endō's art that would ultimately emerge as his hallmark. Let us now turn to the expression of these themes and techniques as evidenced in Endō's early full-length novels.

3

THE SEA AND POISON, WONDERFUL FOOL, THE GIRL I LEFT BEHIND

> Our attitude towards the inner voice alternates between two extremes: it is regarded either as undiluted nonsense or as the voice of God. It does not seem to occur to anyone that there might be something valuable in between. The 'other' may be just as one-sided in one way as the ego is in another. And yet the conflict between them may give rise to truth and meaning – but only if the ego is willing to grant the other its rightful personality.
>
> (C.G. Jung)

In keeping with so many of his contemporaries on the Japanese literary scene, Endō was soon to discover the benefits that tend to accrue to recipients of the Akutagawa Prize. Pressed for manuscripts from all quarters, there followed a series of short stories and novels, mostly building upon the themes broached in *White Man* and *Yellow Man*. At the same time, securement of a position as Lecturer in the Division of Literature at Sophia University provided a modicum of financial security intended to tide the family over until Endō was in a position to devote himself full-time to his literary pursuits. These were hectic years for the author, but such industry was rewarded by the acclaim accorded to novels such as *The Sea and Poison*[1] and *Wonderful Fool* and with the opportunities for foreign travel that accompanied increased notoriety.

Hard work also brought with it a price, however, and by 1960 Endō was forced to seek admission, first, into the Department of Infectious Diseases at Tokyo University and subsequently into Keiō University Hospital suffering from a recurrence of the TB that had contributed to his early return from his period of study in France some seven years earlier. Three years and three major operations later, when Endō completed the last of his periods of protracted hospitalisation, the disease had taken its toll, the works written in the immediate aftermath of this experience suggesting a man seeking relief from physical exhaustion through spiritual enquiry of a different dimension from that evidenced in the earlier works. The process would eventually lead to publication of *Silence* in 1966, the work with which the author established his international reputation. But, in many ways, this was heralded by *The Girl I Left Behind*, a work usually assigned to the *taishū bungaku* ('popular' or 'entertainment literature') as opposed to *junbungaku* ('pure literature') section of his work, but which the author himself saw as bridging the divide between these two categorisations.[2]

Seen in this light, it is possible to delineate a clear progression between the works written before and after the author's hospitalisation. Nevertheless, in that the emphasis in all these works rests on protagonists who come increasingly to question the distinctions traditionally attributed to a series of oppositions, these can all be seen as preparing the ground for the process whereby, in *Silence*, the author attempts a redefinition of such traditional classification. At the same time, closer examination of these works reveals a series of protagonists who come increasingly to recognise a greater complexity to their being than they are initially ready to acknowledge – and, as they do so, all evidence a growing awareness of the 'Self', a growing recognition of some unconscious aspect of their being brought into *rapprochement* with a conscious element. On frequent occasions, this increased self-realisation is supported at the textual level by the image of the 'watching eye' so integral to Endō's novelistic technique. The image of the watching eye may change: it can be seen in different works as that of a dog, a bird, a mother figure, even in some cases, that of Christ Himself. But in each case the effect is the same: in the portrayal of this image of omnipotent vision, Endō sought to highlight the attempt to see through to, and to understand, a deeper level of human existence, and to suggest that it is through awareness of this 'eye', this gaze transcending the lives of the characters in his works, that these are ultimately able to aspire to their own salvation. The result is a body of works in which, increasingly, protagonists come to listen to the voice of their unconscious and the consequent progression from depiction of this realm as predominantly dark to a world in which the impulse towards Evil is balanced by an optimistic, forward-looking element that can ultimately lead to the Jungian view of the unconscious as the repository of both positive and negative forces. This chapter will therefore focus on the period leading up to the publication of

Silence and, in particular, on the three novels already mentioned as contributing most to Endō's burgeoning reputation during this time: *The Sea and Poison*, *Wonderful Fool* and *The Girl I Left Behind*.

The Sea and Poison

Of these, *The Sea and Poison* can be read as the most concerted attempt to that date by the author to penetrate deeper into the realm of the unconscious in the hope thereby of hinting at a greater complexity to human nature than is initially apparent. In this regard, Endō's choice of subject material for this novel – experiments in human vivisection conducted during the Pacific War by the Japanese authorities on American POWs – would appear to be deliberate. In so doing, Endō appears intent on probing the extremes of human behaviour – in the hope thereby of addressing the distinction between 'sin' and some form of absolute 'Evil', evil that does not represent a 'perverted image of the search for Christ' (as discussed in Chapter 1) and consequently possesses no potential for salvation. In Japanese, the distinction is that between *tsumi* (sin, crime) and *aku* (traditional evil), a delineation defined by the scholar whom Endō openly acknowledges as the primary influence on his decision to study the writings of Jung, namely, the Japanese psychologist Kawai Hayao, who has argued:

> Sin has its limits and leads on to redemption. But Evil is limitless and allows for no salvation. Sin is necessary for the establishment of our own individual identity. (The story of the Fall is the ultimate expression of this). In contrast to this, it is Evil that comes into play in the process of soul-making....
>
> In the process of redemption from sin, there are always certain generally-accepted techniques, and group religions come to exert their influence. But in the case of Evil, each individual has no choice but to seek for himself a life-style with which to oppose [the Evil]. Or perhaps, one should say that the 'power' of the individual becomes virtually meaningless.[3]

In choosing to focus once more on an example of inhuman behaviour, Endō was well aware of the dangers inherent in this task. The effect, however, is similar to that already discussed with reference to *White Man*: in highlighting the ability of the individual to inflict unconscionable suffering on fellow human beings, Endō encourages interpretation of the work as contrasting the world of the 'white' prisoners with that of their Japanese captors, seemingly devoid of all awareness of God, sin and death and consequently unable to resist the lure of sin. In keeping with the earlier precedent, however, there is another level to the text – a development during the course of the novel in which erosion of the initial distinction between lack of sin-consciousness and true understanding is reflected in the process of self-realisation at work in the hearts of the various characters. Characters who, at the outset, appear to lack all comprehension of the concept of 'sin', become increasingly aware of the consequences of their actions. But since, in the majority of cases, this remains at the unconscious level, the author can only hint at this by depiction of unfathomable impulses.

The clearest example of such awakening occurs in the person of Suguro, the young hospital intern at the time of the vivisections who is portrayed as conniving in the crime largely out of fear of the adverse effects on his career that would likely ensue from any refusal to co-operate with orders stemming from his superiors. Suguro's progression from being an 'accomplice to crime', however unwilling, to one possessed of an awareness of sin is never explicitly portrayed, but it is clearly hinted at in the depiction of a man increasingly wracked by recognition that his failure to take preventative action in the face of the crime locates him firmly within the ranks of the guilty.

In retrospect, however, the fact that there is more to Suguro than meets the eye can be seen as emphasised from the outset. First introduced in the text as an elderly doctor 'with [a] grey, bloated face'[4] eking out a solitary existence as an unfêted doctor in the suburbs of Tokyo, Suguro's medical ability is immediately acknowledged by the narrator who visits him for pneumothorax treatment:

> Speaking from my own experience, even [the] veteran doctor in Kyodo would slip up once or twice a month and have to withdraw the needle to try again. At times like that, I was seized with pain as though my side had been ripped open.
> This never happened with Dr Suguro. With one thrust he would insert the needle quickly and surely right between the pleura and the lung, lodging it there securely. There was no pain at all. It was done before I could even flinch. (p. 21)

The question of why such a competent doctor appears destined to finish his career in such a 'barren spot' alerts the narrator to the possibility that there is something in Suguro's past preventing him from assuming a position his talent would seem to merit. At the same time, however, the passage highlights the potential for deceptive appearances, suggesting a greater complexity to Suguro than initially implied. Prompted by this realisation, the narrator investigates further, although here, too, the text is at pains to attribute this, not to any conscious determination to ascertain the 'truth', but rather to an unfathomable and unconscious impulse: 'Why I had come all the way up here [to the Fukuoka Medical School in which the vivisections had purportedly taken place], I myself didn't know' (p. 29).

Already the depiction of Suguro as somehow distinct from his contemporaries is established and, as the narrative focus reverts to events leading up to the vivisections, so the image of Suguro as somehow set apart from the other medical personnel in the hospital is reinforced. Unlike Dr Asai, his immediate superior, and the other interns, all of whom look on patients with complicated symptoms as representing 'good opportunities' for research (p. 41), Suguro is portrayed from the start as feeling a stronger sense of attachment to patients as individuals. Troubled by the hardened attitude of his colleagues, Suguro is left 'feeling that he was a cog on one of the gear wheels turning here, whose movements he had no way of understanding' (p. 52). Constant contact with such an attitude does, however, take its toll and, following the death of the 'old lady', a patient to whom he had grown particularly attached, Suguro's attitude appears to harden.

> 'From now on', Suguro thought, 'for myself, for the War, for Japan, for everything, let things go just as they like.' (p. 72)

The passage marks a watershed for Suguro, and from this point on he finds himself increasingly responding to the promptings of his unconscious. Significantly, it is immediately after this incident that Suguro is asked to take part in the vivisection – and he is totally unable to account for his readiness to co-operate in this crime.

> Was it because he was drawn along by Toda? Or was it because of his headache and the nausea churning in the pit of his stomach?...
> 'It's all the same', Suguro kept thinking. 'I was drawn into it because of the blue charcoal flames maybe. Maybe because of Toda's cigarette. Because of one thing, because of another, what does it matter? It's all the same.' (p. 76)

In keeping with the above-mentioned determination on the part of the author to refrain from analysis of unconscious impulses, however, the question is not pursued. Instead, Endō chooses to hint at a different dimension to Suguro's being through presentation of his dream of the time:

> In his dreams he saw himself in the dark sea, his figure a battered husk swept round in the current. (p. 76)

From this moment on, the depiction of Suguro is that of a man troubled by facets of his being that he had not previously acknowledged. To Suguro himself, such growing self-awareness may not be immediately apparent, but there is clear evidence at the textual level of a man struggling to come to terms with aspects of his inner being – of a man engaged in a process of spiritual awakening.

Embroiled as he is in a dilemma of vast ethical proportions, Suguro cannot escape the spiritual implications of his complicity in the crime. During events leading up to the vivisections, he maintains an outward bravado that allows for no such considerations and in response to the specific question offered by his fellow intern, Toda, as to whether Suguro believes in the existence of God, the latter replies with apparent conviction:

> For myself, I can't see how whether there's a God or whether there's not a God makes any difference. (p. 79)

At this point, however, Suguro leaves the room abruptly: he is clearly struggling to accept such a clear-cut denial. Little overt mention is made of this struggle in the ensuing text, but it is traced, in symbolic form, in the references to Suguro's reaction to the poem he had learnt from Toda:

> When the clouds like sheep pass,
> When the clouds swirl like steam,
> Sky, your scattering is white,
> White, like streams of cotton. (pp. 44–5)

For some reason which Suguro himself is unable to identify, the poem always resurfaces in the protagonist's mind at moments of greatest moral dilemma, the image of the 'clouds...like sheep' sufficient to reduce the protagonist to 'a mood of tears' (p. 45). The more Suguro is troubled by this verse, the more its role as an object of his subconscious religious devotion is established. Significantly, however, as increasingly Suguro is obliged to accept that mere non-co-operation in the crime is no vindication, so the poem is superseded by a voice reverberating from deep within his being accusing him of 'always [being] there...always there – not doing anything at all' (p. 150). By the end of the work, such promptings from the unconscious have completely replaced the poem: confrontation with the existence of absolute evil has resulted in Suguro's awakening to the enormity of his sin – and to increased understanding of the complexity of human nature in general, and of his own psychological make-up in particular.

In the case of Suguro, such potential for increased awareness may be in evidence from the outset. In the case of Toda, however, such growth is much more unexpected. At the beginning of the novel, Toda is portrayed as a young intern whose callous attitude towards his work has led him to conclude:

> Killing a patient isn't so solemn a matter as all that. It's nothing new in the world of medicine. That's how we've made our progress! (p. 51)

In part, such callousness can be attributed to an attitude of resignation induced by the war, for as he admits: 'Today everybody is on the way out. The poor bastard who doesn't die in the hospital gets his chance every night to die in an air raid' (p. 42). But the implication that this lack of concern is a reflection of a more fundamental and deep-rooted insensitivity appears confirmed when he dismisses the cover-up of the death of another of the patients, Mrs Tabe, as a 'comedy' (p. 65).

At this stage of the novel, the impression that this is the sum total of Toda's personality is powerful. However, through skilful insertion of several 'flashbacks' to incidents in Toda's childhood, the author is in a position to hint at a greater depth to Toda's being. The technique begins with the protagonist's tacit admission of a distinction between his current self and former self, as he confesses:

> The me who is writing now, today, doesn't look upon the me of that time, the bright little boy, as having been especially crafty. (p. 104)

In so doing, Toda comes to recognise that, even as a child, all his energies had been devoted to careful cultivation of his public persona

– and that his daily routine consisted of a series of 'performances', all designed to reinforce the outward impression of the perfect student. His sense of unease following the arrival of the new pupil, Wakabayashi, is, however, important, for, as he acknowledges following the incident in which he had deliberately solicited praise for intervening in a skirmish, involving Wakabayashi, in the sandpit:

> The uncanny feeling surged up in me that, no doubt about it, here was one person able to see to the bottom of my heart. (p. 110)

The fear of having the contents of his Shadow perceived by a fellow human being is very real for Toda – and leads to an increased determination to fathom his own unconscious being for himself. Immediately after the incident with Wakabayashi, for example, comes another incident – the attempt to atone for an earlier act of deception by presenting his classmate with a pen – that leads to further self-discovery. Toda returns from this act of penitence in a state of confusion as, far from feeling content with himself, his 'heart was blank and empty....The joy and satisfaction which come from doing a good deed – not the faintest hint of anything like this welled up in [his] heart' (p. 113). Toda is here learning the painful lesson, later articulated by Endō, that:

> An action which appears pure and correct may conceal, deep within the unconscious of the individual in question, an egoism, a vanity, a greed or a sense of self-gratification.[5]

The most blatant example of Toda being confronted with the contents of his unconscious bursting forth into consciousness in an act of unfathomable impulse is, however, still to come – in the scene – reminiscent of that in which Mauriac's Thérèse poisons her husband – where the boy Toda steals and kills his teacher's precious butterfly. Significantly, the narrative description of this event stresses that it is the 'stifling heat' of the 'afternoon sun' that incites Toda to commit this act, luring him into a feeling 'very much like lust' (p. 115). Put in these terms, the implication appears clear: this is no premeditated attack – just an involuntary explosion of a previously suppressed impulse that conforms closely with Jung's description of repressed impulses, which, if not corrected, are 'liable to burst forth suddenly in a moment of unawareness'.[6]

As suggested by the above, inclusion of these flashback scenes serves the important function of transforming Toda in the eyes of the reader into a man, not so much devoid of a sin-consciousness, but who, whilst recognising the distinction between right and wrong, has always tried to convince himself that 'looking upon [various episodes] as distasteful and suffering because of them are two different matters' (p. 123). Already there is evidence of a man who, like Suguro, is struggling to come to terms with the ethical implications of the crime in which he is about to become embroiled and vaguely aware that complicity would bring about some form of retribution. As he acknowledges immediately after this:

> I don't know why. I thought at that moment that one day I would be punished. I felt with a sharp insistence that one day I would have to undergo retribution for what I had done so far in my life. (p. 125)

For Toda at this stage, such retribution is envisaged at the societal level: it is only later that Endō was to introduce the concept of an omnipotent being to influence this. But in thus hinting at a sin-consciousness in even the seemingly implacable Toda, such sections cast a fresh gloss onto the depiction of the scenes of the vivisections that follow. Armed with this additional perspective, the reader is alerted to the slightest hint of a conscience penetrating Toda's carefully maintained public facade – hints that might have been overlooked were it not for these earlier suggestions of a more complex being behind the public mask. During the course of the operation, for example, Toda is assailed by a 'strange feeling' as he realises: 'I'm going to be in this film too' and asks himself, 'Afterwards, when the film is shown, will it rouse any special emotions in me?' (p. 144). From this and other similar sections, it is clear that, despite his outward bravado, Toda is becoming increasingly disturbed by his conscience – and it therefore comes as little surprise to see him drawn back to the operating theatre, scene of the crime, after everything has finished. Significantly, whilst there, he bumps into the surgeon responsible for the operation, the 'Old Man', Dr Hashimoto – a strong indication that Toda is not alone in his anguish. With this narrative device, Endō succeeds in implying that the others involved in the conspiracy are equally torn by a similar voice urging them to acknowledge a greater complexity to their being than that they had hitherto recognised.

Seen in this light, the traditional classification of *The Sea and Poison* as a novel portraying the absence of sin-consciousness in 'yellow' society requires modification.[7] Rather than focusing on the lack of guilt evidenced by the various characters, Endō can here be seen shining the narrative spotlight onto the crime of vivisection *per se* and, in so doing, analysing the process whereby the various accomplices are gradually forced to confront the complexity of human nature. As shown above, the various characters *do* become aware of the concept of sin; their problem is that, having detected it, they are unable to handle it. The result is a novel in which the role of the unconscious is acknowledged – although the ensuing image of this realm is more reminiscent of the dark realm as depicted by Freud than the dual image of a realm that serves as both 'the fount of sin and the place where God works' that is developed in later works.[8] The point was keenly felt by the author, who acknowledged in a subsequent discussion:

> My treatment of the unconscious in *The Sea and Poison* – in the portrayal of man drawn towards sin (in the guise of vivisection) – made for painful writing. As I wrote, I kept hoping that this would be transformed into a longing for God. But I ended up unable to discern the [positive element].[9]

To Endō, such works – those in which sin is portrayed but in which there is little sense of empathy with the suffering of those involved and which consequently fail to probe the potential for salvation at the very extremes of evil – had been depicted as resembling 'negatives of life'. What was required, he argued, was the presence of 'God who prints these negatives',[10] and it is this realisation that leads to the more overt references to the concept of an omnipotent being who can influence this process in subsequent novels of this period.

Wonderful Fool

Only two years were to elapse before publication of Endō's next major novel, *Wonderful Fool*, but already there is evidence of an author whose vision of the realm of the unconscious has evolved in the intervening period. Not only is the potential for growth of characters initially portrayed as two-dimensional here exploited at greater length, but the later novel goes a long way to moving the focus away from the sin and weakness of the characters *per se*, emphasising, rather, the potential for salvation, both for the individuals concerned and for those with whom their paths through life cross.

The technique employed to this end is that, outlined above, of the fusion of oppositions traditionally viewed as irreconcilable. In *Wonderful Fool*, the tension at the heart of the novel is that between strength and weakness, and it is through examination of the innate relationship between these two qualities that Endō succeeds in capturing the inner growth within his characters, in particular within his French protagonist, Gaston. From the outset, Gaston is portrayed as an enigma: not only are his motives in coming to Japan unclear, but his actions following his arrival are equally shrouded in uncertainty. From the moment he establishes contact with Takamori, his long-standing penfriend, and Tomoe, Takamori's sister, however, his role resembles that of the fool in traditional drama, a role encapsulated by Roland Barthes as serving as 'the purveyor of double understanding'.[11] The trait is integral to the depiction of Gaston, the process whereby Gaston is transformed in the eyes of his Japanese hosts from a 'simpleton'[12] into a man capable of exerting a subtle, yet all-pervading, influence not only on his friends but even on Endō, the aptly named, self-confessed killer with whom he becomes increasingly embroiled, lying at the heart of the novel. It is this process that epitomises, once more, the technique of paradoxical inversion on which the author's literature was founded.

In keeping with the pattern established earlier, Gaston's eventual emergence as a 'wonderful fool' relies, in large measure, on gradual exposure of elements of his character that initially remain rooted in his unconscious. To this end, initial emphasis rests squarely on the protagonist's ungamely public facade – and on his seeming folly – as he meets Takamori and Tomoe for the first time:

> His face was so sunburned that he could easily have passed for an Oriental, and it was very long – a horseface indeed!
>
> It was not only his face. His nose too was long. And when he opened his huge mouth to laugh, displaying the gums of his teeth, the impression of 'horse' was all the stronger. (p. 39)

As the novel progresses, so Takamori and Tomoe's initial impressions of their visitor are undermined by his generous and warm-hearted nature. In keeping with precedent established in the earlier works, however, Endō does not suddenly endow his protagonist with qualities that he did not formerly possess. Rather, in stressing his humanness, the author seeks to locate within his 'weak' character an inner energy and a consequent capacity for acts of 'strength'. In the case of Gaston, this quality centres around his capacity for love: the Frenchman is possessed of an overpowering, self-sacrificing love of both people and animals that is portrayed as his one great redeeming virtue. With the benefit of hindsight, it is clear that Gaston has always possessed this capacity, but it is only gradually during the course of the novel – as his 'loving trust in others forces all who come into contact with him to face up to themselves and challenges them to change' – that the reader is alerted to such potential in this character.[13] At the same time, the very qualities initially interpreted as signs of weakness come to be recognised as a potential source for Gaston's ultimate salvation.

First to notice that initial impressions of Gaston may be mistaken is Takamori, who from a very early stage is astute enough to offer the following warning to his more impetuous sister, Tomoe: 'It's still too early to tell whether he's a fool or not. He may surprise you' (p. 51). Thereafter, as the drama unfolds, Gaston comes increasingly to act in a way that attracts a reaction of derision, on occasion even of contempt, from both Takamori and Tomoe. It is at these moments, however, that the narrator's 'spirit double' intervenes, coming increasingly to stress another facet of Gaston's being. As he remarks on one occasion:

> Simple Gaston was constitutionally incapable of harboring resentment or hatred towards anyone....Instead, he was quickly moved to trust in the goodwill and friendship of others, or at least to want to trust in them. (p. 83)

Beneath the 'dull-witted' and 'clumsy' persona lies a man who 'wishes to be of help...to all unfortunate people' (p. 100) and it is to this greater complexity to his being that first Takamori and later Tomoe are attracted.

In the case of Takamori, it is following the disappearance of Gaston in the company of the renowned gangster, Endō, that he comes to acknowledge the existence of inexplicable feelings of attraction for their French visitor – as he comes to admit, if only to himself, that 'Gaston has become something of an ideal for me' (p. 132). Thereafter, in a passage that serves as a precursor of similar depictions by Endō of the 'weak' *Kakure* (Hidden) Christians, Takamori concludes:

> Not all men are handsome and strong. There are some who are cowards from birth....But for such a man, a man both weak and cowardly, to bear the burden of his weakness and struggle valiantly to live a beautiful life – that's what I call great....I feel more drawn to Gaston than I would to a splendid saint or hero. (pp. 187–8)

The burgeoning relationship between Takamori and Gaston is clearly integral to the novel, the closeness of the tie emphasised in Takamori's realisation that 'to abandon Gaston now would be like throwing away the best part of myself' (p. 186). For Takamori, by this stage, Gaston has come to assume a significance out of all proportion to his status as a visiting pen-friend whom Takamori had only met a few weeks previously. The influence that Gaston is able to exert on Takamori's daily schedule appears total – to the extent that the latter thinks nothing of entrusting his backlog of work to colleagues and taking off in search of his new friend. And, far from begrudging the time he finds himself devoting to his enigmatic guest, Takamori is by now betraying all the signs of conforming to the Jungian tenet, to which reference has already been made, that 'when we particularly dislike someone, especially if it is an unreasonable dislike, we should suspect that we are actually disliking a quality of our own which we find in the other person'.[14] The more Takamori comes to acknowledge, however unconsciously, the 'indelible marks' that Gaston has left on his life, the better equipped he is to assess the full extent of Gaston's capacity for love of others – and to recognise the superficiality of his own first impressions of the French visitor.

For Tomoe, however, the road to increased self-awareness is not quite so smooth, her ambivalent attitude towards Gaston being indicative of the greater difficulty she experiences in separating his outward appearance from his inner being. And yet, in retrospect, from the outset Tomoe, too, is not totally oblivious to Gaston's potential for good – as evidenced in the following passage shortly after Gaston's arrival:

> Tomoe thought: He may be a coward and lacking in self-respect, but he certainly has a good heart. She felt she had finally come to understand his good qualities, and looked at him now with new eyes. (p. 67)

Such sections, however, reveal more about Tomoe's own lack of self-understanding than her ability to fathom the depths of Gaston's inner being – and she continues to dismiss him in the company of others as 'a fool, a complete idiot' (p. 122). First indications that there may be more to Tomoe's rejection of Gaston than meets the eye are thus limited to those sections of the novel in which the voice of the alternative narrator intrudes overtly into the narrative with commentary on Tomoe's instinctive reactions. An early example occurs in the portrayal of her relationship with her effeminate colleague, Osako – in the observation that, 'for some reason, the more [Osako] abused Gaston, the angrier Tomoe became' (p. 137). At the conscious level, such support for the man she is openly dismissing as 'a complete idiot' would appear excessive. As a manifestation of Tomoe's empathy for Gaston, however, the incident betrays an element of concern at the level of the unconscious with which Tomoe is struggling to come to terms. From this point on, outwardly Tomoe continues to dismiss the visitor as a 'fool'; but increasingly the attention of the reader is drawn to the presence of more complex emotions within her – in the form of the voice of her unconscious increasingly urging her to admit 'that her brother was right in saying that he had a good heart' (p. 172).

In a development remarkably true to real life, however, it is only following Gaston's physical departure from Tokyo that Tomoe comes to acknowledge these conflicting feelings. As she gazes at his train disappearing into the evening gloom, convinced that it is carrying the Frenchman out of her life once and for all, the narrative now provides specific acknowledgement of Tomoe's change of attitude: 'Gaston, who until now had been nothing more than an object of her ridicule and pity, seemed suddenly transformed into a man of extraordinary power' (p. 179). Only now is she in a position to conclude:

> He's not a fool. He's not a fool. Or, if he is, he's a wonderful fool...a wonderful fool who will never allow the little light which he sheds along man's way to go out. (p. 180)

As suggested with this comment, by this point in the novel we have travelled far along the road towards the transposition that lies at the heart of the work – the gradual emergence of Gaston as a Christ-like figure. As discussed earlier, the technique of transposition lies at the heart of Endō's art and, in retrospect, the process can be seen hinted at from the outset of the novel – in the occasional use of Christ-like images and Biblical allusions used in the portrayal of

Gaston. As he leaves Takamori and Tomoe's house for the first time, bound for his own period in the wilderness, for example, the portrayal of Gaston, 'all alone' is preceded by the following Biblical citation: 'The foxes have their holes and the birds of the air their nests' (p. 74). In choosing to cite this passage in the Biblical original, Endō openly acknowledges the implication that Gaston, like the Son of Man, will have 'nowhere to lay his head' as he sets off towards an unknown future. In the sections that follow, moreover, as Gaston comes more and more to manifest his capacity for selfless acts of love, so similarities with the Christ-image become increasingly overt. Even when embroiled in the criminal world of the callous Endō, Gaston's overwhelming love for his fellow human beings remains paramount – to the extent that when Gaston resolves 'not to leave...[but rather] to go with' the cold-blooded murderer (p. 153), this comes to be seen, less as an act of unbridled naivety, more a deliberate attempt to come alongside Endō in his hour of need in the hope thereby of influencing his actions. As may be expected, the effect on Endō is hardly immediate: following his initial encounter with Gaston, Endō struggles at length to resist the increasingly irresistible promptings of his own unconscious. By the end of the novel, however, even Endō is forced to acknowledge his growing respect for his unsolicited companion – as he watches his intended victim, Kobayashi, struggling with Gaston, and the latter taking 'Kobayashi's blows on himself in order to save [Endō] and collaps[ing] in the shallows of the swamp' (p. 231).

The struggle takes place at the 'Big Swamp', a remote spot in the heart of the mountains of northern Japan to which Endō and Gaston have been led by the unwitting Kobayashi. The immediate aim is to recover the bars of silver whose disappearance had resulted in the execution of Endō's brother at the end of the war. For Endō, the gangster who remains convinced that his brother had paid the ultimate price for the treachery of Kobayashi and his accomplice Kanai, this represents the ideal location to dispose of Kobayashi once the latter had served his useful purpose. For Endō, as author, however, selection of the swamp as the setting for the denouement of the novel was of much greater significance: the metaphor of the 'mud-swamp' was one that he had already developed in much of his shorter fiction to date as symbolising the insensitivity to sin to which so many of his products of 'yellow' society are prone. As already noted, for Chiba, in *Yellow Man*, such insensitivity had been depicted as an 'extreme fatigue' – as 'a weariness, murky as the colour of [his] skin, dank and heavily submerged'

(p. 87). Thereafter, the more the author came to identify such lack of energy with an unwillingness to deal effectively with moral issues, the more he resorted to the image of the swamp as symbol of the safe, uneventful life by which many of his characters are ensnared, but to which they remain inexplicably attached.

For Chiba, Suguro, Endō and others, the swamp may appear all-consuming. But what of the potential with which these characters are endowed to extricate themselves from this embrace? As the critic, Mathy, has pointed out, Endō's earliest works of fiction never really come to terms with this issue.[15] With the depiction of Endō, Gaston and Kobayashi flailing about in the 'Big Swamp' at the conclusion of *Wonderful Fool*, however, Endō avails himself of a traditional image, both of 'a world in which every creature devours every other' and of the individual's search for love[16] – and succeeds thereby in engendering the ultimate transposition of Gaston from a figure of ridicule into one whose capacity for life succeeds in effecting changes on all those with whom he comes into contact.

The love that Gaston evidences at the swamp ultimately proves irresistible. More specifically, in the portrayal of Gaston's concern for his companions as a gift volunteered unconditionally, the swamp scene is effective as a symbol of Endō's frequently discussed vision of the maternal nature of Christ's love.[17] Once more, however, one can detect, behind the acknowledged focus on the maternal qualities he sought in Christianity a greater complexity to this symbol, a complexity again derived from the author's interest in Jungian psychology.

It was the Jungian psychologist, Erich Neumann, who explored the image of the swamp, not merely as an expression of the cry for maternal love, but in particular as a symbol of the archetype of the 'magna mater', the great mother.[18] As Neumann is quick to note, the archetype is possessed of a dual nature. On the one hand, the mother figure can be seen as the abundant fount of all things, showering her creatures with her bountiful blessings, the 'protector figure'. At the same time, however, she is the 'terrible mother', luring all creatures inside her towards darkness and death – the devourer and destroyer to which Jung himself made such frequent allusion.

The choice of the swamp as symbol of this duality would seem entirely appropriate. In choosing physically to locate the climactic scene of this novel in a swamp, moreover, Endō draws attention to the process of re-evaluation of Gaston that had long lain at the heart of his literary design. Before the dramatic struggle in the swamp, acknowledgement of the hidden facets to their visitor has been portrayed as a slow and, on occasion, painful process – for Takamori, Tomoe and Endō, the three characters most affected by these latent qualities of the Frenchman. With the unravelling of the symbolic aspect of this scene, however, the implicit recognition evidenced by all three of a greater depth to Gaston than they had initially countenanced carries greater conviction. Not only are all three now willing to acknowledge, however begrudgingly, the influence Gaston has exerted on their lives, but even after Gaston's disappearance, all three would concur with Takamori in his belief that 'Gaston is still alive. One day he'll come lumbering down again...to take upon his back once more the sorrow of people like these' (p. 237).

It is not only Gaston, however, whose outward persona conceals a complex personality. Even in the case of Endō, seemingly the archetypal villain, the novel provides frequent evidence that, behind the cold exterior, lies a measure of compassion that he struggles, on occasion, to suppress. Shortly after Gaston's first encounter with Endō, for example, comes the scene in which, having been able to whip his woman friend with no apparent feelings of remorse, Endō had been drawn to tears as he contemplates his dead brother. True to type, Endō attempts to dismiss such emotion with the simple comment, 'I hate sentimentality'. But, as the narrative is quick to point out: 'He sounded as if he were talking to himself' (p. 134).

Clearly, the problem of coming to terms with alternative facets of his being is one that Endō must address and struggle with for himself. But, as noted above, the narrative appears designed to highlight the role exercised by Gaston in drawing Endō along the road to self-realisation. As the latter stands on the point of murdering Kanai, for example, it is Gaston who attempts to intercede, leaving the narrator to conclude: 'There was no doubt that his heart had been touched by Gaston's plea' (p. 148). And in full accordance with the process of self-discovery outlined by Jung (and discussed by Endō in *Watashi no aishita shōsetsu*), this gradual awakening is accompanied by frequent examples of Endō troubled by an 'inner voice' – the voice of his unconscious – as he struggles to keep this aspect of his being suppressed. As he stands over the prone Kanai, awakening to the realisation that Gaston had removed the bullets from his pistol, it is this voice that he hears: '"No bullets! No bullets!" He seemed to hear someone, *not himself*, shout in his ear in derision' (p. 149, my emphasis). And as Endō seeks to come to terms with the changing reality of the situation, it is this same voice that leads him to conclude:

This man was just pretending to be a fool. In reality, he was a very clever man, aware of everything going on around him. (p. 151)

Later, in the incident with Kobayashi in the swamp, it is this same voice that surfaces as Endō struggles with the trigger: ' "Pull! All you have to do is pull!" *a far-off voice somewhere in his head* ordered' (p. 226, my emphasis). At this point, Endō begins a dialogue with this 'other self', a process that the narrative clearly identifies as the gangster struggling with his own guilty conscience. The more he strives to account for his inability to pull the trigger, the more Endō succumbs to 'the illusion that he had heard this voice before in the long distant past' (p. 226). And as, increasingly, he finds himself troubled by this voice of inner reasoning, so more and more he is obliged to acknowledge this other voice as offering a realistic, alternative course of action. Significantly, therefore, as these 'two voices began to merge in his head' (p. 226), Endō loses consciousness, unable to come to terms with these conflicting elements of his own being.

The effect upon Endō of Gaston's 'quiet diplomacy' is thus incalculable: the man who was content to treat Gaston with total contempt when first they had met is gradually won over by the latter's powerful presence. Not only does he come consciously to entrust him with intimacies that he would normally reserve for his own inner group, but at the unconscious level, he finds himself manipulated by the Frenchman in a manner so subtle and unobtrusive that the fact that both of his intended victims, Kanai and Kobayashi, escape their fate is almost lost amongst the psychological drama.

At first sight, the link between Endō and Gaston may indeed appear tenuous. But viewed in this light, as two men involved in the process of self-discovery and struggling with aspects of their personalities they had previously kept suppressed, the two can be seen as complementary figures, both of whom are able to draw attention to previously unrecognised traits in the other. It is a similar, symbiotic relationship that links Yoshioka and Mitsu in *The Girl I Left Behind* – and it is to a discussion of this novel that the focus of this chapter will now turn.

The Girl I Left Behind

As noted above, the years between composition of *Wonderful Fool* in 1959 and *The Girl I Left Behind* in 1964 represented the nadir of

Endō's fortunes from a medical standpoint. In terms of literary output, too, these were relatively barren years.[19] In that this period of enforced respite provided the opportunity for objective reassessment of the author's corpus to date, however, this was to prove an invaluable break and it is possible to attribute the more intimate relationship between the narrator and his 'spirit double' in the works that appeared following his return to full literary productivity to a more considered approach to his art. In terms of design, therefore, similarities between *Wonderful Fool* and *The Girl I Left Behind* are readily apparent: the focus in both works is on the transposition of the protagonist from abject fool into a figure whose capacity for selfless love is acknowledged by all. The difference lies in terms of narrative approach: whereas in *Wonderful Fool*, the gradual emergence of Gaston as a figure capable of unconditional love is heralded in the very title of the novel and is traced in very deliberate terms, in *The Girl I Left Behind*, the catalyst for Mitsu's ultimate development into a being of Christ-like proportions is explored in greater detail, the consequent re-evaluation that takes place within Yoshioka accordingly more convincingly anticipated. At the same time, in choosing to resort to the image most widely used in Western literature to signify the relationship between God and His creation – that of the lover – Endō can be seen here conforming more closely to the precedent, established by Western Catholic writers, of avoiding a specifically theological vocabulary.

As the author acknowledges in *Watashi no aishita shōsetsu*, in depicting love (and especially passion) Western Catholic authors had traditionally sought to depict God as at work in even the most inauspicious surroundings.[20] With spiritual yearning identified with the image of the individual responding to unfathomable instinct, here was a concrete image from conscious experience that hinted at God as present even in those thoughts suppressed into the unconscious. The symbol was readily adopted by Endō, the desire to detect within even the most mundane experience the potential for increased awareness of a spiritual element to the human condition never far beneath the surface. In his examination of the psychology of his characters in their emerging relationships, therefore, Endō focuses on the lack of drama behind such bonds – in an attempt in this way to suggest a new dimension to the most fundamental of instincts. For, as he argues:

> These events are initially covered by the film of mundane daily conventionality – but, as one grows in experience of

life, this cover drops like a bark – to reveal the thirst for 'the water of eternal life'....Within the mundane reality of human love lurks the desire for the Holy – in the form of the quest for God.[21]

With this acknowledgement, Endō was concerned, not with similarities between the mentality of the lover and that of the believer *per se*, but with the potential with which this invested him to suggest a greater depth to the depiction of relationships that often appear, on the surface, destined to be pursued in the least auspicious of surroundings. The issue is integral to any assessment of *The Girl I Left Behind*, a novel in which the focus upon the lives of two individuals who struggle to make sense of the monotony of their experiences in life to date appears unremitting.

For Yoshioka, the young man so entrapped in his own small world and bent on self-advancement at all costs, relationships with those with whom he comes into contact had always been viewed from a utilitarian perspective. Such a self-serving approach is anathema to Mitsu, the 'country bumpkin',[22] torn between reluctance to respond to Yoshioka's overtures and an equally powerful aversion to inflicting further damage onto the latter's fragile self-esteem. True to type, the two come together as the result of a 'chance encounter' (p. 22): Yoshioka's decision to respond to Mitsu's cry for friendship in a 'lonely hearts' column is explicitly portrayed as a means of 'reliev[ing his own] boredom' (p. 21), rather than as motivated by any genuine desire for friendship. The couple drift apart and duly become established in roles that appear designed to reinforce their respective stereotypes. For Yoshioka, the future upon graduation looks bright: he immediately secures employment in a wholesale business in Tokyo and, before long, finds himself engaged to the niece of the company chairman. Equally predictable is the road towards abject misery travelled by Mitsu following the couple's aborted affair. A string of monotonous jobs ensues, with each seemingly designed to augment the image of Mitsu as caught up in an inexorable downward cycle.

Once more, the stereotypes appear exaggerated. Once more, however, such type-casting serves a vital function, not in reinforcing certain conventional images, but in enhancing the force of the reversal effected by means of the paradoxical inversion at work at the narrative level. As noted earlier, the manner in which the figure of Mitsu, too, is transformed from the butt of so much ridicule into a being whom even the hardened Yoshioka is obliged to describe as an 'ideal woman,...a saint' (p. 22) is heavily reminiscent of a similar development evidenced in the depiction of Gaston, the 'wonderful fool'.[23] In *The Girl I Left Behind*, however, such transposition is enhanced through unwavering focus on the relationship between Yoshioka and Mitsu, which continues to influence the routine lives of the individuals involved long after they have gone their separate ways. Seen thus, and in the light of the author's self-acknowledged aim to attribute a greater significance to the mundane, the novel comes to resemble an examination, not merely of Yoshioka's growing understanding of both himself and of Mitsu, but also of the emerging awareness, within both Yoshioka and Mitsu, of an unfathomable force that retains ultimate control over their destinies. During the course of the novel, this is symbolised by Yoshioka's growing recognition of the 'indelible marks' that individuals in general leave on each other – and, more specifically, of the influence that Mitsu has exerted on his own life.

In keeping with the tradition established in earlier Endō novels, from the outset Yoshioka appears determined to deny this trait. However, his constant assertions that Mitsu is no longer a part of his life come to appear increasingly desperate as the novel progresses and closer examination of the text reveals evidence, almost from the time of their first meeting, suggesting that Mitsu will indeed leave an 'indelible mark' on Yoshioka. First indications that Mitsu will represent more than a casual encounter for Yoshioka are to be seen in the hesitation the latter evidences when tempted to take advantage of Mitsu's naivety in accompanying him to a Japanese-style inn. Having appealed both to her gullibility and to her sensitivity by deliberately emphasising his limp, Yoshioka is nevertheless drawn to conclude: 'I'm the lowest of the low. If I were to take advantage of her kindness for my own gratification now, that would place me beneath contempt' (p. 39). The implication is strong that Yoshioka will ultimately be moved by the goodness of Mitsu's nature – and, for all his seeming lack of genuine feelings for Mitsu, it is not long before he is in a position to admit that: 'Like that of a cloud that appears fleetingly over a desolate mountain landscape in winter, her shadow passed in front of my eyes' (p. 74).

Try as he might, Yoshioka is unable to ignore this 'shadow' – and the lesson is brought painfully home to him when he attempts to replace Mitsu with Miura Mariko, the niece of the company chairman. The more he seeks to convince himself that, having met Mariko, Mitsu is now an irrelevance in his life, the more he is troubled by a voice from within, until he is obliged to conclude:

I remained totally oblivious to reality. To the fact that all our dealings with others, however trivial, are not just destined to vanish like ice in the sun. I was unaware that, even though we may distance ourselves and banish thoughts of a fellow human being to the recesses of our minds, our actions cannot simply disappear without leaving traces engraved in the depths of our hearts. (p. 81)

The voice continues to disturb him – and, in keeping with the precedent Endō had established in his earlier fiction, this often takes the form of Yoshioka involved in dialogue with his 'other self', the voice of his conscience. Having finally brought himself to acknowledge his continuing attachment to Mitsu, for example, he eventually tracks her down to a bar in Kawasaki. At this point, however, Yoshioka enters into heated debate with this 'other self':

'If you hadn't met her that day', the voice muttered, 'she might have led a very different life – a much happier, more uneventful life.'
'It's not my fault.' I shook my head. 'If we spent all our time thinking like that, we'd end up meeting nobody. We wouldn't be able to get on with our daily lives, would we?'
'That's true. That's part of the complexity of life. But never forget! It's not possible for someone to interact with a fellow human being without leaving some traces.' (p. 115)

For Yoshioka, the road towards full appreciation of this fact is long and painful, and it is not until the very end of the novel, when he receives the letter from Sister Yamagata, the nun at the leprosarium that Mitsu attends, initially following the mistaken diagnosis of leprosy and subsequently as a volunteer, that he comes fully to acknowledge the influence Mitsu has exerted on his life. News of Mitsu's tragic death affects Yoshioka more than he would ever have countenanced. The shock is compounded, however, by the realisation that Mitsu had died following an act of characteristic selflessness: her failure to move out of the path of a reversing lorry was occasioned by her overriding concern for the basket of eggs that had been carefully nurtured by the lepers and by her determination not to disappoint them in her promise to translate these into much-needed cash. To Yoshioka, such altruism remains outside his world view. Faced with the facts of Mitsu's self-sacrifice, however, he is obliged to acknowledge that Mitsu was indeed capable of such magnanimous conduct and this, in turn, enables him to draw closer to the full complexity of Mitsu's being. Only now is he in a position to give vent to the feelings of grief that had been welling up in his unconscious. Only now does he appear convinced by his own argument: "This was life. And the undeniable fact was that my path had crossed that of Morita Mitsu in the course of this life' (p. 192).

With these concluding comments, the transposition of Mitsu in the eyes of Yoshioka into a figure of Christ-like proportions is implicitly acknowledged. Again, however, closer textual analysis reveals considerable evidence of the development of Yoshioka's increasing awareness of Mitsu's inner being during the course of the novel. Most significant of these is the growing suggestion that, despite his callous and uncaring persona, there is another, more sensitive aspect to Yoshioka's being that he struggles to keep suppressed. At first, the evidence assumes physical form: whenever Yoshioka treats Mitsu in an uncaring manner, he is depicted as feeling pain in his palsied leg. But as he comes increasingly to take her for granted, so his feelings of guilt increase, leading to various acts of kindness that are prompted, not from any conscious concern, but from a more fundamental recognition, deriving from his unconscious, of the tie that unites them. It is this instinct that inspires him to evince uncharacteristic generosity in lending money to Mitsu when he discovers her reduced to living in abject poverty – and the same unfathomable instinct that can be seen at work in his impulsive decision to send her a New Year's card long after their paths have seemingly diverged once and for all following his marriage to Mariko.

Closer inspection of the text does, however, reveal further indication of the narrator's attempt to prepare the ground for Yoshioka's heightened understanding of human nature. From the outset, for example, there is an implicit comparison of Yoshioka and Mr Kim, the Korean businessman to whom he turns for part-time work – a man for whom first impressions count for everything. Mr Kim's advice to Yoshioka is that, in trying to attract women, the important thing is 'to create a powerful first impression' (p. 19); he betrays no understanding whatsoever of the need to delve deeper, to penetrate beyond the external persona, in order to understand the complete being. Yoshioka, however, appears unconvinced by Kim's argument – hence his reluctance to avail himself of the latter's advice during his first encounter with Mitsu. To be sure, 'first impressions' of Mitsu are not favourable: the portrayal of the embarrassed young woman who arrives at Shimokitazawa station, her friend Yoshiko in tow for moral support, is clearly reminiscent of Takamori and Tomoe's first encounter with Gaston:

> Both of them were wearing brownish sweaters and black skirts like those for sale in any market outside suburban stations. The unsightly wrinkles in their stockings suggested they must have been trying to support them with rubber bands above the knee...
> I had been prepared all along, not for a formal meeting with a society lady, but for a clandestine date with the kind of woman Nagashima had dismissed as a 'country bumpkin'. But as soon as I was left alone with Morita Mitsu, I was assailed by an overwhelming sense of self-pity. (pp. 25–6)

Almost immediately, however, the text offers clues that there is more to Mitsu than meets the eye. Several subsequent incidents draw attention to her incredibly sensitive nature, the palmist at Shibuya being the first to highlight this aspect of her personality in concluding, 'This young girl is far too friendly. She has to be very careful. If not, she'll end up being used by one man after another' (pp. 31–32). At the time, the comment is dismissed as a narratorial aside. In retrospect, however, the warning is prophetic: it is indeed Mitsu's over-sensitivity that leads her to give herself to Yoshioka. Shortly, thereafter, this facet of Mitsu's personality is explicitly acknowledged by the increasingly sympathetic narrator:

> For some reason, ever since childhood Mitsu had been unable to endure the sight of someone looking sad. And such feelings were accentuated when such sadness was on her account. (p. 61)

Already, then, the implication is strong that Mitsu's plain physical appearance masks a heightened sensitivity and it is not long before the process whereby Mitsu, too, will be transposed into a figure possessed of Christ-like qualities becomes more explicit. Confronted by the pitiful sight of Mrs Taguchi, the impoverished wife of Mitsu's uncaring supervisor, for example, one part of Mitsu determines to leave 'as soon as possible', loath to become embroiled in the domestic troubles she has just unintentionally witnessed. At the same time, however, she is aware of a conflicting voice within her urging her to offer assistance to Mrs Taguchi, desperate for financial help in raising her children. At the unconscious level, the voice is rapidly superimposed on to the image of 'the tired face of one gazing down with pity on these lives [and] whispering to Mitsu' (p. 69). When the voice urges her to give up her hard-earned ¥1000 to Mrs Taguchi – at the expense of the cardigan Mitsu had been longing to buy – Mitsu's instinctive reaction is to seek 'desperately to resist that voice' (p. 69), to protest the absence of any connection with the problems of others. By this time, however, there can be no denying its existence – or the nature of the transposition involved. As the voice continues, therefore, Mitsu's thoughts are juxtaposed with those of Christ:

> I know just how much you want that cardigan and how hard you've worked for it. And that is why I'm asking you. I'm asking you to use that thousand yen for that mother and her children instead of for that sweater....
>
> There's something more important than responsibility. The important thing in this life is to link your sadness to the sadness of others. That is the significance of my cross. (p. 70)

By now, Mitsu is clearly identified as a figure destined to share the suffering of those around her. Thereafter, as increasingly she succumbs to her own physical frailty, the depictions of Mitsu's physical appearance become, if anything, even more pitiful. The portrayal of the forlorn young woman just diagnosed with leprosy awaiting the train that will take her to the leprosarium provides a particularly poignant example:

> Mitsu was suddenly overwhelmed by an incredible feeling of anguish welling up from the innermost depths of her being. She was acutely aware as she stood there in the drizzle amongst the Shinjuku crowds – as she stood on the road through life – that she was totally alone. Not just alone, she was more forlorn and forsaken than a suffering puppy. (p. 134)

Even such self-pity is not sufficient to deprive Mitsu of her innate concern for others, however and, confronted with the sight of a sick, old man desperate for a seat on the train, it is Mitsu, as opposed to any of the other healthy passengers, who feels obliged to give up her seat. Her inner spirit of compassion remains undaunted:

for all her own problems, she even finds it in herself to commiserate with a young office worker, recently arrived in Gotenba at the start of a hiking trip with a group of colleagues, who is disappointed by the inclement weather. Inevitably, however, there is a price to pay for such altruism and it is not long before Mitsu, too, finds herself assailed by her *alter ego*. As she stands at the gate of the leprosarium, it is this voice that surfaces, whispering precisely those words of advice that Mitsu most wants to hear:

> 'Shall I go home? Yes, why don't I go home?' *A voice kept whispering in her ear*. All she had to do was to return the way she had come. She had lived quite happily until today. So why not carry on in the same way as though nothing had happened? (p. 141, my emphasis)

Nevertheless, thanks in part to the physical presence of one of the nurses who comes alongside her at this point, in part to the unacknowledged promptings of her unconscious, Mitsu enters the leprosarium, and it is only then, as she finally confronts those who are physically more wretched than herself, that she comes to acknowledge both thoughts as equally true to her 'real self'.

In similar manner, the instinctive feelings of revulsion Mitsu experiences when confronted by the patients are rapidly countered by a sense of shame, but it is not long before she is in a position, once more, to trivialise her own problems and to expend all her energy on care and concern for others. To some extent, this may be an inevitable development, a survival technique that all in the leprosarium are obliged to adopt to a greater or lesser extent. As Mitsu quickly discovers, however, there are those in the leprosarium who continue to bemoan their own fate. And yet, significantly, from this point on, the narrative focuses on those to whom Mitsu finds herself instinctively drawn – and, in particular, on her room-mate, Taeko, who, for all her tragic circumstances, is able to admit:

> We get used to unhappiness. No, we don't just get used to it. Life here has its own joys and happiness. I no longer feel that I have been abandoned here. I feel I've come to a world of a different dimension to the outside world. The joys and happiness of the outside world may be denied us here....But it's possible to discover a purpose in life here that you can't get outside. (pp. 153–4)

For Mitsu, recently arrived in the leprosarium, such reassurance is not readily comprehensible. Already, however, the narrative has provided sufficient evidence to suggest that, if anyone is equipped with the inner strength to live out such optimism, then Mitsu can. By now, the image of Mitsu as seeking more than simply to come to terms with personal misfortune has been established and, as if to reinforce the sense that Mitsu will not succumb to self-pity, the text again stresses the protagonist's overriding concern for her recently acquired companions:

> Mitsu was the kind of person who, when confronted by the misery of another, insisted on sharing that misery and always sought to extend the hand of friendship. (p. 158)

In reaching out to others, Mitsu is only giving expression to an element of herself which, though not necessarily immediately apparent from her outward appearance, was nevertheless an integral part of her 'total self'. The longer she remains in the leprosarium, and the more Taeko and the others help her to see through to these aspects of her unconscious being, the more these qualities come to be accepted as an integral part of the 'real Mitsu'. And yet it is not until Mitsu is told that she has been wrongly diagnosed and is consequently free to leave the leprosarium that the lessons learnt along the road to self-discovery are translated into concrete action – as she finds herself incapable of turning her back on her immediate past. At the rational, conscious level, Mitsu is not able to account for the impulse that causes her to return to the hospital after only a few hours back in the humdrum world she rediscovers outside. But just as Yoshioka had ultimately been obliged to accept that he could not simply discard Mitsu from his life, so Mitsu now comes to recognise that she cannot simply abandon her new-found friends. She comes to acknowledge that to do so would be to 'betray' not only those left behind, but also her own real self (p. 169). The result is a gradual *rapprochement* between Mitsu's public persona and her 'shadow' being – and the consequent recognition by those with whom she comes into contact of her innate selflessness. For Yoshioka, such dawning only occurs at the very end of the novel. In the case of Sister Yamagata, however, this quality is acknowledged at an earlier stage – in the depiction of her allowing Mitsu to return to the leprosarium as a volunteer despite her policy, strictly adhered to until that point, of rejecting such offers of help that occasionally arrive but which, until then, she had dismissed as 'born of sentimentality' (p. 176). As the nun confesses in her letter to Yoshioka:

> At the beginning of this letter, I made so bold as to suggest that charity derives not from sentimentality nor from compassion in the face of suffering, but rather that it requires patient endurance. But, for Mitchan, the desire to empathise with those who suffer was so strong that, unlike us, she had virtually no need of such patient endurance. (p. 187)

By this stage in the novel, the process of 'transposition' is virtually complete: the portrayal of Mitsu during the course of Sister Yamagata's letter is strongly reminiscent of the image of Christ as presented, if not in the Gospel portrayals, then in the concept of Christ, the constant companion (*dōhansha*), which, as we shall see, was subsequently to develop into a major motif of Endō's literature.[24] On the one hand, the Mitsu as described here is the 'little child' established as the model for all human beings in the Gospel accounts. At the same time, in offering to take upon herself the suffering of others, especially little children, she can ultimately be seen as conforming, as closely as any of Endō's creations to date, to a literary embodiment of the figure of Christ Himself.

The parallel is one to which Endō himself has frequently alluded and that he chose to emphasise in the recently written 'Afterword' appended to the English translation of the novel, in which he claims:

> Through the medium of this novel, I sought to portray the drama of 'the Jesus I left behind'. Mitsu can be seen as modelled on Jesus, abandoned by his own disciples; she is modelled on the Jesus whom all Christians are guilty of abandoning on a daily basis in their everyday lives.[25]

It goes without saying that in the analysis of specific texts, such authorial pronouncements on 'literary intent' must be clearly divorced from the immediate task confronting the critic. The mere fact that the author has felt drawn to offer such frequent reminders is evidence, nevertheless, of a consistency of approach that transcends the traditional distinction between 'popular' and 'pure' literature as introduced at the outset of this chapter. As noted earlier, Endō's critics have tended to assign *The Girl I Left Behind* to the former of these two categories and, in so doing, have implied a clear-cut distinction between this and subsequent works, which they have readily depicted as representative of a class of 'purer' literature.[26] To Endō, such categorisation represents an artificial divide, just one more example of an opposition that he has sought to bridge over the course of a lengthy career. Seen thus, *The Girl I Left Behind* comes to assume its place on the continuum, less as an alternative, more popular, approach to the author's by now well-established focus of novelistic concern, more as a compelling example of consistency through diversity. To be sure, the years immediately following publication of the novel were marked by a pronounced shift in the selection of material for Endō's fiction. To view works such as *Silence* and *The Samurai* as somehow representative of an abrupt change of narrative approach is, however, to reckon without the significant contributions to a consistent approach afforded by the novels discussed in this chapter. The novels with which Endō established his international reputation in the late 1960s and 1970s were born of the world of Suguro, of Gaston, and of Mitsu. So, too, were the more recent novels with which this reputation was secured, testimony to the author's conviction that:

> Mitsu has continued to live within me ever since [publication of *The Girl I Left Behind*] and can be seen reincarnated in my most recent novel, *Deep River*, in the person of the protagonist, Ōtsu.[27]

4

SILENCE

> I am not a Christian author. It is just that Catholic padres happen to populate the pages of my works.
>
> (Graham Greene)

After the years spent, quite literally, in a life and death struggle against TB, the reception accorded *The Girl I Left Behind* and other stories of the time must have served as a considerable source of encouragement to Endō.[1] Buoyed by such critical acclaim, he busied himself in the ensuing months with composition of several stories born of his experience as a visiting scholar at the University of Lyons over a decade earlier. Three of these, '*Rūan no natsu*' (A Summer in Rouen), '*Ryūgakusei*' (trans. Araki Thomas) and '*Nanji mo, mata*' (And you, too) would eventually be published in a single volume under the title, *Ryūgaku* (Foreign Studies), despite their disparate subject matter – testimony, if this were still needed, of the multifaceted interpretation the author had come to derive from his own attempts at cross-cultural communication.

More significant in terms of subsequent career development at this time, however, was the increasing interest Endō was coming to show in study of the history of the Christian missions to Japan. In this, as noted earlier, the author's attention was inevitably drawn to the so-called 'Christian century' from the mid-sixteenth century to the mid-seventeenth century when the predominantly Portuguese and Spanish missions strove to plant the seeds of Christianity in a Japan dominated by military authorities increasingly confident of their own position and consequently less and less disposed to tolerate the challenge to national security that was seen in the 'alien' religion. The more he considered the seemingly inexhaustible depictions of courageous martyrdoms in the face of cruel persecution, however, the more he was struck by the 'gaps' in these histories – the unrecorded despair and ignominy endured by those who, for whatever reason, ultimately succumbed to torture, both physical and psychological, and went through the ritual of *efumi* (treading on the crucifix), that most public act of apostasy. Endō was quick to identify with such 'weaklings' and consistently sought to empathise with the feelings of those who, having publicly defiled the image of the Christ to whom they had sworn undying allegiance, were subsequently obliged to live with the sense of guilt and loneliness occasioned by their act. In particular, as noted earlier, the author's attention was piqued by the *Kakure* (Hidden) Christians who, despite acquiescence in the often-annual *efumi* ritual imposed upon them by the shogunate authorities, continued in their attempt to keep the flames of their faith burning, often in the face of incredible personal sacrifice and who persist to this day in their adherence to the religious formulae born of the years of enforced secrecy.[2]

Over the decades, Endō has continued to expound on his feelings of identity with those traditionally dismissed as having succumbed to torture and, in the early 1960s, he made several visits to the Nagasaki district of Kyushu in an attempt to come to a closer understanding of the circumstances surrounding this episode in Japanese history. That such trips were prompted by more than mere intellectual curiosity is, however, evidenced in his oft-repeated claim that, 'If [the Christians of this era] were to be divided into the weak and the strong, I would be among the former'.[3] The realisation may have been painful to Endō, the Catholic adherent. As author, however, such sentiments could not be ignored, for as he continued, 'History knows their sufferings: I believed it was the task of a novelist to listen to their sufferings'.[4] With each visit to Nagasaki and, in particular to the various sites associated with the suppression of Christianity during the early part of the seventeenth century, Endō's tendency to empathise with the *Kakure* psychologically intensified, but as he admits in a subsequent essay, it was the chance examination of a *fumie* statue on display in a Nagasaki museum that was to determine the form his literary investigation of the issue would subsequently assume. Confronted by the reality of the *fumie*, worn and battered from years of (ab)use, Endō confesses to having been overcome by the following three questions:

1   If I had lived in that period of history, would I have stepped on the *fumie*?
2   What did those who stepped on the *fumie* feel?
3   What kind of people trod on the *fumie*?[5]

Questions that may initially have grown out of idle curiosity were soon to emerge as a concerted theological debate in the author's mind and there followed a series of short stories focusing on the mental anguish of those subjected to torture by the shogunate authorities intent on securing apostasy and on the perceived imperviousness of God to the suffering of those forced to endure such treatment in His name. Shortly thereafter, Endō produced the work that was to secure his reputation, not only as a prominent member of the Japanese literary scene, but also as an author of international acclaim.

Endō himself frequently acknowledged the extent to which the novel *Silence* was born of such questioning.[6] At the same time, however, he was quick to recognise the novel as representing a prime example of the manner in which historical 'facts' are ultimately transformed into 'an image and a "truth" transcending the original "fact"'. As he pointed out in *Watashi no aishita shōsetsu*, historical records concerning the mission led by Christovao Ferreira focus on the Jesuit's initial 'success' in Japan and on the number of converts procured in the period preceding his capture.[7] Of greater significance to Endō, the author, however, was the fact that all documentation concerning the historical Ferreira appears to come to an abrupt halt around the year 1632: for, as Endō was all too well aware, such documentation emanated, almost exclusively, from orthodox Jesuit sources. Seen thus, the premise upon which Endō chose to operate – the suggestion that the sudden cessation of all mention of Ferreira in the Jesuit archives reflects an abrupt and total fall from grace as a result of the decision to apostatise – is by no means unreasonable. From this point on, all 'detail' about Ferreira becomes the province of the literary artist and, with his imagination further fired by a few tantalisingly brief references to the subsequent attempt by Giuseppe Chiara (the model for Rodrigues in the novel) to determine the truth about his mentor, Endō proceeded to entrust the rest to the creative forces at work in his unconscious.[8]

The ensuing novel has been subjected to a barrage of interpretations by a variety of critics, most seeking to account for the perceived illogicality of a self-confessed Catholic selecting as the ostensible focal point of his novel the act of apostasy performed by his protagonist, the Portuguese missionary, Rodrigues.[9] Having insisted on entering the country in deliberate violation of the anti-Christian edicts that were being so ruthlessly enforced in Japan at the time in which the narrative is set (early seventeenth century), Rodrigues' ultimate decision, following his inevitable capture, publicly to renounce his God and all that his life to date had stood for has been widely condemned in the Japanese Christian community as an act of heresy. Indeed, several pastors were to go on public record in the months following publication of the novel expressly forbidding their congregations from purchasing a copy of the work. To many of these critics, the novel *Silence* came to be viewed as a misguided attempt by the author to posit an irreconcilable gap, both spiritual and cultural, between East and West, a reading seemingly supported at the textual level by Ferreira who, in a desperate attempt to elicit Rodrigues' apostasy, claims:

> This country is a swamp...a more terrible swamp than you can imagine. Whenever you plant a sapling in this swamp the roots begin to rot; the leaves grow yellow and wither. And we have planted the sapling of Christianity in this swamp....
>
> The Japanese till this day have never had the concept of God; and they never will....The Japanese are not able to think of God completely divorced from man; the Japanese cannot think of an existence that transcends the human.[10]

To critics of this persuasion, Endō is here guilty of giving vent to doubts concerning his faith that verge on the blasphemous – and of blindly echoing the doubts expressed by his literary forebear, Masamune Hakuchō, in asking:

> Why did the Christian padres who came to Japan to preach the Christian gospel instruct their simple Japanese converts to endure the cruel persecution that awaited them? Why did they have to endure persecution in order to reach heaven? Why did they not renounce their faith and escape such cruel persecution? If God is truly the God of loving mercy, how could He criticise those who apostatised under such circumstances?[11]

What possible justification could there be, such critics have asked, for Endō to devote an entire novel to Rodrigues' increasing despair at the apparent 'silence' of God towards those who clung tenaciously to their faith in the face of the cruellest torture and death? According to this line of logic, Rodrigues is here guilty of doubting the very essence of his faith – like the psalmist David in Psalm 13: 1, who cries out in desperation, 'How long wilt thou forget me, O

Lord? For ever? How long wilt thou hide thy face from me?' Indeed, to some, including the influential critic, Professor Yanaihara, such uncertainty was seen as evidence of no more, nor less, than a fundamental absence of faith within the protagonist, Rodrigues, from the outset.[12] Particularly in view of Endō's burgeoning reputation as a prominent, if unorthodox, spokesman for the minority Christian community in Japan, such pessimism did nothing to assist the uphill struggle of proselytisation on which Yanaihara and his fellow believers were engaged.

To Endō himself, however, such criticism, whilst not surprising,[13] was evidence, both of a continuing reluctance on the part of the church to address the tension he had come to perceive between literature and religion and also of a tendency to view the scene in which Rodrigues is finally persuaded to defile the *fumie* with his foot as the culmination of the novel. As Endō was first to acknowledge, interpretation of the novel along the lines outlined above may be readily supported by an analysis of the first eight chapters of the work, chapters in which the primary focus is on the psychological drama played out within the protagonist's mind as he wrestles with his conscience. Significantly, however, the novel does not finish with Rodrigues' act of apostasy. The protagonist may emulate his mentor, Ferreira, in stepping on the *fumie* and in subsequently accepting a Japanese name, a wife and a residence in Nagasaki courtesy of the very authorities who had driven him to apostatise. As Endō is at pains to stress, however, there is evidence in the two concluding chapters and in the extracts from the diary of an officer at the Christian residence (the so-called 'Kirishitan yashiki' section) which follow that, for all his outward capitulation, inwardly Rodrigues is now possessed of a faith more real and more profound than that which had inspired him to risk all in embarking on his mission to Japan in the first place.

Viewed in this light, the novel *Silence* comes to assume a very different complexion. Far from an outburst of despair at the seeming failure of the Christian missions to come to terms with a fundamental reluctance on the part of the Japanese to embrace the 'Western' religion, the novel can now be seen as a protracted attempt to penetrate the depths of the protagonist's inner being – in a desire, similar to that evidenced in the earlier novels, to discern there some archetypal positive quality to human nature. The qualities so overtly attributed to Gaston in *Wonderful Fool* and to Mitsu in the *The Girl I Left Behind* are here subtly interwoven into the psychological make-up of the protagonist, whose increasing sense of solidarity with the

Japanese converts whose destiny he not only shares but ultimately dictates leads to a gradual erosion of the all-consuming self-assurance and unquestioning conviction so prominent at the outset. The more the protagonist is obliged to acknowledge his own weakness in the face of the psychological torture to which he is subjected, the more his initial self-image is challenged. For Rodrigues, the process is necessarily painful; but as one critic has argued:

> The breakdown of layers of false pride and egotistical heroism that create walls between human beings is a prerequisite for entry into Endō's select world of weak but glowingly human characters.[14]

So how does this process of self-discovery work at the textual level? And to what extent does Rodrigues gain entry into 'Endō's select world of weak but glowingly human characters'? The issue lies at the heart of the novel, embodied as it is in the changing depictions of the protagonist's response to adversity as the novel progresses. A discussion of the distinction in the portrayal of Rodrigues before and after his decision to trample on the *fumie* serves to reveal the distance travelled by the protagonist in the course of the novel.

The Rodrigues who arrives in Japan in 1640 would indeed appear to represent the epitome of self-assuredness. Fired by a seemingly unquenchable missionary zeal and enthusiasm to rescue the believers in Japan abandoned to a lonely existence as preservers of a proscribed religion, he appears possessed of the vision of an omnipotent and omniscient God that should be sufficient to equip him with the resilience required to defy all the physical pain his fellow man could inflict upon him. Refusing to heed the advice of his superior, Father Valignano, Rector of the Macao seminary where he is obliged to wait with his companions for a suitable means of transport to Japan, Rodrigues concurs wholeheartedly with the assessment of his colleague, Juan de Santa Maria:

> Our secret mission could with God's help turn out successful....In that stricken land the Christians have lost their priests and are like a flock of sheep without a shepherd. Some one must go to give them courage and to ensure that the tiny flame of faith does not die out. (p. 34)

By this stage, Juan de Santa Maria is stricken with malaria and unable to participate any further in the mission. Rodrigues, however, remains undeterred, convinced that 'it was the great mission of [my companion] Garrpe and myself to tend' the seed of Christianity that had been sown in Japan 'lest it wither and die' (p. 55). Even the coming of the rainy season shortly after their arrival in Japan fails to quench the protagonist's initial enthusiasm, and he continues:

> With the coming of the rain the officials will probably relax their vigilance, so I intend to make use of this opportunity to travel around the neighbourhood and search out the remaining Christians. (p. 60)

Viewed out of context, such evidence suggests a protagonist of unbending principle, a man for whom apostasy, regardless of the provocation, could never be a viable option. That this is not the full extent of Rodrigues' being is, however, to be anticipated from the analyses of earlier Endō protagonists – and closer examination of the text reveals evidence, even at this early juncture, of a greater complexity to Rodrigues' being. Immediately after the above display of optimism, for example, the protagonist is drawn to confess to a lingering uncertainty *vis à vis* God's purpose for the mission in Japan:

> Why has God given our Christians such a burden? This is something I fail to understand. (p. 64)

At this stage, Rodrigues retains his basic determination to maintain a show of optimism for the benefit both of the Japanese converts who increasingly risk life and limb in defying the authorities by secretly visiting the priests and of his superiors back home whose conviction in the significance of his mission he seeks to bolster. Nagging doubts are consequently suppressed for the benefit of public consumption – and he maintains:

> The conviction grows deeper and deeper in my heart that all is well and that God will protect us. (p. 68)

Before long, however, the reality of the choice confronting those who continue to resist the shogunate line is brought home with horrendous force – as Rodrigues is obliged to observe the agonising deaths suffered by two of the local converts, Mokichi and Ichizō, tied to stakes at the shoreline at low tide and abandoned to their inexorable fate by the increasingly callous authorities. Again, Rodrigues' 'public' reaction to these martyrdoms suggests an attempt to cling to his fundamental convictions:

> I do not believe that God has given us this trial to no purpose. I know that the day will come when we will clearly understand why this persecution with all its sufferings has been bestowed upon us – for everything that Our Lord does is for our good. (p. 96)

Such steadfastness is, however, belied by his next words, 'And yet, ...', words that, as noted earlier, serve to combine the protagonist's psychology with the narrator's cognitive activity. Thereafter, true to precedent, it is not long before he gives vent to the deep-rooted sense of uncertainty that this incident has simply served to bring into closer focus. In another letter to his superiors in Lisbon, he argues:

> I know what you will say: 'Their death was not meaningless. It was a stone which in time will be the foundation of the Church; and the Lord never gives us a trial which we cannot overcome'....I also, of course, am convinced of all this. *And yet*, why does this feeling of grief remain in my heart? Why does the song of the exhausted Mokichi, bound to the stake, gnaw constantly at my heart?...
>
> Behind the depressing silence of this sea, the silence of God...the feeling that while men raise their voices in anguish God remains with folded arms, silent. (pp. 104-5, my emphasis)

The perception of God as silent in the face of the suffering of His people is a temptation to which Rodrigues succumbs increasingly as the situation deteriorates. Confronted as he is more by the suffering of the Japanese peasants to whom he seeks to minister than by fear that he himself will be subjected to physical torture, such nagging doubts are even harder to dispel. The perceived obliviousness of God to the protagonist's own needs was a notion that his faith sought to address. But the apparent indifference of God to the cries of anguish, both physical and psychological, of the Japanese converts for whom Rodrigues feels increasingly responsible is more challenging – and Rodrigues' attempts at self-assurance become ever more desperate:

No! No!...If God does not exist, how can man endure the monotony of the sea and its cruel lack of emotion? (But supposing...of course, supposing, I mean.) *From the deepest core of my being* yet another voice made itself heard in a whisper. Supposing God does not exist. (p. 117, my emphasis)

At a rational level, Rodrigues is still in a position to acknowledge that 'if I consented to this thought, then my whole past to this very day was washed away in silence' (p. 118). More and more, however, his inner being is developing into a battleground for conflicting voices, the voice of conscious reasoning increasingly challenged by a voice from a deeper level of his being that calls into question the very nature of the mission in which he is engaged. Seen in this light, the protagonist's inevitable arrest by the authorities following the duplicity of his Japanese 'guide', Kichijirō, is but another stage on his journey, a journey that will ultimately lead to acknowledgement of this inner voice as an equal contributor to his composite being.

At this stage, however, the process of self-discovery is still at an early stage – as testified by the frequency and desperation of Rodrigues' prayers. 'Lord, why are you silent? Why are you always silent?' (p. 153) he continues to cry, only to find his anguish challenged, once more, by that conflicting voice:

What is happening to you?, he asked himself. Are you beginning to lose your faith?, said *the voice from the depths of his being. Yet* this voice filled him with disgust. (p. 157, my emphasis)

That Rodrigues is 'filled with disgust' by this voice is hardly surprising: the thought of abandoning the faith that had ordered his life to date remains unconscionable and, in public at least, the protagonist succeeds in preserving the unquestioning facade which the Japanese converts with whom he shares a cell following his own arrest had come to expect. 'The Lord will not abandon you for ever....The Lord will not be silent for ever' (p. 173), he reassures them. The earnest fervour and frequency with which Rodrigues feels obliged to offer this and similar pronouncements is, however, indicative of the priest's desire to convince, not only his despairing audience, but himself of God's continuing concern – and his words, whilst providing a modicum of solace to his fellow prisoners, serve equally as a fervent prayer. For Rodrigues by this stage, the divide between conviction and despair has never appeared so tenuous and it is not long before he gives full vent to the feelings he had struggled so desperately to suppress. Obliged to watch as his colleague Garrpe struggles with the agonising choice between apostasy – an act that Garrpe is led to believe would lead not only to his own release but, even more significantly, to that of the Japanese peasants whose destiny has been placed in his hands – and martyrdom with its concomitant responsibility for the death of the same, Rodrigues rails at his God:

> There is still time! Do not impute all this to Garrpe and to me. This responsibility you yourself must bear. (pp. 216–17)

Garrpe's decision to conform to the unquestioning dictates of his school – to opt for martyrdom regardless of the inevitable consequences for his fellow prisoners – provides considerable impetus to Rodrigues as he continues his journey of self-discovery and, returned once more to the physical and spiritual loneliness of his cell, his ever-increasing doubts appear to reach their logical conclusion:

> Did God really exist? If not, how ludicrous was half of his life spent traversing the limitless seas to come and plant the tiny seed in this barren island!...How ludicrous was the life of Garrpe, swimming in pursuit of the Christians in that little boat! (p. 223)

We have, of necessity, covered the psychological distance travelled by Rodrigues following his arrival in Japan in some detail. Without this, without the considerable focus on the growing uncertainty experienced by the protagonist at the conscious level as a result of the gnawing 'voice from the depths of his being', Rodrigues' subsequent decision to go through with his outward display of apostasy would remain unconvincing. Equally, without the increasing focus on the seeds of doubt already present in his unconscious being, the protagonist's outward submission to the psychological torture imposed on him (in the form of the clinical attempts by Ferreira, his former mentor, to convince him of the hopelessness of the mission he had set for himself) would lack the all-important ring of authenticity. In practice, however, Ferreira's argument that the seeds of Christianity can never take root in the 'swamp' of Japan is introduced at the very moment that Rodrigues betrays the clearest signs to date that he is coming to acknowledge the significance of the 'voice from the depths of his being', the former's line of logic according cruelly with the 'inner voice' that Rodrigues can no longer ignore:

> The reason I apostatized....I was put in here and heard the voices of those people for whom God did nothing. God did not do a single thing. I prayed with all my strength; but God did nothing....
>
> And while this [suffering] goes on, you do nothing for them. And God – he does nothing either. (pp. 265–6)

By this stage, the die is cast. Rodrigues, deprived of his powers of reasoning as a result of months of psychological confusion, is powerless to counter the carefully calculated force of Ferreira's logic – to the extent that the latter's suggestion that 'Christ would certainly have apostatized to help men' is met simply by a desperate shout of 'No, no!...Stop tormenting me! Go away, away!' (p. 269)

The exchange between the two former colleagues can be viewed as a classic example of the juxtaposition of the voices of God and the Devil – with Ferreira's argument procuring the darkness without which the ray of light within Rodrigues' inner being would lose its dramatic impact. As he now stands before the *fumie*, poised to perform the one action that theoretically would render his entire life to date meaningless, the despair he experiences appears absolute, the darkness, both physical and psychological, in which he is enveloped, seemingly impenetrable. It is at this very moment, however, that 'the first rays of the dawn appear' (p. 271). And in keeping with the seemingly instantaneous victory of light over darkness in the natural world, so the protagonist comes to recognise for the first time in the image on the cross he had studied so often in the past, not the powerful image of dignified beauty of European tradition, but rather the face of a man with the desire simply 'to share men's pain' (p. 271). From a theological standpoint, therefore, there can be no justification for the Christ on the *fumie* to break his silence to the despairing Rodrigues with the words, 'You should trample! I more than anyone know of the pain in your foot. You should trample! It was to be trampled on by men that I was born into this world'(p. 271).[15] From a literary perspective, however, this is the moment of catharsis, the moment in which the symbiotic relationship between light and darkness is brought into the starkest possible relief – through the introduction of 'the glimmer of light, the twilight glow reminiscent of a Rembrandt painting – the light of God's grace' as discussed earlier.

The change effected in Rodrigues' physical circumstances in the wake of this single act of outward renunciation is dramatic. Released from detention and provided accommodation by the very authorities who had succeeded in inducing his apostasy, Rodrigues is no longer obliged to listen to the moans of the Japanese peasants. This dramatic turn-about in his physical fortunes is, however, as nothing when compared with the metamorphosis occasioned on his inner being. To be sure, the protagonist's assertion in the immediate aftermath of his release that 'Lord, you alone know that I did not renounce my faith' (p. 275) may still appear lacking in absolute conviction. Towards the end of the novel, however, the extent to which Rodrigues has indeed heeded the 'inner voice' that represents his guide along the road to self-discovery is reinforced – in the depiction of the protagonist agreeing to hear the confession of Kichijirō, the very man who had betrayed him, Judas-like, to the authorities. To the orthodox church, this decision – the willingness to cling to the vestiges of priesthood even following his public act of renunciation – may be seen as the ultimate heresy. To Rodrigues, however, the reaction of his peers is now of little concern. His journey of self-discovery has removed him from concerns for the reactions of his former colleagues. Instead, he is now armed with a new-found confidence in his continuing and strengthened relationship with God, leading him to conclude:

> No doubt his fellow priests would condemn his act as sacrilege; but even if he was betraying them, he was not betraying his Lord. He loved him now in a different way from before. Everything that had taken place until now had been necessary to bring him to this love. 'Even now I am the last priest in this land.' (p. 298)

Significantly, however, the novel does not end at this point. There now follows a section containing extracts from the diary of an officer at the Christian residence – and it is in this light, as indication that, even following his public fall from grace, Rodrigues continues to be afflicted by pangs of conscience, that this concluding section is best appreciated.[16]

By this stage, the action has moved on some twenty years, with the diary extracts recording the salient events in the last decade of the life of Rodrigues, now living under the assumed name of Okada

San'emon. The intervening years provide invaluable scope for Endō's narrator to adopt a more objective perspective in his portrayal of the protagonist. For all the distance, however, the overriding focus of this brief concluding section is on a man, alone with his thoughts, yet still clinging to the fundamentals of the Christian faith he had purportedly long since renounced. Much of his time is occupied in writing a '*shomotsu*' (lit. book, documents) and, in view of the fact that Rodrigues is writing this 'at the command of Tōtōminokami' (p. 300), it is clear that the *shomotsu* on which he is engaged represents more than a work he is compiling out of interest or to wile away the time. Rodrigues is not simply 'writing a book':[17] he is writing yet another 'disavowal of his religion'. The implications of this are crucial to our understanding of Rodrigues' journey. Even now, some twenty years after his initial apostasy, Rodrigues is still vacillating; the desire to remain faithful to his creed remains in conflict with acknowledgement of the need to adopt a more pragmatic approach towards the authorities.

The fact that Rodrigues continues to trouble the authorities with his persistent interest in the proscribed faith is clearly evidenced by the latter's ongoing persistence that he attach his name to documents of apostasy. There is, moreover, further evidence at the narrative level of Rodrigues' refusal merely to adopt a low profile and to put his past behind him. It is here that the full import of his decision to employ Kichijirō as his servant comes into its own.

On initial reading, the fact that Kichijirō continues to hound the protagonist long after the latter's fall from grace may appear of little note. The young Japanese has, after all, represented a constant thorn in the protagonist's flesh in a relationship that dates back to the time Rodrigues spent in Macao before embarking on his mission to Japan. Closer scrutiny of the relationship that exists between the two men some two decades after the *fumie* scene, however, suggests that there is more to this than mere physical proximity. It is not simply that Kichijirō continues to seek out Okada San'emon's company; the diary extracts reveal the extent and the genuine nature of the understanding that has come to exist between the two – an understanding born of the shared experience of struggling to come to terms with the pain of the apostate. The question of how the two men had come to this understanding may be nowhere explicitly addressed in the narrative. Nevertheless, the few allusions to this relationship that are offered by the officer in his diary serve to reinforce a sense of the strength of this bond – to the extent that, in the depiction of Kichijirō, gaoled for possession of an amulet containing

Christian icons, the narrative implication is strong that such open defiance of shogunal authority has been silently condoned, if not openly encouraged, by Okada.

On the one hand, Kichijirō's continued presence around Okada serves as a constant reminder of the events recounted in the main body of the novel. His narrative role then had been to confront the protagonist with the voice of his own conscience. And, even now, in spite of all that had passed between the two men some two decades earlier, Kichijirō's presence exercises a similar effect on Okada. Daily contact with the man who had once betrayed him to the authorities serves to confront the protagonist with his own inner being. And the more he is obliged to acknowledge the strength of the impulses he discerns there, the more he is obliged to accept the force of the empathy that has emerged between the two men.

The portrayal of Okada and Kichijirō as constant partners on their respective journeys of self-discovery can be seen as the clearest assertion in Endō's *oeuvre* to date of the obligation confronting the author to depict characters engaged in their own 'process of individuation'. In keeping with the Jungian rejoinder of the need for constant acknowledgement of the power of the inner voice, Endō here provides a fitting conclusion to his portrayal of inner growth within his protagonist. As a result of the 'weak' Kichijirō's loyalty, both to Okada himself and to his faith, Rodrigues' fundamental reassessment of his initially unquestioning image of God appears vindicated. Before turning to a consideration of the 'transposition' that occurs within Rodrigues with regard to this image, however, let us briefly consider another technique deployed by the author in an attempt to maintain the narrative spotlight on his protagonist's development as an individuated being – that of manipulation of the narrative perspective.

The drama begins with an objective narrative depiction of the three priests, Rodrigues, Garrpe and Juan de Santa Maria, travelling to Macao in the hope of thereby securing passage to Japan and fulfilling their desire to track down their erstwhile mentor, Ferreira. Following this brief introductory preamble, however, the narrative eye switches to that of Rodrigues – in the guise of the protagonist's letters describing the situation in Japan to his superiors back in Europe. From this point on, it is this single perspective that predominates – as increasingly the narrative assumes the form of Rodrigues' subjective musings. In this, the novel accords closely with the template delineated for the modern subjective novel by Henry James:

From the moment we are inside the mind of a character we are committed to that character's *point of view*. It follows that the more intense the perceiver, the more intense the experience of the reader. The writer must be aware of the limits of the consciousness he is projecting: he must not make a limited mind too perceptive, nor impose limitations where there is abundant capacity for perception.[18]

As Edel points out in his study of the modern psychological novel, the hallmark of such works is not only that the angle of vision is located in one specific consciousness, but also that the illusion is thereby created that 'the reader actually follows the character's flowing thought'.[19] The illusion is present in *Silence*, an illusion effected in large measure by the gradual transition from description of Rodrigues' thoughts and actions to a simple rendering of them. The trait is particularly evident in the portrayals of Rodrigues following his arrest – scenes in which the portrayal approximates the form of 'internal monologue' as originally coined by Dujardin. The portrayal of Rodrigues struggling to reconcile his perception of a silent God with his previously unwavering conviction that 'everything that our Lord does is for the good'; of his desire to save the lives of the peasants in the pit standing in stark contrast to his determination to conform with the dictates of his order: this entire section of the novel conforms closely with Dujardin's encapsulation of:

> that unheard and unspoken speech by which a character expresses his inmost thoughts, those lying nearest the unconscious, without regard to logical organization – that is, in their original state – by means of direct sentences reduced to syntactic minimum, and in such a way as to give the impression of reproducing the thoughts just as they come to mind.[20]

As a result of confrontation with this stream of internal monologue as Rodrigues awaits his destiny, the reader is indeed placed 'largely at the "centre" of the [protagonist's] thoughts – that centre where thought often uses words rather than images'.[21] Inevitably, as the *fumie* scene approaches and the coercion on Rodrigues to comply with the authorities intensifies, so alternative perspectives – most notably those of Kichijirō, Ferreira and Inoue – are introduced into the narrative. There are even descriptions of the neighbourhood in which Rodrigues is being held – details to which the protagonist could not have been privy and which are consequently prefaced with such phrases as 'According to the records'....Even here, however, the narrative focus remains on Rodrigues. For all the depictions of the actions of the others, their emotions are merely hinted at – and the inner drama and tension is consequently augmented in the build-up to the moment of the protagonist's apostasy.

In the light of the above discussion, it is hardly surprising that, once the drama of the *fumie* scene is over, a greater degree of objectivity is reintroduced into the narrative perspective. The bulk of the remaining text assumes the form of extracts from two diaries, the first belonging to Jonassen, a clerk at the Dutch firm on the island of Dejima, the second that of the officer at the Christian residence to which reference has already been made. On the one hand, in reverting to a more detached depiction of the protagonist, these alternative eyes complete the frame within which the narrative drama has been incorporated. At the same time, they offer the reader invaluable critical distance from which to reassess the hitherto protagonist-dominated version of events. Mention has already been made of the efficacy of this final section in drawing attention to the distance travelled by Rodrigues/Okada. Let us now turn to consideration of the manner in which the shifting narrative focus during the course of the novel mirrors the transposition effected within the protagonist with regard to his perception of the God he had sought to convey to the Japanese.

As noted already, Rodrigues arrives in Japan imbued with a seemingly unshakeable conviction in the powerful and glorious Christ image that had been instilled in him during his years at seminary and determined to transmit this sense of majesty to the Japanese. Armed with the vision of a face 'resplendent with the authority of a king' that 'bears the expression of encouragement... filled with vigor and strength' (p. 47), Rodrigues is able to face the future, however uncertain, with assuredness. Already, however, the text provides evidence of the transformation that will subsequently be effected within Rodrigues in the seemingly casual reference to the physical appearance of Christ: 'What did the face of Christ look like? This point the Bible passes over in silence' (p. 46). As the protagonist's physical circumstances deteriorate, so he comes to imagine less a figure of powerful authority, rather a being whose 'clear blue eyes were gentle with compassion', with 'tranquil' features and 'a face filled with trust' (p. 174). But he is still able to gain solace from the conviction that the face that 'from childhood had been for him the fulfillment of his every dream and ideal...even in its moments of terrible torture...had never lost its beauty' (p. 170).

As he languishes in prison, it is to this image that Rodrigues seeks desperately to cling. The more he considers his fate, however, the more he comes to identify, not so much with the glorious miracles of Christ about which he had previously preached with such enthusiasm, more with the psychological pain and suffering – the sense of betrayal – that the latter had been forced to endure. Shortly after his betrayal by Kichijirō, therefore, Rodrigues concludes:

> This case was just like his own. He had been sold by Kichijirō as Christ had been sold by Judas; and like Christ he was now being judged by the powerful ones of this world. Yes, *his fate and that of Christ were quite alike*; and at this thought on that rainy night a tingling sensation of joy welled up within his breast. This was the joy of the Christian who relishes the truth that he is united to the Son of God.
>
> On the other hand, he had tasted none of the physical suffering that Christ had known; and this thought made him uneasy. (p. 203, my emphasis)

Such apparent delusions of grandeur are not entirely unanticipated in the text. Earlier, as he had examined the reflection of his 'tired, hollow face' in a pool, he had been reminded of the face of 'yet another man...the face of a crucified man' (p. 115). For all his realisation that 'he had tasted none of the physical suffering that Christ had known', however, his destiny is being increasingly juxtaposed on to that of Christ – a process that requires a fundamental reassessment within Rodrigues of Christ's relationship with mankind. The image of splendour is not entirely eroded, but the powerful figure whom Rodrigues had earlier been able to follow unquestioningly is gradually transposed into a figure who calls into question the protagonist's earlier vision of majesty. The face on the *fumie* that is eventually placed before him, therefore, is a far cry from this symbol of authority:

> A simple copper medal is fixed on to a grey plank of dirty wood on which the grains run like little waves. Before him is the ugly face of Christ, crowned with thorns and the thin, outstretched arms. (p. 270)

The face with which the protagonist is now confronted is totally 'different from that on which [he] had gazed so often in Portugal, in Rome, in Goa and in Macao' (p. 276). The transposition is significant, for it is at this moment, as he gazes at 'the sunken and utterly exhausted' face, that Rodrigues is in a position to perceive, behind the outward frailty, an inner resilience, a strength that enables his Christ to accept human frailty and to come alongside the individual in moments of need. For Rodrigues, that moment has come – and it is at this point, as the protagonist prepares to lower his foot on to this pitiful figure, that Christ breaks His perceived silence:

> You should trample! It was to be trampled on by men that I was born into this world. It was to share men's pain that I carried my cross. (p. 271)

The image is one to which Endō would frequently return. Here is Christ, the companion (*dōhansha*) figure so prominent in the author's work, a being who, resolved not to look down in judgement, chooses rather to share in the individual's pain and anguish as his 'companion'. For the author intent on exploring the various facets of the inner being of his creations, the symbol is indeed powerful: in thus electing to focus firmly on the compassionate qualities of this 'companion' figure, Endō is better placed to approximate an image of Christ as a positive force which envelops both the individual and his Shadow being, and leads him in the direction of the light. In this, the image of Christ, the constant companion, is a natural sequitur to the notion of the 'third dimension' discussed earlier – and a clear break from the stigma that tended to accrue to the notion of the Shadow as representing the 'other (second) dimension' to human nature, the negative side of the personality. The notion of the positive doppelgänger, to be analysed in the discussion of Endō's subsequent novel, *Scandal*, had been coined, a development that was to have profound implications for the direction of the author's subsequent literature.

Seen thus, the *fumie* scene in *Silence* represents a clear watershed in the author's *oeuvre*. In the depiction of a figure offering, not to release the protagonist from his psychological torment, but rather to share in his suffering, Endō here hints at a fundamental modification to his vision of the faith he had inherited from his mother, a superimposition on to the figure of the harsh, judgmental God of the Old Testament that had so troubled his literary forebears, the qualities of tenderness and compassionate concern he had come to discern in the gospel portrayals of Christ and which he saw as in need of greater emphasis if Christianity were truly to take root in the Japanese spiritual psychology. For the Catholic Endō, the breakthrough was highly significant for, as he was to confess in a subsequent essay:

> In writing *Silence* I felt as though I had buried the distance I had formerly sensed between Christianity and myself. In short, that represents a change from Christianity as a paternal religion to Christianity as a maternal religion. The male image of Christ that the hero started out with is transformed into a female image.[22]

Much has been made by Etō Jun and other critics of the evolution from a paternalistic into a maternalistic vision of the Christian faith in the one novel, *Silence*.[23] To Etō and several other critics writing shortly after its publication, the novel provides irrefutable evidence of an author determined to rectify a perceived imbalance towards the paternalistic in Japanese literary depictions of Christ to that date by superimposing 'the image of the Japanese mother' onto the figure of Christ on the *fumie* that is placed before Rodrigues. According to Etō's reasoning, in placing his foot on the crucifix, Rodrigues is lured by the maternal qualities he comes to recognise in the face on the *fumie*, the protagonist's subsequent act of apostasy interpreted as 'a rejection of the Japanese mother'.[24]

Such a view, whilst highlighting Endō's desire to seek within Christianity those elements most acceptable to the Japanese, fails, however, to detect within this process, not simply a move from one extreme to the opposite, but rather, yet one more example of *rapprochement* between established binary oppositions. To concur with Etō's assessment of the face on the *fumie* as representing merely 'the image of the Japanese mother' is to defer to a traditional opposition between the 'paternal' and 'maternal'. More specifically, however, such an assessment ignores the presence within this depiction of the archetypal figure of the 'Great Mother', an image that, as already noted in the discussion of *Wonderful Fool*, was indebted to Neumann's vision of duality.

As evidenced above, the image of Christ on the *fumie* betrays the very conflicting qualities that Neumann attributed to this archetype – and it is this duality, rather than the simple 'image of the Japanese mother', that lies at the heart of the depiction of the figure on the crucifix. Furthermore in keeping with Neumann's assessment of the archetype, these opposing qualities speak to different levels of the protagonist's being. At the conscious level, the figure is wretched, the contours of the face 'worn down and hollow with the constant trampling' (p. 271) and the words to emerge from that contorted mouth ('You should trample! You should trample!') do indeed seem to lure Rodrigues towards the darkness and death of apostasy. At the same time, however, it is this same figure who paradoxically speaks through such physical frailty imbuing the protagonist with an inner conviction more powerful (and consequently better able to leave a mark on the lives of those around him) than that inspired by his earlier unquestioning faith.

The process is one of fusion of which the author himself was not necessarily consciously aware at the time of writing. In retrospect, however, particularly in the light of his subsequent study of Jungian psychology, Endō was to recognise the significance of this development – and to acknowledge:

> At the time [of composition of *Silence*], I had yet to read any of Jung's works, so I remained totally oblivious to the fact – but the image [on the *fumie*] stems in all probability from the 'magna mater' archetype latent within me. Because I am Japanese – and because I entertain a strong sense of love towards my mother – this 'magna mater' archetype becomes active whenever I think of Christ – and it was this that led to the depiction of that scene.
>
> The image of Christ carved on the *fumie* in *Silence* is a maternal image, a woman seeking to suffer with her child and to share the child's pain. It is not the paternal image to be found in so much Western art, the face of Christ resplendent with majesty and wearing an expression which represents the epitome of order and discipline.
>
> As such, the success of the scene depends on whether it strikes a resonant chord with the 'magna mater' archetype resident in the unconscious of the reader.[25]

With this reassessment, Endō can be seen voicing concern at the somewhat inflexible interpretations that had been assigned to the novel by several of his critics. Just as *Silence* represents less a simple portrayal of 'the image of the Japanese mother', more a depiction of the paradox of strength emerging through weakness, so the vision of the novel as a straight comparison of the 'strength' evidenced by Garrpe and the other martyrs in laying down their lives for their convictions with the 'weakness' of Rodrigues and Ferreira in succumbing (albeit under considerable duress) to the *fumie* is now challenged. For if the image on the *fumie* does indeed 'stem from the "magna mater" archetype latent within' the author, then the vision of Rodrigues succumbing to weakness rather than of a man acknowledging a source of paradoxical strength within his being is brought into question. A novel intent on such a comparison would surely focus on the rights and wrongs of the protagonist's decision to apostatise and on the factual events surrounding his ultimate submission. Were Endō truly intent on bringing into relief the opposing poles of the theological spectrum that would appear to be embodied in Garrpe's unwavering and single-minded obedience on the one hand and in the vacillation and ultimate capitulation to the forces of evil evidenced by Rodrigues on the other, more could surely have been made of the tension between the two men – and of the consequences of the latter's ultimate decision to yield to the pressure exerted on him.

As artist, however, Endō chooses to focus rather on the psychological pain and anguish leading up to the decision to apostatise. To this end, the only torture to which the protagonist is subjected is psychological – the cruel threat that refusal to trample on the *fumie* will result, not merely in Rodrigues' martyrdom (an eventuality for which he has long since sought to reconcile himself), but in that of the Japanese peasants who, despite their own personal apostasies, are still subjected to torture in the 'pit', their destiny entirely in Rodrigues' hands. To the same end, even the issue of whether Rodrigues' apostasy resulted, as promised, in the immediate release of the Japanese converts remains shrouded in mystery: to Endō, the extent to which Rodrigues could have endured physical pain and the consequence of his act for the Japanese peasants in the pit are not the issue. What matters at this stage is *the potential* for a reinterpretation of Rodrigues' act – and the text leaves the reader in no doubt that, if nothing else, Rodrigues' decision to place his foot on the *fumie* has at least opened *the possibility* for a new start and for the release of the Japanese Christians.

As suggested by the above, it is as an exercise of psychological drama that the novel *Silence* is best appreciated. Throughout, the focus remains on the psychological process that anticipates the heightened self-awareness evidenced by the protagonist at the conclusion – and it is through the depiction of the inner pain, endured to a similar degree by Rodrigues and his companion, Garrpe, that the author succeeds in removing the focus from a discussion of the validity of choosing either martyrdom or apostasy in such circumstances. As they await their inevitable capture, both men experience the misery of those for whom God appears silent and both experience, in equal measure, the pain of witnessing the repercussions of their act of 'strength' in coming to Japan in defiance of the shogunate proscription – the torture not of themselves but of those they had sought to encourage. For Garrpe, even this fails to elicit a reassessment of the situation. For Rodrigues, however, the erosion of the clearly defined distinction between strength and weakness begins at this point, hence his struggle to respond to the desperate plea of the 'weak-willed' Kichijirō:

> One who has trod on the sacred image has his say, too. Do you think I trampled on it willingly? My feet ached with the pain. God asks me to imitate the strong, even though He made me weak. Isn't this unreasonable? (p. 186)

By this stage, Rodrigues is armed with the realisation that, whereas the 'strong' martyrs suffer physical pain, the 'weak' apostates are condemned to a life of psychological pain, his vacillation emphasised at the textual level by a further blurring of the boundaries between martyrdom and apostasy. Consequently, when Kichijirō comes to him at the end of the novel with a renewed request for the 'disgraced' priest to hear his confession, Rodrigues' instinctive reaction is to refuse. 'I'm no longer "father"....Go away quickly!...I'm a fallen priest' (p. 296), he entreats Kichijirō. Within seconds, however, Rodrigues finds himself reconsidering: 'It is not man who judges. God knows our weakness more than anyone, reflected the priest' (p. 296). Coming after the protracted psychological torment to which he has been subjected, the *volte-face* is crucial, representing as it does the ultimate textual evidence of an erosion of the distinction between 'strength' and 'weakness' at the psychological level. Rodrigues has come full circle – to the extent that he is now in a position to concur with Kichijirō in claiming:

> There are neither the strong nor the weak. Can anyone say that the weak do not suffer more than the strong? (pp. 297–8)

For Rodrigues, such distinctions are no longer straightforward. The distance he now senses between his fellow priests back home who 'no doubt...would condemn his act as sacrilege' (p. 298) is, in a sense, compensated for by the increased empathy he has come to feel towards Kichijirō. And just as the 'strength' of those who had devoted their entire lives to propagation of the Christian gospel now appears less impressive to Rodrigues, so the 'weakness' of those like Kichijirō – like Ferreira and like Rodrigues himself – who had succumbed to the exigencies of their immediate situations comes to appear less absolute. Again, the notion that, under the circumstances, the act of martyrdom can be seen as more selfish than agreeing to bear the pain of apostasy for oneself is heresy to the theologian. As author, however, Endō is not assessing the validity of either option; rather, by suggesting that in the face of torture both represent two opposing images of life, each involving equal anguish, he succeeds paradoxically in merging these two opposites into alternative expressions of the same concept – that of human love.

The qualities of strength and weakness, symbolised in the text by martyrdom and apostasy, have been effectively fused in the protagonist's mind and, with it, Rodrigues' initial perception of an unfathomable gap between East and West has been eroded, the neat division between the 'monotheistic' West and the 'pantheistic' East no longer readily identifiable. Only now, as Rodrigues appears ready to judge those with whom he comes into contact as individual human beings rather than on the basis of their cultural identity, does the protagonist acknowledge the artificiality of the barriers he and his school had erected to perpetuate this gap. Only now is he in a position to appreciate the full significance of the fact, casually introduced early in the novel but all too readily overlooked, that Inoue, the cruel instigator of the shogunate's most inhuman forms of torture, was 'formerly of [the Christian] faith', that he was 'even baptized' (p. 36). The image of Christianity as a 'Western' religion that Rodrigues had initially sought to impose upon the 'godless' Japanese in defiance of the intransigence of those such as Inoue has now evaporated, replaced in the protagonist's mind by the vision of Christ, the 'companion', that may indeed succeed in penetrating the 'mudswamp' of Japan in a manner not available to the figure of awe and majesty extolled by both Ferreira and Rodrigues prior to their respective acts of apostasy.

During the above discussion, considerable emphasis has been placed on the process whereby Rodrigues emerges, by the conclusion of the novel, as an 'individuated' being, this in an attempt to cast a new light on the much-publicised criticisms of the novel *Silence* as depicting a stubbornly silent God. During the course of the novel,

Rodrigues' channels of communication with his God are certainly challenged – and his dejection at the seeming absence of response to his prayers entails a radical rethink of previously unquestioned assumptions. As noted above, however, for all its focus on the suffering of those who seek to follow the missionaries' call to faith, Endō's portrayal in *Silence* is of a God acutely aware of the suffering being inflicted in His name and resolved to speak *through* His silence. The point is lost on Ferreira; for years, Rodrigues, too, had clung to his plea for some practical manifestation of divine intervention. When this does happen, however, it assumes a form he could never have envisaged (in encouraging him to 'trample' on the *fumie*) and, in keeping with the technique of paradoxical inversion, it is at this moment that Rodrigues comes to acknowledge the true form assumed by the voice of God, leading to his ultimate conviction that:

> Our Lord was not silent. Even if he had been silent, my life until this day would have spoken of him. (p. 298)

Rodrigues' eventual acknowledgement of God speaking through His silence mirrors, in dramatic literary terms, the gospel portrayals of Christ as a response to the doubts, cited earlier, expressed by the psalmist David. For Endō, the juxtaposition would appear crucial – as testified by his well-documented disappointment at the manner in which the original film version of the novel does indeed portray Rodrigues as treading the same forlorn path of despair following abandonment by a silent God as that followed by his mentor Ferreira.[26] In a format reliant on visual appeal, such a denouement would certainly have immediate attraction for a film director. Without some acknowledgement of the focus of the concluding section of the novel, however, such a representation can only serve to perpetuate the line of criticism introduced at the beginning of this chapter – and to elicit an equally strong riposte from the author who, even some thirty years after initial composition of the work, continued to maintain:

> In *Silence*, I sought to portray, not the silence of God – but the way in which God speaks through man....I wanted to show that God, who appears superficially oblivious to human suffering and misery, actually speaks through a medium other than words.[27]

The frequency with which Endō felt himself obliged to offer such retorts suggests an author sensitive to the theological implications of this issue. With this and other similar comments, however, Endō can equally be seen seeking to return the focus of critical discussion towards the individuals who populate his works. In *Silence*, all such discussion must, of necessity, revert to Rodrigues, the character whose increasing awareness of inner growth born of a gradual renunciation of his earlier pride and heroism was to provide a model for all the author's subsequent examinations of the composite individual. Here is the author's most convincing examination to date of human psychology; here, the strongest indications to date of the possibility of reconciliation of seeming oppositions. And yet....

5
THE SAMURAI

> I can't help thinking that even though the praiseworthy act of that soldier was so very great, he'd have committed no sin if in an emergency like that he had renounced, if I may say so, sir, the name of Christ and his own baptism, so as to save his life for good deeds by which to atone in the course of years for his cowardice.
>
> (*The Brothers Karamazov*)

And yet, for all the international critical acclaim afforded the novel *Silence*, the questions remained. Despite receipt, in October 1966, of the prestigious Tanizaki Prize for this work and the enthusiasm with which the English translation (the first of Endō's novels to appear in English translation) was greeted some three years later, critical consensus as to the implications of this success for the author's subsequent narrative development remained divided and the author himself frequently acknowledged the uncertainty he was to experience upon completion of the novel in response to the question, 'Where next?'[1]

In this regard, the criticism offered by several of his Catholic critics that the novel portrayed no more nor less than a lapse of faith in the protagonist, Rodrigues, whilst in no way unanticipated, may well have exerted a more profound psychological influence than the author himself was inclined to acknowledge during this period of transition. To be sure, there was no wavering in the conviction that such criticism entailed a failure to distinguish between theological concerns and the poetics of literature with which he was engaged. But, in keeping with the overzealous denials of so many of his protagonists of any relationship with the world of organised Christianity, so the frequency with which Endō felt obliged to issue such disclaimers lamenting the 'misunderstandings' to which the novel had been subjected suggests an author inordinately concerned with the response the work had elicited in the very theological circles from which he was purportedly intent on maintaining his distance.

The paradox was not lost on the author and, during the next few years, Endō published a series of short stories that betray more than a passing acknowledgement of the critical discussions inspired by the novel. Two in particular are worthy of specific note.

As suggested by the title, the first of these, 'Kageboshi' (Shadows, 1968; trans. 1993),[2] represents the most overt reference in Endō's corpus to date to the concept of the dual-faceted nature of the human composite to which the author had long been attracted – and appears to build very deliberately on the aforementioned heightened self-awareness evidenced by Rodrigues at the conclusion of *Silence*. In the portrayal of the narrator–protagonist writing a letter to his former priest recounting various episodes, mostly unsavoury, from his youth, the narrative design in this latest short story provides the author ample scope for examination of the Shadow being that lurks within both parties. More specifically, with the priest initially established as a symbol of purity, the narrator is early identified as a detective seeking to fathom the 'real' person behind the former's public mask. As he begins his letter, therefore, the protagonist, an aspiring author, is aware of a certain quality about the priest's personality with which he has yet to come to terms. As such, despite frequent attempts to deploy the figure of the priest as a central figure in his novels, the narrator is forced into the following confession:

> Even though you're such a crucial character, virtually every story I've written about you has been a failure. I know why. It's because I still didn't have a firm grasp of who you are.[3]

The desire to unveil the 'real you' persists, however, fanned by a recognition that even this 'pure' priest is as subject to carnal feelings as the protagonist himself. By the end of the story, there is evidence, in the altered assessment of the priest's psychology, that he has succeeded in this task:

> I can no longer think of you as a dynamic missionary brimming with confidence and conviction, nor as a man, standing between lighted buildings and apartment houses where washing hangs out to dry, who looks down on life

from a higher position and passes judgement upon it. Instead, I think of you as a man whose eyes are now no different from the sad eyes of a dog.[4]

The object of the protagonist's concern is now seen, quite literally, as a mere shadow of his former self, reduced, in the eyes of society, to the role of disgraced priest following an affair with a Japanese woman on whom he had taken pity. To the protagonist himself, however, the distinction between the priest's latest persona and his inner being, his Shadow, is now clearly formulated, enabling him to accept, with no apparent perception of contradiction, the strong indications that his mentor's faith is, in fact, as strong as, if not stronger than, before. The image of the priest at the conclusion of the story as he 'quickly and inconspicuously crossed [him]self' is a powerful symbol,[5] not so much of a renewed faith born of hardship, but of a persistent faith, shaken only at the conscious level, but resolute throughout at the level of the unconscious.

The other story of the time that draws significantly on the critical response to *Silence* is '*Haha naru mono*' (Mothers, 1969; trans. 1984), a story that can be seen as adding to the image of God developed in the earlier novel, as representing not merely the strong paternalistic figure of the Old Testament, but also the more maternal figure, the 'compassionate weakling' that Endō strove to highlight in the Christ of the New Testament. As noted in the previous chapter, the literary depiction of Christ as *dōhansha*, the constant companion whose very strength lay paradoxically in his weakness, is integral to the novel *Silence* and other earlier works. But it is here, in 'Mothers', that the author succeeds, as never before, in incorporating within this image the various elements he had been seeking to reconcile.

The text itself is carefully crafted to incorporate both the present and the past. Narrated entirely in the first person by a young novelist engaged in research on Japan's 'Christian century', the story intersperses depictions of his current field trip to the island of Kyushu with a variety of flashbacks – recollections of his childhood and, in particular, of certain incidents involving his mother. The link between the two levels is, however, far from tenuous. The focus of the narrator's research is the *Kakure* Christians but, on discovering the existence of a small number of determined locals who had refused to revert to traditional Christianity even following the re-admission of the foreign missionaries towards the end of the nineteenth century, he finds himself increasingly attracted to the psychology of those who have been forced to come to terms with their own weakness. As the story develops, however, the narrator comes to discern in the experience of the *Kakure* parallels, not merely with so many contemporary Japanese Christians struggling to reconcile the perceived clash between their faith and their native culture, but also with his own experience of having been unable to live up to the expectations of religious piety that his mother had struggled so hard to impose on him.

On the one level, the story contains frequent references to the similarities the narrator perceives between his own situation and that of the *Kakure*. On arrival in Kyushu, for example, he is met by a series of Catholic parishioners who will serve as his local guides. Immediately, he is reminded of the intensity of his mother's faith, but confrontation with such powerful spirituality only serves to heighten his feelings of empathy for the 'weak' *Kakure*, leading him to conclude, 'If I had been born in such a time, I [too] would not have had the strength to endure...punishment'.[6] The more he contemplates their situation, the more he comes to realise that, just as the *Kakure* had been forced to endure the critical gaze of 'stronger' people around them, so he, too, has been subjected to the censorious gaze of others as a result of his callous, occasionally deceitful, treatment of his mother. As he admits,

> I am interested in the *Kakure* for only one reason – because they are the offspring of apostates. Like their ancestors, they cannot utterly abandon their faith...sometimes I catch a glimpse of myself in these *Kakure*, people who have had to lead lives of duplicity, lying to the world and never revealing their true feelings to anyone.[7]

It may be the awareness of this mutual burden of guilt that initially attracts the narrator to the *Kakure*, but the more he comes to contemplate their situation, the more he comes to accept that, just as the *Kakure* had learnt of the impossibility of merely abandoning God with no subsequent pangs of guilt, so too, he is unable to simply forget his own mother. The result is a juxtaposition of scenes devoted to the *Kakure* with those involving recollections of the narrator's mother and the explicit acknowledgement that 'to the *Kakure*, God was a stern paternal figure, and as a child asks its mother to intercede with its father, the *Kakure* prayed for the Virgin Mary to intervene on their behalf'.[8]

This process of fusion of images is gradual, and is accompanied in the narrator's mind by a mellowing of the initial recollections of his mother. As the story develops, so the image of the pious woman with the 'hard, stone-like face' that so troubles him at the beginning is tempered, developing gradually into a more tender, maternal figure who stands 'with her hands joined in front of her, watching [him] from behind with a look of gentle sorrow in her eyes'.[9]

The depiction echoes a recurring image of Endō's literature of the time and represents the author's most concerted attempt to date to fuse the image of the mother with this vision of Christ as man's companion, symbol of love and compassion. Seen in this light, the 'mother' to appear in the story is an idealised figure and again the text provides ample evidence of this intent.[10] In the first flashback scene, for example, the narrator is portrayed as dreaming of his mother standing at his hospital bedside, although, as he subsequently acknowledges, 'My wife...was the one who watched over me through every night after each of my three operations'.[11] Already, reality and imagination have become blurred and, the more the narrator seeks to abandon this image, the more he is forced to recognise the 'mother' as the personification of selfless love – and to acknowledge that, in the creation of this image, he had 'superimposed on the face [of his mother] that of a statue of "Mater dolorosa", the Holy Mother of Sorrows, which [his] mother used to own'.[12]

The result is a single image – a fusion of the mother, of Mary and of Christ – which is the key to an understanding of this and so much of Endō's work and which is overtly acknowledged by the narrator towards the end of the story with the following comment,

> When the missionaries had been expelled and the churches demolished, the Japanese *Kakure*, over the space of many years, stripped away all those parts of the religion that they could not embrace, and the teachings of God the Father were gradually replaced by a yearning after a Mother – a yearning which lies at the very heart of Japanese religion.[13]

Significantly, however, the story does not end with this moment of insight. As this realisation revives memories of his mother, the narrator's thoughts wander to the painting he has just seen – a picture of a Japanese farm woman suckling her baby – and he comes to view this as representative of the 'maternal' element inherent in the Japanese religious sensitivity.

The conclusion is indicative of the extent to which this story, published some three years after *Silence*, has built on the revised image of Christ ultimately accepted by Rodrigues following the shattering of his preconceptions at the moment of apostasy. At the same time, it hints at the direction that the author was to adopt in his literature during the ensuing decade. Having turned his powers of narrative creativity to a literary depiction of the holy, Endō now turned his attention to closer examination of the man behind the image. There followed several trips to the West – and to the Holy Land in particular – and publication, during the course of the 1970s, of a series of works born of this consideration.

Of these, those to attract most critical acclaim were *Iesu no shōgai* (The Life of Jesus, 1973; trans. 1979) and *Kirisuto no tanjō* (The Birth of Christ, 1978) – as suggested by conferral on the former of the International Dag Hammarskjöld Prize in 1978 and on the latter of the Yomiuri Literary Award in 1979. As tentative expositions of the very personal theology the author had long been developing in his fictional worlds, these works reinforce the by now well-worked image of Christ as 'powerless', 'useless', 'incapable of positive achievement'...but utterly loyal as a companion.[14] In addressing this theme from a more specifically Christian perspective – by focusing specifically on the question of how the Christ of the New Testament became the Messiah – however, such works develop the image of each individual as engaged in an intensely personal relationship with Christ, leading ultimately to the conclusion, in *The Birth of Christ*, that:

> What is indisputable is that Christ left an indelible mark on those whose lives crossed His path....
>
> Those who despair of love seek an existence who will not betray their love, those who have abandoned all hope of being understood in their sorrow seek a true understander in the recesses of their hearts. This is not sentimentality or over-dependence: merely a necessary precondition for individuals in their interactions with others.[15]

The citation encapsulates the paradox integral to Endō's vision of Christ, the powerless, yet constant companion. The challenge for Endō as novelist, however, was to incorporate such insights into his fictional worlds – and it is in these terms that the ensuing novel, *The Samurai*, is perhaps best evaluated. Before turning to a more detailed discussion of narrative developments within this latest text, however, let us remain with the broader picture of the development of Endō's *oeuvre* in general in attempting a brief comparison between *The Samurai* and the earlier masterpiece, *Silence*.

In view of the similar historical time period (early seventeenth century) and subject material (the challenge confronting both foreign missionaries to Japan and the native Japanese to whom the 'alien' religion was being introduced) that is evidenced in the two novels, such comparisons are perhaps inevitable, the instinct to place this latest novel at the end of an emerging continuum without consideration for the very real distinctions that exist between the two works undeniable. And it has to be admitted that there is a very real sense in which *The Samurai* draws on much that had already been evidenced in the earlier work. More specifically, in persisting with the fundamental question of 'Where is God as His people suffer?', Endō here remains faithful to the issue that had pervaded, not merely *Silence* but so much of his corpus to date. In *Silence*, the question had been entrusted in large measure to Rodrigues, whose growing concern over the perceived silence of the God he sought to introduce to the Japanese had presaged a heightened awareness of a deeper dimension of his being at which God speaks to him with an intensity he had never previously experienced. In *The Samurai*, this same question is addressed. Here, however, its ramifications are pursued, not merely by the Spanish missionary, Velasco, whose initial self-assurance and confidence are challenged in a far more subtle manner than that revealed in the earlier portrayal of Rodrigues, but also, more objectively, by Hasekura, the junior ranking samurai who travels to Spain and Rome via Nueva España at the behest of his feudal lord. Both men take part in a mission whose ostensible goal is the procurement of trading rights with the outside world for the local hegemon, Lord Shiraishi. Ultimately, however, both emerge as hapless victims of political machinations beyond their control.

The two men are brought together, in typical Endō manner, as a result of a decision to which neither is privy and which they are powerless to oppose. From the moment their paths cross aboard the *San Juan Baptista* at the outset of the mission, however, their destinies are linked and, during the four years they subsequently spend in their ultimately fruitless attempt to convince the Western powers of Japan's suitablity as a trading partner, they come increasingly to manifest a common concern for the same question that had so tormented Rodriques: 'How can one place ultimate trust in a God who remains silent in the face of the seemingly meaningless suffering of His creations?'

Again, as in *Silence*, the only hint of an 'answer' emerges at the very end of the novel. By this stage, both men await execution: Velasco for having defied the shogunate exclusion order that applied to all foreigners but was particularly vigorously enforced in the case of those committed to proselytisation of the Christian gospel; the samurai for having converted, however expediently, to the alien faith and then fallen victim of a changed political landscape on his return to Japan. And it is only then that the two men acknowledge the same deeper dimension to their being, one that can attribute significance to their seemingly meaningless deaths. For Velasco, it is only following his decision to return to Japan, fully aware of the consequences, from the relative safety of Luzon and his consequent inevitable arrest that he acknowledges this inner being. Here for the first time, he comes to grips with the absolute difference between his own human ambitions and the will of God. It is only now as he awaits death that he comes to experience a previously unconscionable degree of love towards his fellow man (epitomised by the care and concern he shows for his cell mate, a priest from the Jesuit order that the Franciscan Velasco had previously despised). For Hasekura, too, it is confrontation with a death that, to the end, defies comprehension at the level of logic (the text throughout has been at pains to stress the depiction of the samurai as guilty of no greater crime than blind obedience to the orders received from his superiors) that elevates him to a greater level of consciousness: as he awaits his summons, he, too, experiences a renewed capacity for love – towards his family, his fellow envoys and retainers and towards Velasco – that affords meaning to an otherwise meaningless destiny.

To the extent that both novels depict the suffering of God in, with and for individual human beings, therefore, the inevitable comparisons may indeed appear justified. What such ready parallels fail to acknowledge, however, is the extent to which questions introduced in *Silence* in general terms are addressed with greater intensity and specificity in the later work. The concern with the historical records relating to Japan's confrontation with Christianity and with the author's perception of a utilitarian tendency in Japanese culture – the predominance of that which Kitamura Tōkoku had portrayed as 'horizontal thought' mitigating against the search for what is eternal or beyond humanity: both of these clearly remain.[16] But in contrast to the focus on the question of whether the Japanese can accommodate Christ as introduced by the European missionaries, a question central to the narrative design in *Silence*, in *The Samurai* the issue is universalised – as both Velasco and Hasekura struggle with the more fundamental concern of 'Who is Christ?' The shift is subtle, but significant, and it is borne out by consideration of the superificial similarities – and differences at a deeper level – between the two Western priests, Rodrigues and Velasco.

Initial examination of these two protagonists suggests considerable analogy between the two. Both arrive in Japan with an apparently unquestioning faith, a set of convictions that is seemingly eroded during the course of the respective novels, gradually but inexorably, in the face of increasing setbacks. For both, however, it is precisely when their purportedly unerring belief is subjected to the severest of challenges and they are close to despair that we sense in them a more profound faith, one born of anguish in the face of harsh reality. Thereafter, buoyed by this increased conviction, both come to discover renewed meaning for their lives, meaning that enables both to justify the performance of acts that, though in contravention of the explicit teachings of the church, are nevertheless seen as conforming to the tenets of a renewed and more personal creed. For Rodrigues this moment arrives with his willingness to hear the confession of his betrayer, Kichijirō, despite his own public act of apostasy: as Rodrigues acknowledges, 'No doubt his fellow priests would condemn his act as sacrilege; but even if he was betraying them, he was not betraying his Lord'.[17] In like manner, confronted with the suicide in Nueva España of Tanaka, one of Hasekura's fellow envoys and fully aware that 'the Church does regard suicide as a mortal sin',[18] Velasco chooses to obey a deeper, unconscious prompting in agreeing to offer the funeral rites to the dead samurai. The narrative emphasis at this juncture is on Velasco's genuine compassion for his fellow travellers, his justification for this act that would officially be denounced as sacrilege – that 'a priest lives to serve others in the world, not for his own sake' (p. 215) – echoing Rodrigues' conviction that his relationship with his Lord may change but will never be severed.

In betraying elements of suffering and servanthood, therefore, both Rodrigues and Velasco can be seen as conforming to Endō's image of Christ, the *dōhansha*. To conclude from this that the psychological journeys undertaken by these two are identical is, however, to ignore the fundamental difference in their respective responses – the fact that Rodrigues arrives at his renewed faith following a public expression of apostasy whereas Velasco ultimately remains true to the official dictates of his faith and returns voluntarily from Luzon to embrace death as a martyr. The pride and arrogance that had dogged his every move earlier in the novel has by now completely dissipated and he can now see a purpose to his death that extends beyond the blind call to a glorious martyrdom upon which his religious order would have insisted. Moreover, far from viewing this simply as a response to his duty as missionary to establish a model of self-sacrifice, Velasco is now in a position to attribute to his death a far greater, more personal significance: in dying he can share a miserable reality with his fellow traveller, Hasekura.

The narrative process whereby these two men, initially poles apart, are gradually reconciled to the point where both are enabled willingly to share this miserable reality is clearly integral to *The Samurai* and represents a significant shift of emphasis from the earlier *Silence* (where, as noted above, a similar *rapprochement* between Rodrigues and Kichijirō is clearly suggested in the concluding section but not developed with anything like the same intensity during the course of the novel). In view of its impact, the manner in which the juxtaposition between the two main characters in the later work is developed throughout the novel will be discussed at greater length later in this chapter. Its significance to any comparative consideration of these two novels cannot, however, be overstated, reflecting as it does a greater commitment to the technique of transposition, cited by Endō at the outset of his career as integral to his art and yet crafted in *The Samurai* in a manner more deliberate and sustained than in any earlier Endō text. The process is evidenced at the superficial level in a manner immediately reminiscent of that deployed in *Silence*: the historical models for the main protagonists are readily discernible in the seventeenth-century archives, the identification between the Society of Peter of the novel with the Jesuit order, the Society of Paul with the Franciscan order overtly acknowledged.[19] As the novel unfolds, however, the technique is clearly developed on a different level – as the purported goal of the mission, a meeting with the Pope, is gradually and imperceptibly transposed into confrontation with a King of a different dimension. The physical images of Christ, the pitiful figure on the crucifixes with which the samurai is constantly confronted along the way and to whom he finds himself inexplicably, yet increasingly, drawn stand in total contrast to the figure of awe and majesty he had envisioned meeting in Rome. The further he travels, however, the more he finds himself juxtaposing his own miserable destiny with that of Christ on the cross until eventually he finds himself possessed of the strength to accept death for His sake. At the time, rejection by the earthly King – the meeting with the Pope when it eventually materialises is a perfunctory affair – is painful, symbolising as it does the ultimate failure of the mission. By the conclusion of the novel, however, Hasekura has indeed secured a more significant meeting with a King[20] – and, in so doing, discovered a previously inconceivable meaning to his entire journey.

The technique is integral to the narrative impact of the novel, *The Samurai*. Even more significant to a comparative discussion of the two novels, *Silence* and *The Samurai*, however, is the manner in which the increased focus on the evolving transposition during the course of the narrative masks one further crucial distinction between the two works, an ironic shift all too easily lost in the search for consistency. The distinction is embodied in the evolving images of Christ nurtured, on the one hand, by Rodrigues, on the other, by Hasekura. For both, the ultimate search may be for a figure of love, a compassionate being who can share their burden. Significantly, however, in sharp contrast to the figure of awe and splendour initially embraced by Rodrigues but gradually transposed into just such a being, Hasekura begins from the opposite end of the spectrum. The Christ to whom he is introduced – the wretched figure of Christ crucified whom he could never envisage worshipping – could not be further divorced from such majesty. The goal, however, remains the same and, though the process may be reversed, it is the samurai's ultimate ability to discern in this image identical qualities of compassionate concern and to acknowledge in this the power of God's grace that ultimately enables him, like Rodrigues, to accept his destiny with dignity.

The comparison – the consideration of the similarities and differences between the two works is essential to an understanding of the position of *The Samurai* as representing the apogee of Endō's prolonged literary concern with the era of Christian persecution in Japan. Having placed the work in context, however, let us now turn to critical discussion of the text itself.

In keeping with precedent established in the earlier works, this latest text was the product of extensive research into an historical figure – the inspiration for Endō in this case was the samurai, Hasekura Tsunenaga – with whom the author had over the years come to experience a profound sense of empathy. The more Endō investigated the archives relating to Hasekura and the mission to Nueva España and subsequently to Europe in which the latter participated, the more he came to sympathise with Hasekura as a hapless pawn of the political authorities. As Endō was quick to discover, historical records concerning Hasekura, as with those concerning the models for Ferreira and Rodrigues in *Silence*, appear to come to an abrupt halt, in this case following the samurai's dutiful return to Japan after a mission that had lasted some four years and had resulted in Hasekura's baptism by the King of Spain's personal chaplain in Madrid. Opinions as to subsequent developments in the life of Endō's model vary: as Gessel acknowledges in his 'Translator's Postscript', some records claim he apostatised shortly after his return to Japan, others that he refused to recant and suffered a fate similar to that endured by Hasekura, and yet others suggest that, in a manner reminiscent of the *Kakure* Christians, he went through with a public act of disavowal of the faith whilst secretly continuing to adhere in the privacy of his own life.[21] To Endō, however, all this represented idle speculation. Of far more interest was the fact that here was another example of a man forgotten by history, another opportunity, as novelist, to depict the individual as he attempts to come to terms with the perceived silence of God. In so doing, in seeking the creation of a protagonist who experiences the true meaning of this silence, Endō, once more, brings his powers of literary imagination to bear on the creation of a character who, in terms of psychology, personality, ideals and lifestyle, projects the essential 'truths' surrounding the historical Hasekura into those periods in which the archives lapse into silence. In this way, in thus breaking the 'silence of history', Endō sought to encapsulate the spirit of a man who would otherwise have remained enshrouded in the oblivion of uncertainty. The result is a masterpiece of imaginative history, a penetrating analysis of questions fundamental to religious experience.

Endō's research into the archives relating to Hasekura and his mission was painstaking and, in 'Ikenie no shisetsu' (The Self-sacrificing Envoy), one of the many short stories written in anticipation of *The Samurai*, the author identified four questions surrounding his life and subsequent historical treatment, questions that would emerge as the central theme of the novel.

1 Why was Hasekura chosen to take part in the mission to Nueva España?
2 Why was he entrusted with a warm letter addressed to the Pope long after the Christian persecution had begun in Japan?
3 Where are the records of the trip, especially those showing how much Hasekura was aware of the false hopes with regard to

evangelism in Japan that both his feudal lord and Velasco passed on to the Pope?
4   If Hasekura was so loyal to orders from above, why have his remains been lost without trace?[22]

The resulting depiction of Hasekura, Tsunenaga's fictional 'other', would appear to remain considerably closer to the archival sources than that evidenced, for example, in the portrayal of Rodrigues in *Silence*. Examining the records, not only in the Sendai region of northern Japan from which the 1613 mission emanated, but also in Mexico, Spain and Rome, Endō unearthed a wealth of information relating to the historical Tsunenaga and it is on the basis of this that the novel *The Samurai* evolved. For Endō, as novelist, however, more interesting than those details he was able to unearth were the series of inconsistencies and discrepancies he discovered there and, more significantly, the gaps in the documentation that piqued his fascination as author.[23] As historian, Endō would have been driven to seek to place on record such lacunae. As author, however, he sought, not to expose these shortcomings nor even necessarily to remain faithful to the various 'facts' surrounding Tsunenaga's mission. Instead, in the manner adopted in the earlier *Silence*, Endō built on the various 'factual' acounts in the creation of a 'truthful' record of the samurai's ultimate destiny.

As noted earlier, the distinction between 'facts' and 'truths' is one to which Endō made frequent reference and, in an article written shortly after completion of the manuscript for *The Samurai*, he concluded:

> *The Samurai* is not intended as a biographical record of his mission to Europe. It is a novel in which I have recreated in my mind several concepts inspired by the life of Tsunenaga.[24]

The 'facts' as portrayed in the novel may not stand up to close scrutiny. As Gessel has pointed out, however, it 'is unquestionably "true" in a broader sense', as a 'true record of the spiritual voyage that is undertaken within one man's heart'.[25] At the level of narrative, the voyage may be undertaken by the samurai, Hasekura. As Endō himself was the first to acknowledge, however, the implications of that voyage run far deeper – to the level of the unconscious – and it is in these terms that the author sought to encapsulate the work. As he remarked in another interview offered shortly after publication of the novel:

> With *The Samurai*, I had no intention of writing a historical novel. I was inspired by the biography of Hasekura and have referred to that, but this is my 'I-novel' (*shishōsetsu*). It is a reconstruction effected within my inner being and is thus far removed from a historical novel in the strict sense of the word.[26]

During the course of this interview with Kaga Otohiko, Endō sought to elucidate on his vision of the novel as 'a reconstruction effected within [his] inner being', claiming in particular that,

> The more I pursued my investigation, the more I came to feel that here was a man on to whom I could reflect myself – that *Hasekura and I were as one*.[27]

Just as the author himself had viewed his baptism as an act of expediency, had subsequently experienced a sense of revulsion at the images of the wretched figure on the crucifixes that adorned not only the churches with which he became acquainted as a youth in Japan, but even the grand cathedrals he encountered during his stay in Europe and had ultimately clung to his faith in response to the unfathomable promptings he perceived as emanating from his unconscious being, so too with Hasekura. Here, too, was a man who, judging from the evidence available to the author, resorted to baptism as an expedient measure, remained perplexed by the miserable image of Christ that represented the object of worship for the Christians he encountered on his journey and whom Endō could consequently justifiably develop into the man who ultimately refuses to balk, even in the face of execution, for beliefs that, to the end, he is unwilling, or unable, to acknowledge at the conscious level.

Viewed in this light, authorial identification with the protagonist, Hasekura, would appear intense, the autobiographical elements incorporated into his portrayal readily identifiable. And, as the author was first to acknowledge, the temptation to perceive his protagonist as a symbol of his own struggle to come to terms with his adopted faith was one with which Endō was constantly confronted as the narrative evolved.[28] To be sure, such author–protagonist parallels may be of passing interest for the light they throw on the evolving theology of an author, still subject to attacks from the more traditional wing of the Catholic community in Japan. In terms of contributing to a critical evaluation of the text itself, however – and this must needs remain the subject at hand – such identification is of mere tangential concern: it is of interest only inasmuch as it provides a framework from which to assess the author's depiction of *The Samurai* as his '*shishōsetsu*'.

In view of the form in which the narrative is structured, it is hardly surprising that much of the critical discussion of the novel in Japan has focused on the task of identifying the parallels between the journeys, both physical and spiritual, undertaken by Endō and his fictional construct, Hasekura. To jump from this to a reading of the novel as *shishōsetsu* is, nevertheless, a major leap of logic, one that is hardly supported by closer textual analysis. Let us turn, then, to a brief consideration of those aspects of the narrative that belie the author's own depiction of the work as a *shishōsetsu*.

Reference has already been made to one quality of the novel that sets it apart from the *shishōsetsu* template: the author's determination to impose an imaginative creativity on to the 'factual' nucleus of his narrative. In sharp contradistinction to the advocacy, noted earlier, by critics such as Kume Masao for 'the recreation of the path trodden in real life by an individual', Endō has brought his powers of literary fabrication fully to bear on his recreation of the life of an historical 'other'. The division is jealously guarded – and highlighted, at the structural level, by the juxtaposition of scenes in which Hasekura's perspective alternates with sections drawn from the diary of Velasco. This splintered narrative perspective is maintained throughout the novel and, although it may not be particularly influential in determining the pace at which the narrative unfurls, the cumulative effect is nevertheless pronounced, ensuring as it does that Hasekura will never achieve the privileged status of the prototypical *shishōsetsu* hero.

Velasco's role in this regard is clearly paramount. Not only does the frequent insertion of extracts from the missionary's diary highlighting the process whereby he is drawn inexorably to empathise with the Japanese envoys provide a forum for alternative views on events as they unfurl that is patently lacking in the *shishōsetsu* model. But, in thereby ensuring that the sensibilities of a single focus figure will not come to dominate, these extracts also raise important questions as to the samurai's qualifications as a reliable and authoritative narrator-cum-story-teller.

Significantly, however, the task of bringing into question the perspective volunteered by the samurai is not restricted to Velasco. Equally telling, though considerably more limited, are the contributions to the overall narrative development of two others whose perspectives intrude, if only briefly, as a welcome foil to those offered by Hasekura and Velasco. The first of these, Yozō, retains to the end his status as loyal and trusted retainer to the samurai. In offering a view of events that frequently anticipates that subsequently to be adopted by his master, however, his perspective serves an invaluable proleptic function that, by its very perspicacity, serves to augment the sense of dramatic irony surrounding events at the conclusion of the novel. The other perspective that contributes to the multiconsciousness narration so integral to the novel is that provided by the renegade Japanese monk encountered by the mission in the hamlet of Tecali as they journey across Nueva España towards the port of Veracruz. Here is a man who, for all his public renunciation of his faith, clings powerfully to his conviction that, 'no matter what the padres might say, I believe in my own Jesus' (p. 120). And it is on those, admittedly rare, occasions when the narrative focus shifts to incorporate this, the most objective view of the events in question, that the true extent of the distance, psychological rather than physical, to be travelled by both the samurai and Velasco is best attested.

Deprived of these alternative views on events – without the suggestions of authorial identification with Velasco's unwavering conviction that, having once turned to Christ, the individual is never abandoned by Him, with the Tecali monk's belief in an intensely personal Christ whose influence on believers is powerful if imperceptible, and with Yozō's instinctive attraction to the miserable figure on the cross – the danger of over-identification with the samurai's vision of events might indeed intrude. As a result of the expanded range of perspective and points of view afforded by these alternative eyes, however, the novel achieves a balance, a symmetry that is absent from the Rodrigues-dominated narrative structure of the earlier *Silence*.

Such balance is carefully crafted, its dramatic impact dependent, less on the diversity of viewpoints thereby introduced, more on the manner in which the varying perspectives, including as they do seemingly irreconcilable attitudes and responses, are subsequently carefully fused. Again, the issue is one to which reference has already been made – its significance to Endō's narrative design hard to exaggerate. Once more, however, it is to *The Samurai* that the reader must turn for the most effective exposition to date of the process whereby a sense of unity is induced by means of fusion of purportedly contradictory elements.

As with several of the earlier novels, attention to the technique is symbolised by the series of overt contrasts the author initially appears intent on establishing at the textual level. From the moment Hasekura embarks on his mission, the small village from which he hails – and the tight community this represents – is clearly placed in opposition to the vast world that lies before him. At the same time, the traditional unquestioning values he cherishes at the outset of the work are implicitly contrasted to the Christian beliefs espoused by Velasco to which he is increasingly drawn. The contrasts are often overtly highlighted, but always behind the establishment of such distinctions lies an equally determined attempt to challenge the traditional basis upon which such oppositions are founded. The challenge is rarely explicit. But, as suggested by the comment of the samurai's patron, Lord Shiraishi, as the envoys prepare to sail from the port of Tsukinoura, the attempt to secure such fusion of traditional differences is significantly cited as the primary objective of the entire mission as envisioned by the shogunate authorities:

> In the land of the foreigners,...the ways of life will probably be different from those here in Japan. You must not cling to Japanese customs if they stand in the way of your mission. If that which is white in Japan is black in the foreign lands, consider it black. Even if you remain unconvinced in your heart, you must wear a look of acquiescence on your face. (p. 49)

The implication at this point would appear to be that the success of the venture on which the envoys are about to embark is dependent on capitulation to the values that they would encounter abroad. Once on board, however, a chance remark by Matsuki, the most self-serving of the envoys, in a discussion with Velasco suggests that, far from an abandoning of the cultural underpinnings that the Japanese envoys were bringing to bear on the mission, the process of fusion during the course of the novel would actually assume the form of a degree of mutual compromise with which the Japanese could readily identify. The following conversation between Hasekura and his fellow envoy, Matsuki, is testimony to this trait:

> 'To be neither hot nor cold, but merely lukewarm...is that what you want, Lord Matsuki?'...
> 'What can I do about it? I was brought up in Japan.... Extremes are not well thought of in Japan.' (p. 75)

From this moment on, the series of extremes initially established in the narrative is consistently challenged, the process whereby these come eventually to be perceived, not as irreconcilable opposites, but as elements of a dynamic tension in which the one is only definable in terms of the other representing the key element bringing together the seemingly disparate threads of the narrative. Let us turn now, therefore to a consideration of the opposition most consistently undermined by this narrative process – that between East and West.

From the moment Endō emerged on the literary scene, the tension between East and West has remained at the heart of his narrative design. In *The Samurai*, once more, the opposition is initially carefully constructed – through the deliberate crafting of the 'eastern' samurai and the 'western' missionary as contrasting figures. Achieved at the narrative level by the above-mentioned juxtaposition of sections entrusted respectively to the first-person and alternative narrators, this is reinforced by the implicit contrast between the small village (and the tight community this encompasses) that represented the extent of the samurai's horizons to date, and the vast world to which Velasco had been exposed. Equally, however, the contrast between the two men is simultaneously embodied in the personal traits attributed to each man. In complete contrast to the depiction of the self-indulgent, often aggressively ambitious Velasco, therefore, lies the portrayal of the samurai, seemingly devoid of worldly ambition and content to eke out an existence for himself and his family in the marshlands of northern Japan.

Introduction to Velasco's worldly ambition and vanity is immediate – in the depiction of the missionary, still convinced of his own worth despite incarceration by the shogunate authorities. As he sits in his prison cell at the outset of the novel ruminating on the future, his conclusion betrays all the pride he had previously brought to bear on his work in Japan:

> If his life were spared, it would be because the statesmen of this country still had need of him. Up until now, they had used him as a translator whenever emissaries had come from Manila, and in fact there were no other missionaries left in Edo who had his fluent command of Japanese. If the covetous Japanese wished to continue their profitable trade relationship with Manila or with Nueva España far across the Pacific Ocean, they could not afford to dispense with him, since he could serve as a bridge for their negotiations.

'I am willing to die if it be Thy will', the missionary thought, lifting his head proudly like a hawk. 'But Thou knowest how much the Church in Japan needs me.' (p. 17)

Thereafter, Velasco is equally quick to attribute his subsequent release to divine acknowledgement of the role he has to play in the future attempts at proselytisation in Japan:

> Thou knowest my abilities....Thou hast need of me, and for that reason rescued me from prison....The missionary sensed that he could use their greed to benefit the missionary cause. (p. 26)

Contrasts with initial portrayals of the samurai could not be more pronounced. To be sure, Hasekura may have the status of samurai and thus purportedly stand at the apex of the Tokugawa social order. But from the beginning, the text is at pains to emphasise his position as low-ranking samurai and his consequent inability to influence the events in which he becomes embroiled. For Hasekura at this juncture, the village in which he had been born and spent his entire life represents the entire world; his determination never to betray his ancestors and relatives living there is a paramount influence on his actions. The image of a man totally caught up in this small world is readily discernible in the depiction of Hasekura, desperate to maintain the aura of communal harmony to which he was accustomed in the face of his uncle's concerted efforts to restore the family to its former glories:

> Without a word of reply, the samurai took some dried branches from the pile beside him and broke them for the hearth. As he listened to the dull snap of the branches, he tried his best to endure these familiar complaints from his uncle. He was mute not from any lack of thought or feeling. It was simply that he was not accustomed to allowing his emotions to show on his face, and that he did not like to disagree with anyone. (p. 11)

The contrast with Velasco remains implicit, but after the two men have come together aboard the ship that will transport them across the Pacific, this is exacerbated by the latter's explicit denunciation of Hasekura as the least attractive of his travelling companions:

Hasekura Rokuemon appears to be more a peasant than a samurai, and is the least impressive of all the envoys. It has not yet been decided whether we shall go to Rome, but I haven't the slightest idea why Lord Shiraishi encouraged me to take along Hasekura if we do. The fellow cuts a sorry figure, and he lacks Matsuki's intelligence. (pp. 59–60)

Equally effective in the establishment of this opposition is the genuine incomprehension evidenced by Hasekura and his fellow envoys at the missionary's seemingly blind devotion to the miserable figure they discern on the crucifix that is never far from Velasco's side. To Hasekura, this figure epitomises all that is unfathomable about the West, his attitude – more that of incredulity than of deep-rooted resistance – apparent in the following narrative depiction:

> The row of beads was made from seeds, and a crucifix dangled from one end of the string. The naked figure of an emaciated man had been carved on the crucifix. The samurai gazed at this man, whose arms were outstretched, and whose head drooped lifelessly. He could not understand why Velasco and all the other foreigners called such a man 'Lord'. To the samurai, only His Lordship could be called 'Lord', but His Lordship was not a wretched, emasculated figure like this. If the Christians really worshipped this emaciated man, then their religion seemed an incredibly bizarre sort of heresy. (pp. 83–4)

The opposition is by now firmly established. In keeping with precedent established in the earlier novels, however, it is precisely at this point – with the antagonism between Velasco and Hasekura seemingly absolute – that the process of fusion comes to the fore, as the contrast between the two is slowly but surely eroded. And once more, it is at the level of the unconscious that the first signs of challenge to the construct are evidenced. Let us examine this process of fusion in terms of narrative developments in the portrayal of, first, Velasco, and thereafter, the samurai.

First indications that there is more to Velasco than meets the eye assume the form, as in the earlier texts, of deliberate narrative subversion of several of the purportedly unquestioning self-assessments offered by the priest himself. His prayer from his prison cell, 'If Thou hast need of me no longer…Thou mayest summon me at any time. Thou knowest better than anyone else that I am not at all attached to this life' (pp. 18–19), for example, is pronounced with apparent conviction. Such selflessness is, however, undermined by the undeniable ambition and self-serving attitude offered in the narrative immediately before and after this prayer, the effect of such juxtaposition being to bring into question whether Velasco succeeds in convincing even himself of his willingness to sacrifice his life for his Lord. Such suggestions of self-deception become more pronounced as the narrative unfolds, the purported altruism behind his determination to become Bishop of Japan consequently subject to increasing suspicion. As he discusses the impending mission with Lord Shiraishi, for example, and catches himself about to ask for that position in return for his services as interpreter for the envoys, Velasco struggles to justify his ambition:

> For a moment [Velasco] was ashamed of his pride, yet at the same time he told himself, 'I do not seek advancement out of selfish interest. I wish to have the position of Bishop so that I may set up a last sturdy line of defence in this country that seeks to proscribe Christianity. I alone can do battle with these cunning, heathen Japanese.' (p. 35)

Once more, the depiction is of Velasco struggling to resist the promptings of his unconscious. Again, the issue of whether he convinces himself of his own logic is the subject of intense narrative scrutiny, the challenge to the initial portrayal of Velasco consequently enhanced.

As long as Velasco seeks to resist the promptings of his unconscious, however, there can be no suggestion of his coming to terms with this more complex being behind the stereotype as introduced at the outset. First to see through to a greater depth to the missionary than he is willing to acknowledge, therefore, is not Velasco himself, but those with whom he interacts. Significantly, the first such insight is offered by Matsuki, the envoy whom Velasco had typecast as 'the most intelligent of the four envoys' (p. 59) following their first meeting. In response to Velasco's persistent attempts to convince the envoys of the efficacy of baptism even if 'their only motive was to benefit their business' (p. 73), Matsuki responds pointedly:

> You're quite a schemer, Lord Velasco. You play upon their greed and make them into Christians. (pp. 73–4)

What has long been evidenced implicitly has now been explicitly acknowledged and the reader subsequently encounters a series of individuals ready to offer equally percipient assessments of the missionary. The Viceroy the mission encounters in Mexico, for example, is in no doubt as to the hidden agenda behind Velasco's supposedly selfless attempts to secure the baptism of the envoys out of missionary zeal, concluding their brief encounter with the penetrating remark:

> You seem to have chosen the wrong profession, Father. You should have become a diplomat instead of a missionary. (p. 104)

Equally perspicacious in his analysis of Velasco's actions is the Bishop of Sevilla, who after welcoming the missionaries and the envoys he has brought from Japan, declares:

> 'My son', the Bishop looked steadily into Velasco's face, 'you are too impassioned. You must examine your heart to be sure that in the future your passion does not do damage to your soul.' (p. 143)

At this stage in the novel, such assessments are entrusted to relatively minor actors in the unfolding drama. Concurrent with these explicit analyses, however, the narrative comes increasingly to focus on signs of Velasco acting in contrast to the stereotypical character attributed to him at the outset. Embroiled in an Indian rebellion between Córdoba and Veracruz, for example, Velasco's courage and powers of leadership are clearly at stake. Loath to proceed, the 'forced smile' he betrays in response to the taunts of cowardice offered by Tanaka, now firmly established as the most intrepid of the envoys following Matsuki's premature return to Japan, is immediately picked up by the narrator: 'It was the first indication of weakness they had ever seen in the missionary' (p. 129). Almost immediately, however, the group is surprised by an Indian woman emerging from the shade of an olive tree begging for assistance for her dying brother – and Velasco's response is equally unexpected, this time in its compassion. Now it is Tanaka and the other envoys who wish to distance themselves as quickly as possible from any signs of trouble, and it is Velasco who, quietly but firmly, reminds them of his 'calling as a Christian padre' (p. 131) as he departs, at considerable risk to his personal safety, to administer the last rites.

The incident represents a significant turning point in the narrative portrayal of Velasco, and there follow increasing suggestions of a man slowly but surely confronting the realities encompassed by his inner being. A passage from his diary shortly after arrival in Spain betrays just such a flash of genuine insight, acknowledging as it does a growing recognition that peace of mind will only come following acceptance of unconscious forces at work on his being. Aroused from sleep by a wet dream, the missionary resorts to his only recourse at such moments, prayer. His own narrative at this point, however, betrays all the pain of growing self-realisation:

> As I prayed, I was suddenly overcome by a terrifying sense of despair. Drop by drop I tasted the poison seeping through my soul, and I felt as though I had just discovered my own ugly face in a mirror. The lusts of my flesh, my hatred for the Jesuits, my almost arrogant confidence in my work in Japan, my thirst for conquest – one after another they surged up from the depths of my soul, to the point that I could no longer feel that the Lord would listen to my prayers and my petitions. I felt as if He were pointing a finger at me, showing me the abominable ugliness of the selfish ambition that lurked behind my prayers and my aspirations. (p. 139)

By this stage, Velasco's powers of resistance are clearly under attack, and there now follows a series of assaults on his public facade from a variety of unconscious sources. First of these is the voice that whispers at his ear, a well-worn image in Endō's literature of the individual wracked by his inner being:

> A voice sounded in Velasco's ears. 'What are you trying to do now? To baptize men who do not believe in the Lord, for your own benefit, is a blasphemy and a profanation. It is an act of arrogance, and through the sacrament of baptism you heap the sins of unbelievers upon the Lord.' (p. 146)

Velasco's initial response is to seek to 'exorcize this voice' (p. 146), but the more he resists, the more he is brought face to face with its stark reality. At the same time, he is increasingly subjected both to 'a searing pain in his chest' and also to 'a voice laughing' at him, two more common symbols in Endō's *oeuvre* of conscious manifestations of the pangs of the unconscious. It is around this time, however, that Velasco is obliged to defend his mission in the face of a concerted attack from Father Valente, representative of the Jesuit order that stands between Velasco and his ambition to receive appointment as Bishop of Japan. To Father Valente, the issue is clear-cut, the divide between East and West unfathomable:

> The Japanese basically lack a sensitivity to anything that is absolute, to anything that transcends the human level, to the existence of anything beyond the realm of Nature: what we would call the supernatural....
>
> Their sensibilities are firmly grounded within the sphere of Nature and never take flight to a higher realm. Within the realm of Nature their sensibilities are remarkably delicate and subtle, but those sensibilities are unable to grasp anything on a higher plane. That is why the Japanese cannot conceive of our God, who dwells on a separate plane from man. (p. 163)

Significantly, the task of advocating a less than absolute divide – the potential for meaningful dialogue between East and West – is now left to Velasco, earlier symbol of Western intransigence. His earlier vision of a clear opposition is now clearly tempered, his vacillation increasing in direct proportion to the uncertainty manifested by Hasekura and the other envoys. Initial attempts to deny the existence of such wavering inevitably founder, his ambiguous feelings exemplified in his less than enthusiastic response to the baptism of the three remaining envoys, an occasion that, in theory at least, represents the fulfilment of all his prayers. Far from a surge of joy, Velasco experiences mixed emotions on this occasion:

> I was seized by the gnawing, hollow feeling that everything I had done was crashing down around me like an avalanche. I felt as though I were seeing before my very eyes all my labours come to naught, all my plans stripped of meaning, and everything I had believed in turning out to be solely for the sake of self-gratification. (p. 179)

Velasco is now approaching the point where he can no longer deny the existence of such instinctive, involuntary responses and such recognition comes in the acknowledgement of a growing sense of camaraderie with his travelling companions. The jealously guarded distance has now evaporated, to be replaced instead by recognition of a distinct empathy born of shared experience:

> This all seems very strange. Before we set out, and throughout the entire journey, I felt as though I were walking a different path from each of you. To be honest, it seemed as if we never communicated with one another. But tonight for the first time I feel somehow that we have all been bound together by a single cord. From now on you and I will be pelted by the same rains, buffeted by the same winds, and we will walk side by side down the same path. (p. 184)

A diary entry of that time reveals a similar bond:

> It was as though a friendship had at last been forged between the betrayed and the forsaken – a mutual sympathy and a mutual licking of wounds. I felt an affinity with those Japanese that I cannot describe. It was as if a firm bond of solidarity that I had never felt before had formed between the envoys and myself. To be honest, I had employed many stratagems up until then, dragging them about by the nose to achieve my own private purposes and taking advantage of their weaknesses....That icy distance that once separated us seemed to exist no longer. (p. 186)

Such emotions may strike Velasco as 'strange' at the conscious level but, hounded by an awareness of the pain and suffering his reckless ambition has caused to others, Velasco at this point is almost ready to beg the envoys' forgiveness. And it is only now, having experienced the pain of humiliation and defeat, that he is able to act as bearer of true love in a way that had been denied to Father Velasco, the confident emissary of the Christian gospel depicted at the outset of the novel.

The distance already travelled by Velasco in his journey of self-discovery is considerable and, once more, this increased understanding, both of his fellow travellers and of himself, is deliberately juxtaposed on to a similar *rapprochement* that occurs, during the course of the novel, between Velasco and his God. His ambition now largely dissipated, Velasco now finds himself pleading, as miserable sinner yet confident in his new-found belief that this is the will of God, that the Council of Bishops authorise his return to Japan.

In keeping with the model established with Rodrigues, there are, inevitably, still those occasions when Velasco manifests outward signs of despairing of God's presence alongside him, most poignant being the entry in his diary as the mission beats a weary retreat across the Atlantic:

> 'It is all...because of Thee. If Thou hadst not brought about such a result, our voyage home would have been filled with joy, and the ship would have rung with the voices of Japanese singing hymns to Thy praise. But Thou didst not desire that. Thou chosest to forsake Japan.' (p. 207)

Far from focusing on Velasco in the depths of despair, however, the narrative at this stage highlights the cathartic effect of such an honest admission – and within a page of recording such concerns, Velasco is driven to acknowledge:

> When I finished writing the letters, my heart was strangely at ease. The realization that the flames of passion which had been my reason for living had now burned themselves out brought me a tranquillity I had not known since our departure from Rome. (p. 208)

The transition effected at this point is clearly depicted in far less dramatic terms than those attributed to Rodrigues as he confronts the *fumie*. The effect on the character concerned, however, is equally marked. The Velasco to emerge from this confrontation with seemingly overwhelming despondency possesses a renewed faith that, whilst still a far cry from the orthodoxy traditionally associated with his religious order, manifests a concern for fellow humans that is rooted in genuine empathy. Examples of the reinvigorated Velasco less concerned with the dictates of his order than with his desire to stand alongside the envoys in times of need now come to proliferate, his release from the straitjacket of rigid dogma nowhere more apparent than in his response to the suicide of Tanaka, who succumbs to the outward failure of the mission. Velasco's justification of his decision to accord Tanaka the trappings of Christian respectability is telling:

> The Church does not allow the sacrament for the dead to be performed for those who take their own lives. But at that moment I no longer cared about the regulations of the Church. I knew the anguish of Tanaka's journey. I knew

what had been in the hearts of Tanaka and Hasekura and Nishi as they persevered with their hopeless mission. (p. 213)

The effect of this and other depictions of the caring Velasco is pronounced, their role in preparing the narrative ground for the missionary's ultimate act of empathy – his decision to forsake the relative security of Luzon for certain capture and death in Japan – highly influential. Seen as a 'rational' response to the impulse towards self-preservation, Velasco's decision can only be portrayed as illogical. Far from an impulsive, unconsidered act, however, the resolve is clearly justified – not at the level of conscious reasoning but as an equally convincing response to unfathomable, yet undeniable promptings from the unconscious. Such justification is paradoxically enhanced by Velasco's inability to comprehend his own impulse:

> 'Japan. The storms of persecution have raged, and you exhibit only enmity towards God. Then why am I drawn to you? Why do I seek to return to you?' (p. 246)

Velasco's willingness to obey such impulses in defiance of his own conscious reasoning is now absolute, the consequent portrayal of integrity correspondingly enhanced. His reaction to his subsequent, inevitable arrest provides perfect testimony to this renewed positive approach to his circumstances:

> I shall calmly accept this fate which God has ordained, just as a fruit absorbs the mellow light of autumn. I no longer consider my own imminent death a defeat....Soon another missionary will stand on the stepping-stone that is me, and he will become the next stepping-stone....
>
> I feel as though the Lord gave me all those setbacks so that He could force me to look this reality in the face. It is as though my vanity, my pride, my haughtiness, and my thirst for conquest all existed for the purpose of shattering everything that I had idealized, so that I could see the true state of the world. (pp. 252, 254)

Armed with such renewed conviction, Velasco can display an optimism that belies his current miserable circumstances. Neither the death in agony of Father Vasquez, the Dominican priest awaiting execution with Velasco, nor the arrival of Father Carvalho, whose mere affiliation to the Jesuit order would have been sufficient to arouse the ire of the earlier Velasco, can shake such new-found hope. The self-depiction in the final testament Velasco writes from his cell is testimony to the distance the missionary has placed between his current self and the ever-confident man depicted at the outset of the novel:

> With each passing moment now I sense my final hour pressing in upon me. Blessed be God, who sends the rains of love upon this rocky, barren land. I hope that each of you will also forgive me my sins. I committed many errors in the course of my life. Like an ineffectual man who tries to resolve everything with one single effort, I now await my martyrdom. May God's will be done in the trackless lands of Japan just as His will is done in Heaven. (p. 263)

The ground for such new-found serenity in the face of martyrdom has been carefully prepared, explicit textual acknowledgement of the missionary's enhanced capacity for love essential to an understanding of the final section of the novel. Taken at face value, Velasco's reaction to news that the envoys, Hasekura and Nishi, have been executed ('a smile of delight appeared on Velasco's blanched lips' (p. 266)) would appear remarkably reminiscent of the initial, stereotyped Velasco. Far from a display of pity for the poor, innocent pawns condemned to death for embracing a baptism for which he was directly responsible and which he had always recognised as expedient, here is Velasco seemingly oblivious to the destiny of his companions. By now, however, the paradox has been exposed, enabling Velasco's smile to be interpreted, not as a sign of callousness, but of joy at the realisation that their faith had indeed taken root and delight both at the strength and boldness of their witness and the anticipation evident in his response, 'Now I can join them' (p. 266).

The image of Velasco as he walks to the stake, therefore, is of a man convinced that in accepting his fate, he is conforming to the will of God. The portrayal is important for, in emphasising the self-conviction manifest by the missionary to the end, the narrative provides powerful evidence that, for all the distance he has indubitably travelled in his journey of self-discovery, Velasco remains fundamentally unchanged: there is a consistency of portrayal here that, whilst accommodating growth, retains the essence behind the public facade. The effect conforms to the model discussed in the Introduction to this study: Velasco has not suddenly and unconvincingly been endowed with qualities which he did not possess at the outset of the novel. Instead, the very qualities initially cited as signs of weakness – single-minded determination, blind ambition, etc. – have come to be seen as the source of his ultimate salvation. The transposition of Velasco from figure of ridicule to powerful witness is now complete, the symbolic fusion of the traditional opposition between strength and weakness thereby effectively sealed. The process is precisely that as depicted by Gessel:

> There is a different reward, one filled with anguish and humiliation, that Endō's God offers to those who can strip themselves of the ego that surrounds them like a protective shield. When they abase themselves and share the burdens of another human being, God shatters His silence and speaks, using the lives of those individuals as the instrument of communication.[29]

The comment encapsulates the process of individuation upon which Velasco is engaged. For Hasekura, the psychological direction in which he is travelling may differ; the end result, however, is remarkably similar. Let us turn then to consideration of the journey towards greater self-realisation as undertaken by the samurai.

As noted above, initial portrayals of Hasekura content with his lot in the marshlands appear uncompromising. Following the shattering of this tranquillity with the order for him to participate in the mission to the West, however, it is not long before some of the painful lessons he is obliged to confront begin the process of shattering his early sense of security. Not surprisingly, primary instigator in the fundamental reassessment of human nature that is forced upon the samurai is Velasco, whose apparently contradictory behaviour is a source of increasing confusion to Hasekura. One moment, he appears to have the interests of others entirely at heart – as, for example, when he voluntarily shares his own dry clothes with those whose own provisions have been saturated in a storm. The next moment, however, he is 'watching with composure' (p. 80) as one of the sailors is flogged as punishment for stealing a watch and several pieces of gold from the captain's cabin. As the narrator observes at this juncture:

> The samurai could not bring himself to believe that this Velasco and the Velasco who had shared his clothing with Yozō were one and the same man. (p. 80)

Already, Hasekura is betraying signs of awareness of a division within the priest – of a greater complexity to his being than was initially apparent. Thereafter, the more the two men keep each other's company, the more the samurai's uncertainty as to Velasco's true intentions intensifies. On one issue, however, Hasekura remains steadfast: the Christ whom Velasco invokes at every opportunity remains a distant concept, one with which he has neither the desire nor the ability to empathise. It is in these terms that the significance of the contribution of the renegade monk the envoys encounter in the hamlet of Tecali is best appreciated.

Overwhelmed by Velasco's portrayal of Christ as a figure of awe and majesty and confused by the seeming discrepancy between this and the pitiful images of Christ on the cross that he actually encounters on his travels, Hasekura's inability to reconcile the two is hardly surprising. Such equivocation, however, only serves to heighten the force of the alternative interpretation offered by the monk as he seeks to account for his continuing adherence to the creed despite his public disavowal of the faith. Pressed by the envoys to account for this apparent inconsistency, he explains:

> I don't believe in the Christianity the padres preach....
> I believe in my own Jesus. My Jesus is not to be found in the palatial cathedrals. He lives among these miserable Indians. (p. 120)

The image of the intensely personal relationship with Christ is clearly reminiscent of that to which so many of the earlier Endō protagonists had aspired, its effect on the confused samurai immediate. Not only does the monk's portrayal of a weak but compassionate Christ cast an element of doubt on to the previously unquestioned depictions routinely offered by Velasco, to date the samurai's only source of information on the subject, it also inspires a telling reappraisal of the nature of his own journey. The blind obedience to his lord's wishes that previously had represented his sole motivation is here being challenged for the first time, his consequent assertion that 'this is a journey we have to make' and his realisation 'that he had changed' (p. 122) suggesting a growing acceptance of unconscious promptings that represent an equally powerful guiding force behind his actions.

Armed with this alternative evaluation of the significance of the figure on the crucifix, Hasekura comes to show increasing signs of vacillation, his confusion augmented by his continuing inability to 'understand why he had become so obsessed with that emaciated man with both hands nailed to a cross' (p. 176). On the one hand, he starts to be troubled by the inevitable alternative 'voice', the voice of temptation attempting to convince him of the innocuous nature of an expedient acceptance of the faith: 'To help your mission, and to help your friends, why can't you become a Christian just for appearance's sake?' (p. 170). Equally powerful, however, is the voice of rational consideration, the reluctance to abandon all that his life in the marshlands of Japan had embodied, which argues:

> 'I...I have no desire to worship you,' he murmured almost apologetically. 'I can't even understand why the foreigners respect you. They say you died bearing the sins of mankind, but I can't see that our lives have become any easier as a result. I know what wretched lives the peasants lead in the marshland. Nothing has changed just because you died.' (p. 173)

The conflict is disturbing, the desire to convince himself that 'this is not me...this is not how I really feel inside' (p. 177) indicative of a man struggling to come to terms with the contents of his unconscious being. Once more, the portrayal is reminiscent of a string of earlier Endō protagonists who, confronted with harsh, inner realities, engage in a desperate, and ultimately forlorn, battle to deny the very existence of such sentiments. And once more, the narrative focus is directed, very specifically, on the inherent paradox of the situation: the fact that the samurai's increasingly undeniable interest in the 'alien' creed is born, not of a growing fascination with its physical embodiments, but of an enduring, and unmistakable, lack of interest in, even aversion to, its substance. For all the above-mentioned vacillation, therefore, Hasekura continues studiously to distance himself from all Velasco's attempts at persuasion, his antipathy towards the crucifixes that appear to confront him at every step if anything intensified in direct proportion to the lure to which he is increasingly subjected from his unconscious.

The impression of a widening rift between different levels of the samurai's being as he continues his journey is pronounced, the tension augmented by inclusion of parallel sections devoted to Velasco's perspective in which the missionary's growing confidence in the ultimate success of the mission is relentlessly addressed. The indirect effect induced by these passages, suggesting as they do a distinct evolution in the samurai's approach to Christianity without recourse to specific depictions of the changing workings of his mind, is powerful, with the result that Hasekura's eventual decision to accept baptism in Spain retains the aura of improbability that distinguishes it from a rational, conscious resolve. Viewed as a response to Velasco's persistent entreaties, interpretation of Hasekura's change of heart may indeed appear as an improbable climb-down, the question of his apparently abrupt capitulation to the faith to which he had maintained a seemingly constant aversion never satisfactorily addressed. Missing from such reservations, however, is a recognition of the distance already travelled by the samurai at a deeper level and of his increasing affinity with the being introduced to him by Velasco but radically transformed in his mind by the quiet portrayal offered by the monk in Tecali.

The outward protestations of disinterestedness persist, however, and even following the baptism service (at which his public avowal of belief is juxtaposed with repeated attempts to convince himself that 'this is not from [the] heart – it is for the sake of [the] mission' (p. 175)), the outward determination to disavow all connection with 'that man' continues. Interspersed between these self-assessments, however, runs the voice of more objective reason, a narrative voice that argues tellingly:

> If this truly was a mere formality, there was no need to keep repeating the same words to himself over and over again. (p. 176)

The *rapprochement* is by now well advanced; all that remains is for Hasekura to come to a conscious recognition of a greater significance to this act than mere expediency. In the narrative that follows, this is mirrored in the increasing concern the samurai directs at his fellow travellers and, in particular, at his ever-loyal retainer, Yozō. More specifically, Hasekura's acceptance of stark reality is embodied in his growing acknowledgement of the steadfastness of his retainer as his ever-constant companion – and the corresponding narrative identification of Yozō with the 'personal' Christ as extolled by the monk at Tecali. The more Hasekura comes to recognise in his servant an inner strength and constancy after which he himself is hankering, the more the image of Yozō as *dōhansha* (man's constant companion) is enhanced. As the samurai sets out, more in desperation than in expectation, for his meeting with the Pope, this quality is duly recognised in the narrative:

> In his present state of despair, forsaken and betrayed from all quarters, the samurai felt that this servant who had attended him faithfully since childhood was the only man he could trust. (p. 202)

During the course of the subsequent abject return to Japan, such fusion of Yozō with the image of Christ is augmented by the deliberately restrained depiction of the relationship between servant and master. In so doing, the image of the retainer, not merely as physical but also as spiritual *dōhansha* is enhanced. Before the samurai is in a position to acknowledge this trait, however, he is still in need of more explicit reassurance. Once more, it is the monk at Tecali who provides the required exegesis – in attempting to account for the paradoxical need for Christ to be portrayed as a figure of misery:

> Because He was ugly and emaciated, He knew all there was to know about the sorrows of this world. He could not close His eyes to the grief and agony of mankind. That is what made Him emaciated and ugly....Do you think He is to be found within those garish cathedrals? He does not dwell there. He lives...not within such buildings. I think He lives in the wretched homes of these Indians....He sought out only the ugly, the wretched, the miserable and the sorrowful. But now even the bishops and priests here are complacent and swollen with pride. (pp. 220–1)

Hasekura's explicit response to this explanation is to maintain a due scepticism. By now, however, the earlier attitude of outright dismissal has clearly mellowed, his subconscious concern betrayed by the fact that 'for the first time the samurai asked the question in earnest' (p. 220). As a result of such narrative subversion, the samurai's repeated protestations that he 'can get by without thinking about Him' (p. 221) are reduced in plausibility. Nevertheless, true to the tradition of emboldening the weakling, it is only following his return to Japan – and rejection by the very authorities who had sent him – that Hasekura is able to fully identify with this being, powerless yet compassionate.

Already, as Hasekura steps ashore after some four years at sea, there is ample evidence that all is not well politically. The reception accorded the returning mission is decidedly muted, attempts to debrief the envoys in the hope thereby of gaining political advantage over neighbouring domains non-existent. For several months, however, the samurai remains oblivious, not only to the implications of this absence of curiosity, but also to the change effected on his inner being. Thereafter, in typical paradoxical manner, it is at the very moment when he starts to comply with his lord's command that he destroy the various Christian artefacts he has accumulated along the way that the truth finally dawns and he comes explicitly to acknowledge a degree of affinity with the haggard figure of Christ he had seen so often on his journey:

> Again the samurai closed his eyes and pictured the man who had peered down at him each night from the walls of his rooms in Nueva España and España. For some reason he did not feel the same contempt for him he had felt before. In fact it seemed as though that wretched man was much like himself as he sat abstractedly beside the hearth. (p. 242)

The carefully crafted distance the narrative had always placed between the samurai and 'that man' is now finally eroded, the admission of a relationship far deeper than anything he had previously envisaged accompanied by a parallel recognition of all that 'that man' had taught him:

> [The monk in Tecali] had wanted an image of 'that man' which was all his own. He had wanted not the Christ whom the affluent priests preached in the cathedrals of Nueva España, but a man who would be at his side, and beside the Indians, each of them forsaken by others. 'He is always beside us. He listens to our agony and our grief. He weeps with us'....The samurai could almost see the face of the man who had scribbled these clumsy letters. (p. 243)

The image is now vivid, but in the ensuing narrative this assumes the form, not of a portrayal of Hasekura fired by a burning desire to emulate Velasco, but rather at his most content when in the presence of his ever-faithful retainer. At the same time comes explicit acknowledgement of the fusion that has occurred in his own mind between Yozō and the man whose presence in his life he can no longer deny:

> The samurai was suddenly struck by the impression that his loyal servant's profile resembled that man's. That man, like

Yozō, had hung his head as though enduring all things. 'He is always beside us. He listens to our agony and our grief'.... Yozō had never abandoned his master – not now or ever in the past. (p. 245)

The transposition of Christ from figure of awe and splendour into a being who can respond directly to the yearning 'in the hearts of men for someone who will be with you throughout your life, someone who will never betray you, never leave you – even if that someone is just a sick, mangy dog' (p. 245) by means of a corresponding reappraisal of the narrative contribution of Yozō is now complete. The latter is now invested with a strength that enables him to reassure his master even as the latter is led away for execution ('From now on,...He will attend you' (p. 262)), his membership of the category of 'hidden saints', which Gessel sees as integral to Endō's art, now firmly secured. The following portrayal could have been written with Yozō specifically in mind:

> Weaving their uncertain way among these calloused, uncaring figures are the 'hidden' saints – those who are failures in the eyes of society but unqualified successes in the areas that really count for Endō: in the expressions of tenderness and concern for the pain of others.[30]

The question of Hasekura's reaction to the cruel fate that awaits him remains unclear, however – portrayal of the scene in which Nishi and he embrace death deliberately avoided. Only indication that the samurai is now able to share the conviction expressed by his loyal servant comes in the portrayal of the former as he 'stopped, looked back and nodded his head emphatically' (p. 262). The scene is depicted with typical Endō restraint, the consequence of such lack of explicit detail being to shift the narrative focus away from the question of how he ultimately responds to the boundless potential with which he is now endowed. Just as, in *Silence*, the narrative avoids reference to the ultimate fate of the Japanese peasants in the pit whose release is potentially secured with Rodrigues' act of apostasy, so here the issue of primary literary concern is not Hasekura's actual response in the face of death, but rather the strength of character that he now visibly evidences and that keeps alive the possibility of death as a martyr. Having driven his protagonist *in extremis*, the sole concern of Endō's narrator at this juncture rests solely with the *potential* for self-determination with which the samurai is now invested, his *actual* reaction at the moment of death consequently scrupulously avoided.

For all the narrative restraint, however, the portrayal of Hasekura finally united in death with Velasco provides invaluable support to the image of two men entirely acceptant of their inevitable destiny, not as a result of any dramatic change of heart, but simply through recognition of their own human weakness and their equally human need for a companion figure. The true nature of the journey upon which both are engaged – a psychological journey in which both are forced to confront their own Shadow being in the form of the voice of their unconscious – is thereby underscored, the initial perception of unfathomable distance between the two now entirely eroded. As both have journeyed towards the Self, both have come to confront a new dimension to their being and, in so doing, have been drawn inexorably closer to each other.

As Jung would have predicted, the process of reconciliation has not been devoid of pain; both men have inevitably striven to resist the subliminal voice that appeared to encourage them to act in ways that could never be sanctioned through logical reasoning. In ultimately coming to acknowledge the futility of such resistance, each may simply be bowing to the inevitable. In so doing, however, both men implicitly acknowledge this as an integral part of the process of individuation upon which each is engaged. The significance of this evolution within Endō's evolving literary world cannot be overstated, the influence it can bring to bear on our reading of *Scandal*, to be discussed in the next chapter, equally hard to exaggerate.

6
SCANDAL

Doppelgänger... so heissen Leute, die sich selbst sehen.
(Jean Paul Richter)

Just as we all have a 'kagebōshi', so we all have a self which we don't show to anyone, whether we are conscious of this or not. This other self is our Shadow. In public, we cover ourselves up. It is normal that, when dealing with others, we exercise the necessary social morality and common sense in order not to offend – and, taking this one step further, we make every effort to advance ourselves. But inside this self which we consciously create lurks another self. This is the suppressed self of which Freud speaks. But Jung thinks of this rather as our self as a work of reparation. In other words, it is an additional self quietly seeking to provide support to those areas lacking in our conscious being. It is this that Jung labeled the Shadow.
(Endō Shūsaku)

The Devil! He's taken to visiting me. He's an impostor.... But *he* is me, Alyosha, *me*! All that is base, rotten, and contemptible in me!
(*The Brothers Karamazov*)

The Samurai was immediately acknowledged by Endō's critics both at home and abroad. In Japan, the novel was awarded the Noma Prize for Literature, a conferral that represented the last of the major domestic literary awards for which Endō was eligible. The English translation that appeared some two years later met with an equally favourable reception, sales for the work soon placing it in contention for the accolade of 'best selling work of Japanese fiction in English translation'.[1]

For Endō, however, there was no let-up in the frenetic pace of creativity, a brief examination of a list of the author's major literary achievements during the early 1980s revealing a constant stream of publications in the wake of the success of *The Samurai*. In addition, election as chairman of the Japan PEN Club in June 1985 brought with it considerable added responsibilities – responsibilities towards the younger generation of Japanese authors, which to the end Endō continued to take extremely seriously. And yet, by the author's own admission, this was also 'a time of transition', a period during which he sought 'a new direction' for his literature.[2]

The result, as noted earlier, was a concerted study of the writings of Jung – and publication, in 1985, of two works born of this reading. Neither *Watashi no aishita shōsetsu* (A Novel I Have Loved) nor *Hontō no watashi o motomete* (In Search of the Real Me) received much critical attention at the time. As precursors to the author's next major work of creative fiction, *Scandal*, published in March of the following year, however, both offer valuable insights into the narrative approach adopted in *Scandal* and, as such, are of considerable interest to the critic for whom this latest novel represents, not some 'radical, new departure',[3] but rather a natural progression, building on the examination of the human composite so integral to the earlier novels.[4]

For the casual reader of *Scandal*, any connection with the author's previous novels may indeed appear tenuous. Far from the intense focus in the earliest works on the potential for redemption for those apparently separated by an unfathomable gulf from the rest of humanity and the more overt examination, in *Silence* and *The Samurai*, of Japan as the 'mudswamp' in which the seed of Christianity appears to struggle in its attempts to take root, here, it would seem, was the abrupt transition that the author had been seeking. Here, it would seem, was the shift in emphasis of which the author spoke so frequently during the 1980s, a move evidenced, not merely in terms of the subject material involved but, more significantly, in terms of development of the jealously preserved author–narrator–protagonist paradigm that must needs represent the core of the author's narrative strategy.

As suggested by the discussion to date, however, all attempts to remove this work from the continuum within Endō's *oeuvre* are fraught with difficulty, the depiction of *Scandal* as representing a 'radical, new departure' masking the continued and more concerted attention afforded by this novel to examination of the forces at work in the human unconscious. It is in this light, as the most complete examination to date of the 'living chaos'[5] at work within each of Endō's creations, that the novel *Scandal* will be considered in this chapter.

In the preceding chapters, much has been made of Endō's relentless scrutiny of the human duality. In *Scandal*, this is incorporated into the very structure of the work – in the person of Suguro, a 'Catholic author' approaching the end of a distinguished literary career, who is identified from the outset as protagonist of the novel. The choice is highly significant: in choosing deliberately to locate his fictional construct in territory traditionally assigned to himself, the author appears intent on locating this work within the remit of 'third-person autobiography' through the establishment of the very 'author–reader pact' that, as noted in the Introduction, has been cited by Philippe Lejeune as integral to the form.[6] At the same time, however, as we shall see, there is an element of subversion at play here, a parody of the *shishōsetsu* form of self-referential narrative, born of the overt emphasis on the potential which this affords him for self-satirisation.

To a readership in Japan privy to an inordinate amount of autobiographical detail concerning the author as a result of constant media attention, the Suguro portrayed in the opening pages as he sets out to receive yet another prestigious literary award, represented none other than Endō's fictional double. Readers who proceeded to read the entire ensuing narrative as some form of literary atonement by an author resolved to expose his 'true' identity were, however, in for a rude awakening. For, from the moment Suguro is disturbed by the appearance of a man, seemingly identical in every physical detail to the protagonist himself, leering at him from the back of the auditorium, Suguro is reduced to an increasingly frenzied state of self-doubt. Attempts to confront this 'impostor' lead Suguro to experience the seamier side of Tokyo's Kabuki-chō, with its seemingly inexhaustible supply of scandal-mongerers bent on destroying the reputation of this popular novelist through exposure of his less salubrious pleasure pursuits. And the more Suguro struggles to uncover and expose the 'truth' concerning this 'impostor', the more he finds his destiny tied up with those who seek his downfall.

The consequent probing of the psychological drama experienced by Suguro is persistent. Thereafter, no doubt inspired by such critical response to view the novel as a thinly disguised autobiographical confession, many would appear subsequently to have felt justified in rushing off to Kabuki-chō in search of Endō's secret haunts![7] What such a reading fails to acknowledge, however, is the carefully crafted and jealously guarded narrative distance that separates Endō both from his ever-complicit narrator and from his hapless protagonist. Through skilful manipulation of the potential with which creation of this literary *alter ego* has presented him for examination of the composite being, the author affords himself a unique opportunity for analysing his literary material, not as belonging to the external world, but as stemming from his own deep consciousness. The result is a literary depiction of the doppelgänger, one that Susan Napier cites in support of her claim that, for all the proliferation of ghosts and monsters in contemporary Japanese literature, 'increasingly, in the modern period, the really monstrous is located inside the self, a feared alter ego'.[8] As Napier points out, a creature of this kind represents 'less a menace to society (although it may be that as well) than a threat to the person it inhabits or to the people immediately around him or her'[9] – and it is significant for the purposes of this discussion that it is to *Scandal* that she turns for 'perhaps the most negative portrayal of the alien within the postwar period'.[10] Let us begin our discussion of the novel, then, with a consideration of the nature of the relationship between Suguro and his 'menacing' double.

The development of Suguro's double during the course of the novel is marked. It first appears at the ceremony at which Suguro is presented with a literary prize for his latest work of fiction – in the guise of 'his own face [wearing]...an expression that could be taken either as a grin or sneer',[11] which Suguro sees at the back of the auditorium during the course of his acceptance speech. But when the image disappears as quickly as it had appeared, the entire incident is immediately dismissed at the textual level as either a chance look-alike or as an optical illusion rooted in the protagonist's own feelings of self-satisfaction. The more prominent the role occupied by Suguro's double becomes, however, the more Endō's narrator appears to challenge such interpretations. With events increasingly enveloped in mystery and no longer answerable to a logical train of thought, the contrast between Suguro and his *alter ego* comes to be blurred, his initial conviction that 'the donning of a different face did not entail artifice of any kind, nor did it connote play-acting or hypocrisy' (p. 28) increasingly subject to scrutiny.

Concern at confrontation with his physical double serves to pique Suguro's professional interest in coming to a closer understanding of the 'inner being' of his creations and the ensuing novel can be read as a literary consideration of the three psychological strategies – suppression, denial and integration – that are available to Suguro in the circumstances. Suguro to date, the Suguro who had attracted an avid and devoted readership as a 'Christian author', had tended to believe only what he saw. Faced with this new reality, he is forced to do more than judge merely on external appearances. At this moment, a chance meeting with the Freudian psychologist, Professor Tōno, provides the protagonist an ideal opportunity to explore the subject in greater detail. But Tōno's description of the phenomenon is deeply disturbing to Suguro:

> A *doppelgänger* or a ghost double...[is] not all that frequent, but there've been two or three reports of the phenomenon at medical conferences. One patient, who was suffering from tympanitis, became neurotic and began to experience auditory hallucinations. He saw himself lying down in front of his own eyes. It was his own corpse lying before him, as I understand it.
>
> [The *doppelgängers* are usually] suffering from neuroses ....They seem to be accompanied by fairly extended spells of insomnia, abnormal body temperature, body-image agnosia, and loss of mental faculties. (p. 139)

Mulling over Tōno's definition, Suguro comes increasingly to acknowledge the existence of a relationship between himself and his double much closer than his earlier conclusions would have countenanced. At this stage, however, the protagonist still seeks to play down the significance of the initial appearance of his double during the course of his speech, trying to convince himself that:

> The figure he had seen from the lectern could have been a hallucination. If not a hallucination, then a vile prank perpetrated by the impostor. It had to be one or the other of these two options. (p. 141)

Already, however, in acknowledging that Suguro is obliged to 'nudge himself towards that conclusion' (p. 141), the text provides ample evidence that Suguro is wavering in his conviction. Nevertheless, despite having come to doubt his original assumptions, Suguro remains incapable of identifying an alternative explanation and it is only when confronted with the sight of his 'double' taking advantage of the innocence of Mitsu, the young girl he had earlier employed to clean his office, that he is in a position to offer a reassessment.

The scene is carefully orchestrated by Madame Naruse, a woman whose 'split' identity as a confirmed sado-masochist who has nevertheless succeeded, at the same time, in earning a reputation as a most caring and sensitive hospital volunteer, provides her with a unique vantage point from which to seek to influence Suguro's understanding of events. As Suguro stands with his eye to the peep-hole in the cupboard in the hotel room to which he has been lured by Madame Naruse with the express purpose of introducing the protagonist to the 'urges in his unconscious' (p. 211), he tries desperately to distance himself from the image of this 'impostor'. For all his incredulity, however, he is unable to tear his eye away from the peep-hole and increasingly he finds himself 'bec[oming] one with the man' (p. 216). As the jangling telephone summons him back to reality, therefore, far from outright dismissal, Suguro is obliged to conclude:

> It couldn't have been [an illusion]. It was all too clear and vivid in his memory. He could no longer call it an illusion, as he had at the prizegiving and the lecture-hall....
>
> What he had seen through the peep-hole had been no illusion, no nightmare....That had been no stranger, no pretender. It had been Suguro himself. It had been *another side of himself, a separate self altogether*. He could no longer conceal that part of himself, no longer deny its existence. (pp. 219, 221, my emphasis)

But even this conclusion is not entirely free of ambiguity: the desire to dismiss the phenomenon as 'a separate self altogether' has not entirely receded. Suguro has nevertheless travelled a long way from his initial terror at seeing the 'impostor' in the auditorium – although significantly, such fear has been replaced, not by relief at the exposure of his double as a fraud, but rather by recognition of a relationship between the two that, in its complexity and intimacy, serves to induce within Suguro a radical reconsideration of human nature. The more he comes to admit the futility of continued pursuit of a physical double, the more he is obliged to acknowledge the fundamentally symbiotic relationship that lies at the core of the human drama. The discovery is hard-earned, the true implications for Suguro only fully identified at the conclusion of the novel – in the scene in which Suguro is informed by his ever-supportive publisher that he has purchased and destroyed some potentially ruinous photographs of Suguro and Mitsu taken by Kobari, the unrelenting journalist in search of a 'scoop' that will destroy Suguro's reputation as a 'Christian author' once and for all. By this stage, the narrative is explicit:

> The photograph and negative had been reduced to ashes. But that man had not been burned to death along with them. He continued to live inside Suguro. With his sneering smile. (p. 234)

An act that was designed to resolve all the problems and appears, initially, to have succeeded in this aim has served, rather, to bring Suguro one step closer to recognition of alternative facets to his being.

Reference has already been made, towards the end of Chapter 1, to Keppler's study of the literature of what he defines as 'the second self' – and the suggestion made that the relationship between Suguro and the shadowy figure who continues to haunt the protagonist in *Scandal* conforms closely to the template Keppler establishes for such works. The question to be addressed at this point, then, is the extent to which, in depicting the protagonist locked in seemingly irresolvable conflict with this figure, Endō's narrator succeeds in establishing the two as 'an inescapable two that are at the same time an indisputable one'.[12] Concomitant to this is the extent to which the process set in motion by the appearance of this alter ego does indeed result in 'a reconciliation of absolute irreconcilables'.[13]

To Keppler, the relationship between the two is inviolable. In contrast to the first self, who tends to remain in the foreground of the reader's perspective and believes himself to be the whole self, the second self represents 'an intruder from the background of shadows', an elusive existence who, regardless of the prominence he may ultimately attain, remains 'half-shadowed'.[14] At the same time, he is 'surrounded by an aura of the uncanny that sometimes makes him seem to belong to a different order of reality from that of the world in which he moves, so that the first self may almost fancy his counterpart to be the product of his own mind'.[15]

We are talking here, then, of more than a Jekyll and Hyde scenario in which the mechanics of the situation make it impossible that the two will ever separate, let alone confront each other – in which the very presence of the 'other' as an external, independent existence is explicitly ruled out. To Keppler, a double of this sort, while sharing 'a basic psychical identity with the first self,...lacks any convincing simultaneous identity of its own'. It is, in short, too subjective; it is '"self", but not "second"'.[16] At the same time, however, as the narrative unfurls, so increasingly it comes to challenge the suggestion that what we have here is little more than mere physical duplication – that which Keppler categorises as an 'objective second self' in which the double 'possesses external reality, clearly independent of the first self, but lacks any sort of inward linkage or continuity with the latter; it is "second", but not "self"'.[17]

Keppler's definition is useful – and examination of the preceding paragraphs reveals a degree of conformity in the case of the novel *Scandal* that serves to counter the argument, raised by several critics, that, with the identity of the double shrouded in mystery until the end, the conclusion of the novel is altogether too '*aimai*' (vague).[18] The figure who appears to Suguro at the back of the auditorium is indeed 'an intruder from the background of shadows', an elusive existence who remains 'half-shadowed'. The result, as already noted, is that Suguro does indeed 'fancy his counterpart to be the product of his own mind'.

The question of the identity of this double is clearly very real to Suguro, the temptation for the reader to search the text for explicit answers deliberately incited by the narrator. On this point, however, Keppler is insistent:

> The question may sometimes occur to us, as we read, whether if we knew all the facts we might decide he was all one thing or all the other, all physical duplicate or all hallucination; *but the question must never be answered; we must always be forced to keep a foot in the camp of either possibility.*[19]

The caveat is crucial to our understanding of *Scandal*. It is this quality of paradox that makes Suguro's double such a complicated figure to pin down. At the same time, it is this same quality that provides the relationship between the two with a reciprocity – in that both remain intent on unmasking the 'true' identity of the other – that would otherwise be lacking.

But where does this leave us? Does this being who continues to determine Suguro's course of action throughout the novel conform to Keppler's model of the second self as 'a logical impossibility…an always contradictory being, a paradox of simultaneous outwardness and inwardness, of difference from and identity with the first self'?[20] The question is perhaps best answered through consideration of the affinity that develops between Suguro and his double and of the ways in which the various manifestations of this affinity during the course of the narrative accord closely with the minimum prerequisites for a 'first self–second self relationship' as delineated by Keppler.

Of the various ways in which an affinity between the first and second selves may be manifest, Keppler begins with the presence of 'inexplicable emotional reactions to each other, usually antagonism'.[21] Immediately, similarities between this model and the relationship that develops between Suguro and his double are readily discernible. For from the moment Suguro detects the disturbing presence at the back of the auditorium, his response betrays all the hallmarks of one unable to fathom, let alone control his emotional reactions. The more he pursues this figure, the more elusive it becomes. As Madame Naruse and the others he encounters during the course of his search never fail to point out, however, Suguro displays little evidence of a desire to rationalise the situation: instead, his response is impulsive, the product of an outpouring of emotional anger induced by what he perceives as the audacity of his double in challenging his hitherto unsullied reputation.

Second in Keppler's list of the ways in which such an affinity is typically displayed is through 'an insistent preoccupation with each other that may be quite unwilled by either or even consciously willed against by both'.[22] Again, the portrayal appears to invite ready comparison with the situation enacted in *Scandal*, a novel whose narrative suspense derives almost entirely from Suguro's inability to divorce himself from concern for his reputation inspired by appearance of the double – and from the latter's persistent ability to hound the protagonist at the most inconvenient of moments. Suguro spends his time consciously willing against the appearance of his tormentor. Equally, however, there is a strong implication embedded within the narrative that the double, too, is a reluctant player in this drama: the suggestion is ever-present that if Suguro had not remained so determined to defend his hard-earned public reputation, none of the ensuing charade would have been required.

The next characteristic of the affinity traditionally established between first and second selves as cited by Keppler is 'intimate insight into each other's mind and soul, more often displayed by the second self but sometimes shared by both and to both incomprehensible'.[23] Here, too, applicability to the novel *Scandal* is pronounced. For it is the seeming ability of Suguro's double to fathom the recesses of Suguro's mind and consequently to make his appearances at those very moments when the protagonist is most susceptible to self-doubt that characterises the relationship between the two. First appearance of the double occurs at a reception held in Suguro's honour. More specifically, it is timed to occur at the very moment when Suguro is engrossed in his acceptance speech – and revelling in the adulation of friends and critics alike. He is at his most relaxed, his defences lowered. And it is at this moment, as if by instinct, that the double chooses to make his appearance. In the ensuing drama, the double reappears on frequent occasions. In each case, however, the timing appears deliberate. It is indeed as if he shares intimate insights into Suguro's psychology and is consequently in a position to cause maximum disruptive effect.

The fourth hallmark Keppler attributes to the first self–second self relationship is that of 'behavior to each other, or attitude toward each other, frequently as astonishing to them as it is to us'.[24] Again, comparisons with *Scandal* reveal the latter's close approximation to the template. Suguro's astonishment at the behaviour of his double requires little comment: that he is troubled by what he sees as an inexplicable phenomenon may be an entirely natural response. Of perhaps greater significance at this juncture is the extent to which the protagonist astonishes himself on occasion at his own reactions to the presence of his double. At the outset, Suguro can do little more than attempt to make some kind of sense of the appearance of his double and of the rumours about his private life that simultaneously begin circulating in the reception hall as a result of the comments offered by the woman claiming to have met him in Kabuki-chō. Time should, in theory, provide him with the opportunity to offer a more measured response. In practice, however, his subsequent behaviour, inspired by the determination to unmask the 'impostor', is punctuated by an uncharacteristic desperation. Aware of the potentially destructive direction that events appear to be following, he becomes increasingly powerless to control his response to conform to his hitherto unsullied reputation – and no-one is more surprised than Suguro himself.

By way of example, one need look no further than Suguro's response to the world of sado-masochism to which he is introduced by Madame Naruse. Troubled by the self-confessed fascination with 'an aesthetics of ugliness' (p. 160) of the various women with whom his life had become embroiled since the encounter with his double, Suguro consults his mentor, Professor Tōno. The latter's attempt to assuage the protagonist's burgeoning self doubt brooks little compromise:

> The fear that a child experiences when it leaves the uterus is extreme, and it lingers in the depths of its heart. That fear is never extinguished. Even after he grows to maturity, it remains a part of his unconscious mind. It is linked to the fear of death and, conversely, is also transferred into a profound longing to revert to the foetal state, to live once again within the amniotic fluids. Masochism just might be a deformation of this urge to subsist within the uterine waters. (p. 133)

To Suguro at this stage, the predilection for sado-masochism evidenced by these women appears as the perversion of a warped mind. The more his shadowed self adds to this sense of insecurity, however, the more he comes to visualise the frightening potentialities lurking within himself – and the more he astonishes himself in his response to his new-found companions. As long as Suguro continues in his attempts to convince himself of the need to hunt down and expose his physical double, such surprise at his own behaviour appears destined to continue. It is only when he is in a position to acknowledge his own 'irrational' actions as valid, as impossible to deny or even to ignore as any of his more carefully considered responses, that the element of astonishment can be removed.

The final characteristic Keppler identifies within the typical example of literature of the second self is that, in virtually all cases, it is the second self who appears, unexpected and uninvited, to initiate the subsequent drama. By definition, therefore, primary narrative focus will rest on the actions of the second self – and on the reactions of the first self. As Keppler suggests, 'we tend to be interested in what is *done by* the second self, and in what *happens to* (or within) the first self'.[25] This may be inevitable: we are more aware of the reactions of the first self, not necessarily because they are more important to us, but simply because the fact that they derive from the first or foreground self makes them more readily accessible. The fact nevertheless remains that, in *Scandal*, given the strong narratorial identification with Suguro, we are indeed privy to the actions of his double (if only as they impinge on the protagonist's consciousness), but the narrative momentum is driven by the persistent emphasis on Suguro's reactions to the situation in which he finds himself embroiled.

Before returning to consideration of the text of *Scandal* itself, however, there remains one further element of Keppler's study that should help our understanding of the relationship between Suguro and his double. From the outset, Keppler is at pains to stress that the relationship between the two selves may be anything from one of malevolence to misunderstood and resisted benevolence. Clearly, the former is the more usual – and in such cases, Keppler suggests that the 'evil' second self tends to assume the guise of either 'pursuer' or 'tempter'. Again, the description could have been written with the novel *Scandal* in mind. We shall return to consideration of the consequence of this pursuit later in this chapter. At this stage, however, let us bear in mind the suggestion that, in Keppler's estimation, remains implicit in all 'evil second selves':

> The combination of things that gives him his special power to victimize the first self – his terrifying alienness together with his no less terrifying familiarity, his unaccountable malice together with his unaccountable insight – is the same combination which characterizes the spirit of Evil by whatever name it is known, that superhuman force of darkness in the universe.[26]

The depiction captures the paradox of simultaneous identification and separateness embodied in all such relationships. It also serves to presage the conclusion, offered by Keppler towards the end of his study, that 'evil and darkness characterize only one side of the second self, which is counterbalanced by the side of goodness and light' and that this makes him an ideal 'instrument of self-exploration, self-realization, of expanded rather than contracted being'.[27] Here, in essence, is an encapsulation of the role assigned to Suguro's double in *Scandal*. His task is to make Suguro more aware of his own Self – and to accompany the insecure protagonist in his first tentative steps along the road to self-discovery and wholeness of self. Without this presence, Suguro would have remained possessed of his conviction that he had 'looked upon hideous things in all their hideousness' (p. 136), totally oblivious to the fact that, shut up in his study and absorbed in creation of his next literary 'success', he had unwittingly been obstructing the path to greater self-awareness. The double is integral to the process of individuation upon which Suguro is involved and, by the end of the novel, Suguro does indeed encounter his shadowed self – precisely in the shocking realisation that there is no true 'double' or 'impostor', merely his own personal unconscious. Seen thus, the experience of confronting his double has certainly 'yielded a great deal'. In the first chapter of this study, reference was made to Keppler's claim that, in the majority of such cases, some harm will inevitably ensue from the process. In *Scandal*, the 'harm' is clearly delineated. But, true to form, this is indeed 'a harm that stirs awake, that lances through the comfortable shell of self-complacency or self-protection, that strips away all masks of self-deception, that compels self-awareness and in the agony of the process brings self-enlargement'.[28]

The above discussion has portrayed Suguro as true to type for a first self troubled by the appearance of his second self. In *Scandal*, however, the scenario is further complicated by the presence of the journalist, Kobari, who, lacking that certain human tenderness evident even in Kichijirō in *Silence* and Nezumi in *Shikai no hotori* (Beside the Dead Sea, 1973), can be viewed as the first Endō character to be left unsaved – and who, in complementing the positive qualities with which Suguro is endowed, fulfils a function very similar to that of the double as initially identified by Suguro. Let us turn, then, to a discussion of the relationship between Suguro and Kobari and, in particular, to consideration of the role exercised by the latter as a further manifestation of Suguro's alter ego.

At the outset of the novel, the divide between the two men could not be more pronounced: the two are enmeshed in a battle of wits, with the careers of both men seemingly dependent upon exposure of the other. That there is more to this apparent animosity is to be inferred from the preceding consideration of the relationship between Suguro and the 'impostor' – and examination of the tie that comes to link Suguro and this other perceived tormentor reveals a connection between the two that accords, again with considerable fidelity, to Keppler's prerequisites for a first self–second self relationship. Here, again, is a relationship characterised by 'inexplicable emotional reactions' to each other, usually antagonistic in nature; by insistent and involuntary 'preoccupation' with each other; by 'intimate insights into each other's mind and soul'; and by behaviour or attitudes towards each other 'frequently as astonishing to them as it is to us'. Here, once more, is a classic example of a narrative in which the focus rests squarely on the actions of the one (Kobari) and the reactions of the other (Suguro). In sum, with Kobari, whose desire to unearth the 'real' Suguro is increasingly depicted as born, not of altruistic interest, but of his need to eradicate his own unfulfilled desires, we have a further classic example of the 'evil' second self as 'pursuer' and as 'tempter'.

Early indications that Suguro and Kobari are destined to emerge as more than conflicting elements of some binary opposition assume the form of the gradual erosion of the stereotype to which each character originally appears to have been assigned. Just as Suguro is increasingly exposed as a more 'complex' being than that of the persona that he had traditionally presented to his reading public, so Kobari is shown to be possessed of a variety of motivations and agendas – aspects of his being with which he has yet to be reconciled. The longer his claim of some 'scandal' surrounding Suguro remains unsubstantiated, the stronger the narrative implication that Kobari conforms to the Jungian model of resentment – and to Keppler's model for the second self: those qualities that he finds unattractive in Suguro appear increasingly to reflect those qualities he has sought to suppress within himself. The claim by Hina, one of the girls to whom he turns for information about Suguro, that, 'You've sniffed out an image of yourself in Mr. Suguro and you hate him for it' (p. 160) is initially strongly refuted by Kobari. In the ensuing scene, however, Kobari is portrayed as hounded by dreams of becoming the object of laughter and ridicule – and when this is juxtaposed on to a similar dream in which Suguro is dogged by the words of King Lear ('Pray, do not mock me: I am a very foolish fond old man' (p. 166)), the suggestion is reinforced that both men, for all their apparent occupation of opposing extremes of the spectrum, are actually linked in a symbiosis remarkably similar to that depicted as existing between Suguro and the 'impostor'. Both struggle to resist what appears to each as the promptings of the Devil. In the case of Suguro, the intervention of the Devil assumes the guise of his inordinate fear of death; for Kobari, such urgings only serve to exacerbate the inexplicable feelings of hatred he has come to nourish towards Suguro.

With the narrative distance between Suguro and Kobari increasingly brought into question, another dichotomy comes to be blurred. Kobari, initially convinced of the holiness of the crusade upon which he is embarked, is no longer possessed of any such conviction. And Suguro, whose primary concern at the beginning had focused on the potential damage that Kobari could inflict on his career, now comes to view himself, less as a victim of some malicious personal vendetta, more as embroiled in a psychological drama in which content takes precedence over outcome. In the process, the distinction between 'follower' and 'followed', initially so clear in the depiction of Kobari in pursuit of a 'scoop' concerning Suguro, becomes blurred and, as more and more Suguro appears intent upon pursuit of his inner self, so the assailed comes to be cast in the role of assailant. In like manner, as Suguro's determination to expose his double assumes ever-increasing intensity, so, too, does Kobari's sense of being manipulated, in true Jungian fashion, by Suguro's unconscious – hence his confession that he is unable to recognise the motivation for his actions. To be sure, the desire to expose what he views as Suguro's hypocrisy persists, but in a more positive sense, he is also clearly motivated by something intangible, a force he senses emanating from Suguro's double. Seen in this light, the novel can be represented as shown in the following terms:

```
              → Kobari →
           ↗              ↘
         ↗                  ↘
       ↗                      ↘
  Suguro's double  ← ← ← ←  Suguro
```

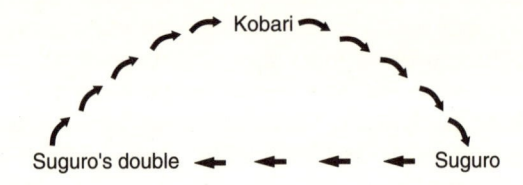

Figure 6.1

The picture of Suguro to have emerged from the preceding analysis is of a man conforming to the task that Jung assigned to the individual: 'If...a person wants to be cured it is necessary to find a way in which his conscious personality and his shadow can live together'.[29] In so doing, moreover, he comes to correspond closely to Jung's definition of the 'mature' being:

> The first half of life...is the period of life when the individual makes use of his 'superior' function to gain his ends...when the busy, successful man is so intent on his pursuit of wealth and power that he has no time to give to the cultivation of his inner life....It is about the mid-point of life that he must rediscover those aspects of himself which have been neglected.[30]

At the same time, however, as Christian, Suguro is possessed of a vision of God as creator of all mystery in the world, and his belief in a single integrated world created by an omnipotent God is subsequently applied to those with whom he comes into contact – with each human being seen as none other than a single, integrated whole. Again, the potential for absolute opposition is apparent: confronted by the varying manifestations of his double, Suguro is obliged to address the ultimate mystery – the realisation that maybe he is not unique after all – and yet to admit this is to bring into question the existence of a single, omnipotent God. As with other oppositions in Endō's works, the duality is initially presented as unfathomable – and the effect is heightened by the gulf that initially appears to exist between Suguro and the other characters with whom he comes into contact.

Most notable in this regard is Madame Naruse, the other character by means of whom the author seeks to emphasise the duality of Suguro's nature. For all her carefully cultivated public persona as a devoted hospital visitor, here is a woman equally at home, it would seem, in the murky world of Kabuki-chō to which Suguro finds himself increasingly lured in his search for the 'truth'. To Madame Naruse, there is no inconsistency at work here and yet, as she confides in a letter to Suguro, it was in her husband that she had first recognised the potential for a split personality within the human being. In the letter, remarkable as much for its unsolicited nature as for the frankness of its contents, she confesses that she did not hate her husband on discovery that he had been responsible for the murder of innocent Chinese peasants during the War:

> For the first time I had become aware that within my husband, who behaved sometimes like a younger brother to me, lay the silhouette of a totally different man, and the realisation that these two contradictory aspects had fashioned the man I married was both startling and thrilling to me. (p. 122)

Madame Naruse detects male drive in her husband's action and, in an attempt to fulfil the role of the 'everlasting woman', she seeks to probe deeper. In so doing, however, she exposes the demonic impulses latent within her own being and is forced to recognise:

> You might want to ask, which of these two is the real Mariko? All I can say is that both of them are me. You might ask, don't the contradictions between the two cause you any torment? Yes, sometimes when I think about those contradictions, I horrify myself. I am repelled by myself. But there are also times when I am not, and there is nothing I can do about it. (p. 126)

In this, Madame Naruse represents a sharp break with the more traditional Endō female character: much less of the Eve-like temptress, she exposes her own dark interior in a way that appears designed to emphasise her distinct dual nature. Her role is to show

Suguro that the man he sees as his double is none other than himself – and that neither his Christianity nor his art is capable of shielding him from the volcanic magma, the 'rage' she sees as hidden within every being. In this, too, it is to her late husband that she turns: it is his depiction of the human heart that she adopts in an attempt to heighten Suguro's awareness of these unconscious powers:

> There are several rooms inside the human heart. The room at the lowest level is like the store-room you have here in your home, Mari – it has all kinds of things stored up in it. But late at night, the things you've locked up and forgotten in there begin to move. (p. 111)

To Suguro, at this stage, such a notion represents totally unexplored territory. He feels distinctly challenged not only by the thoughts expressed in her letter, but also by all that her current lifestyle symbolises, and he confesses:

> Never before had he met, or even written about, such a woman. A woman so shot through with contradictions. A woman who seemed so cold-hearted, only to be transformed the next moment into a startlingly gentle and caring individual. (p. 183)

Madame Naruse's role within the novel both as signifier of the voice of Suguro's unconscious and in highlighting the contrast between sin (with its concomitant potential for salvation) and absolute Evil, is thus clearly fundamental, and in seeking a Mephistopholean figure in the novel, the reader is quickly drawn to Endō's female protagonist. Even more significant, however, is her role in drawing Suguro's attention to the fact that, in presenting his pure and clear countenance to the world, he was indebted to the work of his Soul, operating on his unconscious being. Influenced by Madame Naruse, Suguro becomes increasingly reluctant to dismiss the double as mere impostor or optical illusion and comes to view this, rather, as a manifestation of a cry from the Soul. At the same time, Suguro appears more and more concerned that thoughts that, as Christian, he had been forced to dismiss, had been abandoned along the path leading to his Soul, thereby blocking further communication between his Soul and his conscious being. The result is a growing realisation that he had hitherto devoted so much time to cultivation of his public persona that he had neglected to nurture his own Soul – with the result that it had become infected.

Through Madame Naruse, therefore, Suguro comes to learn the painful lesson that to ignore the Soul at the expense of the body is to nurture only one side of the personality. Significantly, it is at moments when this relationship is at its lowest ebb – as the 'cog-wheels rotating at the very core of his heart suddenly went beserk' (p. 77) – that the attempts by the Soul to improve this relationship intensify.

The 'cog-wheel' metaphor suggests a distinct worsening of the relationship between heart and Soul and, on such occasions, in true Jungian fashion, the attempts by the Soul to improve this relationship assume various guises. Particularly prominent in *Scandal* is the stream of hoax phone calls, powerful images of the voice crying *de profundis* – out of the darkness of the Soul.[31] Suguro himself appears to recognise the import of the jangling telephone:

> The sound impressed [Suguro] as being like a groan from the depths of a human heart. The fathomless pit yawning at the bottom of that heart. The echo of a wind coursing through that pit. Something he had not yet described in any of his novels. (p. 129)

As with other such calls, however, Suguro cannot bring himself to answer the phone: he is not yet in a situation in which he is able to hear the cries emanating from his own Soul. But the voice from the darkness does add further depth to Suguro's self-scrutiny, removing it to a new dimension – that of the unconscious. Such scrutiny, however, remains internalised and Suguro's attempts at *rapprochement* with his own Soul remain foiled, obstructed by the tantalising divide he comes to perceive increasingly clearly between his conscious and unconscious being. Towards the end, however, there is clear evidence that the bridge he has sought to construct between the two is almost in place – in the scene in which Suguro walks away from Kobari and the hotel in which he had been brought face to face with his double:

> A myriad white flecks hit by the street-lights whirled ahead of him. The thin flakes of snow seemed to emit a profound light. The light was filled with love and compassion, and with a maternal tenderness it seemed to envelop the figure of the man. His image vanished.

He felt a rush of vertigo. He peered into the space where the man had disappeared. The light increased in intensity and began to wrap itself around Suguro; within its rays the snowflakes sparkled silver as they brushed his face, stroked his cheeks and melted on his shoulders. (p. 222)

The all-pervasive light envelops both Suguro and his double, and Suguro himself appears closer to an acceptance of this as an embracing of his entire being, Soul and body, conscious and unconscious. The light appears rooted in the Soul and, whilst inflicting pain on his physical being, it is this Soul that he comes to see as furnisher of infinite peace. The result, by the end of the novel, is the depiction of a man more ready than any previous Endō protagonist to accept the various dimensions of his being. As the novel closes, Suguro is still being troubled by the unanswered telephone calls: the Soul has yet to finish its interrogation. Significantly, however, by this stage, Suguro is no longer forced to endure this cry alone; in stark contrast to the earlier calls, his wife is now an equal actor in the psychological drama, inextricably caught up in her husband's double identity. As the phone rings, it 'jangle[s] insistently. Summoning him. Her eyes wide open, his wife heard it too' (p. 237). Suguro is now only too well apprised of the lesson of his Soul: he now realises the futility of seeking to limit the aspects of his being he reveals to those with whom he interacts, particularly his wife. Compared with the man who had been so distraught when confronted by his 'other face' (p. 14) at the outset of the novel, Suguro now appears much better equipped to cope with whatever his self-examination might reveal – and to confront a different level of reality from before.

Before concluding this discussion of *Scandal*, however, there remains one further aspect of the work that enhances its status as Endō's most complete examination to date of the workings of the unconscious. As already indicated, dreams, perceived by Jung and many schools of psychoanalysis as one of the most reliable means of access to the workings of the human unconscious, exercise a significant role in the development of the narrative – and the focus of this chapter will now turn to a discussion of this element within the novel.

Once more it was in the critical study, *Watashi no aishita shōsetsu*, that Endo acknowledged his indebtedness to Jungian psychology for his appreciation of the insights afforded by dreams in the formulation of the integrated individual. Before reverting to the novel in hand, therefore, a brief examination of those elements of Jungian dream psychology to which Endō makes specific reference as having a particular bearing on his subsequent literary texts should facilitate the process of analysing the significance of the various dreams that pervade the novel, *Scandal*.

Identifying the contents of dreams, along with the sudden surfacing of inexplicable impulses, as the most effective means of access to the workings of the unconscious, Jung was at pains to assail the widely held view of dreams as reproductions of actual, recent events, claiming rather that:

> The general function of dreams is to try to restore our psychological balance by producing dream material that re-establishes, in a subtle way, the total psychic equilibrium.[32]

In this, Jung appears to be highlighting the voice of the unconscious speaking through dreams – a voice that, in his opinion, should never be ignored. He was, however, equally ready to recognise the role of dreams in pointing to character strengths and weaknesses in order to rectify an unbalanced image that one individual may hold of another, as well as in highlighting various hidden conflicts within the individual by revealing an unknown aspect of his, or her, character.

Dreams were thus clearly defined as powerful signs to which the individual needs to remain sensitive. However, in recognising the tendency for a dream to possess overtones, to 'stand...for something more than its obvious and immediate meaning'[33] with the result that full significance cannot readily be grasped intellectually, Jung was further arguing the role of dream as symbol. As he continued:

> No matter what fantastic trappings one may put upon an idea [that has been reached as a logical conclusion or by deliberate intent], it will still remain a sign, linked to the conscious thought behind it, not a symbol that hints at something not yet known. In dreams, symbols occur spontaneously, for dreams happen and are not invented; they are, therefore, the main source of all our knowledge about symbolism.[34]

Even such symbols, however, require differentiation: the distinction between the conscious use of symbols and those, such as dreams, that stem from the unconscious was one to which he made frequent reference:

> We constantly use symbolic terms to represent concepts that we cannot define or fully comprehend....But this conscious use of symbols is only one aspect of a psychological fact of great importance: Man also produces symbols unconsciously and spontaneously, in the form of dreams.... As a general rule, the unconscious aspect of any event is revealed to us in dreams, where it appears not as a rational thought but as a symbolic image.[35]

Dreams are thus seen as evidence of the individual striving towards unity – a unity in which divisions are to be replaced by consistency, oppositions balanced and the conscious to be viewed in symbiotic relationship with the unconscious. In representing the voice of the unconscious, however, dreams are inevitably subject to the distinction, integral to Jung's vision, between the personal and collective realms within this inner being, and the positing of both 'personal' and 'collective' dreams was thus fundamental to Jung's code of interpretation. As the product of the personal unconscious, the former remain concerned with personal aspects of the dreamer's life. More important to Jung, however, were those 'collective' dreams that present archetypes from the collective unconscious, and consequently hold significance for others as well as for the dreamer. Such dreams are often vivid and make use of surprising, even incomprehensible, symbols, their relationship to the dreamer consequently difficult to trace.

Having outlined, in brief, Jung's basic approach to dreams, however, the question at this point must be the extent to which Endō has heeded these lessons – or, more fundamentally, the extent to which the novel *Scandal* conforms to this paradigm. One Jungian tenet to which the author appears intent on adhering is one that stems from the above-mentioned technique of fusion of apparent opposites – in this case, in the form of the gradual blurring of the distinction between 'personal' and 'collective' dreams. Just as the self/*alter ego* dichotomy, initially established as evidence of the existence of polar opposites, grows weaker as the novel progresses, so the narrator comes increasingly to impute a universal, 'collective' significance to the various dreams that Suguro experiences – early examples of which appear intensely personal.

The first dream recorded in the novel is that in which Suguro dreams of his literary forebear, Akutagawa Ryūnosuke, entering the world of the dead (p. 27). At this stage, death is very clearly on Suguro's mind and the dream appears as little more than the necrophilic leanings of a man confronted by old age. In both of his next two dreams (pp. 35, 36), however, Suguro finds himself confronting mirrors, a distinct Jungian symbol of the individual and his Shadow – of coming to terms with the full implications of this darker side of his being. Equipped with such information, Endō's reader is placed in a privileged position: he/she is in a position to provide a reasoned retort to the narratorial aside that '[Suguro] couldn't understand why lately mirrors were always showing up in his dreams' (p. 36). Already, however, Suguro is troubled by the content of his dreams: they appear to be hounding him in a manner similar to that of the doppelgänger he had earlier detected.

In keeping with the theme of pursuit, however, as the novel continues, Suguro dreams more and more of being followed. The more he is hounded by Kobari, the more his dreams suggest a man desperate to extricate himself from the thick fog in which his life has become embroiled. The dream in which he associates his destiny with that of King Lear, however, offers symbolic evidence of escape from this endless cycle. Determined to throw off his pursuer, Suguro dreams of hiding in a doorway, only to sense his assailant giving up the chase:

> Just then he noticed a faint light beginning to flicker through the fog. It did not emanate from the bleary house lamps. The source of the light seemed to be somewhere at the top of the hill, emitting a glow as if in response to Suguro's prayer. It shone through the stagnant fog and narrowed to a focus upon him. He had the distinct impression that some volitional force was trying to catch hold of him, but strangely he could discern no ill-will or malice in that force; in fact, the moment his body was enveloped in a deep, soft light he felt an indescribable peace within all his senses....No longer did anything restrain him. The heavy weights that had burdened his mind were gone. (pp. 167–8)

The image of light appears to offer the potential for release from Suguro's anguish. With the ensuing image, however, such grounds for optimism are called into question – as the source of light is linked with the world of death. Death is very clearly his assailant –

although, by the end of the dream, this no longer represents the source of fear that it had earlier in the novel:

> Suguro was steeped in an immense pool of joy as he wondered if this was what death was really like. He was amazed to find that death had a visage utterly unlike the fearsome aspect he had long dreaded. There was not a trace of menace or condemnation in the light that enfolded him in its arms. (p. 168)

By now, Suguro has grown enough in awareness to recognise that the light of the world beyond death – as well as the feeling of joy with which it instils him in his dream – represents a distinct idealisation of death. But this is nevertheless sufficient, not merely to remove some of his earlier fear, but also to encourage him to seek to maximise his own life. Significantly, therefore, his next dream involves Mitsu, symbol of his determination to gain a clearer understanding of the workings of his own Soul:

> In his dreams he was rubbing his own unsightly cheek against Mitsu's. He was compelled by the hope that in so doing he could extend his own dwindling life by another year or two. (p. 173)

Suguro is by now firmly embarked upon the road towards rebirth as a more complete person, possessed of both conscious and unconscious aspects to his personality and it is in this context that his final dream, in which the dankness of his study is compared with the amniotic fluids within the womb, and in which Suguro dreams of resisting the natural impulse towards birth, assumes added significance. By this stage, as already noted, Suguro has come to recognise the existence of his Shadow as part of himself, however loathsome, and this dream can thus be seen as representing, in symbolic fashion, the final stage of the process of rebirth as individuated being.

As Jung himself emphasised, the task for the individual is not to seek to rid himself entirely of dreams – and clearly, for Suguro, there is no lessening either of the intensity of his dreams, or of the significance he subsequently attaches to them. In true Jungian fashion, moreover, Suguro refuses to embark too readily on the process of dream analysis. Indeed, his initial reaction is to dismiss them entirely: following his first dream about Mitsu, he concludes:

> Because it was a dream, he did not feel responsible for it.
> There was no need to feel embarrassment or shame over a
> dream. (p. 36)

Nevertheless, Suguro has yet to confront the question: if not himself, then who should be responsible for his dreams? And even were he ready to embark on such a line of reasoning, at this stage of the work, he is in no position to provide an answer. By the end of the novel, however, the implication is strong that Suguro has come to see these dreams as deriving from his inner being. As Christian, moreover, he is coming to acknowledge an immediate correspondence between this realm and the Soul – and to a vision of the latter as responsible, not only for forging the fusion between the conscious and unconscious elements of his being, but also, more specifically, for those aspects of his unconscious that had found expression through dreams.

Seen in these terms, depiction of the novel *Scandal* as representing, not a watershed in the author's *oeuvre* but a logical sequitur to the examinations of the composite individual that pervade the author's entire work, appears more convincing. Just as those critics who over the decades have mined works of the *shishōsetsu* tradition in search of biographical information concerning the author have consistently chosen to overlook the element of 'fictional complicity'[36] that is integral to this form, so those who have dismissed *Scandal* as a somewhat faltering attempt on Endō's part to mark out a new literary terrain, appear to offer scant regard to a deeper level to the narrative at which the concerns embodied within Suguro come to reflect, very closely, those raised by earlier Endō protagonists. To be sure, the decision overtly to highlight the attempt to probe the conscious persona of his protagonist (by presenting him in the guise of a carefully constructed authorial double and in subsequently focusing on Suguro's own pursuit of his *alter ego*) sets the work apart from the author's earlier examinations of human nature in terms of content. Viewed as a literary portrayal of a protagonist brought face to face with his own shadow being and obliged as a result to accept the need for acknowledgement of this in the formulation of his previously carefully cultivated self-image, however, the novel assumes its place as a natural successor to *Silence* and *The Samurai* and the earlier narratives.

The true significance of the novel *vis à vis* the earlier Endō texts certainly merits reassertion. At the same time, however, it is hard to exaggerate the importance of *Scandal* in opening up a new perspective for incorporation into critical discussions of the narrative deployment of 'the splintered range of perspective and point of view' discussed at the beginning of this study.

The full extent of this legacy will be examined in greater detail in the discussion of the novel, *Deep River*, that follows. At this stage, suffice it to say that there is evidence, in the depiction of both Suguro and Madame Naruse in the concluding section of *Scandal*, of a narrator intent upon leaving unresolved the fruits of the exploration of the psychological dramas in which his creations are embroiled, thereby opening up new avenues of investigation for his subsequent work. Mention has already been made of the manner in which Suguro is abandoned at the end of the novel listening forlornly to the sound of the 'jangling' telephone and thereby left with the ultimate question of 'whether, in the future, he will intone the music of destruction or of rebirth' unresolved.[37] Equally significant, however, is the nature of Madame Naruse's disappearance at the conclusion of the novel: in this way, she can be seen as preserved, unfathomed whether by author, narrator, protagonist or reader, for a subsequent role as expositor of the seemingly paradoxical function of the human unconscious. That role is subsequently assumed by Mitsuko in *Deep River* and it is to a consideration of this novel that we now turn.

7
DEEP RIVER

> Rebirth is an affirmation that must be counted among the primordial affirmations of mankind. These primordial affirmations are based on what I call archetypes. In view of the fact that all affirmations relating to the sphere of the suprasensual are, in the last analysis, invariably determined by archetypes, it is not surprising that a concurrence of affirmations concerning rebirth can be found among the most widely differing peoples.
>
> (C.G. Jung)

In the light of Endō's burgeoning reputation as a potential Nobel laureate, the barrage of critical appraisal to which the novel, *Scandal*, was subjected is hardly surprising. Several critics, including Kawai Hayao, wrote in glowing terms of the novel's 'success' in penetrating further than any previous Endō novel the world of the unconscious.[1] Others, however, were less enthusiastic, choosing to view the work as, at best only partially successful as an attempt to forge a new direction for the author's subsequent work. The following comment, by Moriuchi Toshio, is representative of those who reserved judgment, anxious to see where this new path would lead:

> The work reads like an autopsy of the soul of a Catholic author...but it lacks depth. If Suguro were truly a Catholic author, he should leave the world of this novel. Instead, he starts asking the question, 'Why?' (At this late stage in his career!) and thereby confuses his reader....The 'Christian author', Suguro, should be done with delving into the dark recesses of his soul, the scene of carnage in his heart. He should know that faith brings not only peace, but also fear and terror to the heart....Faith is something that exists

before God – and, at such times, our human nature is destroyed. To live in the righteousness of God is to find rebirth through destruction of the Self. I am fascinated to discover whether, in the future, Suguro will intone the music of destruction or of rebirth.[2]

The challenge was clear and, in the months following publication of the novel, Endō spoke of his determination to persist with his attempts 'to confront the forces of Evil, head-on',[3] justifying this pursuit with the following explanation:

I can't help wondering whether even the world of ugliness which currently lies before me may not be a rite of passage, a preparation for the world to come. I have no idea what this world might have to offer us. And yet, I cling to a faint hope that even this world of ugliness might be enveloped in light.[4]

The implications for Endō were far-reaching and, in keeping with precedent, more than half a decade was to elapse before the literary formulation of this latest search was to appear – in the form of the novel, *Deep River*. For all the time lapse, however, the basic scenario for this latest novel was taking shape even before completion of *Scandal*. Two decisions in particular, acknowledged in a discussion to mark publication of the earlier novel, were destined to have significant implications for *Deep River*. The first of these concerned the character of Madame Naruse, whom Endō vowed to 'reincarnate' in his next novel. Another admission, hardly designed to take Endō's critics by surprise yet nevertheless highly influential in determining the narrative tenor of the subsequent work, was the determination, not merely to persist with his examination of the unconscious forces at work in the lives of his creations, but to locate the novel in 'India, land of the unconscious'.[5]

Endō made several trips to India in the late 1980s and early 1990s, each designed to bring the author face to face with the backdrop to the novel in gestation. During the course of these visits, the author found himself inexorably drawn to the holy city of Vârânasi. Here, at the confluence of the Ganges and the Yamunā rivers, the author detected a location rich in symbolism, an echo of the collective unconscious in which the lives of all mankind, regardless of background and life experiences, can be seen brought together into the flow of the great river. The symbolism of the Ganges is central to the novel and we shall be returning to this aspect later in this chapter. At this stage, however, suffice it to say that Endō recognised in this a convergence and ultimate fusion of life and death, beauty and ugliness, hope and despair, that served as a perfect symbolic end-point for the searches embodied in the Endō protagonists considered in the previous chapters. As he remarked at the time:

> It is a great river in which life and death live side by side. Going to India, you come to sense the existence of another great world of a different dimension that coexists with our world.[6]

The visits to India also had considerable repercussions on the role of Madame Naruse – or Mitsuko – as protagonist of the novel. The more Endō strove to portray the symbiotic relationship between the various, seemingly conflicting, qualities within the single character and to adopt the symbol of the Ganges as the great river affirming this process, the more he was drawn to depiction, not of a search carried out in isolation, but as part of a much larger process. The 'subsidiary' characters consequently grew in significance, and Mitsuko's role as unquestioned protagonist was subverted by the increasing importance attached, not merely to Ōtsu, the 'weak' and 'powerless' voice whom, try as she might, Mitsuko is unable to leave behind, but also to a series of other fellow travellers brought together on the tour to India that forms the narrative basis for the novel.

As Endō admitted in a discussion with Kaga Otohiko, the decision to shift the narrative focus away from Mitsuko and to increase the cast of characters evolved gradually.[7] Thereafter, the more he became embroiled in the very personal searches for lost love – for a light that can envelop even the 'world of ugliness' in which each of these protagonists is embroiled, the more Endō was drawn to accept the gauntlet thrown down by Moriuchi: to address the question of whether his protagonists would 'in the future...intone the music of destruction or of rebirth'. The consequent aim was highly explicit:

> My aim is to focus, not on the psychological worlds of the characters, but on the issues that trouble their souls – and to cut everything else that one normally includes in a novel. I know of no example of a Japanese novel, be it popular or psychological, in which all the characters are engaged in searching their souls. So I decided to give it a try.[8]

The determination to 'search the souls' of his literary creations represents a logical progression. The empty lives and absence of hope and dreams for the future betrayed by Endō's protagonists from the outset had been painfully exposed in *Scandal*; the requirement now was for a work that would delve deeper into the causes of such 'aloneness' and, in so doing, provide a fresh perspective on the concerted search for identity that had pervaded Endō's entire *oeuvre*.

It is in this context – as an exploration of the possibilities for 'rebirth' of the individual – that the novel *Deep River* fits neatly into our continuum. Before turning to the novel itself – to a consideration of the extent to which the various characters do indeed confront their individuated beings on the banks of the Ganges – let us consider briefly another aspect of the novel that serves to locate it fairly and squarely within Endō's corpus whilst, at the same time, offering a fresh approach to familiar material.

The issue of religious syncretism has served as a constant subtext to this study of Endō's fiction. From the author's earliest critical writing, the question has never been far beneath the surface, the relationship between the Christian monotheistic vision and a pantheistic world view a constant refrain. As already noted, however, the approach has not been entirely uncontroversial and Endō has been obliged to endure criticism, especially from the traditional Christian community, for his willingness to engage in such inter-faith dialogue. For Endō, however, the issue was not only intimately linked to the East–West divide he had been so consistently challenging, it was also a necessary corollary of the search for the self with which he was absorbed. His was the approach of G.W. Houston, who has argued:

> If a Christian dialogues with a Buddhist, he need not lose his faith, nor must he convert. He must first try to understand. There must be an arena of openness and expression. Once this takes place, one can rediscover one's own roots. This of all things modern civilisation needs to do. We are all eroding at the roots.[9]

In *Deep River*, this issue of religious syncretism is explicitly highlighted, both in the decision to locate the novel in India and in the nature of the tour on which the various characters come together: as the tour guide, Enami, explains at the pre-departure informational meeting, although the tour is nominally scheduled to take them to various Buddhist holy sites, it also provides the opportunity to visit a series of Hindu temples.

For all the seeming consistency of the refrain, however, comparison of the syncretic vision embodied in the latest novel with that developed in the earliest texts (and, as discussed earlier, delineated in early articles, such as 'The gods and God') bears testimony to the considerable distance travelled in the interim. Gone is the simple contrast between 'monotheism', with its 'absolute division between God, angels and man', and the 'pantheistic' world of the East in which 'everything represents an amalgam and extension of the individual'.[10] In its stead lies a more sophisticated approach, one indebted in equal measure to the Buddhist preoccupation with 'knowing the self' and to the Christian focus on redemption. For Endō, the development was integral to the narrative design for *Deep River* and, in a discussion with William Johnston, translator of *Silence* and authority on Christian–Buddhist dialogue, he acknowledged his fascination with 'the search, not for Christianity, not for Buddhism, but for a "third religion"…one that was divorced from institutionalised religion such as Christianity, or Buddhism, or Islam'. Here was the call for 'a religion that transcends sectarianism…a great life force' whose relationship with Christianity Endō was committed to clarifying.[11]

The vision is integral to *Deep River* and whilst we must be constantly mindful of the need to avoid falling into the very trap, delineated at the outset of this study, of reading Endō's texts as theological tracts as opposed to literary constructs, the above discussion provides a useful context for consideration of that aspect of the novel that marks it out from the previous texts: the more concerted focus on the concept of rebirth.

Reference has already been made to Moriuchi's concern that future Endō protagonists intone the music, not of destruction, but of rebirth. Implicit in this comment is a reading of the Endō narrative to date as embroiling the protagonists in a journey of self-discovery that ultimately proves inconclusive. To be sure, as noted in our discussion of the earlier texts, the journeys invariably bring those involved face to face with aspects of their being previously suppressed into the unconscious. The questions, however, remain. Have the protagonists themselves been willing and able to assimilate such newly acquired self-knowledge? And to what extent have they availed themselves of this growing awareness to release themselves from the shackles of the past? In short, to what extent have their respective processes of individuation resulted in a sense of rebirth? It is in these terms – as a more positive approach to the concept of rebirth – that the ensuing discussion of *Deep River* will evolve.

First indications within the novel of the significance to be attached, not merely to the process of evolving self-awareness but to the desire for rebirth born of renewed optimism is provided by Endō's title for the novel and the decision to cite the Negro spiritual of the same name as a prologue. The spiritual, born of decades of slavery in the American South and replete with its dreams of freedom from persecution in the promised 'campground', focuses on the River Jordan, the 'deep river' that represents the final obstacle separating the Jews from the promised land of Israel. Here was a river symbolising, not so much removal of the memories of slavery, but rather their desire to take this burden with them to the promised land. So near and yet so far, before their eyes lay the land of renewed hope and new beginnings – the vision of rebirth that Endō discerned in the Ganges and adopts as his central metaphor.

In the narrative that follows this citation, the desire for rebirth is incorporated, as noted earlier, in the symbolic setting of the drama beside the Ganges. It is Mitsuko, towards the end of the novel, who points out to her fellow travellers that 'the Hindus apparently call the Ganges the river of rebirth'.[12] In the preceding narrative, however, much has already been made of the significance of the river in which the positive, life-giving force of water is inextricably linked with its negative, destructive force and which consequently serves to affirm both the positive and negative experiences in the lives of those who assemble on its banks. Throughout, the emphasis is on the universal, unchanging qualities of the holy river and on the extent to which the memories and wishes that unite all mankind at the unconscious level are incorporated into its depths. Equally significant, especially to our reading of the text as a 'novel of rebirth', however, is the constant flow of the river: as it disgorges into the ocean, so the eternal cycle of departure and return is symbolically completed. In Endō's novel, the cycle of unopposable history is given concrete form – in the manner in which the group of unrelated tourists comes together in a concerted search for renewal.

In keeping with precedent established in the earlier novels, the narrative focus on *rapprochement* between the various characters is highlighted through initial emphasis on the differing motives behind the searches upon which each is engaged. All embark on the tour with differing, and specifically individual, agendas and all appear oblivious to the needs and concerns of their fellow travellers. The distinctions, emphasised at the textual level by the structuring of the novel into a series of 'case studies', nevertheless mask a crucial link: they are united in their determination to put the past behind them and in their desire for rebirth. In the process, each examines his or her inner horizons in a manner not achieved by earlier Endō protagonists leading to closer adherence to the process defined by Jung as the 'enlargement of personality' than that evidenced in the previous novels. Each, in short, can be viewed as conforming to Jung's original template:

> What comes to us from outside, and, for that matter, everything that rises up from within, can only be made our own if we are capable of an inner amplitude equal to that of the incoming content. *Real increase of personality means consciousness of an enlargement that flows from inner sources.*[13]

The motives behind the various searches for renewal may differ considerably between the various characters. Of greater significance to our reading of *Deep River* as a novel of rebirth, however, are the differing interpretations each places on the very concept of rebirth itself. Here again, the Jungian model provides a useful approach – one that, in identifying five discrete variants of the concept of rebirth, should serve as a convenient benchmark against which to gauge the respective quests. Let us briefly summarise these five forms of rebirth as outlined by Jung in his lecture at the Eranos meeting of 1939.[14]

The first type of rebirth addressed by Jung is that of metempsychosis, or transmigration of the soul, in which prolongation of life is achieved by passing through different bodily experiences (although 'it is by no means certain whether continuity of personality is guaranteed or not'). Second, Jung cites reincarnation, a concept that implies that human personality be regarded as both continuous and accessible to memory and that generally refers to rebirth in a human body. Third in Jung's list is resurrection, the 'reestablishment of human existence after death', which necessarily involves 'the change, transmutation, or transformation of one's being' and which Jung specifically defines more broadly than 'the Christian assumption that this body will be resurrected'. As a fourth variant, Jung posits the concept of 'rebirth within the span of individual life', acknowledging that, on the one hand, this may be 'a renewal without any change of being, in as much as the personality which is renewed is not changed in its essential nature, but only its functions, or parts of the personality are subjected to healing, strengthening, or improvement', but equally that it can involve 'total rebirth of the individual', a transmutation implying 'a change of [the individual's] essential nature'. Finally, Jung discusses a form of 'indirect rebirth' in which 'the transformation is brought about not directly, by passing through death and rebirth oneself, but indirectly, by participating in a process of transformation that is conceived of as taking place outside the individual. In other words, one has to witness, or take part in, some rite of transformation'.

As Jung was the first to acknowledge, the list may not be exhaustive: it would nevertheless appear to 'cover at least the cardinal meanings'.[15] And consideration of the novel, *Deep River*, within these parameters reveals evidence of all five aspects of rebirth, differences closely preserved in the Japanese original. Let us turn, then, to the text itself – to consideration of the manner in which, as each of the primary characters continues his or her search for something to assuage the emptiness of their routine lives, so each is depicted as drawn, inexorably, towards one of the five categories.

The novel begins with the coming together of a group of individuals, with seemingly little in common and all 'seem[ing] to be going to India with different feelings' (p. 32). United only in their sense of being abandoned and alone, all are depicted, in typical Endō manner, as victims of a society in which a series of man-made organisations appears to exist with the sole purpose of trampling on the individual. The differences between them are deliberately accentuated. From this point on, however, the text depicts a growing *rapprochement*, a coming together of differences and an intertwining of the various lives that represent the central narrative strategy of the novel. At first, the tiny threads that are unearthed linking the various characters in the past would appear inconsequential. The discovery that one of the tourists, Mitsuko, had nursed the dying wife of another, Isobe; Mitsuko's discovery that Ōtsu, the man she had toyed with at college parties but had long since claimed to have abandoned, had preceded her, first to France and subsequently to India: the flimsy links are presented as mere coincidences, an all too convenient literary device designed to provide a semblance of inter-relatedness to disparate material. As the drama unfolds, however, and as the extent to which the characters are indeed linked in their search for answers to certain fundamental questions that have resonated throughout Endō's corpus becomes apparent, so the significance of these 'coincidences' as both inevitable and meaningful is unearthed. There is an element of synchronicity here that conforms with the Jungian template more closely than in the previous novels.

But what is this 'meaning'? And to what can we attribute the eventual forging of links between the various fellow travellers far stronger than the norm for a tour of this nature? To a large extent, it is the confrontation with death and rebirth (in its variant forms) that effects the fusion of differences so unlikely at the outset.

Turning first to metempsychosis, distinguished as *tensei* throughout the Japanese original, this is presented as the missing link for all the Japanese tourists as they arrive at Vârânasi. Troubled by the sight of the Indians desperate to reach the Ganges before they die, it is only once they come to see the role exercised by the river on the lives of those who reach its banks (in assisting in this process of metempsychosis) that they, too, can share in appreciation of the awesome power of the river. Only then can they appreciate the implications of the explanation of this significance which Ōtsu, by now working amongst the *harijans*, the 'untouchables' shunned by the rest of society, offers to Mitsuko:

> Every time I look at the River Ganges, I think of my God. The Ganges swallows up the ashes of every person as it flows along, rejecting neither the beggar woman who stretches out her fingerless hands nor the murdered prime minister, Gandhi. The river of love that is my God flows past, accepting all, rejecting neither the ugliest of men nor the filthiest. (p. 185)[16]

Only now can they begin to fathom the reasons behind Ōtsu's decision to devote his life to the dead and dying.

Turning next to the concept of reincarnation (*umare-kawari* or *migawari* in the original), this receives extensive consideration in the novel as a result of the pledge, made by Isobe's wife on her deathbed, that she would 'be reborn (*umare-kawaru*) somewhere in the world' and her demand that her husband 'look for [her]...find' her (p. 19). The words continue to haunt Isobe, inducing him to make contact with those involved in a research project at the University of Virginia at which specific instances of 'reincarnation' were being examined. The trail leads him to northern India, to the village of Kamloji near Vârânasi, to investigate the claim made by a 5-year-old girl, Rajini Puniral, that she had spent a previous life as a Japanese. In this, however, Isobe is not alone. Numada, a fellow traveller, is also dogged by thoughts of reincarnation and has determined to purchase and subsequently release into the jungle a myna bird – in memory of the bird that he sees as having 'died in place of' himself (*migawari ni natte kureta* (p. 82)) whilst he was undergoing a life-threatening operation.

Resurrection, or *fukkatsu*, the third variant of rebirth delineated by Jung and addressed in the novel, represents a constant refrain throughout the novel. It is with this concept that Ōtsu struggles most as he attempts to come to terms with the orthodox Christian theology with which he is confronted at the various seminaries he attends. In keeping with the Jungian model, he finds himself unable, or unwilling, to limit his understanding of the concept in Christian terms and it is this that encourages him to quit his formal studies and to seek a broader interpretation amongst the Hindu *sâdhus*. Indeed, the entire novel can be viewed as an attempt to reconcile the Christian vision of resurrection with the other forms of rebirth as distinguished by Jung.

The fourth category, that involving rebirth within the span of the individual life, or *renovatio* as Jung describes it, also exercises a central function within the novel. As the tourists depart for India, leaving their humdrum lives behind them, each can be seen as searching for a 'healing, strengthening, or improvement' of the 'functions, or parts of the personality'. The quest is intensely personal, representing as it does a logical extension of 'the search for the real self' that has exercised the various Endō protagonists considered in this study and about which the author wrote so extensively in the years leading to publication of *Deep River*.[17] The search is clearly not devoid of pain and, in keeping with the precedents considered in previous chapters, often involves characters in direct confrontation with their own double.

First to sense the presence of his own doppelgänger in the novel is the war veteran, Kiguchi, whose trip to India is motivated by the desire to perform a memorial service for the numerous friends and colleagues who had perished in the infamous 'death march' through the Burmese jungle at the end of the Pacific War. Aware that his own survival was thanks, in no small measure, to the selfless care of his friend, Tsukada, Kiguchi's recollection of those days, 'as they dragged their legs along in utter exhaustion' (p. 86), incorporates a hazy differentiation between his physical self and 'an exact replica of himself walking alongside him'.

> 'Walk! You must keep walking!' His double, or perhaps the Kiguchi who was about to collapse physically, had bellowed

at him. 'Walk! Keep walking!'...He was certain that his exact duplicate had stood at his side, berating him. (p. 87)

The 'exact replica of himself', 'his double', or 'his exact duplicate' – all translations of the same *mō hitori no jibun* in the original – continues to haunt Kiguchi, his release from its clutches finally achieved only as he stands beside the Ganges intoning the sutras and concluding that, like good and evil, the two aspects of his being are linked in a symbiotic relationship: they stand 'back to back with each other, and they can't be separated the way you can cut things apart with a knife' (p. 200).

Equally disturbed by the presence of a doppelgänger standing alongside her is Mitsuko who, in keeping with the model established with Madame Naruse in *Scandal*, is aware of conflicting impulses within her being – the one drawing her to devote much of her free time to care of the sick and elderly as a hospital volunteer, the other attracted, in spite of herself, to the 'freshly severed head and blood flecked lips' of the Hindu goddess, Kâlî. Significantly, moreover, as she 'flicked back and forth between the photos and paintings [of Kâlî, Mitsuko] *felt that both images were herself*' (p. 115, my emphasis).

Awareness of this *alter ego* is something with which, over the years, Mitsuko has learnt to live. And as the narrative explicitly acknowledges shortly after this, those times in which the two appeared as conflicting voices within her were the source, not so much of concern, as of acceptance of a greater complexity to her being than was appreciated by those with whom she came into contact:

> On...occasions, she heard another voice identical to hers saying: '*This invalid isn't going to get better....*' None of the nurses or doctors was aware of her two faces...*Ōtsu wrote that God has many faces*, she suddenly thought,...'*And so do I*'. (pp. 124–5, emphasis in original)

For all this apparent acceptance, the presence of this alternative self is nevertheless enough to induce Mitsuko to travel to India – 'to search out the darkness in her own heart' (p. 58) and, once more, it is only in the depiction of Mitsuko as she stands alone with her thoughts on the banks of the Ganges at the end of the novel that the narrative alludes to the potential for reconciliation of these disparate voices.

The examples are by no means exhaustive: there are occasions in the lives of each of the tourists when they are forced to confront similar echoes of their unconscious being. Ōtsu, too, is similarly troubled, his quest for the being whom, in deference to Mitsuko, he refers to as his 'Onion', offering the most consistent challenge to the caricature of the weak and ineffective victim of circumstances depicted at the outset. The narrative effect in each case is, however, the same: the more the initial portrayal of the individual is subverted, the more these characters come to appear engaged in a dialogue with the self that identifies them as engaged in the process of individuation.

Let us turn now to the fifth and final form of rebirth as identified by Jung. Here, as noted above, the relevant metamorphosis is effected indirectly and involves the individual's participation in, or at the very least, witnessing of some rite of transformation. The rites in question in *Deep River* are the various rites of passage performed by the Ganges: the seemingly endless procession of funerals of those for whom death beside the 'deep river' represented the apogee of freedom, and the wedding procession in which Mitsuko and Numada become inadvertently embroiled during their search for Ōtsu. In each case, identification with the group lies at the heart of the experience and, as such, each is subject to the caveat, offered by Jung, with regard to the collective experience of transformation:

> If any considerable group of persons are united and identified with one another by a particular frame of mind, the resultant transformation experience bears only a very remote resemblance to the experience of individual transformation....If, therefore, I have a so-called collective experience as a member of a group, it takes place on a lower level of consciousness than if I had the experience by myself alone.[18]

In short, the danger in such circumstances is that 'the change does not last'. But as Jung proceeded to point out:

> The inevitable psychological regression within the group is partially counteracted by ritual, that is to say through a cult ceremony which makes the solemn performance of sacred events the centre of group activity and prevents the crowd from relapsing into unconscious instinctuality.[19]

Provided, then, that the ritual is of sufficient intensity to retain the individual's attention and that there is 'relation to a centre which expresses the unconscious through its symbolism', Jung argues in favour of the possibility of a 'comparatively individual experience [of rebirth] even within the group'.[20] The centre in *Deep River* is the Ganges, the force of the various rituals performed on its banks extended during the course of the narrative to include one more: the tour itself.

The transformation of the tour to India from a convergence of unrelated individual journeys to a group experience in which the various participants do indeed attain 'a comparatively individual experience' of rebirth represents a central strand of the narrative in *Deep River*. Until the group arrives at the Ganges in Vârânasi, not only is the group identification relatively weak, but the interest that each participant shows in the quests driving the others is limited. Confrontation with the various 'cult ceremon[ies]' serves as a clear catalyst, however, and from then on, each participant becomes exercised, not only by successful accomplishment of his or her own respective mission, but increasingly, in assisting others in pursuit of their goals. Thus Numada accompanies Mitsuko in her search for Ōtsu, Mitsuko involves herself closely, both with Isobe's search for his reincarnated wife and with Kiguchi's determination to perform an appropriate memorial ritual for his fallen war comrades. And Enami, the tour leader, identifies more and more with the individual concerns of each of his clients. In so doing, the various missions are valorised until, by the end, each does indeed come to assume the aspect of 'the solemn performance of sacred events'.

But how are we to account for this elevation? To what can we attribute the transformation of these intensely personal quests into the nature of sacred rituals? It is perhaps in this regard that the role of Ōtsu as unwitting orchestrator of events is best considered. Let us turn, then, to analysis of the influence exercised by Ōtsu, reluctant protagonist, as the (predominantly absentee) instigator of the processes of rebirth upon which the various other characters are engaged.

First introduction to Ōtsu appears, in Chapter 3, through the eyes of his fellow student, Mitsuko, who succumbs to pressure, in the form of promptings, both from her unconscious and from her peers, to ridicule the reticent young man whose presence, under normal circumstances, she would have scarcely deigned to acknowledge. From this moment on, Ōtsu's presence is all-pervasive, his perspective on events essential in bringing together the various threads into a consistent narrative. Admittedly, for all but Mitsuko, he remains of little more than peripheral interest – an eccentric young Japanese whose work amongst the *harijan* untouchables is attributed to an esoteric spirituality with which they are unable to identify. And yet Ōtsu's is a unifying presence, bringing together, if only at the unconscious level, all the tourists, even those who remain nameless in the text. His perspective on events in the narrative is introduced sparingly. When provided, however, his view serves to complement that of the other protagonists providing a welcome contrast to the self-scrutiny indulged in, not merely by Mitsuko, but by the others desperate to fulfil their mission as they had initially envisaged it. The effect of the insights thereby provided is subtle. Particularly when directed at Mitsuko, however, the eye is perceptive – and it is therefore wholly appropriate as the first to really penetrate the workings of another's mind. Significantly, however, the converse perspective is equally hard to locate: the developing portrayal of Ōtsu is limited, coloured by the almost exclusive reliance upon Mitsuko's vision of events. And yet, towards the end of the novel, as the drama shifts to presentation through a third-person narrative, so a more objective viewpoint emerges, one that appears to combine the perspectives of all the other characters. As the hitherto conflicting perspectives are fused, so some of the questions surrounding Ōtsu's influence on the narrative – and his connection with the Endō protagonists discussed in previous chapters – become clearer.

The evolution is crucial to the narrative, Ōtsu's transformation from the inept social misfit depicted at the outset into the figure of strength and conviction by the end reminiscent of so many of the earlier Endō protagonists. Gaston in *Wonderful Fool*, Mitsu in *The Girl I Left Behind*: the process of sanctification of the weakling has represented a constant refrain in this study. And the similarities are not limited to form; in substance, too, Ōtsu's vision of a seemingly unfathomable divide between East and West is clearly reminiscent of similar views expressed by a series of earlier Endō protagonists – Tanaka in *Foreign Studies* springs readily to mind – who ultimately succumb to such distinctions. Ōtsu's view, expounded upon in a letter to Mitsuko, would appear to brook no compromise:

> After nearly five years of living in a foreign country, I can't help but be struck by the clarity and logic of the way Europeans think, but it seems to me as an Asian that

there's something they have lost sight of with their excessive clarity and their overabundance of logic, and I just can't go along with it. Their lucid logic and their way of explaining everything in such clear-cut terms sometimes even causes me pain....An Asian like me just can't make sharp distinctions and pass judgement on everything the way they do. (pp. 117–18)

The West may seem far divorced from Ōtsu's immediate world; certainly the God to whom he is introduced in the Western seminaries is one with whom Ōtsu struggles to identify. In his own way, however, he clings to a vision of a more personal relationship with a being who is always alongside: the *dōhansha* figure, already discussed in relation to the earlier texts. Ōtsu's vision of a powerless, yet compassionate God is evidenced in his observation to Mitsuko that, 'even if I try to abandon God,...God won't abandon me' (p. 42). For Ōtsu, this figure represents the ultimate influence behind all his decisions; here is the being – and as he readily admits, whether he be called God, Tomato, or even Onion is of no concern – who offers him the absolute reassurance he seeks:

Just as my Onion is always beside me, he is always within you and beside you, too. He is the only one who can understand your pain and your loneliness. One day he will transport you to another realm. We cannot have any idea when that will be, or how it will happen, or what form it will take. He makes use of every means. (p. 120)

The portrayal epitomises the concept of the *dōhansha* so carefully cultivated throughout Endō's *oeuvre*. Of greater relevance to a discussion of the narrative development of Ōtsu in the novel, however, is the extent to which this image is subsequently fused with that of Ōtsu himself. For Endō, the issue was central to the narrative design of the novel and, as he argued in the above-mentioned interview with Kaga Otohiko:

Christ Himself takes the form of...Ōtsu in this novel. Perhaps I should call it an imitation of Christ, but I have tried to juxtapose the life of Ōtsu on to that of Christ, the failure.[21]

Again, the technique has been discussed in relation to several of the earlier novels. And, as noted earlier, there are certainly clear similarities between the manner in which Ōtsu emerges as the narrative embodiment of his own view of Christ – as the archetypal *dōhansha* figure himself – and a similar juxtaposition in the cases of, for example, Gaston and Mitsu. The titles of the chapters focusing on Ōtsu drawn straight from the Book of Isaiah, the manner in which Mitsuko juxtaposes the image of Ōtsu carrying the dying for cremation beside the Ganges with that of Christ bearing His cross to Golgotha: the text is replete with images that serve to reinforce this superimposition.

As always, however, focus on the similarities between this and earlier texts provides, at best, an incomplete picture. We have now travelled a long way from the more straightforward attempts to depict 'a God with whom the Japanese can identify', never far below the surface of discussions of the various novels up to, and including *Silence*. And it is in his ability to offer a revised vision of the potential for rebirth for the various members of the tour that Ōtsu's contribution to the narrative is most revealing.

The spiritual awakening attributed to Ōtsu as he works amongst the dying beside the Ganges is a far cry indeed from that evidenced by any of the previous Endō protagonists – with one significant exception. The vision is of a God, not as some supernatural, omnipotent being but as a 'great life force' (*ōki na inochi*), which envelops, not just the individual but the whole natural world. Here is an image of divinity whom Ōtsu identifies as 'not so much an existence (*sonzai*) as a force' (*hataraki*; lit. work), and whom Ōtsu does not so much 'believe in' (*shinkō ja nai*) as 'depend upon' and 'trust' (*shinrai shite imasu*, p. 66) – one that is reminiscent of that depicted by the renegade Japanese monk at Tecali in *The Samurai*. For Ōtsu, as for the Tecali monk, the image is of 'an entity that performs the labours of love' (*ai no hataraku katamari*, p. 64), an 'entity of unbounded gentleness and love' (*mugen no yasashisa to ai no katamari*, p. 67). In comparison to the earlier *dōhansha* figures, the image incorporates one significant modification: its removal from any specific cultural or systematic context.

In retrospect, Ōtsu's claim that, in living our religious lives within a particular cultural or sectarian context, the individual stands to lose sight of the fundamental essence of God as a 'great life force' can be seen incorporated in the portrayal of the Tecali monk committed to ending his days divorced from both his native and spiritual homes. For Ōtsu, however, the absence of any such limitations is integral to his interpretation of divinity and his journey from Japan via France and Israel to India can readily be viewed as the narrative embodiment of the author's determination, cited earlier, 'to clarify the relationship between the great life force and Christ'.

As long as he remains in Europe, Ōtsu struggles to find a suitable outlet for his conviction in the possibility for reconciliation of differences and the 'harsh criticism' he receives for his 'heretical' views remains a source of genuine incomprehension. But even at this stage, the source of Ōtsu's struggle is clearly formulated in his own mind. He is convinced that:

> God has many different faces. I don't think God exists exclusively in the churches and chapels of Europe. I think he is also among the Jews and Buddhists and the Hindus. (p. 121)

The road that will ultimately take Ōtsu to Vârânasi is already well-prepared, the warm welcome he receives from the Hindu *sâdhus* on arrival there eliciting little surprise. To him, the decision to work alongside the *sâdhus* in helping the untouchables represents no inherent contradiction for, as he confidently declares in response to Mitsuko's query as to whether he has converted to Hinduism, 'No, I'm...I'm just like I've always been. Even what you see here now is a Christian priest. But the Hindu *sâdhus* have welcomed me warmly' (pp. 180–1). For all his outward appearance, Ōtsu remains wedded to the ideal of the *dōhansha* that had earlier led him to pursue his studies in France. It is his conviction of the centrality of selfless love at the core of all religious schema that has been hardened in the light of confrontation with European orthodoxy. And at the heart of this conviction lies the example he attributes to 'the Onion':

> If the Onion came to this city, he of all people would carry the fallen on his back and take them to the cremation grounds. Just as he bore the cross on his back while he was alive....In the end, I've decided that my Onion doesn't live only within European Christianity. He can be found in Hinduism and in Buddhism as well. This is no longer just an idea in my head, it's a way of life I've chosen for myself....
>
> When the Onion was killed...the disciples who remained finally understood his love and what it meant. Every one of them had stayed alive by abandoning him and running

away. He continued to love them even though they had betrayed him. As a result, he was etched into each of their guilty hearts, and they were never able to forget him. The disciples set out for distant lands to tell others the story of his life....After that, he continued to live in the hearts of his disciples. He died, but he was restored to life in their hearts. (pp. 184–5)

The section is worthy of citation in full. Not only does it provide the most concerted attempt in Endō's entire corpus to encapsulate the essence of the *dōhansha*. It also provides testimony to the paradox inherent in the depiction of Ōtsu: that in helping the dying he is, in fact, contributing to his own fulfilment. The paradox is crucial. Without it – without Ōtsu's persistence in the face of all manner of adversity – all the suffering and concerns of the others would indeed seem meaningless. Without it, the depiction of Ōtsu as the embodiment of strength through weakness would disintegrate.

The above discussion has sought to throw light on to the guiding principle behind Ōtsu's decision to devote his life to helping the sick and dying in Vârânasi. In so doing, it has highlighted a vision, central to the narrative development of *Deep River*, remarkable in its similarities to that held by a group to which, as already noted, Endō had long been attracted: the *Kakure* (Hidden) Christians. Let us dwell briefly on the similarities – as the comparison provides valuable insights into the nature of the influence exercised by Ōtsu on the journeys undertaken by the various tourists, albeit vicariously.

Given the need for both Ōtsu and the *Kakure* to seek to perpetuate their faith in an environment in which Christianity was at best tolerated, at worst forcibly suppressed, such similarities may be hardly surprising. The Hinduism that Ōtsu encounters at Vârânasi raises profound questions in the protagonist's mind as to the 'absolute' nature of Christianity – in a manner reminiscent of the subtle, yet all-pervading influence exerted, again unconsciously, by the indigenous religions of Japan on the initially unquestioning faith the *Kakure* inherited from the Christian missionaries in the sixteenth and early seventeenth centuries. The effect in both instances is similar: in challenging the orthodoxies, these indigenous influences highlight the integral nature of the soul. A verse from the *Kakure* 'Konchirisan no ryaku' serves to emphasise this centrality:

Of all that is important to man, none is more so than salvation of the *anima*, or soul. As Jesus, the very saviour of all mankind, said, 'What shall it benefit man if he inherit the whole world though he lose his soul?' Or as He said elsewhere, 'No amount of wealth can purchase salvation for the soul'.[22]

The verse is explicit in its extolling of the soul. And it is this very lesson – the importance of plumbing the depths of his own being in search of his soul – that Ōtsu appears to heed through adversity and that ultimately leads to his selfless efforts on behalf of those dying beside the Ganges. In helping those in need, Ōtsu strives for their salvation, not in a physical sense, nor even in an orthodox Christian sense, but salvation for their *anima*, the soul at the heart of their being. Thereafter, a similar process can be seen effected on the lives of the Japanese tourists. Each has been depicted as travelling to India engaged in a search. As the narrative progresses, so the object of this search comes to be identified, as a result of juxtaposition with scenes of Ōtsu's altruistic devotion, as the *anima*. And as each experiences their moment of epiphany beside the Ganges, so they come, not only to recognise the absence of the help of the *anima* in their lives to date, but also to acknowledge it as essential to human existence.

The discovery is profound and shared by all the tourists. Nowhere, however, is it more in evidence, nor explored more explicitly within the narrative, than in the person of Mitsuko. Let us turn, then, to consideration of the process of rebirth inherent in the portrayal of Mitsuko – and the extent to which this is reflected in her evolving response to Ōtsu's presence in her life – as the drama unfolds.

In view of the shared name and the author's own comments to the effect that Mitsuko represented an extension of the portrayal of Madame Naruse in *Scandal*, the temptation to view Endō's latest female protagonist simply in these terms is strong. Certainly, the similarities are marked. At the same time, however, for all the validity of such ready comparisons, there is a depth to the exploration of Mitsuko's inner being in *Deep River* that is largely absent from the depiction of Madame Naruse in *Scandal*. Exposure of the emptiness within Mitsuko is more pronounced and the consequent search for something in which Mitsuko can place her trust is pursued with an intensity missing in the earlier *Scandal*, in which her narrative role is limited to serving as catalyst for the changes effected within Suguro. In contrast to Madame Naruse, the relatively uncomplicated symbol of the coexistence of good and evil and the chaos of life whose volunteer work appears as a clear reflection of an abiding love for others, Mitsuko in *Deep River* is a complex being, desperate in her search for something, yet unable to identify the object of her pursuit. At the same time, there are indications, right from the outset, of a woman more acutely aware of the need to acknowledge the existence of both conscious and unconscious elements within the human composite: her description of the comments of the terminally ill wife of Isobe is couched in terms designed to draw attention to this divide:

> She said her conscious mind had slipped out of her body and was looking down from the ceiling at the shell of her body lying on the bed. (p. 15)

Already, Mitsuko is marked out as more sensitive to the complexities of human nature than the other hospital workers. In the section that follows, a section devoted to portrayal of her student days, the emphasis once more is on a woman clearly distinguished from those around her:

> Unlike her school-friends who thought only of the commonplace lives (*seikatsu*) they would be leading in the years ahead, she had wanted to live fully (*jinsei ga hoshikatta*). (p. 33)

The translation is highly effective in capturing the explicit distinction between those intent on pursuit of a future unburdened by spiritual concerns (those who seek an uncomplicated daily routine, or *seikatsu*) and those, like Mitsuko, for whom the future represented a search (those who crave a guiding principle on which to construct a more meaningful *jinsei*). It is this desire to 'live fully' that is the guiding force behind Mitsuko's search, a quest born of intense loneliness, which Mitsuko herself struggles to comprehend. On the one level, she responds to such uncertainty with a desperate attempt to follow the example of her peers and content herself with a trouble-free *seikatsu*: it is this that convinces her of the harmless nature of the taunts directed at fellow-student, Ōtsu, for his reluctance to join in the conventional student pursuits, and this that motivates her to consent to marry the uncomplicated Yano. But, as she sits with him in their Paris hotel on their honeymoon, so the doubts surface:

> *Look at yourself.* Mitsuko took herself to task. *You still haven't abandoned your true feelings. Weren't you planning to bury yourself in your husband?...Just what is it you want?... Just what is it you're searching for?* (pp. 56–7, emphasis in original)

The object of her quest may remain cloaked in uncertainty but, as if by impulse, Mitsuko abandons her husband to enjoy the traditional delights of Paris while she herself resolves to visit the region of Les Landes, near Bordeaux, an area that she associates, not only with the murderous instincts evidenced by Thérèse in Mauriac's classic, but with Ōtsu who, until recently, had represented the butt of her ridicule. The impulse is hard to fathom. But as she surveys the barren scene that greets her on arrival, Mitsuko is struck by a realisation that will have far-reaching implications: 'Mitsuko knew that she had left her husband in Paris and come to this rustic area in order to search out the darkness in her own heart' (p. 58). The realisation may come as a surprise to Mitsuko herself. But, in placing the spotlight very clearly on the workings of her own unconscious being, it provides an invaluable counter – an explanation of sorts – to Mitsuko's frequent protestations concerning her own inability to understand the lure that Ōtsu exercises on her.

The contrast between Mitsuko's lack of conscious interest in Ōtsu and the attraction he continues to hold for her at the level of the unconscious is carefully crafted. From the outset, he is portrayed as 'inept': 'he had no charm as a man, had nothing in his looks that might appeal to her, and he always aroused her feelings of contempt' (p. 116). The ensuing narrative, however, hints at the influence he will continue to exercise on the direction to be assumed by Mitsuko's search:

> *Yet*, in a realm completely removed from the one where Mitsuko and her friends lived, he had had everything snatched away from him by his Onion. While at the base of her heart she rejected everything Ōtsu stood for, she could not feel indifferent towards him. For whatever reason, even though she tried to obliterate him with an eraser, he would not go away. (ibid., my emphasis)

As the tour of India progresses, so Mitsuko's sense that 'the unseen Ōtsu was leading her about by the nose' (p. 167) is enhanced. At the same time, however, irritated by the 'cheap sympathy' she discerns in the attitude of her fellow travellers towards the poor and destitute who dog their every move, Mitsuko's response is unequivocal: 'She no longer wanted imitations of love. She wanted real love and nothing less' (p. 161). The realisation represents the first indication that Mitsuko's search will ultimately not remain fruitless. Significantly, it occurs following intense narrative focus on the role of the Hindu deities, especially Kâlî, mother goddess who serves at the same time as guardian of the dead, and Châmundâ, goddess of passion and suffering, as symbols of reconciliation. Let us briefly examine the narrative effects of this symbolism on Mitsuko's emerging self-awareness.

Mitsuko's fascination with the Hindu deities is manifest as soon as the group arrives in India. Encouraged by the like-minded tour guide, Enami, to experience for herself 'the stifling air, the dark subterranean interior [and] the eerie sculptures' (p. 138) of the various Hindu holy sites (temples that 'most Japanese found boring' (p. 137)), it is not long before she is in a position to acknowledge her avid interest 'not in the India where Buddhism was born, but in the India of Hinduism, in which purity and defilement, holiness and obscenity, charity and brutality mingled and coexisted' (p. 151). It is in these environments that Mitsuko comes alive, here that she appears best able to fathom her own unconscious instincts. Here, in these powerful symbols of all facets of life, are the clearest embodiments in Endō's entire *oeuvre* of the Great Mother archetype in which the forces of good and evil coexist.

Reference has already been made in earlier chapters to Endō's deployment of the archetype of the Great Mother. As Neumann himself has noted in his study of the archetype, however, nowhere is this fusion of opposing qualities 'incorporated in more grandiose form' than in the statues of Kâlî and Châmundâ.[23] Here on the one hand is the 'Terrible Mother...dark, all-devouring time, the bone-wreathed Lady of the place of skulls'. Here, at the same time, though, is the compassionate protector figure, the goddess to whom 'is due the life-blood of all creatures since it is she who has bestowed it'.[24] Her role is half that of torturer, half that of compassionate companion determined to lead the individual to salvation, as typified in the following depiction in the tales of the *Hitopadesa*:

> In her 'hideous' aspect, the Goddess Kâlî, the 'dark one' raises the skull full of seething blood to her lips; her devotional image shows her dressed in blood red, standing in a boat floating on a sea of blood: in the midst of the life

flood, the sacrificial sap, which she requires that she may, in her gracious manifestation as the World Mother, bestow existence upon new living forms in a process of unceasing generation, that as world nurse she may suckle them on her breasts and give them the good that is 'full of nourishment'.[25]

Depictions of the dual-faceted nature embodied in these deities abound in *Deep River*. Her interest initially piqued by Enami's portrayal of Kâlî and Châmundâ at the pre-departure informational meeting as 'earth-mother goddesses:...while they are gentle deities at times, they are also fearsome beings' (p. 31), Mitsuko's first exposure to them comes in the form of a collection of photographs of Kâlî in the New Delhi National Museum:

> [The photographs] depicted the savagery of the goddess Kâlî, who stuck out her long, snakelike tongue as she trampled on her husband Siva....
>
> The goddess Kâlî was gazing towards her, her arms outstretched, her eyes brimming with gentleness. Her lips had – or had Mitsuko just imagined it? – curled into a smile. On the next page, that smiling Kâlî sucked warm blood from the blood-soaked demon Raktavîja. She held up a freshly severed head, and blood flecked her lips as she poked out her long tongue. (p. 115)

From this moment on, Mitsuko is captivated by the intrinsic power of these effigies, her immediate response betraying their symbolic force:

> Earlier that evening she had told Isobe: 'I think I may have come here in search of something, too.' Was it the inept Ōtsu she was searching for? Or was she, like Thérèse Desqueyroux, looking for what lay in the depths of her heart? (p. 115)

The more Mitsuko finds herself discerning in these images the coexistence of good and evil, the more she finds herself experiencing a powerful sense of empathy with these deities. Indeed, as she scrutinises the tension inherent in these images, so she comes to see these as no more, nor less, than 'images of herself' (ibid.): in confronting these icons, Mitsuko finds herself confronting herself.

The juxtaposition is reinforced in the narrative portrayal of her next visit to a temple:

> They walked down the abraded stone steps. For an instant Mitsuko had the impression that she was beginning the descent into the depths of her heart. She felt both the anxiety and the pleasure of peering into the interior of her heart with a microscope. (p. 138)

In the description of the figures that confront her in the dimly lit sanctuary – and in Enami's interpretation of their allure, the emphasis is very firmly on the conflicting attributes combined within these images:

> Many of the Indian goddesses take on not only gentle forms, but also frightening visages. I suppose that's because they symbolize all the activities of life, both birth and, simultaneously, death....
>
> This goddess is called Châmundâ....Her breasts droop like those of an old woman. *And yet* (*demo*) she offers milk from her withered breasts to the children who line up before her. Can you see how her right leg has festered as though afflicted with leprosy? Her belly has caved in from hunger, and scorpions have stung her there. Enduring all these ills and pains, she offers milk from her sagging breasts to mankind. (pp. 138–40, my emphasis)

As noted in the earlier discussion of *Silence*, the force of the conjunction *demo* (and yet) is to shift the narrative focus away from the speaker's consciousness towards the narrator's portrayal of events and, in so doing, to place greater emphasis on the opposition inherent in these icons. There follows a series of descriptions of these goddesses, offered both by Enami and by the narrator, each marked off by a similar conjunction:

> She...she displays all the sufferings of the Indian people. All the suffering and death and starvation that the people of India have had to endure over many long years come out in this statue. She has contracted every illness they have suffered through the years. She has tolerated the poison of cobras and snakes. *Despite it all* (*sore na no ni*), she...as she

pants for breath, she offers milk to mankind from her shrivelled breasts....

[This was] an image not of a mother's plentitude and gentleness but of an old woman reduced to skin and bones and gasping for breath. *Despite it all* (*ni mo kakawarazu*), she was still a mother. (pp. 140–1, my emphasis)

The effect of these images, especially that of Châmundâ, on Mitsuko is profound and the more the text comes to stress the strong connection between this and the river to which the group is headed, the 'great mother Ganges' (p. 141), so the sense of discovery of 'the Asian mother who groans beneath the weight of the torments of this life' comes to 'pierce Mitsuko's heart' (p. 175). There is a life force that she comes to discern in these images to which Mitsuko finds herself drawn and, as more and more she comes to detect in this a symbol of the 'real love' for which she has been thirsting, so she finds herself increasingly juxtaposing the image onto that of Ōtsu for whom such love has come to assume the form of an unwavering commitment to selfless acts of care and concern for those in greatest need. It is entirely appropriate, therefore, that Mitsuko's eventual meeting with Ōtsu should occur shortly after her latest meditation in front of the statue of Châmundâ. Equally appropriate is that the meeting should take place beside the Ganges, the river by which she is reminded of the symbiotic relationship between life and death. The more she contemplates the Ganges, the more she is attracted to its ability to envelop all pain and suffering. In so doing, she is reminded of the image of Christ she vaguely recalls from the Kultur Heim, oasis of Christianity at which she had directed her scorn during her student days.

The transformation effected within Mitsuko as a result of her encounter beside the Ganges is depicted in restrained terms, typical of Endō's *oeuvre*. Drawn to an attitude of prayer by the intensity of the experience, her instinctive response is to dismiss this as a charade – as 'just a fabricated prayer' (p. 210). In a passage reminiscent of the scene from *Scandal* in which Suguro watches as his double is enveloped in the light 'filled with love and compassion', the ensuing narrative sees Mitsuko enveloped in a sense of awe and mystery:

At the end of her range of vision, the river gently bent, and there the light sparkled, as though it were eternity itself. (ibid.)

For Suguro, as noted in the previous chapter, the light enables him to identify more closely with his double – to discern in this an embracing of his entire being, conscious and unconscious. For Mitsuko, however, the awakening is even more dramatic – as she comes to perceive herself as part of the great river of humanity:

> *I have learned, though, that there is a river of humanity. Though I still don't know what lies at the end of that flowing river. But I feel as though I've started to understand what I was yearning for through all the many mistakes of my past....What I can believe in now is the sight of all these people, each carrying his or her own individual burdens, praying at this deep river.* At some point, the words Mitsuko muttered to herself were transmuted into the words of a prayer. *I believe that the river embraces these people and carries them away. A river of humanity. The sorrows of this deep river of humanity. And I am part of it.* (pp. 210–11, emphasis in original)

No other Endō protagonist travels as far as Mitsuko in pursuit of their processes of individuation. Here is the prime example of an individual for whom consideration of her own unfathomable instincts leads to acceptance of the alternative, often conflicting facets of her being (which over the years she has struggled to reconcile) as integral to her individuated self. As she stands beside the Ganges, Mitsuko's renewal is complete, enabling her to empathise with her fellow travellers whose own, intensely personal searches had earlier failed to arouse her interest. She is now in a position to reassure Isobe, whose search for physical evidence of his reincarnated wife had ultimately proven abortive, that 'at the very least, I'm sure your wife has come back to life inside your heart' (p. 214). She is now in a position to acknowledge the presence of 'the Onion...reborn in the lives of other people...reborn in Ōtsu' (p. 215).

Seen thus, the portrayal of Mistuko in this, Endō's final novel represents a fitting culmination to Endō's corpus. Incorporating so many of the qualities of earlier protagonists, the sense of rebirth attained by Mitsuko can, in a very real sense, be attributed to confrontation with the *dōhansha*, the weak yet compassionate being who, as we have seen, has come alongside the various earlier protagonists as they continue their journeys. Initial depictions of Mitsuko at University, striving desperately to lure Ōtsu away from the Kultur

Heim are thus reminiscent of the protagonist in *White Man* as he taunts Jacques and Marie-Terèse. Her subsequent unfathomable fascination with Ōtsu is heavily reminiscent of the unwitting influence that Endō's 'wonderful fools' (notably Gaston and Mitsu) are able to exercise on those with whom they come into contact. At the same time, moreover, the portrayal of Mitsuko, drawn to a deeper understanding of those around her as a result of consideration of her own inner being, provides an interesting new perspective on the much-discussed concluding sections of *Silence* and *The Samurai*. In the former, for all the absence of any conscious decision, Rodrigues and Kichijirō nevertheless find themselves sharing each other's lives in the 'kirishitan yashiki'. In the latter, Hasekura moves from resolute rejection of God to a willingness to embrace death in his name. In neither case, however, are the motivating factors behind these conclusions addressed with the intensity evidenced in the depiction of Mitsuko. Yes, *The Samurai* includes the figure of the Tecali monk, whose role in bringing Hasekura to an acceptance of his destiny pre-empts the similar function exercised by Ōtsu in bringing Mitsuko to greater awareness of 'something great and eternal' (p. 211). It is nevertheless in *Deep River* – and, in particular, in the portrayal of Mitsuko's emergence as an individuated being – that these issues are pursued to a logical conclusion.

The sense of regeneration attained by Mitsuko as she bathes in the holy waters of the Ganges surrounded both by bathers and the ashes of the dead represents a deliberate focus at the conclusion of the narrative. At the same time, the suggestion, implicit rather than explicit, of the potential for a similar transformation effected in the lives of her fellow travellers is carefully crafted. For Numada, author of children's stories who is determined, in some way, to offer thanks for what he sees as the self-sacrifice of the myna bird that had died whilst he himself had been on the operating table, the moment of truth comes as he purchases a similar myna bird in Vârânasi and releases it into the wild as a token of the love he had received from animals in the past. As he does so, he awakens to the force of love, feelings that, though 'of no marketable value in the world of human affairs' (p. 204), he is nevertheless powerless to suppress.

Another to experience similar feelings of rebirth at Vârânasi is Kiguchi, whose simple prayer intoned beside the Ganges for the repose of the souls of his fallen comrades, enables him to expiate the memories of the death and suffering he had witnessed in Burma at the end of the war. As he performs the brief ceremony, his voice is carried along by the river:

> The river flowed by. The River Ganges moved from north to south, describing a gentle curve as it went along. Before his eyes Kiguchi saw the faces of the dead soldiers on the Highway of Death, those lying prone on the ground, and those with their faces turned to the sky. (p. 201)

As Kiguchi stands there, the river serves as a reminder of the powerless love he had received from his friend, Tsukada, as he himself had lain close to death beside the Highway of Death. And for Kiguchi, who knows only the world of the Buddhist sutras, it is at this moment, as he comes to acknowledge that 'Good and evil are as one' (p. 200), that his eyes are truly opened to the promised world of rebirth.

The other character whose rebirth beside the Ganges is hinted at in the narrative is Isobe. His quest for his reincarnated wife may have proven unsuccessful in the form in which he had envisioned it. But as he sits beside the river and watches 'as it silently flowed from south to north', he, too, is struck by a powerful realisation – of the 'depths of affection for him [that] were buried in his wife's heart' (p. 188). The impassioned plea, 'Darling!...Where have you gone?' persists. But, in observing that 'he had never called to his wife with such raw feeling when she had been alive' (ibid.), the narrative implicitly acknowleges the change that has been effected within Isobe. The conclusion he draws from this realisation – that 'there is a fundamental difference between being alive and truly living' (*seikatsu to jinsei to ga konponteki ni chigau*, p. 189) serves to reduce the distance between Isobe and Mitsuko for whom, as we have noted, the distinction had always been important. It may do little to assuage the sense of loneliness he continues to feel. But in portraying this cry, too, as ultimately subsumed by the great river, the narrative emphasis is on the extent to which, once more, the seeds of renewal have been planted:

> The river took in his cry and silently flowed away. But he felt a power of some kind in that silvery silence. Just as the river had embraced the deaths of countless people over the centuries and carried them into the next world, so too it picked up and carried away the cry of life from this man sitting on a rock on its bank. (ibid.)

Not merely for Mitsuko, then, but for her fellow travellers as well, the seeds of transformation have been planted as a result of their respective experiences beside the Ganges. This is not, however, necessarily to suggest that all will now be well – that they are leaving India with the answers to the questions that had drawn them to participate in the tour in the first place and will now be spared the sense of loneliness that had afflicted them all prior to the tour. They had arrived in India as a group of isolated individuals and, in a very real sense, they will leave India similarly alone. But their eyes have been opened – and it is here, in the *potential* for regeneration attributed to each of these individuals in these concluding portraits, that the force of the narrative impact lies.

We have noted the tendency to avoid explicit focus on outcomes – to remain at the level of enhanced potential for self-determination – in earlier novels. Nowhere, however, is this more in evidence than at the conclusion of *Deep River* – with the portrayal of Ōtsu, hovering between life and death following a savage beating by the crowd. True to character, the attack is largely self-inflicted: it is Ōtsu's willingness to intervene in the dispute between Sanjō, one of the tourists whose sole interest lies in securing a prize-winning photograph of a funeral at the *ghâts*, and the crowd, angered at his insensitivity, that incites the attack. The drama ends with Enami's report that Ōtsu had taken 'a sudden turn for the worse' (p. 216). The novel, which had started with the death and dreams of rebirth of Mrs Isobe, has now come full circle – to the suggestion of Ōtsu's potential death and rebirth.

Ultimately, however, Ōtsu's fate is left hanging in the balance. As with the peasants in the pit in *Silence* whose destiny, even following Rodrigues' act of apostasy, is studiously avoided by the narrative, so the question of whether Ōtsu will live or die is no longer relevant. Rather the emphasis has shifted from reality to potential and, in so doing, the narrative reinforces the enduring image of Ōtsu as a man whose life to date, far from a futile attempt to save those who are beyond salvation, had exercised a profound influence on all those with whom he had come into contact. He is now ready to cross over the deep river. The river, for its part, will continue to flow, unchanging, enveloping both the living and the dead in a constant cycle.

AFTERWORD

In his 'Sōsaku nōto' (Composition notes) written as he worked on *Deep River*, Endō was candid as to the physical struggle which composition of this, his last major work, represented.[1] The 'Notes' read as little more than sporadic diary entries for the period 1990–3, but the overall tenor is of a man struggling to complete one last work of art whilst battling against the ravages of increasing uncertainty regarding the direction the novel was assuming and against bouts of illness. Indeed, towards the end of the 'Notes', the author admits to having 'quite literally, whittled away at [his] own flesh and bones' in his battle to see this final work through to completion.[2]

The determination to craft *Deep River* into an appropriate epilogue to a career that had spanned some forty years is evident on every page of the 'Notes'. The overwhelmingly positive response to the work when it appeared in 1993 must therefore have come as considerable relief to the author.[3] For many, their response to the work was encapsulated by Yasuoka Shōtarō, who depicted the novel as 'incorporating every element of Endō's art, from the earliest texts to the present'.[4] And there was more than one critic ready to characterise the work as '*Endō bungaku no sōkessan*' (a final reckoning on Endō's entire *oeuvre*).[5] To the critic, Kawamura Minato, this sense of synthesis is attributable to 'a new element in Endō's art: a more positive approach towards the concept of *tensei* (rebirth) which until now had been rejected, both consciously and unconsciously, as non-Christian, and a more active attempt at syncretism of the various pantheistic faiths, of other major religions including Buddhism, Hinduism and Islam'.[6] Others sought to attribute this sense of novelty to what Inoue Yōji described as the author's deployment of 'the Ganges mandala, the mother Ganges which envelops all things, life and death, the beautiful and the ugly', citing this as an appropriate symbol with which to encapsulate a career devoted to the reconciliation of a series of oppositions.[7]

Critical response to *Deep River* may have been predominantly favourable. Underlying such critical comment, however, there continued to lurk the amorphous depictions of Endō as 'Japanese Catholic author'.[8] In view of this, we should not be suprised by the extent to which the numerous *tsuitōbun* (valedictory messages) contained in the various *tokushū* (special editions) of literary journals devoted to Endō's literary career, which appeared following the author's death in the Autumn of 1996, are dominated by discussion of Endō's legacy as 'Christian author'[9] To be sure, as noted at the outset of this study, such portrayals are convenient, in their own way, in encapsulating the literary concerns of an author whose struggle with the Catholic orthodoxy represented the catalyst for so much of his creative art. At the same time, however, what of the need to beware of the oversimplifications and the misunderstandings that tend to accrue to such loosely defined signifiers?

It was with this in mind that we began this study with an attempt to place Endō in the *shōsetsu* tradition of Japan. More specifically, it was in an attempt to identify the literary, as opposed to the theological context for Endō's writing that emphasis was placed on the author's relationship with the *Daisan no shinjin* literary grouping that emerged out of the ruins of war. Here, we suggested, was a group of authors – one to which Endō has traditionally been seen as, at best, a peripheral figure – who, whilst inheriting the pre-war *shishōsetsu* tradition, were so insistent in their assaults on the all-powerful literary self of pre-war personal fiction. In their resort to autobiographical material as the basis for so many of their fictions, the influence of the *shishōsetsu* tradition is readily identifiable. The difference, however, lies in the persistent questioning of the suitability of the self to serve as the mainstay of their 'fictions' – and in the narrative perspective from which this is addressed. These postwar authors had posited an increased distance between themselves and their materials – and, it is at this level, as an author at the vanguard of a tradition of fractured narrative perspective, that the depiction of Endō as representative member of the *Daisan no shinjin* literary coterie was supported. Here was a group of authors linked in their attempts to rebuild the literary 'I' – even if their means of pursuing this goal may have differed from individual to individual.

In view of the paucity of critical consideration of Endō's relationship with fellow members of the *Daisan no shinjin* to have

AFTERWORD

emerged during the course of his career, the relative dearth of any such discussion within these valedictory messages may appear as of little note. As already suggested, however, a glance at the list of authors and critics called upon to write these final tributes is highly revealing: not only does this list reveal a predominance of authors whose names have been linked, at one time or another, with the *Daisan no shinjin*,[10] but the recollections incorporated within these short messages concentrate on personal memories of incidents involving Endō during their formative years as authors, the late 1940s and 1950s, a time when these other authors were invariably discussed in terms of their *Daisan no shinjin* affiliation.

There is, furthermore, one notable exception to the absence of critical discussion of Endō's links with the *Daisan no shinjin*: the discussion, appropriately entitled 'Endō Shūsaku to Daisan no shinjin' (Endō Shūsaku and the *Daisan no shinjin*), conducted by Yasuoka and Kojima, two integral members of the coterie, and Ōkubo Fusao, whose own reputation as both critic and author has been intimately linked with the group.[11] The choice, both of these three contemporaries to conduct this keynote discussion and of the title subsequently assigned to this, serves to re-emphasise, if only by default, the strength and significance of the lifelong ties that Endō forged with his peers on the literary scene shortly after the Pacific War. Of even greater interest, however, is the interest, initially expressed by Ōkubo but subsequently shared by all three panellists, in the claim, 'often repeated by Endō, that if the literature of the *sengoha*, the first group of post-war writers, is a literature of strength, then ours [that of the *Daisan no shinjin*] is a literature of weakness'.[12] To Ōkubo, it is this comment that is cited as the clearest evidence that 'Endō is not a pure *Daisan no shinjin* member' (*junsui no Daisan no shinjin de wa nai*). His reasoning, however, is revealing:

> The pure *daisan no shinjin* authors are Yasuoka Shōtarō, Shōno Junzō and Yoshiyuki Junnosuke. But Endō is slightly different, isn't he? [He] writes of Jesus Christ. The typical *daisan no shinjin* author doesn't write of such great and powerful beings (*erai, rippa na kata*).[13]

But here, surely, is the point: is it not this trait, more than any other, that highlights the intimate connection between Endō and the *Daisan no shinjin*? For the Christ of whom Endō writes is no 'great and powerful being': he is a weakling, the very weakling upheld by the panellists as the hallmark of the protagonists who populate the pages of the work of the *Daisan no shinjin*. But he is a weakling who is able and willing to come alongside his creations, to share their pain as a *dōhansha*.

The concept has represented a constant refrain in the studies of the individual novels by Endō in the preceding chapters. In each case, we have seen this incorporated into the portrayals of characters whose initial self-confidence and assuredness is gradually undermined, eroded by the process of active engagement with a series of 'others' (depicted as either discrete individuals or as integral parts of their own complex being with which the protagonists are gradually reconciled). It is these 'others' who, for all their 'weakness' (typically identified as a lack of conviction in their own self-worth), nevertheless succeed in setting an example of integrity that the seemingly self-reliant protagonists struggle, in vain, to resist.

These 'others' represent an irresistible force for change within the various dramas. Equally important, however, are their roles as mirrors of that other layer of narrative that lurks behind, or transcends, the narrator's consciousness. Here is the alternative narrative voice in the discourse, one that, during the course of the dramas, comes to challenge the initially confident voice of the 'I-narrators' and slowly but surely, undermines the initial confident narrative portrayals. This voice is never vociferous; indeed, there are occasions when it appears to be too humble and self-effacing for its own good. There is nevertheless a persistence to this voice whereby, inexorably, it succeeds in making itself heard over the protestations of self-worth of the 'I-narrator'. It is these moments, distinguished in the texts as the moments of quiet self-awakening for the protagonists, that represent the true climaxes of the narratives. It is at these moments – moments in which the protagonists' actions are belied by their words – that the full extent of the process of reconciliation at work in the narratives is evidenced.

Reconsidered in this light, the first such moment of reconciliation in Endō's *oeuvre* is provided by the protagonist in *White Man* in his realisation of the mark that Jacques had left on his life, a realisation that stands in sharp contrast to the callousness he had evidenced as he witnessed Jacques' torture. This is followed by the ultimate admission by Dr Suguro in *The Sea and Poison*, that his 'always [being] there...not doing anything at all'[14] as he witnessed the vivisections performed on the American POWs was tantamount to complicity in the crime; by the ultimate, somewhat begrudging,

AFTERWORD

admission by both Takamori and Tomoe of the power of the example set for them by Gaston, the 'wonderful fool'; and by Yoshioka's demurring admission in *The Girl I Left Behind*, that he cannot simply dismiss Mitsu's death with a perfunctory 'So what?' In these, the early Endō narratives, the realisations are consciously acknowledged, albeit begrudgingly, at the conclusions of the dramas.

By contrast, in the later novels, the realisation tends to remain at the unconscious level, signified in the text, not by any statement of insight on the part of the protagonists, but in the commentary provided by that which was identified earlier, using Gessel's terminology, as the 'voice of the narrator's doppelgänger'. The portrayal of Rodrigues, in *Silence*, continuing to return to Christian practices (and thus constantly obliged to add his signature to documents of apostasy drawn up by the shogunate authorities) standing in sharp contrast to the superficial depiction of the denounced priest, apparently willing to conform with the shogunate demands that he emulate Ferreira; that of Hasekura, in *The Samurai*, ultimately embracing death as a martyr for a faith that, as he had continued to assert, had been adopted merely as a 'matter of expediency'; of Suguro, in *Scandal*, troubled to the end by those empty phone calls in spite of his persistent attempts to convince himself that the problem has been resolved; and of Mitsuko, in *Deep River*, persisting in her fascination with Ōtsu in spite of her frequent attempts to convince herself that he had long since been reduced to an irrelevance in her life: in each of these cases, consideration of the extent to which these protagonists ultimately achieve reconciliation with these alternative facets of their being is entrusted to 'the voice of the narrator's doppelgänger'. In each case, moreover, it is this voice that gives clearest expression to the distance travelled by these protagonists during their respective journeys of individuation.

The portrayal in each case has been of protagonists struggling to come to terms with an *uchinaru koe* (voice from within). Reconciliation, when it transpires, may represent the culmination of a painful process. The consequences for the individuals concerned are nevertheless, quite literally, life-changing – changes that conform to the template for this process as depicted by Jung:

> By paying attention to the voice within, the individual achieves a new synthesis between consciousness and unconsciousness – a sense of calm acceptance and detachment and a realisation of the meaning of life.[15]

APPENDIX A
A brief biography of Endō Shūsaku

1923 Born in Tokyo, the second son of Endō Tsunehisa and Iku.
1926 Moves with his family to Dalian in occupied Chinese Manchuria.
1933 Returns to Japan with his mother to live with an aunt in Kōbe following his parents' divorce.
1934 Receives baptism into the Catholic tradition.
1943 Enters Keiō University, but is soon mobilised to work in a munitions factory in Kawasaki.
1945 Returns to Keiō University where he enters the Department of French Literature.
1947 His first articles (including 'Kamigami to kami to' (The gods and God) and 'Katorikku sakka no mondai' (The problems confronting the Catholic author)) are published.
1948 Graduates from Keiō University.
1950 Sets sail for France as one of the first officially sponsored Japanese students to study abroad after the War. Determines to study the writings of various 'French Catholic authors' at the University of Lyons.
1952 Transfers to Paris but, almost immediately, is hospitalised with pleurisy.
1953 Is obliged to return to Japan in February.
1955 Publishes his first novellas, *Shiroi hito* (White Man) and *Kiiroi hito* (Yellow Man) and is awarded the 33rd Akutagawa Prize for the former.
1956 Assumes post as Instructor at Jōchi (Sophia) University.
1957 Publishes *Umi to dokuyaku* (The Sea and Poison).
1958 Receives the 5th Shinchōsha Prize and the 12th Mainichi Culture Prize for the above.
1959 Publishes *Obakasan* (Wonderful Fool).

APPENDIX A: A BRIEF BIOGRAPHY OF ENDŌ

1960 Returns to France to collect materials for a study of the Marquis de Sade, but suffers a relapse of his pleurisy. Returns to Japan and remains hospitalised for most of the ensuing three years. Publishes *Kazan* (Volcano).
1964 Publishes *Watashi ga suteta onna* (The Girl I Left Behind).
1965 Publishes *Ryūgaku* (Foreign Studies).
1966 Publishes *Chinmoku* (Silence) and *Ōgon no kuni* (The Golden Country). Receives 2nd Tanizaki Prize for the former.
1967 Assumes post as Lecturer on the theory of the novel at Seijō University.
1968 Publishes 'Kagebōshi' (Shadows). Assumes post as Chief Editor of the journal, *Mita bungaku*.
1969 Publishes 'Haha naru mono' (Mothers).
1973 Publishes *Iesu no shōgai* (A Life of Jesus) and *Shikai no hotori* (Beside the Dead Sea).
1974 Publishes *Kuchibue o fuku toki* (When I Whistle).
1978 Receives International Dag Hammarskjöld Prize for *A Life of Jesus*. Publishes *Kirisuto no tanjō* (The Birth of Christ).
1979 Receives the Yomiuri Literary Award for the above and the Artistic Academy Award for services to literature.
1980 Publishes *Samurai* (The Samurai) and receives the Noma Literary Prize.
1985 Is elected President of the Japan P.E.N. Club. Receives honorary doctorate from University of California at Santa Clara. Publishes *Watashi no aishita shōsetsu* (A Novel I have Loved) and *Hontō no watashi o motomete* (In Search of the Real Me).
1986 Publishes *Sukyandaru* (Scandal).
1987 Receives honorary doctorate from Georgetown University.
1988 Is selected as 'Person of Cultural Merit' bunka kōrōsha.
1991 Receives honorary doctorates from John Carroll University and Fujen University, Taipei.
1993 Publishes *Deep River*.
1994 Receives the Mainichi Cultural Arts Award for the above.
1995 Receives the Order of Cultural Merit (*bunka kunshō*).
1996 Dies on 29 September.

(The above is based on the biographical sketch provided for Endō by Hiroishi Renji in *Shōwa bungaku zenshū 21*, Tokyo, Shōgakkan, 1987, pp. 1,004–9)

APPENDIX B
Synopses of the works discussed

White Man

The first person protagonist is born in pre-war Lyons of a puritan mother and profligate father. Despite his mother's protection, he is introduced to the world of sin and lust by the family maid, whom he catches deriving obvious pleasure from beating the family dog. His sensitivity thus aroused, he sets out to explore this forbidden world – and, on a trip to Aden with his father, is enthralled by a young couple performing a suggestive street mime. But he is still looked upon as an innocent boy by those around him. Eventually he enters law school, only to reveal his base desires once more by stealing some of the female students' underwear. He is caught by Jacques, a student from the local seminary, and the two realise that they both have their crosses to bear through life. Meanwhile, the threat of war and Nazi invasion looms – but the two men realise that the Nazis do not have a monopoly on evil.

Jacques keeps sending Christian tracts to the protagonist – with various sections underlined. He is particularly drawn to the psychological pain suffered by Christ both at the Last Supper as He confronted Judas and in the Garden of Gethsemane. The protagonist starts to wonder about the nature of 'betrayal'. He overhears Jacques attempting to prevent two female students from attending a dance with the argument that, with the Jews being massacred, this is no time to be attending a dance. One of the students, Monique, storms off, but the other, Marie-Terèse, is torn. Eventually the protagonist decides to go behind Jacques' back. He invites Marie-Terèse to dance with him – and, still in confusion, she reluctantly accepts. Jacques turns up at the dance and is most disappointed to learn of the protagonist's deception and betrayal.

During the summer, the protagonist mulls over the question of

APPENDIX B: SYNOPSES

original sin – realising that man is powerless to overcome this. This helps him to understand why, with the Nazis drawing ever closer, university lectures carry on as if nothing is wrong. His mother eventually dies, but his overwhelming emotion is one of 'freedom' – the same freedom he had earlier experienced in Aden and as he had watched the maid beating the dog. He learns that Marie-Terèse has entered a convent – and assumes that this is at Jacques' instigation. He visits the local church in the hope of seeing them both there and cannot understand a Christ who allows such inhumanity to continue. Equally, however, he cannot fathom Jacques in forcing Marie-Terèse into the convent. This, too, appears to him as an act of tyranny; it is only in scale that this differs from Nazi atrocities.

Eventually the Nazis enter Lyons and arbitrarily arrest five locals to avenge a murdered colleague. The protagonist is struck by the question of why these five individuals had been selected for such treatment. He concludes that fate is in total control of their lives – and that it will be fate that determines whether they live or die.

It is at this time that the protagonist sees an advertisement placed by the Gestapo who are looking for help from bilingual citizens. Remembering his German father and betraying his mother's dying wish that she be accepted as French, he applies and is accepted. He is now party to the cruellest of tortures. At first, he is shocked by the callousness shown by the Nazi interrogators, but he is soon caught up in the sadistic pleasure they appear to experience. Before long, he is displaying a callousness to rival that of his Gestapo employers, betraying virtually no consciousness of sin or betrayal. One day, Jacques is brought in for interrogation. The protagonist watches as his former friend is tortured and then calmly offers him a cigarette. Jacques can only repeat his Christian conviction of his duty to stand up for – even to die for – the truth. The protagonist duly informs him that it was just this self-sacrificing spirit he had discerned within Christianity that had led him to join the Nazis. He realises that, unlike Judas, Jacques will never sell his soul and thereby betray his Lord, but he continues by explaining that he hates just such a heroic attitude. He also despises the hypocrisy of those willing to face death in the cause of righteousness, suggesting that, as individual human beings, they are equally as prone to evil as their neighbour. He acknowledges that, in attacking Jacques, he is attacking all those who live with an illusion of salvation. Jacques accepts his punishment, but refuses to hand over his cross. Next up before the Gestapo is Marie-Terèse and, once more, the protagonist uses the example of Judas in attacking her.

APPENDIX B: SYNOPSES

Throughout all this, the protagonist is struggling over the question of 'providence'. What fate or force was it that had brought the three of them together again? He concludes that the triangular relationship had been destined to reappear – and now each of them must either betray others (by divulging truths) or be betrayed (because of the stubbornness of the others and their own refusal to talk). He realises that, in making this decision, they would be betraying, not merely each other, but also the whole concept of 'providence'. At the same time, however, he realises that there exists a further element to their triangle: he is struck by a certain beauty to Marie-Terèse in her suffering, one that he had never before noticed. As the two of them listen to Jacques' pleas for mercy from his captors, she assumes the air of a 'saint' to him. Later that evening, they learn that Jacques has committed suicide by biting off his tongue and the protagonist is wracked by the portrayal of suicide as the ultimate evil. At the same time, however, he feels a greater sense of grief at Jacques' death than he had ever felt for his mother. He is struck by the pointlessness of this death and the realisation that evil continues despite all Jacques' attempts to live according to the dictates of his faith.

Yellow Man

Chiba, a young Japanese medical student writes to Father Brou, a Catholic priest being held in one of the wartime camps. He senses an irreconcilable difference between Europeans and Japanese – and wonders how the latter can ever believe in the 'European God'. He argues that the Japanese are different, both physically and mentally: they lack any consciousness of sin or of a single God. He recalls how the priest had tried to convince him that God transcends race and colour and had forced him to memorise the 'Ten Commandments' – and how meaningless this had all appeared to him. Meanwhile, the student has contracted TB and wishes to be left alone, but the words of the priest continue to haunt him: for all his cynicism, he cannot reject Christianity that easily. At the same time, he begins an affair with his cousin, oblivious to the fact that the latter is engaged; in view of the uncertain future, the two have determined to live for the present.

As he ponders his 'sin', the protagonist is drawn to Father Durand, the former priest who had been excommunicated following an affair with Kimiko, a troubled parishioner. The letter is purportedly to inform Father Brou that Durand has died, but, as he writes, the student recalls being drawn inexorably to Durand's house as a young man – even though the local believers are convinced that the latter will go to Hell for his sin.

The narrative switches to Durand's diary – to the section recalling his secret visits to the church even following his excommunication. He cannot help comparing his sin with that of Judas and wonders why Christ had been so harsh on Judas if He were truly convinced of the possibility for redemption of all sins and if He realised that he would die for Judas' sake the following day. Durand recalls how he had arrived in Japan ready to commit his entire life to propagation of the gospel, how he had been suicidal following his 'fall' and his cowardice thereafter in the face of the Military Police who were seeking out foreigners. He had accepted money from Father Brou, his former colleague, and had been impressed by this display of true Christian love.

Durand recalls how he had first encountered Kimiko following the Great Kanto flood as Kimiko had set out alone having lost her entire family in the deluge. He had taken pity on her and offered to help her if necessary. Within three days, she had turned up at his home – and he learns of her past and of the fact that she is pregnant. His parishioners insist that he abandon her, but Durand is unable to do so – and the two are drawn together by their mutual sense of rejection. Durand dreams constantly of the hell that awaits him, but, unlike Judas, he is too weak to hang himself for his betrayal. He finds himself ever more distant from God – and is aware that he is losing his consciousness of both sin and death. In this, he concludes that he is becoming increasingly close to his Japanese hosts.

Durand slips a pistol into his former colleague's study, knowing that it will be discovered by the military police and, despite knowing the extent of Durand's treachery, Chiba fails to inform the authorities. Equally, Chiba is wracked by the memory of his failure to push the alarm bell when he had come across a dying patient. In this sense, both can empathise with Judas. But equally both are aware of the pain that is experienced by the betrayer. There is, however, a fundamental distinction between the two men (symbolised in their difference in skin colour): whereas the former is plagued by thoughts of God's judgement and visions of hell and shows considerable concern for those around him, Chiba appears resigned to his fate.

One day, Durand visits his former colleague, mainly to check whether the pistol remains where he had hidden it. But as pretext for this, he lectures Father Brou on his belief that Christianity and Japan are mutually exclusive. But, try as he might, he cannot alter the fact that the Christianity he seeks to renounce continues to haunt him. The final episode is related by Chiba, who informs Father Brou how he had received from Durand on Christmas Eve what appears to be a suicide note. To Chiba, the fact that Durand is able to commit suicide is evidence of his absorption into Japanese society – though he is equally convinced that it had been Durand's consciousness of sin that had led him to that pass. He is nevertheless drawn to report all this to the incarcerated Father Brou, evidence that, for all his railing at the 'white' religion, it continues to haunt him and play a significant role in his life.

The Sea and Poison

When the protagonist visits his local doctor for pneumothorax treatment for his TB, he senses that there is more to the elderly Doctor Suguro than meets his eye. His investigations lead him to the Fukuoka University medical school where he discovers a hospital afflicted by an uneasy sense of doom. Briefly the prevailing politics within the department are outlined: the dean of the school has recently died and there is considerable competition to succeed him in this post. In particular, the chiefs of first and second surgery are manoeuvring to succeed him in the vacant post. Favourite for the job is Dr Hashimoto, chief of first surgery, who decides to bring forward the date for operating on a patient, Mrs Tabe, in the hope that success in this operation will enhance his election prospects. (He is aware that, as a close relative of the late dean, her speedy recovery would ingratiate him with the dean's faction.) Unfortunately, however, the operation is unsuccessful and Mrs Tabe dies on the operating table and there follows an attempt by Dr Hashimoto and his staff to make it appear as if the death had happened in her room during recovery. To regain lost prestige, Dr Hashimoto decides to curry favour with the medical staff of the Army's Western Command by agreeing to perform some vivisections on a few American prisoners of war for scientific purposes. From then on, the drama centres on those who get caught up in the steadily escalating web of criminal behaviour. Chief among these and protagonist of the novel is Dr Suguro, at that stage a young intern who becomes embroiled largely on account of his inability to stand up for his principles – and who provides a perfect focus for a novel dealing with the question of guilt consciousness. By the end, he has become vaguely aware that he is guilty, not only of cowardice, but also of wrongdoing – and it is this awareness that he will carry with him to the grave.

Wonderful Fool

The ungainly Gaston, a self-styled descendant of Napoleon, arrives in Japan and places himself at the hospitality of his pen-pal, Takamori. The latter is intrigued by his unconventional friend, but his sister, Tomoe, is contemptuous of Gaston's apparent stupidity. Refusing to explain the purpose behind his visit to Japan, he takes his leave of them as if on the spur of the moment. It is only at this point that Takamori and Tomoe realise the extent of their fascination and growing feelings of affection for Gaston; the more they think about him, the more they are intrigued by their visitor. After leaving his hosts, Gaston unwittingly helps a prostitute thief – and his life changes. The lady introduces him to a palmist, but on his first night working as the latter's assistant, he is abducted by a criminal by the name of Endō.

Endō is bent on revenge for his murdered brother and thinks that Gaston may be useful in helping him to evade the police dragnet. Gradually, the full extent of his predicament dawns on Gaston, but rather than seeking to extricate himself, he insists on remaining with Endō in the hope of reforming him. He removes the bullets from Endō's gun – with the result that when Endō has his victim cornered, the latter is able to escape. Furious, Endō beats Gaston unconscious – and the latter is ultimately returned to Takamori's safe-keeping. But by this stage, Gaston is intent on saving Endō from the consequences of his sins and, knowing that the latter had gone off to Yamagata Prefecture in search of his other victim, he again leaves his hosts without ceremony and follows after Endō. Once more, he becomes embroiled in Endō's plots: this time he plans to have his victim lead him to some stolen silver before killing him. Again, Gaston attempts to intercede and is almost drowned for his pains. Following a fight between Endō and his victim, Endō is left in critical condition – and Gaston disappears. There is no further news, despite the efforts of Takamori and Tomoe to track him down in Yamagata. It is only then that the police investigation reveals that Gaston had come to Japan with a missionary zeal determined to save the Japanese from the 'mudswamp' in which he sees their society as mired. The only explanation for Gaston's disappearance is the egret seen returning to the sky.

It is through the overpowering self-sacrificing love for his fellow humans that Gaston succeeds in pointing to the way out of the swamp. In order to become capable of love, the denizens of the swamp must first be loved. Significantly, at the end, even Endō is induced by this appeal to spare his intended victim.

The Girl I Left Behind

Yoshioka and Nagashima are two young men caught up in a monotonous student life routine. The former, in particular, spends his days whiling away the time in his room and looking for casual labour. All the time, though, he is wishing for more excitement in his life. One day, on a whim, he responds to an advertisement in a 'lonely hearts' column and, before long, he is waiting for Mitsu to turn up for a blind date. When she arrives, not only is she accompanied by her friend, Yotchan, she also strikes Yoshioka as being the archetypal 'country bumpkin'. After Yotchan leaves, he spends the evening initiating Mitsu into the night life of Shibuya. As the evening wears on, Yoshioka determines to take advantage of the latter's innocence. After plying her with drink, Yoshioka invites her to accompany him to 'one more place', but, on the way, they stop at a palmist's stall. Mitsu is advised that she is too sensitive and caring and that, unless she is careful, she will be exploited by men. She is also warned of an unexpected turn of events in her life in the next few years. The couple move on to a Japanese inn where Yoshioka overcomes Mitsu's resistance by appealing to her sensitivity. (He claims that he has never had success with women because of a limp brought on by childhood polio.)

The next day, the two go their separate ways to continue their humdrum lives. Both, however, are keenly aware that their paths through life have crossed and neither can put the other out of their thoughts. Mitsu in particular has been struck by Yoshioka and is desperate to hear from him. At the same time, she makes an effort to make herself more appealing to him and has her eyes on a cardigan. The days drag as she saves up to buy it, but on pay day, as she leaves work to go to the shops, she bumps into the wife of her boss who is experiencing financial difficulties as a result of her husband's excesses. True to character, Mitsu takes pity on her and hands over her hard-earned money, knowing that, in so doing, she will have to forego the cardigan. Shortly thereafter, she resolves to visit Yoshioka in his apartment, but on arrival there, she learns from his landlady that he has disappeared without trace.

APPENDIX B: SYNOPSES

Meanwhile, as far as Yoshioka is concerned, Mitsu represents no more than a memory from the past. On graduation, he enters a nail wholesale business and soon finds himself on the ladder to success. He is determined to make a success of the job and his prospects are enhanced as a relationship develops between himself and Mariko, niece of the chairman of the company. He works hard to impress her and, in so doing, Mitsu's existence becomes less and less real to him. For all that, however, he cannot put her out of his mind and as a result of a series of chance meetings with friends of Mitsu, he learns just how fate has treated her and how low she has fallen in life. When they do eventually meet up again, Mitsu looks bedraggled and forlorn and informs Yoshioka that she has been suffering from a mysterious spot on her wrist and sent to a hospital in the countryside. From her description, he realises that the hospital in question is a leprosarium and cannot believe this turn of events.

The same holds true for Mitsu, who struggles to comprehend the reason for her fall – especially as she had been brought up to believe that leprosy was a disease that only afflicted those with an evil karma. She makes her way to the leprosarium in Gotenba where she is immediately struck by the positive atmosphere and the optimism displayed by the patients despite having lost all tangible connection with the outside world. In particular, the story of Taeko, her roommate who had been struck down by the disease as she stood on the verge of marriage and a successful career as a pianist, is almost more than Mitsu can bear.

After several weeks in which she is unable to show her face to the other patients, Mitsu gradually adapts to life in the hospital – but it is at this point that she is informed that her diagnosis had been mistaken and she is free to leave and return to Tokyo. Her initial sense of euphoria is, however, quickly tempered by the realisation that, in so doing, she would be turning her back on her new-found friends and, despite travelling to the station, she cannot bring herself to board the train. She returns to the leprosarium and begs to be allowed to stay on as a volunteer. By this stage, Mitsu's caring and sensitive nature has been widely acknowledged and the ground is prepared for the tragedy that will strike at the conclusion of the work.

On another whim, Yoshioka, by now happily married to Mariko and moving rapidly up the company ladder, decides to send Mitsu a New Year's greeting card. A few weeks later, he receives a reply from a Sister Yamagata, the nun for whom Mitsu had worked at the leprosarium. The letter recounts events leading up to Mitsu's tragic death. It transpires that, on Christmas Eve, Mitsu had volunteered to take some of the eggs carefully nurtured by the patients to the local market where, under a long-standing agreement, they could be sold to provide cash for the patients. On the way, however, she had been involved in an accident in which a lorry had reversed into her. Sister Yamagata explains how, if it had not been for her concern for the patients' precious eggs, Mitsu would in all probability have been able to jump out of the way. On account of her selfless concern for others, however, she had insisted on cradling the eggs as she fell – as a result of which she had fallen into a coma from which she never recovered. Apparently her dying words had been 'Goodbye, Yoshioka-san'.

Even at this point, Yoshioka tries to convince himself that this was an accident with absolutely no bearing on his own life. By now, however, he has come to realise the full extent of the impact Mitsu had exercised on him and he concludes that, not only was he unable to deny Mitsu's presence in his life, but that if the God, of whom Sister Yamagata had spoken in her letter, truly existed, perhaps He spoke to his creations through such incidents.

Silence

The story is set in the early seventeenth century – with the Tokugawa shogunate increasingly confident in its own resourcefulness and consequently more and more willingly to banish the Christian missions who have been proselytising in Japan for the past century. Word reaches the Jesuit mission in Europe that one of their number, Father Ferreira, has apostatised, albeit under duress, in Japan and three of his former pupils volunteer to make the hazardous crossing to Japan in the hope that they can track him down and lay such rumours to rest. Only two, Rodrigues and Garrpe, make it to Japan, where they are immediately forced into hiding. Initially, however, they are well cared for by the local converts who provide for them under pain of death if captured. As the shogunate net draws in, the two priests are left more and more to their own devices and eventually they agree to separate in the belief that they stand greater chance of avoiding capture when alone. Before long, however, the inevitable happens and both men are hauled before the shogunate authorities; in the case of Rodrigues, he is betrayed by his own 'interpreter', Kichijirō, whom the group had met in Macao and who had been their sole source of information about conditions in Japan before their arrival.

The remainder of the drama focuses on the mental torment

APPENDIX B: SYNOPSES

endured by Rodrigues. He is forced to watch as Garrpe jumps from a boat and drowns rather than succumb to the shogunate demands that he apostatise, and as two Christians from the local village are cruelly tied to stakes in the sea at low tide and forced to await a slow and agonising death. All the time, Rodrigues is assured that all that is required of him is a 'pro forma' apostasy: if he were only to place his foot on the *fumie* (crucifix) brought out for this purpose and publicly to disavow his God, he will secure release, not only for himself, but for the various other Japanese Christians who are being tortured more to place psychological pressure on Rodrigues than to secure their own apostasy.

It is at this moment that Ferreira appears. He confirms the rumours about his own apostasy and tries to convince Rodrigues that Christianity can never take root in the 'mudswamp' of Japan. Continued defiance of the authorities is a pointless exercise in self-deception, he suggests, and he calls on Rodrigues to go through with the ceremony of apostasy, if only to spare the lives of the Japanese converts whose groans from the pit in which they are being tortured represent a constant reminder to Rodrigues of the price he is being forced to pay for continued affiliation to the proscribed faith.

Rodrigues' mood swings from despair at a 'silent' God who can sit back and allow his creations to suffer in this way to a determination to cling to all that his faith demanded even under pain of death. The moment of truth occurs as he is led outside and a *fumie* placed at his feet. As he hesitates, it is the voice of Christ on the cross he hears, a voice that encourages him to trample on the *fumie*: 'it was to be trampled on by men that I was born into this world', the voice suggests. As he places his foot on the *fumie*, dawn breaks and a cock crows in the distance.

Following his expedient apostasy, Rodrigues is feted by the Japanese authorities. Provided with accommodation, a Japanese name and a Japanese wife, the final portrayal suggests that Rodrigues has gone the same way as his mentor, Ferreira. For a discussion of the implications of the closing section of the narrative, however, see the discussion in Chapter 4.

The Samurai

Another work set in the second half of the Christian century in Japan (1549–1650), *The Samurai* focuses on the effects of the era of Christian proselytisation on several low-ranking samurai whose families have long since been reduced to virtual oblivion. One in particular, Hasekura Rokuemon, is determined to recover his family lands from the shogunal authorities, but all attempts to convince his master of the validity of these claims fall on deaf ears. His opportunity arises, however, when he is selected as an envoy to travel to Nueva España to try to establish lucrative trading contacts for his domain in the New World. The request comes from his master and is accompanied with an understanding that, were he to be successful on this mission, the lands will be returned. Hasekura has little choice but to obey and, a few months later, he and his fellow envoys board the ship. They are accompanied by the go-between, Velasco, a self-serving missionary who dreams of becoming Bishop of Japan and expelling the Jesuits. They also bear letters for the authorities in Nueva España from the Tokugawa shogun.

Following an arduous voyage during which Velasco tries his best to convince the envoys to accept Christian baptism as a means, however expedient, of securing an audience with the appropriate authorities in Nueva España, they arrive in Acapulco. They move on quickly to Mexico, where several of the merchants who had travelled with them go through with the ceremony of baptism, convinced that this is a small price to pay for success in their mission. The four samurai, however, refuse, whereupon Velasco convinces them that the only way to ensure the success of their mission is to travel on to Spain and to meet the Spanish King. Matsuki, one of their number, refuses and returns home to a hero's welcome and immediate promotion. But the others, Hasekura, Tanaka and Nitta, accept their lot and set off for Spain.

Again, the journey is arduous and fraught with danger. Once in Spain, the Council of Bishops convenes to hear Velasco debate the Franciscan policy on the mission to Japan with Father Valente, a Jesuit on the Council. The Council appears on the point of deciding in favour of Velasco (and agreeing to accord the envoys ambassadorial status) when Valente produces a damning report of Christian persecution being perpetrated by the shogunate. The report comes with 'proof' that the envoys' feudal lord has renounced his earlier claim to be favourably disposed towards the faith. By this stage, even the envoys are willing to embrace baptism, if only for the sake of expediency, but their petition is rejected nevertheless. They appeal to the Pope in Rome, but to no avail. They are now left with no alternative but to embark, empty-handed, on the long and hazardous journey home.

Four years after leaving, they return to Japan – to discover circumstances very different from those they had left. Persecution of the Christians is now in full swing and their admission that they had embraced Christianity, 'if only for the sake of the mission', is widely criticised. Following recantation, they are initially allowed to return home where they must remain inconspicuous. But the authorities, desperate for scapegoats from the former domainal regime that had been responsible for sending the envoys, eventually orders their execution. Meanwhile, Velasco, who had earlier left the envoys and stayed back in Manila, returns to Japan, is arrested on arrival and shares the same fate as the envoys.

Scandal

Suguro is a novelist approaching the end of a literary career in which he has built up a reputation as a 'Catholic author'. The story begins with Suguro being feted at a reception to mark receipt of yet another literary award and basking in the praise being heaped on him by critics and friends alike. As he stands at the podium to make his acceptance speech, however, he is disturbed by the appearance of a man, seemingly identical in every physical detail to Suguro himself, leering at him from the back of the auditorium. From this moment on, he is reduced to an increasingly frenzied state of self-doubt as he resolves to confront and consequently expose this being whom he seeks to dismiss as either a chance look-alike or an optical illusion. His efforts in this regard lead him to experience the seamier side of Tokyo's Kabuki-chō with its seemingly inexhaustible supply of scandal-mongers bent on destroying his hard-earned reputation through exposure of his less salubrious pleasure pursuits. In particular, it is from some of the women he encounters on his search that he is introduced to the 'aesthetics of ugliness'. Most notable in this regard is the figure of Madame Naruse, whose reputation as a caring and sensitive hospital volunteer belies her self-professed fascination with sadomasochism. At the same time, Suguro is hounded by a journalist, Kobari, who has been striving for some time now to expose the truth that hides behind the veneer of respectability surrounding what he sees as Suguro's carefully cultivated public persona.

The more Suguro struggles to track down the 'impostor', however, the more his fascination with the whole concept of the doppelgänger is piqued. All attempts to expose a physical double appear doomed to failure, and increasingly he is obliged to acknowledge a relationship between himself and this double that is more intimate and more complex than he had hitherto countenanced. Eventually, he throws himself at the mercy of Madame Naruse, who has promised to bring Suguro face to face with the 'impostor'. The meeting takes place in a hotel room. Far from the clear-cut resolution he had anticipated, however, Suguro is obliged to watch through a peep-hole as his double takes advantage of Mitsu, the maid whom Suguro had recently hired.

Suguro is obliged to leave the hotel with the situation still unresolved and as he does so, he watches first as his double is enveloped in 'a light filled with love and compassion' as he disappears into the distance and then as 'the light increased in intensity and began to wrap itself around Suguro'. The image suggests that the bridge Suguro had sought to create between himself and his double is now almost in place and, when he hears from his ever-supportive publisher that he has purchased and destroyed some potentially ruinous photographs of Suguro and Mitsu taken by Kobari, the situation appears to have been resolved.

Significantly, however, the narrative concludes with acknowledgement that this being 'continued to live inside Suguro…with his sneering smile' and leaves Suguro troubled once more by the jangling telephone that had served as a constant symbol of the voice of his unconscious.

Deep River

Isobe watches as his wife succumbs to the ravages of cancer and contemplates a lonely future. With almost her final breath, however, Mrs Isobe expresses her conviction that she will be born again and prevails on her husband to search for her after her death. The words haunt Isobe in the days following the funeral and he establishes contact with a University of Virginia research team who are investigating just such scenarios. He is informed by the head of this team that the only person on their records with claims to have been Japanese in a previous existence is a young girl, Rajini Puniral, who inhabits the tiny village of Kamloji in Northern India. Buoyed by this news, Isobe signs up for a tour of northern Indian holy sites, determined to find an opportunity to visit the village and to question the young girl who has been making such claims.

At the pre-departure briefing session, Isobe meets his fellow travellers, all of whom have shown interest in the tour as the next step in a personal quest. These include Mitsuko, a young woman all too well aware of the pain and suffering she has inflicted on others in the past and determined to use the tour as a springboard to a more meaningful future. As she talks with Isobe, it transpires that she had been the hospital volunteer at his wife's deathbed and the two establish an immediate rapport. Unknown to Isobe, however, there is a darker side to Mitsuko's past, a past that includes the psychological torment she had inflicted on the shy and devout Ōtsu during her university days and a marriage that had appeared doomed from the moment she had taken time out from her honeymoon in Paris to travel to the south of France in search of Ōtsu (who at this stage was attending seminary in Lyons).

For all her inability to fathom the impulse, Mitsuko continues to feel drawn to track down Ōtsu and it is the rumour that he has moved on to the holy city of Vârânasi beside the Ganges that entices Mitsuko to join the tour. Other fellow travellers include Numada, an author of children's literature who has come to India to purchase and release a myna bird as a token of gratitude for the bird who had died whilst Numada had been undergoing a life-threatening operation: to the latter, the bird had died 'in his stead'. Another traveller, Kiguchi, has spent the past fifty years seeking to find a suitable means to honour his comrades who had succumbed to disease and starvation during the infamous retreat along the Burma Road. In particular, Kiguchi is obsessed by the memory of his friend, Tsukada, who had quite literally saved Kiguchi's life by searching out food as the latter lay stricken: only later had he learnt that it had been the flesh of his fallen comrades that had sustained him in his time of need. The tour party also includes the Sanjōs, a young honeymooning couple whose desire to enjoy the trip is tempered by the husband's determination to take advantage of this opportunity to take some prize-winning photographs and by the wife's resentment that she had been deprived of her dream honeymoon in Europe. The tour is led by Enami, a seasoned traveller to India who is intent on shaping the tour itinerary to his own tastes.

Once in India, the travellers become immersed in their own agendas. Isobe tracks down the village in question, but his attempts to discover whether the young girl is really a reincarnation of his wife prove inconclusive. Numada releases a bird into the wild and Kiguchi offers prayers for his fallen comrades beside the Ganges. The main focus, however, is on the relationship between Mitsuko and Ōtsu, who by this stage is sharing his life with a group of Hindu ascetics seeking to provide a semblance of dignity to the thousands who make their way to the holy city of Vârânasi to die beside the Ganges. For all her attempts to convince herself that

Ōtsu has long since ceased to exercise any significance on her life, Mitsuko is nevertheless drawn to search him out among the dying on the banks of the Ganges. When they do eventually establish contact, however, Ōtsu explains how he has found purpose to his life in caring for the dying and expresses his determination that nothing should prevent him from continuing to work for the Hindu *ashram*.

As the tour draws to a close, all the actors are drawn towards the River Ganges, which emerges as a powerful symbol of the cycle of life and death. The drama concludes with Sanjō, the cameraman, stealing a shot of a Hindu funeral (in spite of frequent warnings of the potential consequences of such insensitivity). Ōtsu's attempts to intervene in the consequent skirmish provide Sanjō with the opportunity to run away. Ōtsu subsequently bears the full brunt of the mourners' wrath and is transported to hospital in critical condition. As the tourists depart from Calcutta airport, Enami's phone call to the hospital reveals that 'Ōtsu has taken a turn for the worse'.

NOTES

INTRODUCTION

1 A typical example of such depictions is that which appeared in *The National Catholic Reporter*, which referred to Endō as a 'Catholic writer billed as Japan's Graham Greene'.
2 Miyoshi, Masao, 'Against the native grain: The Japanese novel and the "postmodern" West', in Miyoshi Masao and H.D. Harootunian (eds) *Postmodernism and Japan*, Durham, Duke University Press, 1989, p. 146. An earlier version of this essay was published in *Critical Issues in East Asian Literature: Report on International Conference on East Asian Literature*, 13–20 June 1983 (Seoul).
3 Ibid., p. 143.
4 Ibid., p. 144.
5 Ibid., p. 155.
6 Fowler, Edward, *The Rhetoric of Confession:* Shishōsetsu *in Early Twentieth Century Japanese Fiction*, Berkeley and Los Angeles, University of California Press, 1988, p. ix.
7 Miyoshi, op. cit., p. 159.
8 Fujii, James, *Complicit Fictions: The Subject in the Modern Japanese Prose Narrative*, Berkeley and Los Angeles, University of California Press, 1993, p. 23.
9 Ibid., p. 11.
10 *Endō Shūsaku bungaku zenshū* (The Complete Works of Endō Shūsaku), Tokyo, Shinchōsha, 1975 (hereafter *ESBZ*), vol. 10, pp. 20–9. I have placed the terms 'Catholic author' and 'influence' in inverted commas to draw attention to the problems surrounding both terms as suggested above.
11 The following discussion of trends in the early twentieth-century Japanese *shōsetsu* is necessarily brief. For more detailed discussion the reader is referred to several more detailed studies, including the works by Karatani, Walker, Fowler, Hijiya-Kirschnereit and Suzuki. As evidenced by the frequent footnotes, I have relied extensively on these works in this section of the Introduction.
12 Karatani Kōjin, *Origins of Modern Japanese Literature*, Brett de Bary (trans.), Durham, Duke University Press, 1993, p. 61.
13 Ibid., p. 69.

NOTES

14 Ibid., p. 61.
15 Ibid.
16 Ibid., p. 69.
17 Ibid.
18 Ibid., p. 77.
19 Washburn, Dennis, *The Dilemma of the Modern in Japanese Fiction*, New Haven and London, Yale University Press, 1995, p. 66.
20 Watt, Ian, *The Rise of the Novel*, Berkeley and Los Angeles, University of California Press, 1957, p. 177.
21 This claim is made in Fowler, op. cit., p. 80. Similar claims are advanced in Suzuki, Tomi, *Narrating the Self: Fictions of Japanese Modernity*, Stanford, Stanford University Press, 1996 and Walker, Janet, *The Japanese Novel of the Meiji Period and the Ideal of Individualism*, New Jersey, Princeton University Press, 1979.
22 Mathy, Francis, 'Kitamura Tōkoku: The early years', *Monumenta Nipponica*, 18: 1–2 (1963), p. 1. The following discussion of Kitamura is indebted to Mathy's study comprising this essay and the two articles that appeared subsequently: 'Kitamura Tōkoku: Essays on the inner life', *Monumenta Nipponica*, 19: 1–2 (1964), pp. 66–110 and 'Kitamura Tōkoku: Final essays', *Monumenta Nipponica*, 20: 1–2 (1965), pp. 41–63.
23 This charge was levelled against Tōkoku by Yamaji Aizan, his former mentor.
24 Karaki Junzō. Cited in Mathy, 'Kitamura Tōkoku: Essays on the inner life', op. cit., p. 66.
25 Walker, op. cit., p. 69.
26 Mathy, 'Kitamura Tōkoku: Essays on the inner life', op. cit., p. 79.
27 Walker, op. cit., p. 66.
28 Cited in Walker, op. cit., p. 75.
29 Cited in Mathy, 'Kitamura Tōkoku: Essays on the inner life', op. cit., p. 103.
30 Mathy, 'Kitamura Tōkoku: The early years', op. cit., p. 1.
31 Karatani, op. cit., p. 71.
32 Walker, op. cit., p. 280.
33 Fowler, op. cit., p. 76.
34 Rubin, Jay, 'My individualism', *Monumenta Nipponica*, 34: 1 (Spring 1979), p. 25.
35 Napier, Susan, *The Fantastic in Modern Japanese Literature: The Subversion of Modernity*, London, Routledge, 1996, p. 117.
36 Hibbett, Howard, 'Natsume Sōseki and the psychological novel', in D. Shively (ed.) *Tradition and Modernization in Japanese Culture*, New Jersey, Princeton University Press, 1971, p. 313.
37 Hijiya-Kirschnereit, Irmela, *Rituals of Self-Revelation: Shishōsetsu as Literary Genre and Socio-cultural Phenomenon*, Cambridge, Mass., Harvard University Press, 1996, p. xiii.
38 Keene, Donald, *Dawn to the West: Japanese Literature in the Modern Era*, vol. 1, New York, Holt, Rinehart & Winston, 1984, p. 221.
39 Suzuki, op. cit., p. 11.
40 Ibid., p. 40.
41 Ibid.
42 Ibid., p. 41.

43 Walker, op. cit., p. 116, n. 25.
44 Kume Masao, ' "Watakushishōsetsu" to "shinkyō" shōsetsu' (The I-novel and the state-of-mind *shōsetsu*), in Miyoshi Yukio and Sofue Shōji (eds) *Kindai bungaku hyōron taikei*, vol. 6., Tokyo, Kadokawa shoten, 1973, pp. 50–1.
45 This was the title of an essay, by Ikuta, which appeared in *Shinchō*, July 1924.
46 Suzuki, op. cit., p. 51.
47 See, for example, the view of the *shishōsetsu* as expressed by one exponent, Mushanokōji Saneatsu, who wrote: 'What is of utmost importance is my Self (*jiga*), the development of my Self, the growth of my Self, the fulfillment of the life of my Self (*jiko*) in the true sense of the word. I chose writing for this purpose...because I love my Self, want to develop my Self, and want to give life to my Self....I will not sacrifice my Self for anything' (cited in Suzuki, op. cit., p. 52).
48 Lejeune, Philippe, 'Autobiography in the third person', *New Literary History*, 9 (Autumn 1977), pp. 27 ff.
49 Cf. note 43 above.
50 Cited in Fowler, op. cit., p. 48.
51 The ensuing discussion of the trend towards the divided narrative perspective in the literature of the *Daisan no shinjin* is indebted to Van C. Gessel's studies of their literature. Cf. *The Sting of Life*, New York, Columbia University Press, 1989 and 'The voice of the doppelgänger', *Japan Quarterly*, 1991: 2, pp. 198–213.
52 Although, as Gessel asserts, Endō was a regular attender of the *Daisan no shinjin* meetings following his return from France in 1953, his name is rarely mentioned in connection with this grouping by Japanese critics who tend to limit their discussions to its founder members.
53 Satō Haruo, cited in Suzuki, op. cit., p. 55.
54 Ibid., p. 56.
55 'Discourse on fiction of the self', in Paul Anderer (ed. and trans.) *Literature of the Lost Home: Kobayashi Hideo – Literary Criticism, 1924–1939*, Stanford, Stanford University Press, 1995, p. 92.
56 Ibid., p. 93.
57 Needless to say, for all this identification, it is important, even in the pre-war *shishōsetsu*, to distinguish between authors and their protagonists. As Fowler notes, 'Author and persona even in a *shishōsetsu* are *not* fully interchangeable, because authorial "presence" must always be, in the final analysis, a product of representation....To confuse persona with author...no matter how close the resemblance, is to confuse the telling with lived experience' (Fowler, op. cit., p. 9).
58 Hijiya-Kirschnereit, op. cit., p. 85.
59 Ibid., pp. 323–4.
60 Suzuki, op. cit., p. 59.
61 Cited in Kersten, Rikki, *Democracy in Postwar Japan: Maruyama Masao and the Search for Autonomy*, London, Routledge, 1996, p. 21.
62 For a detailed examination of such 'fantastic' elements in post-war Japanese literature, see Susan Napier's fascinating study, *The Fantastic in Modern Japanese Literature*, op. cit.

NOTES

63 At the heart of the *sengoha* group were authors such as Noma Hiroshi, Haniya Yutaka, Shiina Rinzō and Ōoka Shōhei. It was Shiina, in particular, who so consistently evoked the need to 'endure' (*taeru*) the current reality amidst the 'ruins' of Japan in the immediate aftermath of the Pacific War.
64 For a detailed discussion of the formation of this group and its fluctuating membership, see Gessel, *The Sting of Life*, op. cit., esp. Chapters 1 and 2.
65 Cited in ibid., p. 48.
66 For a detailed analysis of this debate, see Kersten, *Democracy in Postwar Japan*, op. cit.
67 Gessel, The Sting of Life, op. cit. p. 27.
68 See, for example, Torii Kunio, 'Sengo ni okeru shishōsetsu-teki ishiki' (The I-novel consciousness in the post-war period), *Kokubungaku: Kaishaku to kyōzai no kenkyū*, 11: 3 (March 1966), pp. 53–8.
69 Torii Kunio, 'Sengo bungaku ni okeru Daisan no shinjin no ichi' (The position of the *Daisan no shinjin* in post-war literature), *Nihon kindai bungaku*, 56 (1968), p. 66.
70 The depiction is that of Kume Masao in ' "Watashishōsetsu" to "shinkyō" shōsetsu', op. cit., p. 53.
71 'Watashi no bungaku to seisho' (My literature and the Bible), *Kirisutokyō bunka kenkyūjo kenkyū nenpō*, 12 (1980), pp. 15–16. Here, as elsewhere, I have continued to use 'novel' as translation for '*shōsetsu*' in the original Japanese. It should be noted, however, that the term is subject to the provisos outlined earlier.
72 Ueda Miyoji, Akiyama Shun and Abe Teru, 'Daisan no shinjin no kōzai' (The strengths and weaknesses of the *Daisan no shinjin*), *Mita bungaku*, 59:1 (1972), pp. 16–17.
73 Anderer, Paul, (ed. and trans.) *Literature of the Lost Home: Kobayashi Hideo – Literary Criticism, 1924–1939*, op. cit, 1995, p. 69 ff.
74 Fowler, op. cit., pp. 54, 57.
75 Cited in Suzuki, op. cit., p. 4.
76 Ueda *et al.*, 'Daisan no shinjin no kōzai', op. cit., p. 14.
77 Ibid.
78 Yamamoto Kenkichi *et al.*, 'Daisan no shinjin; sengo bungaku; heiwaron' (The *Daisan no shinjin*; Post-war literature; Discourse on peace), *Kaizō*, 36 (1955), p. 163.
79 Ibid.
80 The term is coined by Irmela Hijiya-Kirschnereit to underline the centrality of a single protagonist, closely identified with the author, in the pre-war *shishōsetsu*. Cf. *Rituals of Self-Revelation*, op. cit., pp. 70 ff.
81 This characterisation of the *shishōsetsu* is that of Endō, in *Ningen no naka no X* (The 'X' within Man), Tokyo, Chūō kōronsha, 1978, p. 161.
82 Torii Kunio, 'Yasuoka Shōtarō: hōhō to ichi – Senzen shishōsetsu to no renzoku to danzetsu' (Yasuoka Shōtarō: Style and reputation – continuities and discontinuities with the pre-war *shishōsetsu*), *Kokubungaku: Kaishaku to kyōzai no kenkyū*, 22: 10 (1977), p. 91.
83 Gessel, Van C., 'The voice of the doppelgänger', op. cit., p. 199.
84 Ibid.

NOTES

1 TOWARDS RECONCILIATION

1 This point is manifest mainly in the paucity of critical discussion of Endō's role within this literary grouping. For an exception, see Yasuoka Shōtarō, Kojima Nobuo and Ōkubo Fusao, 'Tsuitō zadankai: Endō Shūsaku to daisan no shinjin' (Commemorative discussion: Endō Shūsaku and the *Daisan no shinjin*), *Bungakkai*, 50(12) (December 1996), pp. 210 ff.
2 Those that do exist tend to assume the guise of a letter to a clearly identified reader or a diary entry in which the focus is more on the character's mental discourse than on factual detail.
3 'Watashi no bungaku to seisho' (My literature and the Bible), *Kirisutokyō bunka kenkyūjo kenkyū nenpō*, 12 (1980), pp. 15–16.
4 One has only to look at the names of those selected to offer valedictory tributes to Endō in the commemorative editions of the various literary journals produced on the occasion of Endō's death to determine the lifelong significance of the ties Endō forged with fellow members of the *Daisan no shinjin*.
5 This is the title of an interview given by Endō that appeared in *Chesterton Review*, 14: 3 (1988), p. 499.
6 Ibid.
7 I am thinking here in particular, of the protagonist of *Shiroi hito* (White Man), Suguro in *Umi to dokuyaku* (The Sea and Poison) and Tanaka in *Ryūgaku* (Foreign Studies).
8 As further evidence of the absence of a single focus figure in *Deep River*, note the gradual shift, discussed in Chapter 7, from emphasis on Mitsuko to equal prominence given to Ōtsu.
9 Cited by Kazusa in a lecture delivered at the Centre for the Study of Christian Arts, Tokyo, 26 May, 1997.
10 Endō, 'Awanai yōfuku' (Ill-fitting Clothes), in *Endō Shūsaku bungaku zenshū ESBZ*), vol. 10, Tokyo, Shinchōsha, 1975, p. 374.
11 Mathy, Francis, 'Shusaku Endo: Japanese Catholic Novelist', *Thought*, Winter 1967, p. 592.
12 Interview with Tanaka Chikao. Cited in ibid., p. 609.
13 'Watashi no bungaku' (My Literature), *ESBZ*, vol. 10, p. 370.
14 Here, in addition to Endō, I am thinking of such authors as Shimao Toshio, Shiina Rinzō, Miura Shumon, Miura Ayako, Sono Ayako, Takahashi Takako, Yasuoka Shōtarō and Ariyoshi Sawako.
15 In several of his early essays, Endō dwells on this clear-cut division between East and West as a prelude to his concerted attempt (to be discussed later) to challenge the notion of the unfathomable divide between the two. See, for example, 'Kamigami to kami to' (The gods and God), *ESBZ*, vol. 10, pp. 14 ff.
16 Endō has frequently used the term *sanbunhō* (trichotomy) to describe this perceived division. See, for example, Endō and Yashiro Seiichi, '*Sukyandaru* no kōzō: ningen no tajūsei ni tsuite' (The structure of the novel *Scandal*: Concerning the multifaceted nature of humankind), *Shinchō* (83(4), (1986), p. 197.

NOTES

17 'Nihonteki kanjō no soko ni aru mono: metafijikku hihyō to dentōbi' (That which lies at the heart of the Japanese sensibility: Metaphysical criticism and the traditional aesthetic), *ESBZ*, vol. 10, p. 146.
18 'Furansowa Mōriakku' (François Mauriac), *ESBZ*, vol. 10, p. 94.
19 'Katorikku sakka no mondai' (The problems confronting the Catholic author), *ESBZ*, vol. 10, p. 28.
20 'Shūkyō to bungaku' (Religion and literature), *ESBZ*, vol. 10, p. 119.
21 'Katorikku sakka no mondai', op. cit., pp. 20–1.
22 Ibid., pp. 21, 23.
23 'Watashi ni totte no kami' (God as I see Him), *Seiki*, 354 (1979), p. 62.
24 Cited in *Ningen no naka no X* (The 'X' within Man), Tokyo, Chūō kōronsha, 1978, p. 137.
25 Interview with Kaga Otohiko, 'Taidan: *Samurai* ni tsuite' (Discussion: About *The Samurai*), *Bungakkai*, 34: 8 (1980), p. 206.
26 Gibson, Boyce, *The Religion of Dostoevsky*, London, SCM Press, 1973, p. 54.
27 In this regard, one could mention, in particular, Shiina Rinzō and Shimao Toshio who were quick to acknowledge their literary debt to Dostoevsky.
28 'Katorikku sakka no mondai', op. cit., p. 27.
29 *Watashi no aishita shōsetsu* (A Novel I have Loved), Tokyo, Shinchōsha, 1985, pp. 21, 30.
30 Cohn, Dorrit, *Transparent Minds: Narrative Modes for Presenting Consciousness in Fiction*, New Jersey, Princeton University Press, 1978, pp. 135–6.
31 Ibid., p. 46.
32 Ibid., p. 56.
33 Ibid., p. 61.
34 Ibid., p. 77, emphasis in original.
35 Ibid., p. 105.
36 *Watashi no aishita shōsetsu*, op. cit., p. 13.
37 Ibid., p. 20.
38 Ibid., p. 33.
39 Ibid., p. 13.
40 Ibid., p. 33.
41 See, for example, 'Literature and religion, especially the role of the unconscious: The Voice of the Writer, J.K. Buda (trans.), *Collected Papers of the 47th International PEN Congress*, Tokyo, 1986, pp. 29–37.
42 Jung, C.G., 'Conscious, unconscious and individuation', *The Collected Works of C.G. Jung*, London, Routledge & Kegan Paul, 1953–77; (hereafter *CWJ*), vol. 9.i, pp. 275–6.
43 Ibid., p. 288.
44 'The detachment of consciousness from the object', *CWJ*, vol. 13, p. 45.
45 'The practical use of dream-analysis', *CWJ*, vol. 16, p. 152.
46 'The development of personality', *CWJ*, vol. 17, p. 180.
47 'The anguish of an alien', *Japan Christian Quarterly*, 40: 4 (Fall 1974), p. 184.

NOTES

48 'Introduction to the religious and psychological problems of alchemy', *CWJ*, vol. 12, p. 31. Endō makes a similar claim in *Watashi no aishita shōsetsu*, op. cit., p. 176.
49 'The psychology of the unconscious', *CWJ*, vol. 7, p. 65, n. 5.
50 'Psychology and religion', *CWJ*, vol. 11, p. 76.
51 'The undiscovered self', *CWJ*, vol. 10, p. 293.
52 *Watashi no aishita shōsetsu*, op. cit., p. 72.
53 Neumann, Erich, *The Great Mother*, R. Manheim (trans.), New York, Pantheon Books, 1955, pp. 75–6.
54 Use of the masculine pronoun here is deliberate since the Endō protagonist is predominantly male.
55 *Volcano*, R. Schuchert (trans.), New York, Taplinger, 1978, p. 127.
56 Cited in 'Katorikku sakka no mondai', op. cit., p. 25.
57 Ibid.
58 *Watashi no aishita shōsetsu*, op. cit., pp. 176–7.
59 Ibid., p. 167.
60 *Ningen no naka no X*, op. cit.
61 *Watashi no aishita shōsetsu*, op. cit., p. 175.
62 Ibid., p. 146.
63 Ibid., p. 152.
64 Ibid., p. 154.
65 Ibid., p. 70.
66 'Kamigami to kami to' (The gods and God), *ESBZ*, vol. 10, pp. 18–19.
67 'Author's Introduction', in Endō, *Foreign Studies*, M. Williams (trans.), London, Peter Owen, 1989, p. 11.
68 For a relatively recent discussion of Endō's views on this issue, see *Kirishitan Jidai: Junkyō to kikyō no rekishi* (The Christian Era: A History of Martyrdom and Apostasy), Tokyo, Shōgakkan, 1992.
69 Again, this aspect of Endō's art is clearly indebted to Western precedent: in a discussion with myself in July 1993, Endō acknowledged his indebtedness in this regard to the precedent established, in particular, by Graham Greene in the person(s) of Francis Andrews in *The Man Within* and by Dostoevsky in the portrayal of Golyadkin in *The Double*.
70 Keppler, C.F., *The Literature of the Second Self*, Tucson, University of Arizona Press, 1972, p. 1. Keppler uses the term 'second self' instead of 'doppelgänger' (which 'suggests duplication, either physical or psychological, or both') or 'inner self' (which is 'too limited, suggesting a twofoldness which is purely internal'). In view of its wider currency, I have chosen to persist with the term doppelgänger – but would concur with Keppler's caveat against the suggestion of simple duplication.
71 Ibid., p. 204.
72 Ibid., p. 10.
73 Ibid., p. 206.
74 Ibid., pp. 194–5.
75 Ibid., p. 195.

NOTES

2 WHITE MAN, YELLOW MAN

1 Endō wrote extensively of the feelings of humiliation he endured aboard the *Marseille* and following his arrival in France. See, for example, 'Shusse-saku no koro' (Around the time of my first novels), *ESBZ*, vol. 10, pp. 376–91.
2 'Kamigami to kami to' (The gods and God), *ESBZ*, vol. 10, p. 14.
3 Ibid., p. 17.
4 The above is a synopsis of the views expounded in 'The gods and God', in particular.
5 Hiroishi Renji, *Endō Shūsaku no subete* (Everything about Endō Shūsaku), Tokyo, Chōbunsha, 1991, p. 48. Cf. Hasegawa Izumi (ed.) *Akutagawa-shō jiten* (A Dictionary of the Akutagawa Prize), *Kokubungaku: Kaishaku to kanshō*, 42:2 (January 1977), p. 198.
6 *Shiroi hito, Kiiroi hito*, Tokyo, Shinchōsha bunkō, 1983, p. 53 (my emphasis). All subsequent citations from these novellas are taken from this edition.
7 See, for example, 'Watashi to Kirisutokyō' (Christianity and I), *ESBZ*, vol. 10, p. 355.

3 THE SEA AND POISON, WONDERFUL FOOL, THE GIRL I LEFT BEHIND

1 This novel was awarded the 5th Shinchōsha Literary Prize and the 12th Mainichi Shuppan Prize.
2 Endō made this point to me when requesting the translation of the novel, which I completed in 1994.
3 Kawai Hayao, 'Tamashii e no tsūro toshite no *Sukyandaru*' (*Scandal* as an avenue to the soul), *Sekai*, 491 (August 1986), p. 102.
4 *The Sea and Poison*, M. Gallagher (trans.), Tokyo, Tuttle, 1973, p. 21. All subsequent citations from this novel are taken from this edition.
5 *Watashi no aishita shōsetsu* (A Novel I have Loved), Tokyo, Shinchōsha, 1985, pp. 74–5.
6 Storr, A. (ed.), *Jung: Selected Writings*, London, Fontana, 1983, p. 88.
7 See, for example, Heremann, Marc, 'The problem of evil and the perception of it in the novels of Endō Shūsaku', unpublished paper, 1987, for such a treatment of this novel.
8 *Watashi no aishita shōsetsu*, op. cit., p. 74.
9 Endō and Satō Yasumasa, *Jinsei no dōhansha* (The Constant Companion through Life), Tokyo, Shunjūsha, 1991, p. 109.
10 Cited in Takahashi Takako, 'Endō Shūsaku-ron' (A study of the writings of Endō Shūsaku), *Hihyō*, 5 (Summer 1966), p. 104.
11 Barthes, Roland, *S/Z*, R. Miller (trans.), London, Jonathan Cape, 1975, p. 145.
12 *Wonderful Fool*, F. Mathy (trans.), Tokyo, Tuttle, 1974, p. 39. All subsequent citations from this novel are taken from this edition.
13 The depiction is that of Mathy in the Introduction to his translation of the novel, op. cit., p. 8.
14 The depiction is that of Frieda Fordham in her study, *An Introduction to Jung's Psychology*, London, Penguin Books, 1959, p. 49.

NOTES

15 Mathy, Francis, 'Shūsaku Endō: The second period', *Japan Christian Quarterly*, 40: 4 (Fall 1974), p. 216.
16 Neumann, Erich, *The Origins and History of Consciousness*, R. Hull (trans.), London, Routledge & Kegan Paul, 1954, p. 27.
17 For a discussion of Endō's focus on the maternal aspects of Christianity, see Kazusa Hideo, 'Kaisetsu', *Gendai Nihon kirisutokyō bungaku zenshū*, vol. 10, Tokyo, Kyōbunkan, 1973, pp. 165–96.
18 Cf. Neumann, E., *The Great Mother*, R. Manheim (trans.), New Jersey, Princeton University Press, 1963.
19 This is not to deny the significance of works such as *Volcano* and *Seisho no naka no joseitachi* (The Women of the Bible, 1960) or of short stories such as 'Watashi no mono' (My Belongings, 1963; trans. 1985) that were penned in between protracted periods of hospitalisation.
20 *Watashi no aishita shōsetsu*, op. cit., pp. 62 ff.
21 Ibid., p. 73.
22 *The Girl I Left Behind*, M. Williams (trans.), London, Peter Owen, 1994, p. 26. All subsequent citations from this novel are taken from this edition.
23 It was the critic, Takeda Tomoju, who noted the symbolism of the name, Mitsu – as an 'inversion of evil' (Japanese: *tsu-mi*). Cf. Endō and Satō Yasumasa, *Jinsei no dōhansha*, op. cit., p. 129.
24 It was this image of Christ, the *dōhansha*, that Endō sought to develop, more explicitly, in works such as *Iesu no shōgai* (A Life of Jesus, 1973; trans., 1978).
25 'Author's Afterword', *The Girl I Left Behind*, op. cit., p. 196.
26 One critic to have argued for such a distinction is Hiroishi Renji in his study, *Endō Shūsaku no subete* (Everything about Endō Shūsaku), Tokyo, Chōbunsha, 1991.
27 'Author's Afterword', *The Girl I Left Behind*, op. cit., p. 196.

4 *SILENCE*

1 For examples of this positive response to the works discussed in the previous chapter, see, for example, Kazusa Hideo, *Endō Shūsaku-ron* (A Study of Endō Shūsaku), Tokyo, Shunjusha, 1987, and Hiroishi Renji, *Endō Shūsaku no subete* (Everything about Endō Shūsaku), Tokyo, Chōbunsha, 1991.
2 For a fascinating study of the significance of the *Kakure* beliefs and rituals, see Turnbull, Stephen, *The Kakure Kirishitan of Japan: A Study of their Development, Beliefs and Rituals to the Present Day*, Folkestone, Japan Library, 1998.
3 'Concerning the novel *Silence*', *Japan Christian Quarterly*, 36: 2 (Spring 1970), p. 101.
4 Ibid.
5 'The anguish of an alien', *Japan Christian Quarterly*, 40: 4 (Fall 1974), p. 180.
6 See, for example, 'Concerning the novel *Silence*', op. cit.
7 *Watashi no aishita shōsetsu* (A Novel I have Loved), Tokyo, Shinchōsha, 1985, p. 154 ff.

NOTES

8 In a brief 'Postscript' included in the original Shinchōsha edition of the novel, Endō briefly addresses the issue of his faithfulness to historical sources re Chiara. According to Endō, the historical Chiara was born in Sicily, arrived on Chikuzen Ōshima in southern Japan in search of his mentor in 1643, was captured almost immediately and sent to Edo where he was tortured by Inoue. Following his eventual apostasy, he was given leave to live in the 'Christian mansion' (*Kirishitan yashiki*), married, and survived until 1685. Endō goes on to stress the importance of 'maintaining the distinction between my protagonist and the historical Chiara' (*Chinmoku*, Shinchōsha, 1966, pp. 256–7).

9 See W. Johnston's 'Translator's Preface', in *Silence*, London, Peter Owen, 1996, pp. 16–17 for a discussion of the negative reception accorded the novel by the Japanese Christian community. The issue is also addressed in Takeda Tomoju, *Endō Shūsaku no sekai* (The World of Endō Shūsaku), Tokyo, Kōdansha, 1971. For Endō's response to such criticism, see Endō and Kaga Otohiko, 'Taidan: Saishinsaku *Fukai kawa*: Tamashii no mondai' (A discussion of the recent novel, *Deep River*: The question of the soul), in Endō Shūsaku *et al.*, 'Tokushū: Endō Shūsaku: Gurōbaru na ninshiki' (Special edition: Endō Shūsaku: A global awareness), *Kokubungaku: Kaishaku to kyōzai no kenkyū*, 38: 10 (1993), p. 16 ff.

10 *Silence*, W. Johnston (trans.), London, Peter Owen, 1996, pp. 237, 241. All further references to the novel are taken from this edition.

11 'Chichi no shūkyō: haha no shūkyō' (Paternal religion, maternal religion), *ESBZ*, vol. 10, p. 181.

12 This view is cited by William Johnston in his translator's preface to *Silence*, op. cit., p. 17.

13 See the author's 'Postscript' in which Endō acknowledges his awareness that his portrayal of Rodrigues' faith (which he describes as 'close to Protestantism') will 'obviously induce criticism in theological circles' ('Postscript' to *Silence*, op. cit., p. 256).

14 Van Gessel, *The Sting of Life*, New York, Columbia University Press, 1989, p. 253.

15 I have amended Johnston's translation of '*fumu ga ii*' from 'Trample!' to 'You should trample'. The original Japanese is not an imperative – and the quiet encouragement encompassed in the expression, 'You should trample' seems more in keeping with Endō's well-worn image of the *dōhansha*, the constant companion in times of trouble. One could also make a case for 'You may trample'. But I feel that 'should trample' serves better as an echo of Christ's pressing words, offered to Judas at the Last Supper ('That thou doest, do quickly' (John 13: 27)) – an echo that is picked up in the subsequent lines, 'It was to share men's pain that I carried my cross....Far in the distance, the cock crew'.

16 Unfortunately, this has been relegated to the status of an 'Appendix' in the English translation. The Japanese original, however, makes no such distinction between this section and the preceding chapter and, as suggested earlier, my interpretation relies heavily on a reading of the final two chapters and the 'Kirishitan yashiki' section as one consistent narrative.

NOTES

17 The English translation suggesting that Rodrigues is 'engaged in writing a book' (p. 300) is unfortunate. It should however be noted that this diary entry is lodged between two entries that portray Rodrigues 'engaged in writing a disavowal of his religion'. The original Japanese prefaces the first and third mention of this *shomotsu* with the phrase '*shūmon no*' (of [his] religion), but there is nothing to suggest other than that the second mention of the *shomotsu* refers to this same document of apostasy.
18 This encapsulation of James' ideas is in Leon Edel's *The Modern Psychological Novel*, New York, Grosset and Dunlap, 1964, pp. 51–2; emphasis in original.
19 Ibid., p. 50.
20 Cited in ibid., p. 54.
21 Ibid., p. 58.
22 Cited in Takano Toshimi, 'Endō bungaku ni okeru Iesu-zō' (The image of Christ in the literature of Endō), in Takeda Tomoju *et al.*, 'Tokushū: Endō Shūsaku' (Special edition: Endō Shūsaku), *Kokubungaku: kaishaku to kanshō*, 51:10 (1986), p. 50.
23 See, for example, Etō Jun, 'Seijuku to sōshitsu: "haha" no hōkai' (Maturity and loss: The collapse of the mother), in *Gendai no bungaku*, 27, Tokyo, Kōdansha, 1972, pp. 84 ff.
24 Ibid., p. 86.
25 *Watashi no aishita shōsetsu*, op. cit., p. 85.
26 On several occasions in private conversation, Endō spoke of his disappointment at the interpretation of the novel as portrayed in the original film version by Shinoda Masahiro.
27 *Nihon Keizai shinbun* (October 17, 1993), p. 32.

5 THE SAMURAI

1 Endō admitted to these concerns in Endō and Kaga Otohiko, 'Taidan: *Samurai* ni tsuite' (Discussion: About *The Samurai*), *Bungakkai*, 34: 8 (1980), p. 200 ff.
2 An earlier translation of this story did appear in *The Bulletin of the College of Biomedical Technology* (Niigata University), 1: 1 (1983), but is not widely accessible.
3 'Shadows', in *The Final Martyrs*, V. Gessel (trans.), London, Peter Owen, 1993, p. 30.
4 Ibid., p. 56.
5 Ibid., p. 57.
6 'Mothers', in *Stained Glass Elegies*, V. Gessel (trans.), London, Peter Owen, 1984, p. 122.
7 Ibid., p. 126.
8 Ibid., p. 129.
9 Ibid., p. 130.
10 This intent is embodied in the title of the story, '*Haha naru mono*' (lit. 'Maternal beings').
11 'Mothers', op. cit. p. 112.
12 Ibid., p. 130.
13 Ibid., p. 135.

NOTES

14 All these depictions appear in *Iesu no shōgai* (A Life of Jesus), Tokyo, Shinchōsha, 1973.
15 *Kirisuto no tanjō* (The Birth of Christ), Tokyo, Shinchōsha, 1978, p. 250.
16 Cf. Satō Yasumasa, 'Modern Japanese Christian Literature after the Second World War', in I. Boyd (ed.), 'Christian writers of Japan', *The Chesterton Review*, 14: 3 (August 1988), pp. 416.
17 *Silence*, W. Johnston (trans.), London, Peter Owen, 1996, p. 298.
18 *The Samurai*, V. Gessel (trans.), New York, Aventura, 1984, p. 214. All subsequent citations from this novel are taken from this edition.
19 See the footnote on p. 17 of the translation of *The Samurai* in which the translator acknowledges the author's own vacillation between the two sets of terms between the original and published versions of the novel.
20 This would explain the choice of *Ō ni atta otoko* (The Man who met a King) as Endō's working title for the novel.
21 Gessel, V., 'Translator's postscript', *The Samurai*, New York, Aventura, 1984, p. 270.
22 Takeda Tomoju, *Chinmoku igo* (Endō's Literature since *Silence*), Tokyo, Joshi Paolo-kai, 1985, pp. 331–2.
23 See 'Watashi no bungaku to seisho' (My literature and the Bible), *Kirisutokyō bunka kenkyūjo kenkyū nenpō*, 12 (1980), pp. 15 ff. for the author's examination of the mistakes he discovered in the archives relating to Tsunenaga.
24 'Samurai o kaki-oete: watashi no kinkyō' (On finishing writing *The Samurai*: an account of my recent circumstances), *Shinkan nyūsu*, 1980: 4.
25 Gessel, V., 'Translator's postscript', op. cit., p. 271.
26 Endō and Kaga Otohiko, '*Taidan:* Samurai *ni tsuite*' op cit., *Bungakkai*, 34: 8 (1980), pp. 201–2.
27 Ibid., p. 200, my emphasis.
28 See 'Samurai *o kaki-oete: watashi no kinkyō*', op. cit.
29 Gessel, V., *The Sting of Life*, New York, Columbia University Press, 1989, p. 256.
30 Ibid., p. 267.

6 *SCANDAL*

1 Information provided by Endō's London publisher, Peter Owen.
2 Endō made this point to me in an interview in Tokyo in April 1988.
3 Cf. Moriuchi Toshio, 'Review of the novel, *Scandal*', *Tosho shinbun* (12 April 1986).
4 For another discussion of *Scandal* as a logical extension of the earlier works, see Satō Yasumasa, in 'Sukyandaru *o tōtte*, Fukai kawa *e*' (Through *Scandal* to *Deep River*), in Endō *et al.*, 'Tokushū: Endō Shūsaku: Gurōbaru na ninshiki' (Special edition: Endō Shūsaku: A global awareness), *Kokubungaku: Kaishaku to kyōzai no kenkyū*, 38: 10 (September 1993), pp. 46–54.
5 *Watashi no aishita shōsetsu* (A Novel I Have Loved), Tokyo, Shinchōsha, 1985, p. 13.

253

6 Lejeune, Philippe, 'Autobiography in the third person', *New Literary History*, 9 (Autumn 1977), pp. 27 ff.
7 Following publication of the novel in 1986, there were several reports in the national media of proprietors of bars in Kabuki-chō claiming a stream of reporters and clients intent on checking on the extent to which Suguro's behaviour is a direct reflection of the author's own leisure pursuits.
8 Napier, Susan, *The Fantastic in Modern Japanese Literature: The Subversion of Modernity*, London and New York, Routledge, 1996, p. 95.
9 Ibid.
10 Ibid., p. 126.
11 *Scandal*, V. Gessel (trans.), London, Peter Owen, 1988, p. 14. All subsequent citations from this novel are taken from this edition.
12 Keppler, C.F., *The Literature of the Second Self*, Tucson, University of Arizona Press, 1972, p. 1.
13 Ibid., p. 10.
14 Ibid., p. 3.
15 Ibid., p. 11.
16 Ibid., p. 10.
17 Ibid., pp. 9–10.
18 The depiction is that of Nishitani Hiroyuki in '*Sukyandaru*', in Yamagata Kazumi (ed.) *Endō Shūsaku: sono bungaku sekai* (Endō Shūsaku: His Literary Worlds), Tokyo, Kokken shuppan, 1997, p. 268. See also Moriuchi Toshio 'Review of the novel, *Scandal*', op. cit., for a similar portrayal of *Scandal*.
19 Keppler, C.F., *The Literature of the Second Self*, op. cit., p. 10, my emphasis.
20 Ibid.
21 Ibid., p. 11.
22 Ibid.
23 Ibid.
24 Ibid.
25 Ibid., p. 25.
26 Ibid., p. 56.
27 Ibid., p. 208.
28 Ibid., pp. 194–5.
29 Jung, 'Psychology and religion', *CWJ*, 11, p. 77.
30 Storr, A., *Jung*, London, Fontana/ Collins, 1973, pp. 85–6.
31 Symbolically, these phone calls tend to occur during the course of Suguro's dreams – a reflection of Jung's belief that the creation of dreams was one of the primary functions of the Soul (cf. 'The Practical Use of Dream Analysis', *CWJ*, 16, pp. 139–61).
32 Jung, 'Approaching the unconscious', in Jung and von Franz, M. (eds) *Man and his Symbols*, London, Aldus Books, 1964, p. 50.
33 Ibid., p. 55.
34 Ibid.
35 Ibid., pp. 21, 23.
36 I have borrowed this term from the title of James Fujii's recent study of the contemporary Japanese prose narrative tradition.

NOTES

37 Moriuchi Toshio, 'Review of the novel, *Scandal*', op. cit.

7 DEEP RIVER

1 Kawai Hayao, 'Tamashii e no tsūrō toshite no *Sukyandaru*' (*Scandal* as an avenue to the soul), *Sekai*, 491 (1986), pp. 96–104.
2 Moriuchi Toshio, 'Review of the novel, *Scandal*', *Tosho shinbun* (12 April 1986). For another negative response to *Scandal*, see Satō Yasumasa, 'Gurōbaru na jidai ni mukatte' (Towards a global era), Yasuoka Shōtarō *et al.*, 'Tsuitō: Endō Shūsaku' (Commemorative edition: Endō Shūsaku), *Shinchō*, 93: 12 (December 1996), pp. 198–9.
3 Endō and Kaga Otohiko, 'Taidan: Saishinsaku *Fukai kawa*: Tamashii no mondai' (A discussion of the recent novel, *Deep River*: The question of the soul), in Endō *et al.*, 'Tokushū: Endō Shūsaku: Gurōbaru na ninshiki' (Special edition: Endō Shūsaku: A global awareness), *Kokubungaku: Kaishaku to kyōzai no kenkyū*, 38: 10 (1993), p. 7.
4 Cited in Kawashima Hidekazu, '*Fukai kawa* no jikken: Ai no gensetsu o megutte' (Experiment in *Deep River*: On the statement of 'Love'), *Kirisutokyō bungaku kenkyū*, 12 (1995), p. 13.
5 This agenda for the future is outlined in Endō and Yashiro Seiichi, '*Sukyandaru* no kōzō: ningen no tajūsei ni tsuite' (The structure of the novel *Scandal*: Concerning the multifaceted nature of humankind), *Shinchō*, 4 (1986), pp. 186–200 and 'Muishiki o shigeki suru Indo' (India: Stimulus of the unconscious), *Yomiuri shinbun* (March 1990).
6 Endō, *Fukai kawa o saguru* (In Search of the *Deep River*), Tokyo, Bungei shunju, 1994, pp. 18–19.
7 Endō and Kaga Otohiko, 'Taidan: Saishinsaku *Fukai kawa*: Tamashii no mondai', op. cit., p. 6 ff.
8 Ibid., pp. 7–8.
9 Houston, G.W. (ed.) *The Cross and the Lotus: Christianity and Buddhism in Dialogue*, Delhi, Motilal Banarsidass, 1985, p. 7. In his '*Fukai kawa* sōsaku nikki', Endō admitted that he was deeply influenced in this regard by John Hick's (1985) *Problems of Religious Pluralism* (cf. '*Fukai kawa* sōsaku nikki' (Composition notes for *Deep River*) *Mita bungaku*, 76:50 (Summer 1997), p. 12).
10 'Kamigami to kami to' (The gods and God), *ESBZ*, vol. 10, pp. 18–19.
11 *Fukai kawa o saguru*, op. cit., pp. 181–2.
12 *Deep River*, V. Gessel (trans.), London, Peter Owen, 1994, p. 200. All subsequent citations from this novel are taken from this edition.
13 'Concerning rebirth', *CWJ*, 9i, p. 120 (my emphasis).
14 This lecture was subsequently revised and published as 'Concerning rebirth', op. cit., pp. 113–50. All citations in the following paragraph are taken from the first section of this essay, pp. 113–15.
15 Ibid., p. 113.
16 Here I have been forced to depart from the published translation and the Japanese original, which refer to 'my Onion' (*tamanegi*) instead of 'my God'. This euphemism was born of Mitsuko's exasperation with Ōtsu's constant reference to God and their agreement (on p. 63 of the translation) to refer instead to this being as 'Onion'.

NOTES

17 See, for example, the series of articles incorporated in *Hontō no watashi o motomete* (In Search of the Real Me), Tokyo, Kairyūsha, 1985.
18 'Concerning Rebirth', op. cit., p. 125.
19 Ibid., pp. 126–7.
20 Ibid., p. 127.
21 Endō and Kaga Otohiko, 'Taidan: Saishinsaku *Fukai kawa*: tamashii no mondai', op. cit., p. 11.
22 Cited in Kawamura Minato, 'Indo ni *anima* o motomete' (In search of the *anima* in India), in Endō *et al.*, 'Tokushū: Endō Shūsaku: Gurōbaru na ninshiki', op. cit., p. 67.
23 Neumann, E., *The Great Mother*, R. Manheim (trans.), New York, Pantheon Books, 1955, p. 150.
24 Ibid., p. 152.
25 Cited in ibid.

AFTERWORD

1 These notes were discovered by Endō's widow, Junko, shortly after his death, and published posthumously in *Mita bungaku*, 76:50 (Summer 1997), pp. 10–54.
2 On frequent occasions, Endō speaks of the '*yūutsu na kimochi*' (feelings of melancholy) that were with him as he wrote (e.g. ibid., p. 49). The statement about having 'whittled away at his own flesh and bones' appears in the final entry, for 25 May 1993, which was penned from his hospital bed following his fifth major operation. Cf. ibid., p. 50.
3 For examples of this positive response, see Endō *et al.*, 'Tokushū: Endō Shūsaku: Gurōbaru na ninshiki' (Special edition: Endō Shūsaku: A global awareness), *Kokubungaku: Kaishaku to kyōzai no kenkyū*, 38: 10 (1993), pp. 6–135 (a special edition of the journal devoted to Endō's work, inspired in no small measure by the considerable media interest in *Deep River*); cf. also the warm words of praise offered to Endō by Ōe Kenzaburō, his long-term rival for the mantle of 'Japan's foremost contemporary author', in ' "Nihon no katorikku" ou: sei no taidō zentai arawasu' (In search of a Japanese Catholicism: Exposé of a whole attitude towards life), *Asahi shinbun* (yūkan), 23 and 24 June 1993.
4 Endō, Inoue Yōji and Yasuoka Shōtarō, ' "Shin" to "katachi" *Fukai kawa* o tegakari ni' ('Faith' and 'form': A reading of *Deep River*), *Gunzō*, 48:9 (1993), p. 199.
5 See, for example, Inoue Yōji, who describes *Deep River* as 'a fitting climax to Endō's career because it brings together all the mysteries of our existence in one final reckoning' (in ibid., p. 209); and Satō Yasumasa, who depicts the novel as a 'final reckoning on Endō's literature in an increasingly global age' (in 'Gurōbaru na jidai ni mukatte' (Towards a global age), in Yasuoka Shōtarō *et al.*, 'Tsuitō: Endō Shūsaku' (Commemorative edition: Endō Shūsaku), *Shinchō*, 93: 12 (December 1996), p. 199).
6 Kawamura Minato, 'Indo ni *anima* o motomete' (In search of the *anima* in India), Endō *et al.*, 'Tokushū: Endō Shūsaku: Gurōbaru na ninshiki', op. cit., p. 65.

NOTES

7 Endō, Inoue Yōji and Yasuoka Shōtarō, ' "Shin" to "katachi" ', op. cit., p. 209. Another critic to comment positively on Endō's use of the Ganges as powerful symbol of reconciliation was Satō Yasumasa, in '*Sukyandaru o tōtte, Fukai kawa* e' (Through *Scandal* to *Deep River*), in Endō *et al.*, 'Tokushū: Endō Shūsaku: Gurōbaru na ninshiki', op. cit., pp. 46 ff.

8 See, for example, Tsuge Teruhiko, 'Iesu-zō: "Endō shingaku" no enkan ga tojiru toki' (A portrait of Jesus: When the circle of 'Endō's theology' is closed), ibid., pp. 75–9, and Ōe Kenzaburō, ' "Nihon no katorikku" ou: sei no taidō zentai arawasu', op. cit.,p. 8.

9 See *Gunzō*, *Bungakkai* and *Shinchō* (all 1996: 12) for these messages. Typical examples of this trait include Miura Shumon's portrayal of Endō as 'using the knife of Catholicism to analyse the psychological make-up of Japan and the Japanese' (*Katorikku to iu mesu o tsukatte, Nihon ya Nihonjin no shinsei o bunseki shite miseta*), *Bungakkai*, (1996), p. 228; and Nakamura Shin'ichirō, who describes Endō's 'life mission' as 'the *Japanisation* of the Catholic faith' (*Katorikku shinkō no Nihonka*), ibid., p. 237, emphasis in original.

10 Most notable in this regard are Yasuoka, Miura Shumon and Kojima Nobuo, all of whom feature in all three of the *tokushū* cited above.

11 Yasuoka, Kojima Nobuo and Ōkubo Fusao, 'Tsuitō zadankai: Endō Shūsaku to Daisan no shinjin' (Commemorative discussion: Endō Shūsaku and the *Daisan no shinjin*), *Bungakkai*, 50 (December 1996), pp. 210–23.

12 Ibid., p. 214.

13 Ibid., p. 215. Ōkubo also cites Agawa Hiroyuki as another 'atypical' member of the *Daisan no shinjin* who wrote of 'great and powerful beings', in his case 'naval captains'.

14 *The Sea and Poison*, M. Gallagher (trans.), Tokyo, Tuttle, 1973, p. 150.

15 Storr, A. (ed.), *Jung: Selected Writings*, London, Fontana, 1983, p. 19.

SELECTED BIBLIOGRAPHY

Aeba Takao (1967) 'Katorikku to Nihon bungaku' (Catholicism and Japanese literature), *Kokubungaku: Kaishaku to kanshō*, 32: 24–8 (June).
—— (1993) 'Ajia-shizen no naka no ai' (Love in the natural beauty of Asia), *Shinchō*, 90(8): 222–5 (August).
Anderer, Paul (1995) (ed. and trans.) *Literature of the Lost Home: Kobayashi Hideo – Literary Criticism, 1924–1939*, Stanford: Stanford University Press.
Arana, Victoria (1981) ' "The line down the middle" in autobiography: critical implications of the quest for the self', in C. Hallam (ed.) *Fearful Symmetry: Doubles and Doubling in Literature and Film*, Tallahassee: University of Florida Press, pp. 125–37.
Barthes, Roland (1975) *S/Z*, R. Miller (trans.), London: Jonathan Cape.
Booth, Wayne (1983) *The Rhetoric of Fiction*, 2nd edn, Harmondsworth and New York: Penguin.
—— (1988) *The Company We Keep: An Ethics of Fiction*, Berkeley and Los Angeles, University of California Press.
Boscaro, Adriana (1981) 'The meaning of Christianity in the works of Endō Shūsaku', in P.G. O'Neill (ed.) *Tradition and Modern Japan*, Tenterden: Paul Norbury Publications, pp. 81–90.
Boyd, Ian (1988) (ed.) 'Christian writers of Japan', *The Chesterton Review*, 14 (3): 365–506 (August).
Brannen, Noah *et al.* (1967) 'Japanese literature and religion: a round-table discussion', *Japan Christian Quarterly*, 33 (1): 74–80 (Spring).
—— (1988) 'Japan through Asian eyes', *Japan Christian Quarterly*, 54: 132–79.
Breen, J. and Williams, M. (1993) (eds) *Japan and Christianity: Impacts and Responses*, Basingstoke: Macmillan.
Breuer, Hans-Peter (1988) 'The roots of guilt and responsibility in Shūsaku Endō's *The Sea and Poison*', *Literature and Medicine*, 7: 80–106.
Cohn, Dorrit (1978) *Transparent Minds: Narrative Modes for Presenting Consciousness in Fiction*, New Jersey: Princeton University Press.
Culler, Jonathan (1975) *Structuralist Poetics: Structuralism, Linguistics and the Study of Literature*, Ithaca: Cornell University Press.

BIBLIOGRAPHY

Durfee, Richard (1989) 'Portrait of an unknowingly ordinary man: Endō Shūsaku, Christianity, and Japanese historical consciousness', *Japanese Journal of Religious Studies*, 16 (1): 41–62.

Eakin, Paul (1985) *Fictions in Autobiography: Studies in the Art of Self-Invention*, New Jersey: Princeton University Press.

Edel, Leon (1964) *The Modern Psychological Novel*, New York: Grosset and Dunlap.

Endō Shūsaku (1955) *Shiroi hito, Kiiroi hito* (White Man, Yellow Man), Tokyo: Kōdansha; Tokyo: Shinchōsha bunkō, 1983.

—— (1957) *Umi to dokuyaku* (The Sea and Poison), Tokyo: Kōdansha; M. Gallagher (trans.), Tokyo: Tuttle, 1973.

—— (1959) *Obakasan* (Wonderful Fool), Tokyo: Chūō kōronsha; F. Mathy (trans.), Tokyo: Tuttle, 1974.

—— (1960) *Kazan* (Volcano), Tokyo: Bungei shunjū; R. Schuchert (trans.), New York: Taplinger, 1978.

—— (1960) *Seisho no naka no joseitachi* (The Women of the Bible), Tokyo: Kadokawa shoten.

—— (1963) 'Watashi no mono' (My belongings) (trans. 1985), *Endō Shūsaku bungaku zenshū* 4, pp. 203–22.

—— (1964) *Watashi ga suteta onna* (The Girl I Left Behind), Tokyo: Bungei shunjū; M. Williams (trans.), London: Peter Owen, 1994.

—— (1965) *Ryūgaku* (Foreign Studies), Tokyo: Bungei shunjū; M. Williams (trans.), London: Peter Owen, 1989.

—— (1966) *Chinmoku* (Silence), Tokyo: Shinchōsha; W. Johnston (trans.), Tokyo: Sophia University and Tokyo: Tuttle, 1969; London: Penguin and London: Peter Owen, 1996.

—— (1966) 'Ōgon no kuni' (The golden country), *Bungei*, 5 (5):76–127 (May); F. Mathy (trans.), Tokyo: Tuttle, 1970.

—— (1968) 'Kagebōshi' (Shadows), *Shinchō*, 65(1): 52–72 (January).

—— (1970) 'Concerning the novel *Silence*', *Japan Christian Quarterly*, 36 (2): 100–3 (Spring).

—— (1973) *Iesu no shōgai* (A Life of Jesus), Tokyo: Shinchōsha; R. Schuchert (trans.), New York: Paulist Press, 1978.

—— (1973) *Shikai no hotori* (Beside the Dead Sea), Tokyo: Shinchōsha.

—— (1974) *Kuchibue o fuku toki* (When I Whistle), Tokyo: Kōdansha; V. Gessel (trans.), London: Peter Owen, 1979.

—— (1974) 'The anguish of an alien', *Japan Christian Quarterly*, 40 (4): 179–95 (Fall).

—— (1975) *Endō Shūsaku bungaku zenshū* (The Complete Works of Endō Shūsaku; cited as *ESBZ*), 11 vols, Tokyo: Shinchōsha. This is still the only collection of Endō's work. It contains the originals of all Endō's works discussed in this book up to 1973 (with the exception of *Watashi ga suteta onna* (The Girl I Left Behind)). Volume 10 contains various of the critical articles written by Endō and cited in this study, including 'Kamigami to kami to' (The gods and God), pp. 14–19; 'Katorikku sakka no mondai' (The problems confronting the Catholic author),

BIBLIOGRAPHY

pp. 20–9; 'Furansowa Mōriyakku' (François Mauriac), pp. 92–103; 'Shūkyō to bungaku' (Religion and literature), pp. 112–24; 'Nihonjinteki kanjō no soko ni aru mono: metafijikku hihyō to dentōbi' (That which lies at the heart of the Japanese sensibility: Metaphysical criticism and the traditional aesthetic), pp. 146–51; 'Chichi no shūkyō: Haha no shūkyō' (Paternal religion: Maternal religion), pp. 179–88; 'Watashi to kirisutokyō' (Christianity and I), pp. 353–59; 'Watashi no bungaku' (My literature), pp. 365–72; 'Awanai yōfuku' (Ill-fitting clothes), pp. 373–76; and 'Shusse-saku no koro' (Around the time of my first novels), pp. 376–91.

—— (1977) *Nihonjin wa kirisutokyō o shinjirareru ka* (Can the Japanese Believe in Christianity?) Tokyo: Kōdansha.

—— (1978) *Ningen no naka no X* (The 'X' within Man), Tokyo: Chūō kōronsha.

—— (1978) *Kirisuto no tanjō* (The Birth of Christ), Tokyo: Shinchōsha.

—— (1979) 'Watashi ni totte no kami' (God as I see Him), *Seiki*, 354: 62–8 (November).

—— (1980) *Samurai* (The Samurai), Tokyo: Shinchōsha; V. Gessel (trans.), London: Peter Owen, 1982; New York: Aventura, 1984.

—— (1980) 'Watashi no bungaku to seisho' (My literature and the Bible), *Kirisutokyō bunka kenkyūjo kenkyū nenpō*, 12: 1–21.

—— (1980) '*Samurai* o kaki-oete: watashi no kinkyō' (On finishing writing *The Samurai*: An account of my recent circumstances), *Shinkan nyūsu*, 4.

—— (1981) 'Jushōshiki no yoru' (The evening of the prize-giving ceremony), *Umi*, 13(6): 18–26 (June).

—— (1983) 'Aru tsuya' (A certain vigil), *Shinchō*, 80(1): 87–95 (January).

—— (1983) 'Rokujussai no otoko' (A sixty-year-old man), *Gunzō*, 38(4): 49–62 (April).

—— (1984) *Saigo no junkyōsha* (The Last Martyrs), Tokyo: Kōdansha.

—— (1984) *Stained Glass Elegies*, V. Gessel (trans.), London: Peter Owen.

—— (1985) *Watashi no aishita shōsetsu* (A Novel I have Loved), Tokyo: Shinchōsha.

—— (1985) *Hontō no watashi o motomete* (In Search of the Real Me), Tokyo: Kairyūsha.

—— (1986) *Sukyandaru* (Scandal), Tokyo: Shinchōsha; V. Gessel (trans.), London: Peter Owen, 1988.

—— (1986) '*Sukyandaru* no kōzō' (The Structure of *Scandal*), *Shinchō*, 83(4): 186–200 (April).

—— (1986) 'Literature and religion, especially the role of the unconscious', The Voice of the Writer, J.K. Buda (trans.), Tokyo: *Collected Papers of the 47th International PEN Congress*, Tokyo, pp. 29–37.

—— (1988) 'The deep inside of man', *Chesterton Review*, 14 (3): 499 (August).

—— (1990) 'Muishiki o shigeki suru Indo' (India: stimulus of the unconscious), *Yomiuri shinbun* (March).

BIBLIOGRAPHY

—— (1992) *Kirishitan Jidai: Junkyō to kikyō no rekishi* (The Christian Era: A History of Martyrdom and Apostasy), Tokyo: Shōgakkan.
—— (1993) *The Final Martyrs*, V. Gessel (trans.), London: Peter Owen.
—— (1993) *Fukai kawa* (Deep River), Tokyo: Kōdansha; V. Gessel (trans.), London: Peter Owen, 1994.
—— (1994) *Fukai kawa* o saguru (In Search of the *Deep River*), Tokyo: Bungei shunjū.
—— (1997) '*Fukai kawa* sōsaku nikki' (Composition notes for *Deep River*), *Mita bungaku*, 76(50): 10–54 (Summer).
Endō Shūsaku *et al.* (1974) 'Naze "Iesu" o kaku ka' (Why do we write of Jesus?), *Bungakkai*, (February) 152–75.
Endō Shūsaku *et al.* (1987) 'Tokushū: Nihonjin to kirisutokyō' (Special edition: The Japanese and Christianity), *Chishiki*, 72: 56–125 (December).
Endō Shūsaku *et al.* (1988) *Endō Shūsaku to kataru: Nihonjin to kirisutokyō* (Conversations with Endō Shūsaku: The Japanese and Christianity), Tokyo: Joshi Paolo-kai.
Endō Shūsaku *et al.* (1993) 'Tokushū: Endō Shūsaku: Gurōbaru na ninshiki' (Special edition: Endō Shūsaku: A global awareness), *Kokubungaku: Kaishaku to kyōzai no kenkyū*, 38 (10): 6–135.
Endō Shūsaku and V. Gessel (eds) (1994) *Endō Shūsaku to Shūsaku Endō: Amerika 'chinmoku to koe': Endō bungaku kenkyū gakkai hōkoku* (Silences and Voices: The Writings of Shūsaku Endō: Proceedings of the Symposium on Endō's Literature), Tokyo: Shunjūsha.
Endō Shūsaku, Inoue Yōji and Yasuoka Shōtarō (1991) 'Shūkyō to fūdo' (Religion and cultural climate), *Gunzō*, 46(9): 156–77 (September).
—— (1993) ' "Shin" to "katachi": *Fukai kawa* o tegakari ni' ('Faith' and 'Form': A Reading of *Deep River*), *Gunzō*, 48(9): 198–219 (September).
Endō Shūsaku and Kaga Otohiko (1980) 'Taidan: *Samurai* ni tsuite' (Discussion: about *The Samurai*), *Bungakkai*, 34 (8): 200–11 (August).
Endō Shūsaku and Miyoshi Yukio (1973) 'Bungaku: Jakusha no ronri' (Literature: The logic of the weakling), *Kokubungaku: Kaishaku to kyōzai no kenkyū*, 18(2): 10–29 (February) .
Endō Shūsaku and Ōhara Yasue (1981) 'Taidan: Nihonjin to kirisutokyō' (Discussion: The Japanese and Christianity), *Chishiki*, 24: 206–16.
Endō Shūsaku and Satō Yasumasa (1991) *Jinsei no dōhansha* (The Constant Companion through Life), Tokyo: Shunjūsha.
Endō Shūsaku and Tanaka Chikao (1966) 'Taidan: Fumie no kokoro' (Discussion: The spirit of the *fumie*), *Kumo*, 10: 5–15 (May).
Endō Shūsaku and Yamagata Kazumi (1987) 'Tsumi kara shi e: Endō Shūsaku no sekai' (From sin to death: The world of Endō Shūsaku), *Fukuin to sekai*, 42(12): 6–18.
Endō Shūsaku and Yashiro Seiichi (1986) '*Sukyandaru* no kōzō: ningen no tajūsei ni tsuite' (The structure of the novel *Scandal*: Concerning the multifaceted nature of humankind), *Shinchō*, 83(4): 186–200 (April).

BIBLIOGRAPHY

Endō, Tasuku, et al. (1994) (eds) *Kirisutokyō bungaku jiten* (A Dictionary of Christian Literature), Tokyo: Kyōbunkan.

Etō Jun (1972) 'Seijuku to sōshitsu: "haha" no hōkai (Maturity and loss: The collapse of the mother), in *Gendai no bungaku*, vol. 27; Tokyo: Kōdansha, pp. 5–133.

Etō Jun et al. (1996) 'Tsuitōbun: Endō Shūsaku' (Commemorative messages: Endō Shūsaku), *Bungakkai*, 50(12): 224–51 (December).

Fordham, Frieda (1959) *An Introduction to Jung's Psychology*, London: Penguin Books.

Fowler, Edward (1988) *The Rhetoric of Confession: Shishōsetsu in Early Twentieth Century Japanese Fiction*, Berkeley and Los Angeles: University of California Press.

Fujii, James (1993) *Complicit Fictions: The Subject in the Modern Japanese Prose Narrative*, Berkeley and Los Angeles: University of California Press.

Fukuda Kōnen (1966) 'Sengo bungaku-ron oboegaki: Daisan no shinjin no ichizuke' (Thoughts on post-war literature: The position of the *Daisan no shinjin*), *Bungakkai*, 20(11): 135–44 (November).

Gallagher, Michael (1993) 'For these the least of my brethren: The concern of Endō Shūsaku', *Journal of the Association of Teachers of Japanese*, 27 (1): 75–84 (April).

Gendai Nihon kirisutokyō bungaku zenshū (Anthology of Modern Japanese Christian Literature) (1972–74), 18 vols, Tokyo: Kyōbunkan.

Genette, Gerard (1980) *Narrative Discourse*, J. Lewin (trans.), Blackwell: Oxford.

—— (1982) *Figures of Literary Discourse*, A. Sheridan (trans.), New York: Columbia University Press.

Gessel, Van (1982) 'Voices in the wilderness: Japanese Christian authors', *Monumenta Nipponica*, 37 (4): 437–57 (Winter).

—— (1984) 'Translator's Postscript', *The Samurai*, New York: Aventura.

—— (1989) *The Sting of Life: Four Contemporary Japanese Novelists*, New York: Columbia University Press.

—— (1991) 'The voice of the doppelgänger', *Japan Quarterly*, 2: 198–213.

—— (1993) 'Endō Shūsaku: his position(s) in postwar Japanese literature', *Journal of the Association of Teachers of Japanese*, 27 (1): 67–74 (April).

—— (1994) 'Tsudoi no chi ni ikitai: *Fukai kawa*-kō' (I want to go to the campground: Thoughts on *Deep River*), in Endō Shūsaku and V. Gessel (eds) *Endō Shūsaku to Shūsaku Endō: Amerika 'chinmoku to koe': Endō bungaku kenkyū gakkai hōkoku* (Silences and Voices: The Writings of Shūsaku Endō: Proceedings of the Symposium on Endō's Literature), Tokyo: Shunjūsha, pp. 197–213.

—— (1997) 'Endō Shūsaku', in V. Gessel (ed.) *Dictionary of Literary Biography*, Detroit, Washington DC and London: Bruccoli, Clark & Layman, pp. 37–51.

Gessel, Van et al. (1991) *Gunzō: Nihon no sakka: Endō Shūsaku, 22* (Japanese Authors: Endō Shūsaku, 22), Tokyo: Shogakkan.

BIBLIOGRAPHY

Gibson, Boyce (1973) *The Religion of Dostoevsky*, London: SCM Press.
Goebel, Rolf (1988) 'Rediscovering Japan's Christian tradition: Text-immanent hermeneutics in two short stories by Shūsaku Endō', *Studies in Language and Culture*, 14: 157–72.
Hallam, Clifford (1981) 'The double as incomplete self: Toward a definition of the doppelgänger', in C. Hallam (ed.) *Fearful Symmetry: Doubles and Doubling in Literature and Film*, Tallahassee: University of Florida Press, pp. 1–31.
Hasegawa Izumi (ed.) (1977) 'Akutagawa-shō jiten' (A Dictionary of the Akutagawa Prize), *Kokubungaku: Kaishaku to kanshō*, 42(2) (January).
Heremann, Marc (1987) 'The problem of evil and the perception of it in the novels of Endō Shūsaku', unpublished paper.
Hibbett, Howard (1971) 'Natsume Sōseki and the psychological novel', in D. Shively (ed.) *Tradition and Modernization in Japanese Culture*, New Jersey: Princeton University Press, 305–46.
—— (1974) 'Introspective techniques in modern Japanese fiction', in A.R. Davis (ed.) *The Search for Identity*, Sydney: Angus & Robertson.
Hick, John (1985) *Problems of Religious Pluralism*, Basingstoke: Macmillan.
Higgins, Jean (1987) 'East–West encounters in Endō Shūsaku', *Dialogue and Alliance*, pp. 12–22.
Hijiya-Kirschnereit, Irmela (1996) *Rituals of Self-Revelation: Shishōsetsu as Literary Genre and Socio-cultural Phenomenon*, Cambridge, Mass.: Harvard University Press.
—— (1997) 'Naze shishōsetsu na no ka' (Why *shishōsetsu?*), Lecture delivered to Tōhō gakkai, Tokyo, 30 May.
Hiroishi Renji (1991) *Endō Shūsaku no subete* (Everything about Endō Shūsaku), Tokyo: Chōbunsha.
—— (1991) *Endō Shūsaku no tate-yoko* (The Warp and Woof of Endō Shūsaku), Tokyo: Chōbunsha.
Houston G.W. (ed.) (1985) *The Cross and the Lotus: Christianity and Buddhism in Dialogue*, Delhi: Motilal Banarsidass.
Howard, Yoshiko (1996) 'The warp and the woof of Endō Shūsaku's Novel, *Fukai kawa* (Deep River)', *Kirisutokyō bungaku kenkyū*, 13: 1–17.
Inoue Yōji et al. (1977) 'Tokushū: Endō Shūsaku' (Special edition: Endō Shūsaku), *Kikan sōzō*, 3: 13–103.
Izumi Hideki (ed.) (1979) *Endō Shūsaku no kenkyū* (Studies on Endō Shūsaku), Tokyo: Jitsugyō no Nihonsha.
Johnston, William (1996) 'Translator's Preface', *Silence*, London: Peter Owen, pp. 1–18.
Jung, C.G. (1953–77) *The Collected Works of C.G. Jung*, 20 vols, London: Routledge & Kegan Paul; cited in *CJW*. It contains most of the articles by Jung cited in this study, including: 'Archetypes of the collective unconscious' (vol. 9i, pp. 3–41); 'Concerning rebirth' (vol. 9i, pp. 113–50); 'Conscious, unconscious and individuation' (vol. 9.i, pp. 275–89); 'The practical use of dream-analysis' (vol. 16, pp. 139–61); 'Introduction to

the religious and psychological problems of alchemy' (vol. 12, pp. 1–37); 'Psychology and religion' (vol. 11, pp. 3–107); 'The undiscovered self' (vol. 10, pp. 245–305); 'Synchronicity: An acausal connecting principle' (vol. 8, pp. 417–58); 'The development of personality' (vol. 17, pp. 167–86); and 'The psychology of the unconscious' (vol. 7, pp. 3–117).

—— (1958) *The Undiscovered Self*, London: Routledge & Kegan Paul.

—— (1968) *Aion: Researches into the Phenomenology of the Self*, 2nd edn, London: Routledge & Kegan Paul.

Jung, C.G. and von Franz, M. (1964) (eds) *Man and his Symbols*, London: Aldus Books.

Kaneko Tateo (1996) 'Nihon ni okeru kirisutokyō juyō no mondai: Endō no *Chinmoku* kara *Fukai kawa* made' (The question of Christian reception in Japan: Endō Shūsaku: From *Silence* to *Deep River*), *Hikaku shisō kenkyū*, 22: 27–33 (March).

Karatani Kōjin (1980) *Nihon kindai bungaku no kigen* (The Origins of Modern Japanese Literature), Tokyo: Kōdansha.

—— (1993) *Origins of Modern Japanese Literature*, B. de Bary (trans.), Durham: Duke University Press.

Kasai Akio (1986) 'Endō Shūsaku: *Samurai* ni tsuite' (Endō Shūsaku: A discussion of *The Samurai*), *Kirisutokyō bungei*, 4: 82–97.

—— (1987) *Endō Shūsaku-ron* (A Study of Endō Shūsaku), Tokyo: Sōbunsha.

—— (1989) '*Chinmoku*: "Chichi no shūkyō no kirisuto" kara "haha no shūkyō no kirisuto" e no tenkan' (*Silence*: The transformation from 'Christ of a paternal religion' to 'Christ of a maternal religion'), *Kirisutokyō bungaku kenkyū*, 6: 69–71.

Kasai Minoru (1997) 'Endō Shūsaku's *Deep River* and the face of Jesus', Lecture delivered at the International Christian University, Tokyo, 28 May.

Katō, Shūichi (1965) 'Japanese writers and modernization', in M. Jansen (ed.) *Changing Japanese Attitudes Towards Modernization*, New Jersey: Princeton University Press.

Kaufman, G. (1985) 'Towards the reconception of Christ and salvation', in G. Kaufman (ed.) *Theology for a Nuclear Age*, Manchester: Manchester University Press.

Kawai Hayao (1986) 'Tamashii e no tsūro toshite no *Sukyandaru*' (*Scandal* as an avenue to the soul), *Sekai*, 491: 96–104 (August).

Kawashima Hidekazu (1993) *Endō Shūsaku: Ai no dōhansha* (Endō Shūsaku: The Constant Companion of Love), Osaka: Izumi shoin.

—— (1995) '*Fukai kawa* no jikken: Ai no gensetsu o megutte' (Experiment in *Deep River*: On the statement of 'love'), *Kirisutokyō bungaku kenkyū*, 12 : 13–24.

Kazusa Hideo (1973) 'Kaisetsu' (Critical commentary), in *Gendai Nihon kirisutokyō bungaku zenshū*, vol. 10, Tokyo: Kyōbunkan pp. 165–96.

—— (1987) *Endō Shūsaku-ron* (A Study of Endō Shūsaku), Tokyo: Shunjūsha.

—— (1997) 'Endō Shūsaku', Lecture delivered at the Centre for the Study of Christian Arts, Tokyo, 26 May.

Kazusa Hideo *et al.* (1988) 'Tokushū: Tōhoku Ajia no kirisutokyō bungaku' (Special edition: Christian literature of northeast Asia), *Fukuin to sekai*, 43 (3): 1–40.

Keene, Donald (1984) *Dawn to the West: Japanese Literature in the Modern Era*, vol. 1, New York: Holt, Rinehart & Winston.

Keppler, C.F. (1972) *The Literature of the Second Self*, Tucson: University of Arizona Press.

Kersten, Rikki (1996) *Democracy in Postwar Japan: Maruyama Masao and the Search for Autonomy*, London: Routledge.

Kojima Nobuo (1971) 'Hōyō kazoku' (Embracing family), in *Kojima Nobuo Zenshū*, vol. 3, Tokyo: Kōdansha.

Kojima Nobuo, Hirano Ken and Yasuoka Shōtarō (1968) 'Zadankai: Bungaku ni okeru "watashi" to wa nani ka' (A round-table discussion: What is the "I" in literature?), *Bungei*, 7 (8): 234–55 (November).

Kubota Gyōichi (1989) *Kindai Nihon bungaku to kirisutosha sakka* (Modern Japanese Literature and Christian Authors), Osaka: Izumi shoin.

Kumai Kei (1997) 'Nihonjin no tsumi no ishiki mitsumete' (Scrutinising the Japanese sin consciousness), *Nihon keizai shinbun*, (15 August).

Kume Masao (1973) ' "Watakushi" shōsetsu to "shinkyō" shōsetsu' (The I-novel and the state-of-mind *shōsetsu*), in Miyoshi Yukio and Sofue Shōji (eds) *Kindai bungaku hyōron taikei*, vol. 6, Tokyo: Kadokawa shoten, pp. 50–7.

Lejeune, Philippe (1977) 'Autobiography in the third person', *New Literary History*, 9: 27–50 (Autumn).

Lewell, John (1993) *Modern Japanese Novelists: A Biographical Dictionary*, Tokyo: Kodansha.

Mathy, Francis (1963) 'Kitamura Tōkoku: The early years', *Monumenta Nipponica*, 18 (1–2): 1–44.

—— (1964) 'Kitamura Tōkoku: Essays on the inner life', *Monumenta Nipponica*, 19 (1–2): 66–110.

—— (1965) 'Kitamura Tōkoku: Final essays', *Monumenta Nipponica*, 20 (1–2): 41–63.

—— (1967) 'Shūsaku Endō: Japanese Catholic novelist', *Thought*: 585–614 (Winter).

—— (1967) 'Endō Shūsaku: *White Man, Yellow Man*', *Comparative Literature*: 58–74 (Winter).

—— (1973) 'Endō Shūsaku's "mudswamp Japan" ', in Japan PEN Club (ed.) *Studies on Japanese Culture*, vol. 1, Tokyo: Japan PEN Club, pp. 331–8.

—— (1974) 'Shūsaku Endō: The second period', *Japan Christian Quarterly*, 40 (4): 214–26 (Fall).

—— (1987) 'Shūsaku Endō: Japanese Catholic novelist', *Month*, 5: 174–8.

Matsuda Kiiichi (1966) 'Shinjitsu no Fereira' (The historical Ferreira), *Kumo*, 10: 16–20 (May).

BIBLIOGRAPHY

Miyano Mitsuo (1989)'*Chinmoku* no naka no mō hitotsu no sashie' (Another picture of *Silence*), *Kirisutokyō bungaku kenkyū*, 6: 66–8.

Miyauchi Yutaka (1971) 'Sakka to shūkyō: Endō Shūsaku-ron' (The author and religion: A study of Endō Shūsaku), *Bungei*, 10 (11): 214–30 (October).

Miyoshi, Masao (1989) 'Against the native grain: The Japanese novel and the "Postmodern" West', in Masao Miyoshi and H.D. Harootunian (eds) *Postmodernism and Japan*, Durham: Duke University Press, pp. 143–68.

Moriuchi Toshio (1986) 'Review of the novel, *Scandal*', *Tosho shinbun* (12 April).

Muramatsu Takeshi *et al.* (1975)'Tokushū: Endō Shūsaku' (Special edition: Endō Shūsaku), *Kokubungaku: Kaishaku to kanshō*, 40(7): 6–176 (June).

Napier, Susan (1996) *The Fantastic in Modern Japanese Literature: The Subversion of Modernity*, London: Routledge.

Neumann, Erich (1954) *The Origins and History of Consciousness*, R. Hull (trans.), London: Routledge & Kegan Paul.

—— (1955) *The Great Mother*, R. Manheim (trans.), New York: Pantheon Books.

Ninomiya, Cindy (1990) 'Endō Shūsaku: Bridging the gap between Christianity and Japanese culture', *Japan Christian Quarterly*, 56 (4): 227–36 (Fall).

Ōe Kenzaburō (1969) *A Personal Matter*, J. Nathan (trans.), New York: Grove Press.

—— (1993) '"Nihon no katorikku" ou: sei no taidō zentai arawasu' (In search of a 'Japanese Catholicism': Exposé of a whole attitude towards life), *Asahi shinbun* (yūkan), (23 and 24 June).

Ogawa Kunio *et al.* (1981) 'Tokushū 2: Katorikku sakka gunzō' (Special edition 2: A profile of Catholic authors), *Kokubungaku: Kaishaku to kanshō*, 46(10): 137–81 (October).

Quinn, Philip (1989) 'Tragic dilemmas, suffering love and Christian life', *Journal of Religious Ethics*, 17: 151–83 (Spring).

Rimer, Thomas (1993) 'That most excellent gift of charity: Endō Shūsaku in contemporary world literature', *Journal of the Association of Teachers of Japanese*, 27 (1): 59–66 (April).

Robinson, Lewis (1985) 'Images of Christianity in Chinese and Japanese fiction', *American–Asian Review*, 3: 1–61 (Fall).

Rosenfield, Claire (1963) 'The shadow within: The conscious and unconscious use of the double', *Daedalus*, 92: 326–44 (Spring).

Rubin, Jay (1979) 'My individualism', *Monumenta Nipponica*, 34 (1): 21–48 (Spring).

Saeki Shōichi, Ueda Miyoji, Isoda Kōichi and Aeba Takao (1980) 'Zadankai: Shishōsetsu' (A round-table discussion: The *Shishōsetsu*), *Bungakkai*, 34(2): 148–75 (February).

BIBLIOGRAPHY

Saitō Kazuaki (1984–97) (ed.) *Kirisutokyō bungaku kenkyū* (Studies of Christian Literature), vols 1–14, Tokyo: Nihon kirisutokyō bungakkai jimukyoku.

Sako Jun'ichirō (1964) *Kindai Nihon bungaku to kirisutokyō* (Modern Japanese Literature and Christianity), Tokyo: Bunka shinsho.

—— (1966) 'Sengo bungaku no shūkyō-teki jōkyō' (The position of religion in postwar literature), *Hihyō*, 5: 33–45 (Summer).

—— (1977) *Shiina Rinzō to Endō Shūsaku* (Shiina Rinzō and Endō Shūsaku), Tokyo: Nihon kirisutokyōdan shuppankyoku.

Sasabuchi Tomoichi (1968) 'Kindai Nihon bungaku to kirisutokyō' (Modern Japanese literature and Christianity), *Kokubungaku: Kaishaku to kyōzai no kenkyū*, 13 (2): 40–8 (February).

—— (1973) 'Meiji Taishō-ki no kirisutokyō bungaku to Arishima Takeo: Kindai kirisutokyō bungaku-shi e no futatsu no shiten' (Christian literature of the Meiji and Taishō eras and Arishima Takeo: Two perspectives on the history of modern Christian literature), *Bungaku*, 47 (3): 1–56 (March).

—— (1975) (ed.) *Kirisutokyō to bungaku* (Christianity and Literature), 3 vols, Tokyo: Kasama shoin.

Sasabuchi Tomoichi *et al.* (1974) 'Tokushū: Shūkyō to bungaku' (Special edition: Religion and literature), *Kokubungaku: Kaishaku to kanshō*, 39(7): 6–153 (June).

Satō Yasumasa (1963) *Kindai Nihon bungaku to kirisutokyō: shiron* (Modern Japanese Literature and Christianity: A Preliminary Thesis), Tokyo: Sōbunsha.

—— (1969) 'Shūkyō to sono dozokka' (Religion and its indigenisation), *Kokubungaku: Kaishaku to kanshō*, 34(12): 38–50 (November).

—— (1974) *Bungaku: sono uchi naru kami: Nihon kindai bungaku ichimen* (Literature: The Internal God: A View of Contemporary Japanese Literature), Tokyo: Ōfusha.

—— (1977) 'Jiishiki no kussetsu' (The collapse of consciousness of the self), *Kokubungaku: Kaishaku to kanshō*, 42(11): 65–72 (September).

—— (1983) (ed.) *Kanshō Nihon gendai bungaku: Shiina Rinzō, Endō Shūsaku, 25*, (Appreciation of Contemporary Japanese Literature: Shiina Rinzō and Endō Shūsaku, 25), Tokyo: Kadokawa shoten.

—— (1992/3) 'Kindai Nihon bungaku ni okeru kirisutokyō to romanshugi' (Christianity and Romanticism in modern Japanese literature), *Kirisutokyō bungaku kenkyū*, 9/10: 61–8.

—— (1994) *Satō Yasumasa chosaku-shū: Endō Shūsaku to Shiina Rinzō, 7* (The Collected Writings of Satō Yasumasa: Endō Shūsaku and Shiina Rinzō, 7), Tokyo: Kanrin shobo.

Satō Yasumasa (1981–97) *et al.* (eds) *Kirisutokyō bungaku kenkyū: Kyūshū shibu* (Studies of Christian Literature: Kyushu Branch), vols 1–16, Kyushu, Nihon kirisutokyō bungakkai jimukyoku: Kyushu shibu.

Scholes, Robert (1974) *Structuralism in Literature: An Introduction*, New Haven and London: Yale University Press.

BIBLIOGRAPHY

—— (1982) *Semiotics in Interpretation*, New Haven and London: Yale University Press.

Selden, Ramon (1985) *Contemporary Literary Theory*, Lexington: University Press of Kentucky.

Shimao Toshio (1977) *Shi no toge*(The sting of death), Tokyo: Shinchōsa.

Shimane Kunio (1989) 'Endō Shūsaku to G. Gurīn: *Chinmoku* ni okeru Gurīn no eikyō' (Endō Shūsaku and Graham Greene: The influence of Greene on *Silence*), *Kirisutokyō bungaku kenkyū*, 6: 19–36.

Shimazaki Tōson (1974) *The Broken Commandment*, K. Strong (trans.), Tokyo: University of Tokyo Press.

Shimizu Shigeo (1983) *Bungaku to shūkyō* (Literature and Religion), Tokyo: Kyōiku shuppan sentā.

Smart, Ninian (1993) *Buddhism and Christianity: Rivals and Allies*, Basingstoke: Macmillan.

Storr, Anthony (1983) *Jung*, London: Fontana/ Collins.

—— (1983) (ed.) *Jung: Selected Writings*, London: Fontana.

Stratford, Philip (1964) *Faith and Fiction: Creative Process in Graham Greene and Mauriac*, New York: University of Notre Dame Press.

Strong, Kenneth (1973) 'Downgrading the *kindai jiga*: Reflections on Tōson's *Hakai* and subsequent trends in modern literature', in Japan PEN Club (ed.) *Studies on Japanese Culture*, vol. 1, Tokyo: Japan PEN Club, pp. 406–11.

Sumiya Mikio (1961) *Kindai Nihon no keisei to kirisutokyō* (The Structure of Modern Japan and Christianity), Tokyo: Shinkyō shuppan.

Suzuki, Tomi (1996) *Narrating the Self: Fictions of Japanese Modernity*, Stanford: Stanford University Press.

Swain, D. (1980) (ed. and trans.) 'Christian influences on Meiji Literature: A round-table discussion', *Japan Christian Quarterly*, 46 (4): 201–14 (Fall).

Takadō Kaname (1966) 'Kirisutosha no bungaku no kanōsei' (The possibilities for Christian literature), *Fukuin to sekai*, 2: 44–52 (January).

—— (1967) 'The challenge of Christian literature', *Japan Christian Quarterly*, 33 (2): 81–6 (Spring).

—— (1972) 'Postwar Japanese Christian writers', *Japan Christian Quarterly*, 38 (4): 185–92 (Fall).

—— (1980) 'Endō Shūsaku: Dōke naru "haha" e no akogare' (Endō Shūsaku: yearning for the comic 'mother'), *Kokubungaku: Kaishaku to kanshō*, 45(4): 131–50.

Takahashi Takako (1966) 'Endō Shūsaku-ron' (A study of the writings of Endō Shūsaku), *Hihyō*, 5: 100–11 (Summer).

Takayama Tetsuo (1975) 'Kanashimi no seika: Endō Shūsaku' (The sanctification of suffering: A study of Endō Shūsaku), *Mita bungaku*, 62 (4): 56–70 (April).

Takayanagi Shun'ichi (1991) 'Iesu to gendai bungaku' (Jesus and contemporary literature), *Jōchi daigaku Kirisutokyō bunka kenkyūsho*, 10: 13–37.

BIBLIOGRAPHY

—— (1995) 'Fukai kawa: tensei to dōhansha' (*Deep River*: Reincarnation and the constant companion), *Kirisutokyō bungaku kenkyū*, 12: 1–11.

Takeda Tomoju (1971) *Endō Shūsaku no sekai* (The World of Endō Shūsaku), Tokyo, Kōdansha.

—— (1973) 'Kami no tankyūsha: Endō Shūsaku' (The searcher after God: Endō Shūsaku), *Seiki*, 274: 68–77 (March).

—— (1973)'Shūkyō to bungaku: Watashi no naka no sengo bungaku' (Religion and literature: My reading of post-war literature), *Seiki*, 278: 76–85 (July).

—— (1974) *Kyūkon no bungaku* (Literature of Salvation), Tokyo: Kōdansha.

—— (1974) *Nihon Kirisutosha sakka-tachi* (Japanese Christian Authors), Tokyo: Kyōbunkan.

—— (1975) *Endō Shūsaku no bungaku* (The Literature of Endō Shūsaku), Tokyo: Seibunsha.

—— (1980) *Sengo bungaku no dōtei* (The Direction of Postwar Literature), Tokyo: Hokuyōsha.

—— (1985) Chinmoku *igo* (Endō's Literature since *Silence*), Tokyo: Joshi Paolo-kai.

Takeda Tomoju *et al.* (1986) 'Tokushū: Endō Shūsaku' (Special edition: Endō Shūsaku), *Kokubungaku: Kaishaku to kanshō*, 51(10): 6–167 (October).

Tamaki Kunio (1977) *Gendai Nihon bungei no seiritsu to tenkai* (The Emergence and Development of the Contemporary Japanese Creative Arts), Tokyo: Ōfūsha.

—— (1982) 'Endō Shūsaku *Shūkyō to bungaku* no igi' (The Meaning of Endō Shūsaku's *Religion and Literature*), *Nihon bungei kenkyū*, 34 (1): 13–25.

Taylor, Charles (1989) *Sources of the Self: The Making of the Modern Identity*, Cambridge: Cambridge University Press.

Toda Yoshio (1982) (ed.) *Nihon katorishizumu to bungaku* (Japanese Catholicism and Literature), Tokyo: Ōmeidō.

Torii Kunio (1966) 'Sengo ni okeru shishōsetsu-teki ishiki' (The I-novel consciousness in the postwar period), *Kokubungaku: Kaishaku to kyōzai no kenkyū*, 11 (3): 53–8 (March).

—— (1968) 'Sengo bungaku ni okeru daisan no shinjin no ichi' (The position of the *Daisan no shinjin* in post-war Literature), *Nihon kindai bungaku*, 56: 55–66 (October).

—— (1977) 'Yasuoka Shōtarō: hōhō to ichi – Senzen shishōsetsu to no renzoku to danzetsu' (Yasuoka Shōtarō: style and reputation – continuities and discontinuities with the pre-war *shishōsetsu*), *Kokubungaku: Kaishaku to kyōzai no kenkyū*, 22(10). 85–92 (August).

Tsujihashi Saburō (1976) *Kindai bungakusha to kirisutokyō* (Modern Novelists and Christianity), Tokyo: Ōfūsha.

BIBLIOGRAPHY

Turnbull, Stephen (1998) *The Kakure Kirishitan of Japan: A Study of their Development, Beliefs and Rituals to the Present Day*, Folkestone: Japan Library.

Ueda Miyoji, Akiyama Shun and Abe Teru (1972) 'Daisan no shinjin no kōzai' (The strengths and weaknesses of the *Daisan no shinjin*), *Mita bungaku*, 59(1): 5–24 (January).

Ueda Tetsu (1972) *Shinkō: Kindai Nihon bungaku to kirisutokyō* (A Reassessment: Modern Japanese Literature and Christianity), Tokyo: Miyairi shoten.

Uyttendaele, Francis (1972) 'Shūsaku Endō', *Japan Christian Quarterly*, 38 (4): 199–205 (Fall).

Walker, Janet (1979) *The Japanese Novel of the Meiji Period and the Ideal of Individualism*, New Jersey: Princeton University Press.

Washburn, Dennis (1995) *The Dilemma of the Modern in Japanese Fiction*, New Haven and London: Yale University Press.

Watt, Ian (1957) *The Rise of the Novel*, Berkeley and Los Angeles: University of California Press.

Webber, Andrew (1996) *The Doppelgänger: Double Visions in German Literature*, Oxford: Clarendon Press.

Williams, Mark (1988) 'Meiji intellectuals and the spirit of the West: A consideration of the influence of Christianity on the literature of Kitamura Tōkoku', *Japan Christian Quarterly*, 54 (4): 208–33(Autumn).

—— (1991) 'Shadows of the former self: Images of Christianity in contemporary Japanese literature', unpublished Ph.D. thesis, University of California, Berkeley.

—— (1993) 'From out of the depths: The Japanese literary response to Christianity', in J. Breen and M. Williams (eds) *Japan and Christianity: Impacts and Responses*, Basingstoke: Macmillan, pp. 156–74.

—— (1994) 'Kōteiteki na hitei: Endō bungaku ni okeru zoku no seika' (Sanctification of the weak in the literature of Endō Shūsaku), K. Ōno, (trans.), in Yamagata Kazumi (ed.) *Sei naru mono to sōzōryoku* (The Holy and the Powers of the Imagination), vol. 2, Tokyo: Sairyūsha, pp. 345–65.

—— (1994) ' "Hontō no jiga" no tsuikyū no mondai' (The search for the "True Self" in the Literature of Endō Shūsaku), in Endō Shūsaku and V. Gessel (eds) *Endō Shūsaku to Shūsaku Endō: Amerika 'chinmoku to koe'*: *Endō bungaku kenkyū gakkai hōkoku* (Silences and Voices: The Writings of Shūsaku Endō: Proceedings of the Symposium on Endō's Literature), Tokyo: Shunjūsha, pp. 133–58.

—— (1995) 'In search of the chaotic unconscious: A study of *Scandal*', *Japan Forum*, 7 (2): 189–205 (Autumn).

—— (1996) 'Inner horizons: Towards reconciliation in Endō Shūsaku's *The Samurai*', *The Japan Christian Review*, 62: 74–96.

—— (1997) '*Ryūgaku*: Ishiki to muishiki no sekai' (*Foreign Studies*: The Worlds of the Conscious and Unconscious), in K. Yamagata (ed.) *Endō Shūsaku: sono bungaku sekai* (Endō Shūsaku: His Literary Worlds),

Tokyo: Kokken shuppan, pp. 131–47.

Williams, Philip (1983) 'Images of Jesus in Japanese fiction', *Japan Christian Quarterly*, 49 (1): 12–22 (Winter).

Wills, Elizabeth (1992) 'Christ as eternal companion: A study in the Christology of Shūsaku Endō', *Scottish Journal of Theology*, 45: 85–100.

Yamagata Kazumi (1994) (ed.) ' "Sei naru mono" to "sōzōryoku": hitosu no shikaku e no kokoromi' ("The Holy" and "The Powers of the Imagination": Towards a perspective), in *Sei naru mono to sōzōryoku* (The Holy and the Powers of the Imagination), 2 vols, Tokyo: Sairyūsha, pp. 9–36.

—— (1997) (ed.) *Endō Shūsaku: sono bungaku sekai* (Endō Shūsaku: His Literary Worlds), Tokyo: Kokken shuppan.

Yamagata *et al.* (1987)'Tokushū: Kirisutokyō bungaku no kanōsei' (Special edition: The possibilities for Christian literature), *Fukuin to sekai*, 42 (6): 1–49.

Yamamoto Kenkichi *et al.* (1955) 'Daisan no shinjin; sengo bungaku; heiwa-ron' (The *Daisan no shinjin*; Postwar Literature; Discourse on Peace), *Kaizō*, 36: 158–68 (February).

Yanagida Tomotsune (1971) *Sakka to shūkyō ishiki* (Authors and Religiosity), Tokyo: Ryokuchisha.

Yasuoka Shōtarō (1984) *A View by the Sea*, K. Lewis (trans.), New York: Columbia University Press.

Yasuoka Shōtarō *et al.* (1996) 'Tsuitō: Endō Shūsaku' (Commemorative edition: Endō Shūsaku), *Shinchō*, 93 (12): 172–229 (December).

Yasuoka Shōtarō *et al.* (1996) 'Tsuitō: Endō Shūsaku' (Commemorative edition: Endō Shūsaku), *Gunzō*, 51 (12): 102–45 (December).

Yasuoka Shōtarō, Kojima Nobuo and Ōkubo Fusao (1996) 'Tsuitō zadankai: Endō Shūsaku to daisan no shinjin' (Commemorative discussion: Endō Shūsaku and the *Daisan no shinjin*), *Bungakkai*, 50(12): 210–23 (December).

Yonekura Mitsuru (1983) *Kindai bungaku to kirisutokyō* (Modern Literature and Christianity), Osaka: Sōgensha.

Yoshida Toyoko (1984–5) 'Kirisutokyō to Nihon bungakusha: 1' (Christianity and the Japanese author: Part 1), *Seiki* (September–May).

—— (1985–6) 'Kirisutokyō to Nihon bungakusha: 2' (Christianity and the Japanese author: Part 2), *Seiki*, (June to March).

—— (1986–7) 'Kirisutokyō to Nihon bungakusha: 3' (Christianity and the Japanese author: Part 3), *Seiki*, April–February).

INDEX

Agawa Hiroyuki 257 n. 13
Akiyama Shun 20
Akutagawa Prize 19, 60, 76, 225
Akutagawa Ryūnosuke 33, 187
Arishima Takeo 33
Ariyoshi Sawako 246 n. 14
archetypes 50

Barthes, Roland 86
Baumann, Emile 3
Bergson, Henri 36–7, 39
Bernanos, Georges 3, 31
Beside the Dead Sea: *see Shikai no hotori*
Birth of Christ, The: *see Kirisuto no tanjō*
Bordeaux, Henri 3, 36
Bourget, Paul 3, 36
Buddhism 194–5, 207, 212, 218, 220
Bungakkai 10
bunka kōrōsha 226
bunka kunshō 226

Camus, Albert 17
Châmundâ 212–5
Chiara, Giuseppe 107, 251 n. 8
Chinmoku 1, 29–30, 54–5, 74, 77–8, 104, 107–32, 135–42, 145, 155, 164, 167, 178, 189, 206, 214, 217, 219, 224, 226, 235–6
Christianity 47, 142, 215; emphasis of maternal in 91, 121–5, 132–5, 139–40, 143, 149, 159, 162–4, 205–6 ; and 'inner life' 7; and *Kakure* 53–4, 87, 106, 132–4, 141, 208–9; and literature 3, 7, 33–40, 49–50, 77, 89–90, 94–5, 98–100, 103, 105, 115–17, 120–4, 127, 137, 161–2, 170, 172, 191–2, 221–3; protagonists attracted to in spite of self 63–6, 137, 139–40, 145–6, 158–63, 180–3, 189, 227–30; and religious syncretism 194–5, 197–200, 206–9, 220; viewed as Western import 7, 9, 25–6, 32–4, 59, 63, 73–5, 105–15, 120, 128, 132–40, 150, 154–6, 159–61, 167, 205–6, 229–31, 235–8
Claudel, Paul 3
Cohn, Dorrit 40–2

Dag Hammarskjöld Prize, International 135, 226
Daisan no shinjin 5, 7, 14, 221–3, 257 n. 13; and 'other self' 23–4; and *shishōsetsu* 14–24, 221
Dazai Osamu 33
de Sade, Marquis 226
Deep River: *see Fukai kawa*
dōhansha (constant companion) 103, 115, 122, 127, 132, 135, 138, 161–2, 205–8, 216, 223
Dominican order 156
doppelgänger 22–4, 28, 55–7, 248 n. 70, 166, 168–78, 187, 200–2, 224, 238–9
Dostoevsky, Fyodor 36, 38–9, 41, 54, 247 n. 67, 248 n. 69, 58, 130, 166

INDEX

du Bos, Charles 3
Dujardin, Edouard 119

Edel, Leon 119
Eliot, T.S., 25
Emerson, Ralph Wardo 9
Endō Iku 225
Endō Junko 256 n. 1
Endō Shūsaku: baptism of 30–1, 59, 143; and Christianity 25–6, 30–40, 74, 105–8, 122–3, 135–40, 143, 167, 222–3; critical response to 107–9, 130–1, 166–7, 194, 220–1; and *Daisan no shinjin* 5, 7, 14, 17–24, 25–30, 221–3; and *doppelgänger* 24, 28, 55–7, 122, 168–78, 187, 200–3, 224, 238–9; 'facts' vs 'truths' 29–30, 50–1, 142–4; and France 3–4, 58–60, 76, 225–6; and French Catholic authors 3–4, 31–2, 34–9, 58–9, 94, 225; and hospitalisation 77, 93–4, 105, 226; and Jung 43–7, 54–5, 78, 83, 91–2, 124, 167, 179–80, 183–6, 188, 197–203; and Mauriac 43, 49, 83; and resolution of dichotomies 51–4, 58–61, 68–74, 77–9, 86, 108–9, 117, 123–7, 145–9, 178–80, 186–9, 193–7, 207, 221; and the 'third dimension' 39, 46, 122
Endō Tsunehisa 225
Etō Jun 123

Foreign Studies: see *Ryūgaku*
Fowler, Edward 2–4, 7, 10, 12, 21
Franciscan order 137, 139, 237
Freud, Sigmund 36–7, 39, 85, 166
Fujen University 226
Fujii, James 3–4
Fukai kawa 29, 40, 55, 104, 190–219, 220–1, 224, 226, 239–41
Fukuzawa Yukichi 8
fumie 106, 109–10, 115, 117, 119–20, 121–5, 128, 155, 236

Ganges, River 192–4, 196, 199, 201–3, 206, 209, 215–9, 220–1, 240–1
genbun itchi 5
Georgetown University 226
Gessel, Van 18–19, 23–4, 141, 142, 158, 164, 224
Gestapo 62–4, 67, 228
Gibson, Boyce 38
Gide, André 3, 21, 36
Girl I Left Behind, The: see *Watshi ga suteta onna*
'Gods and God, The': see 'Kamigami to kami to'
Goethe, Johann Wolfgang von 21
Golden Country: see *Ōgon no kuni*
Great Mother, archetype of 91–2, 123–4, 212
Green, Julien 3
Greene, Graham 1, 37–8, 242 n. 69, 105

'Haha naru mono' 132–5, 226
Hamlet 25
Haniya Yutaka 245 n. 63
Hasekura Tsunenaga 140–2
Hibbett, Howard 11
Hick, John 255n. 9
Hijiya-Kirschnereit, Irmela 11, 16
Hinduism 195–6, 200–1, 207–8, 212, 220, 240–1
Hiroishi Renji 226
Hitopadesa 212
Hontō no watashi o motomete 167, 226
Houston, G.W. 194

Iesu no shōgai 135, 226
'Ikinie no shisetsu' 141
Ikuta Chōkō 13
In Search of the Real Me: see *Hontō no watashi o motomete*
'indirect rebirth' 198, 202–3
individuation, process of 44–6, 57, 61, 118, 127–8, 158, 165, 177, 188, 195–6, 202, 216–7
inner life: *see naibu seimei*
inner voice 16, 42, 45–6, 77, 82, 92–3, 96–7, 99–101, 113–16, 118, 152, 160–1, 224

INDEX

Inoue Yōji 220, 256 n. 5
interiority, discovery of 4–7
Islam 195, 220
Itō Sei 13, 16
Izutsu Toshihiko 50

James, Henry 118–9
Japan P.E.N. Club 167, 226
Jesuits (Society of Jesus) 107, 137, 139, 157, 235, 237
John Carroll University 226
Johnston, William 195
Jordan, River 196
Joyce, James 37
Jung, Carl G. 25, 43–8, 50, 54–5, 61, 76, 77, 78, 83, 91–2, 118, 124, 165, 166, 167, 179–80, 183–8, 191, 197–203, 224

Kaga Otohiko 143, 193, 205
'Kagebōshi' 55, 131–2, 226
Kakure (Hidden) Christians 53, 87, 106, 132–3, 141, 208–9; and 'Konchirisan no ryaku' 208
Kâlî 201, 212–13
'Kamigami to kami to' 52, 59, 61, 68, 195, 225
Karaki Junzō 243 n. 24
Karatani Kōjin 4–6, 10; *see also* 'discovery of interiority'
'Katorikku sakka no mondai' 3, 34, 225
Kawai Hayao 78, 191
Kawamura Minato 220
Kazan 48, 226
Keene, Donald 12
Keiō University 31, 76, 225
Keppler, Carl 55–6, 172–9
Kiiroi hito 40, 48, 52, 60–1, 68–76, 90, 225, 229–31
Kipling, Rudyard 58
Kirisuto no tanjō 135, 226
Kitamura Tōkoku 5–10, 12, 33, 137; and *naibu seimei* 6–10
Kobayashi Hideo 15, 21
Kojima Nobuo 17, 222; and *Hōyō kazoku* 26
Kuchibue o fuku toki 226
Kume Masao 13, 144

Kunikida Doppo 5, 10, 12, 33
Kuwabara Takeo 16

Lejeune, Philippe 13, 168
Life of Jesus, The: see *Iesu no shōgai*
Lyons, University of 105, 225

Macarthur, General Douglas 17
Mainichi Cultural Prize 225
Mainichi Cultural Arts Award 226
'Marseille' 58
Maruyama Masao 16
Masamune Hakuchō 33, 108
Mathy, Francis 7, 9, 10, 91
Mauriac, François 3, 31, 35, 43, 49; and *Thérèse Desqueyroux* 43–4, 83, 211, 213
Meiji Constitution (1889) 6
metempsychosis 197–9
Miura Ayako 246 n. 14
Miura Shumon 17, 246 n.14, 257 n. 9
Miyoshi, Masao 1–4, 12
Mori Ōgai 20; and *botsurisō ronsō* 20
Moriuchi Toshio 191–3, 195
'Mothers': *see* 'Haha naru mono'
Mushanokōji Saneatsu 244 n. 47

Nagasaki 106, 109
Nakamura Mitsuo 21
Nakamura Murao 12
Nakamura Shin'ichirō 257 n. 9
Napier, Susan 11, 169
narrated monologue 40–2
narrativity, theories of 40–2, 50–1, 142
Natsume Sōseki 10–11, 33; and 'Watashi no kojinshugi' 11
Naturalism 6, 11–12
neo-Confucianism 6
Neumann, Erich 48, 91, 123–4, 212
Ninomiya Sontoku 8
Noma Hiroshi 245n. 63
Noma Prize for Literature 166, 226
Novel I Have Loved, A: see *Watashi no aishita shōsetsu*

Obakasan 40, 53, 76, 78, 85–94, 109,

123, 204, 206, 217, 223–4, 225, 232–3
Ôe Kenzaburō 14, 242 n. 3; and *Kojinteki na taiken* 14
Ōgon no kuni 226
oki-kae: see transposition
Ōkubo Fusao 222
Ōoka Shōhei 242 n. 63

paradoxical inversion 47–8, 52, 61–2, 70–1, 86, 95–6, 128
People's Rights, movement of 6–8
'Problems Confronting the Catholic Author, The': *see* 'Katorikku sakka no mondai'
Proust, Marcel 3, 36–7, 39
psycho-narration 40–1, 125–6

quoted monologue 40–2

rebirth 48, 188, 190, 191–2, 193–202, 206, 209–10, 216–9, 220
reincarnation 197, 199–200, 218
Rembrandt 49, 115–16
renovatio 197–8, 200–2
resurrection 197, 200
Richter, Jean Paul 166
Rivière, Jacques 39
Rubin, Jay 11
Ryūgaku 48, 105, 204, 226

Samurai 29, 44, 55, 104, 130–67, 189, 206, 217, 224, 226, 236–8
Sartre, Jean Paul 17
Satō Haruo 242 n. 53
Satō Yasumasa 242 n. 5, 242 n. 7
Scandal:see *Sukyandaru*
Schopenhauer, Arthur 1
Sea and Poison, The: see *Umi to dokuyaku*
Seijō University 226
sengoha 17–18, 222
Shadow 47–9, 83, 102, 122, 131–2, 165, 166, 172–8, 187–9; *see also* 'Kagebōshi'
Shiga Naoya 19, 23
Shiina Rinzō 242 n. 63, 242n. 14, 242 n. 27

Shikai no hotori 178, 226
Shimao Toshio 17, 27–8, 242 n. 14, 242 n. 27; and *Shi no toge* 26
Shimazaki Tōson 10, 12, 33; and *Hakai* 10
Shinchōsha Prize 225
Shinoda Masahiro 242 n. 26
Shirakaba-ha 15
Shiroi hito 29, 30, 40, 48, 52, 60–8, 70, 76, 78, 217, 223, 225, 227–9
shishōsetsu 2–4, 13–16, 19–24, 27, 143–4, 168, 189, 221
Shōno Junzō 222
shutaisei debate 18
Silence: see *Chinmoku*
sin-consciousness, perceived absence of in Japan 62–3, 68–74, 78–9, 84–5, 90–1, 230
Sono Ayako 242 n. 14
Sophia University 76, 225
subjectivism in modern Japanese literature 4–24
Sukyandaru 40, 55, 122, 165–90, 191–2, 194, 201, 209, 215–16, 224, 226, 238–9
Suzuki, Tomi 12, 16
synchronicity 199

Takahashi Takako 242 n. 14
Tanizaki Prize 130, 226
tenkō 14–15, 17
Third generation of new writers: *see Daisan no shinjin*
Tokyo University 76
Torii Kunio 19
transposition 20, 50–1, 89, 94, 99, 103, 118, 120–2, 139–40, 157–8, 163–4
Tsubouchi Shōyō 20; and *botsurisō ronsō* 20

Ueda Miyoji 21
Umi to dokuyaku 30, 40, 48, 54, 76, 78–85, 223, 225, 231–2
unconscious: and dreams 184–9; conflict with conscious 28, 43–6, 51, 57, 64–5, 71, 77, 79, 86–7, 102, 156, 183–5, 188–9, 195–6, 209–10, 211–12, 215–16, 224;

275

nature of 25, 44–7, 78, 85, 94, 167, 176, 177–8, 202–3; and religion 39–40, 47, 132; role of in creation of literature 34, 38–44, 46, 49–53, 85–6, 107–8, 119, 124, 142–3, 149, 190, 191–3, 223–4; symbols of 24, 192–3, 196, 202–3, 239; and third dimension 39; and unfathomable impulses 45–6, 49–50, 63–5, 67–8, 71–3, 80–1, 83, 88–9, 90, 93, 97–8, 114, 151–2, 160, 170–1, 180–3, 192, 204; voice of 77, 89, 92, 99–101, 138, 150, 152–3, 156, 159–60, 165, 182, 201–3
University of California, Santa Clara 226
Uno Kōji 13, 14

Vârânasi 192, 199, 203, 207–8, 217, 240
Volcano: see *Kazan*

Walker, Janet 8, 9, 12–14

Washburn, Dennis 6
Watashi ga suteta onna 29, 40, 53, 77, 78, 93–104, 105, 109, 204, 206, 217, 224, 226, 233–5
Watashi no aishita shōsetsu 43–4, 46–7, 51, 92, 94–5, 107, 167, 184, 226
Watt, Ian 7
When I Whistle: see *Kuchibue o fuku toki*
White Man: see *Shiroi hito*
Wonderful Fool: see *Obakasan*

Yamaji Aizan 243 n. 23
Yamamoto Kenkichi 18, 21
Yanaihara Tadao 109
Yasuoka Shōtarō 17, 23, 28, 246 n. 14, 220, 222; and *Kaihen no kōkei* 26
Yellow Man: see *Kiiroi hito*
Yokomitsu Riichi 15
Yomiuri Literary Award 135, 226
Yoshiyuki Junnosuke 17, 222